THE LIFE OF
SIR EDWARD MARSHALL HALL

Sir Edward Marshall Hall was one of the great legal 'characters'. With his eyeglass, his array of bottles of medicine, his enormous bulk and his incapacity which gave him the privilege of addressing the court seated on an air cushion, he was a famous figure in the courts of his day. But he was not simply a figure of fun. He was, in addition, one of the great criminal advocates of his day, and this book has been acclaimed as a classic of legal biography. Marshall Hall is most celebrated as a brilliant advocate for the defence, and the book is enlivened not only by his own larger-than-life personality, but by the highly eccentric character of many of the people he was called upon to defend.

This is also a highly entertaining book. Marshall Hall's headlong unconsidered oratory often brought him into violent disagreement with the Bench and the Press, and the very generous quotations from his cases which the book contains, emphasise the fact that the theatre lost a great comedy actor when Hall decided to become an advocate.

MARSHALL HALL IN ROBES

THE LIFE OF
SIR EDWARD MARSHALL HALL

EDWARD MARJORIBANKS, M.P.

With an Introduction
by
THE RIGHT HON. THE EARL OF BIRKENHEAD
P.C., G.C.S.I., D.L.

CEDRIC CHIVERS LTD
PORTWAY
BATH

First published 1929
by
Victor Gollancz Ltd
This edition published
by
Cedric Chivers Ltd
by arrangement with the copyright holder
at the request of
The London & Home Counties Branch
of
The Library Association
1972

SBN 85594 709 8

Printed in Great Britain by
Redwood Press Limited, Trowbridge, Wiltshire
Bound by Cedric Chivers Ltd, Bath

A GREAT ADVOCATE

Fold the worn silk ; and let the wig be laid
    Into its battered box : their use is done
    For ever : now the final cause is won,
The long term closes ; the last speech is made.
No prisoner at the Bar may seek his aid ;
    No judge will hear him now': beneath his flail
    No witness now shall writhe—no felon quail,
No jury by his eloquence be swayed.

The Roman head on Saxon shoulders set,
    The silver hair ; the tall heroic frame
Are seen no more ; but some will not forget
    And, till they die, must reverence the name
Of him, who, as they struggled in the net,
    Rose in his strength, and to their rescue came.

E. M.

(*Morning Post, Feb.* 1927.)

CONTENTS

ILLUSTRATIONS

INTRODUCTION

MR. EDWARD MARJORIBANKS has in these pages discharged, with conspicuous ability, a work of loyalty to an old and well-loved friend. The late Sir Edward Marshall Hall is fortunate in his biographer. Mr. Marjoribanks is fortunate in his subject.

Marshall Hall was a man for whom a stranger, seeing him at any moment in his career, even the earliest, even the darkest, must have predicted success. He was a man of remarkable appearance. Very greatly above the average height, admirably proportioned, exceptionally handsome, he radiated vigour, courage, and personality. And behind this magnificent façade lay qualities of character hardly less admirable. Whoever reads these pages will learn with how much adversity, both in his public and private affairs, Marshall Hall had to contend. It is not, I think, the least tribute to a man who, successful as he became, was nevertheless bitterly unhappy at various stages of his life, that never could his acquaintances trace in him the existence of the suffering which often overshadowed, without darkening, his fine nature.

Courage was his outstanding characteristic. He was utterly fearless in the service of what he conceived to be his duty, both as an advocate and in other, less vicarious, paths of life. Mr. Marjoribanks's chapters reveal how often Marshall Hall disdained the prudent dictates of self-interest when he imagined that the interest of his clients was at stake. The élan with which he swept down upon a doubtful jury, brushing aside their prejudices, and persuading them against their will, sometimes possibly against their better judgment, into accepting his own sanguine view of his client's innocence, won many a day which a more timorous, if not less skilful, advocate must have given up for lost.

He had, of course, the defects of this outstanding quality. He was often headstrong, where caution would have been the wiser policy. Even so, it was himself, and not his clients, who suffered from this. When he quarrelled with a judge in open court, which occurred more than once, he drew down the lightning of judicial disapprobation wholly upon his own shoulders ; the jury probably tended *ipso facto* to become more sympathetic towards his client than would otherwise have been the case. But these outbursts did Marshall Hall himself great disservice.

The worst of them occurred at a moment when more than ever his interests demanded that he should be suave and discreet. In the first years of this century he had opened up what appeared to be a most promising political and legal career. He had won Southport for the Unionists ; he was confidently named for proximate law office ; his practice, besides being most remunerative, had the advantage, so valuable to the ambitious lawyer, of bringing his name constantly into public notice. Then, suddenly, a crushing conjunction of disasters overwhelmed him. In the General Election of 1906—an even grosser example of electoral irresponsibility than that which we have recently witnessed—he lost his seat in Parliament, and saw his hopes of political advancement shattered, it must have seemed irretrievably. At the same time, by some freak of fate, or possibly, by some newly developed twist in his character, there came that series of unfortunate conflicts with the Bench which for a time shattered and almost destroyed his practice. It was said that an income of some £5,000 a year—in those days worth at least double to a man of his tastes what it is to-day— was swiftly reduced to little more than £1,000.

The world, and especially the legal world, which knew him hitherto as a fortunate and confident creature, waited, in some cases not without malice, to see him break beneath these combined blows. But he demonstrated that the fears of his friends, and the hopes of his enemies, were unwarranted. Never for one moment did he falter. As he had been in the early years of successful progress, as he was to be in his later years of regained triumph, so he remained in those dark hours. His proud courage, his undaunted self-reliance, his natural cheerfulness, conquered the hearts of even those who had wished him ill. A few difficult years sufficed to restore his fortunes. By that time, I believe, he had not an enemy in the world ; and no single person moved in the whole wide range of his acquaintance but admired him and wished him well.

He was for many years one of the most prominent advocates of his day. The reason lay much more in his human qualities

INTRODUCTION

than in any special claim to legal erudition. He was a diversely equipped advocate ; he did not profess to be even a considerable lawyer. Not the least of his charming qualities was a shrewd and candid knowledge of his own deficiencies. When a difficult point of law arose in the course of a case, he would openly request his junior to argue it. So disarming a gesture from the most confident of pleaders could not but warm the hearts of the fascinated jury.

To watch him in court was an educational process in the study of human nature. Where such an attitude was not impossible, he always believed (or so it must appear to the beholder) to be profoundly, passionately convinced of the integrity of his clients; he threw round them the glamour of his appearance and his personality like a cloak to ward off unmerited misfortune ; he fixed the jury with an eye which compelled consideration and demanded assent from every reasonable man, even the most sophisticated. And so he won his cases and his fame.

During the last years of his life he suffered seriously in health. Illness compelled him, ever a keen lover of sport and the open air, to deny himself more and more the pleasures he loved. He bore this as serenely as the other blows which had befallen him. Many another man would have broken under this final affliction, but he withstood it with his accustomed cheerfulness.

Marshall Hall was a giant among men ; in heart as in stature.

BIRKENHEAD.

July 1929.

AUTHOR'S NOTE

I wish to make it clear that I alone am responsible for the selection of the material used in this book ; and that neither the executors nor Lady Marshall Hall share the responsibility with me.

E. M.

PERDITÆ

CHAPTER I

Youth

THE advocate has been, since the days of the Greek and Roman democracies, an essential and popular figure in European civilised society. " There he goes," said the plebs, impressed and admiring, as Hortensius or Cicero swept into the forum ; and the crowds whispered and made way, and sometimes roared with vehement applause, as the magnificent figure of Edward Marshall Hall was seen hurrying into the Old Bailey, or coming out after one of his great triumphs. He was as well known as any man in England, and millions read of his doings with interest and awe day by day, and year by year, for over a quarter of a century. But fame can be fleeting, and forensic oratory is often written on the sand, and it is time that some record was made of the career of this remarkable man.

Now it is difficult for any man, however wise or eloquent, to speak for himself, when fortune, reputation, happiness, life itself, are in jeopardy and rest on the decision of strangers, sworn before God to find an impartial verdict from the evidence brought before them. Hence has arisen the honourable and necessary profession of the advocate ; it is indeed a high and responsible calling ; for into his keeping are entrusted the dearest interests of other men. His responsibility is wider in its scope than a physician's, and more direct and individual than that of a statesman ; he must be something of an actor, not indeed playing a well-learned part before painted scenery, but fighting real battles on other men's behalf, in which at any moment surprise may render all rehearsal and preparation futile. " My profession," once said Sir Edward Marshall Hall, " and that of an actor are somewhat akin, except that I have no scenes to help me, and no words are written for me to say. There is no back-cloth to increase the illusion. There is no curtain. But, out of the vivid, living dream of somebody else's life, I have to create an atmosphere—for that is advocacy."

The advocate must have a quick mind, an understanding heart, and charm of personality. For he has often to understand another man's life-story at a moment's notice, and catch up overnight a client's or a witness's lifelong experience in another profession ; moreover, he must have the power of expressing himself clearly and attractively to simple people, so that they will listen to him and understand him. He must, then, be histrionic, crafty, courageous, eloquent, quick-minded, charming, great-hearted. These are the salient qualities which go to make a great advocate, and Marshall Hall possessed them all to such a marked degree that he became the best-known advocate of his day, despite other characteristics which would have meant certain failure to a lesser man. He was hot-tempered, and undoubtedly indiscreet, two grave defects in an advocate. His intense love of the dramatic often led him astray, but strangely enough it sometimes guided him to ultimate victory by devious paths that no other pleader could have found. But must not a great advocate be learned in the law ? This proposition Marshall Hall would have stoutly denied, and the great success which he won in his profession is a conclusive argument against its universal truth. " *You* must take this point," he would whisper loudly in court to his junior ; " there's some law in it." He dreaded the Court of Appeal, and only appeared once in the House of Lords. But his forty-four hard-working years at the Common Law Bar, twenty-four of which were spent as a leading counsel, must constitute a record of modern times among men of his eminence, who usually desert the battle and toil of the Bar for the dignity and comparative ease of the Bench, or else retire on their laurels long before they complete such a service. This book will very largely be the story of his battlefields, often the story of victory, sometimes of defeat, but always that of a very brave soldier of fortune, whose bright sword was eagerly sought to the last.

Edward Marshall Hall was a great and remarkable personality; but his character was composed of many contrary things : to his dying day he retained all the buoyancy, and some of the immaturity, of youth. Endowed with pre-eminent personal beauty of the most virile type, and standing six feet three inches high, his life after middle age was a long fight against physical pain. He was at once the most sympathetic and the most egotistical of men ; he was very hot-tempered and very warm-hearted. While he made no secret of his ignorance of the law, his name was better known to the public than that of any among his most learned friends, even those whom he would have openly acknowledged as his betters ; for Marshall, though his best friend would have admitted his vanity, was not a conceited man, and was the first to recognise a superior. Of all leading counsel, his name was most frequently in the newspapers, and most rarely in the official law reports. He adored animals, yet was as fond of shooting as any man in England. In spite of his unrivalled experience of mankind's wickedness and weakness, and the most grievous tragedy in his own life, he remained till the end quite unhardened, a tremendous optimist and naïve as a child. Without real scholarship or learning, he had an unerring eye for beautiful things, whether flowers, jewels, or works of art ; and he turned this gift to great financial advantage. He was most generous, but drove as hard a bargain as any dealer, and would give away quite casually to a friend the fruits of hours of hard bartering. He would have been a prince among jewellers or art-dealers ; and his appearance and voice would have made him the Shakespearean actor of his time. But it was a fortunate thing that fate saved him for the Bar, a profession in which no special gifts or knowledge are wasted.

As a counsel, his was not a star that rose steadily in the legal firmament, nor indeed did it decline : all his strength and fire remained to the end, and he was a greater artist in the Stella Maris trial, as an old and sick man, than he was when he defended the Yarmouth murderer in the pride of his youth and strength. But he had his periods of eclipse, from which a less brave man would probably never have recovered. Twice it seemed as if the day were over, but with indomitable courage he fought through the dark days that seemed to promise failure, and he died in harness at the very height of his powers and reputation. Altogether there is no doubt or wonder that to the people at large he was one of the most popular and fascinating figures of the time : he was the very man to catch the public eye, and win the popular affection ; and it is no disrespect to say that he appreciated these things to the full. This book will be an attempt to put his achievement and his personality before his many admirers; his great trials, already well known, will be retold, but I shall also try to show something of the personality of this valiant and lovable man, who led this most strenuous life in spite of much physical suffering, who could not recognise defeat, and who could smile bravely before the world in the face of the deepest personal sorrow.

He was born at 30 Old Steyne, Brighton, on the 16th of September, 1858. His father was a Dr. Alfred Hall, a well-known physician in that town for many years. The family had come from Swanwick Grange, near Alfreton in Derbyshire, where the name of Hall was so common that the bearers of it were distinguished as "Butcher" Hall, "Baker" Hall, and "Lawyer" Hall. But he had generations of gentlefolk behind him. Dr. Hall's father was "Lawyer" Hall, having been first a solicitor, then a barrister, and finally a Commissioner in Bankruptcy. An elder brother, Frederick Hall, went to Brighton, and practised as a barrister; he was a justice of the peace, and busy in local government work. Dr. Hall first practised as a physician in Glasgow, where he met his wife, the daughter of James Sebright, an official in the postal service, about whose birth Marshall Hall cherished a romantic story. If it could have been proved true, it would have given him the right, after the death of his elder brother, to claim from the Committee of Privileges an ancient peerage; but the elder brother lost whatever documents there were, and Marshall never seriously considered taking the matter up. At all events, Miss Sebright was a beautiful woman, and it was from her that Marshall inherited his remarkable looks. Marshall himself was the youngest of ten children, four of whom died in infancy. The nearest to him was twelve years older than he was, so that he had most of the disadvantages and none of the advantages of being an only child. His name "Marshall," together with the fact that his father was a well-known doctor, have given the impression that he was the son of the celebrated Dr. Marshall Hall, who originated the world-wide method of restoring to life the apparently drowned. This was not so, but when this great physician lay dying at Brighton in 1857, Dr. Alfred Hall was called in to attend him, and the latter, being a great admirer of his distinguished colleague and patient, asked leave to call his next child, if it should be a son, by his first name.

Marshall Hall was devoted to his father and mother; and the urn containing his ashes was buried, in 1927, at his earnest request by their side at Tunbridge Wells. His mother died there in 1889, and his father died at Brighton in 1897 at the age of 85. Among his most treasured papers was found an envelope, inscribed " E. M. Hall, with Mother's love. Read it, dear one, every day," and containing, in his mother's hand, the words of the hymn, " O Jesus, I have promised to serve Thee to the end."

The strong local connection was of the greatest use to Marshall Hall, and indeed gave him the avenue to success, while London work was slow in coming to him. His father also imparted to him a sound knowledge of medicine, which was invaluable to him in the poisoning cases in which he acted when at the height of his career. Marshall was always interested in medicine, made out his own prescriptions, and had a real knowledge of drugs.

The member of his family to whom he was most devoted was his eldest sister, Ada, who married Arthur, the only brother of the celebrated Radical, Henry Labouchere, millionaire, journalist, and wit. Like her brother, she had wonderful looks, and was described by two critical judges, General Sir Henry de Bathe and Sir Douglas Straight (the well-known journalist and criminal barrister), as the most beautiful woman they had ever seen. She and her brother must have made a handsome pair. Sir Arthur Pinero, on seeing Marshall forty years ago for the first time at a party given by Corney Grain, the Society entertainer of the 'eighties, was struck with amazement as he looked across the room at what seemed to him to be " a revelation of manly beauty." He and Marshall were introduced, and became lifelong friends. Marshall thought the world of this sister. He came to her with all his troubles, for counsel and sympathy, both as a boy and a man. He was heart-broken by her death in 1905, and he ascribed to her inspiration whatever success he had in life.

She was married when Marshall was eight years old. He took the event as a personal grievance, and became so naughty and wayward that he had to be sent to school. On one occasion he caught a hamperful of little crabs, and let them loose in the moonlight, while the band was playing and the ladies were promenading on the Brighton Front. Marshall's first school was kept by a clergyman. This gentleman had a cesspool in his garden, as a result of which Marshall caught typhoid fever ; he also had a beautiful daughter named Jessie, with whom Marshall fell ardently in love. No permanent harm was done by either of these two early infections, but Marshall returned home once more to plague the residents of Brighton.

He had already, as quite a small boy, acquired that passionate love of firearms which was to stand him in good stead in so many of his great trials. But the great advocate and actor who gave his famous demonstration with the revolver in the cases of Laurence, Fahmy, and Smith was once a very naughty little boy who took shots at an advertisement on Brighton Old Pier with his first pistol. This was the first of an enormous collection of pistols, and it was the one he loved best, because he was robbed of it under the following circumstances. Marshall was on the pier, and chose as his bullseye the " o " of the word " Royal " which ran along an advertisement on a hoarding. He hit the bull, but was filled with alarm when an old gentleman of ample proportions leapt up from behind the board, clad in a bath towel, and exclaiming that he had been shot. As Marshall was the only person near by, and was holding a still smoking pistol, the old gentleman accused him ; indeed, as he himself admitted, the evidence was overwhelming against him. He was being haled off to the police station, when counsel for the defence appeared in the form of a dear old lady, called Mrs. Terry, who sold brandy-balls and other delicacies at the end of the pier. She told the irate old gentleman that Marshall was a nice little boy, and that he (the old gentleman) ought to be ashamed of himself and get dressed. This had a sobering effect on the old fellow, who discovered that he had not been shot after all, and contented himself with reading Marshall a lecture and confiscating the pistol. This, said Marshall, in later years, was positively the only occasion on which he was arrested for attempted murder.

He had another and a less ignominious story to tell about this same pistol, and, if he was right, a very remarkable meeting took place between a veritable king of criminals of one generation and the greatest " counsel for the defence " of the next. On this occasion he had been practising with his pistol in the safer seclusion of the garden at Warnham Court, Horsham, his sister Ada's place, when three suspicious individuals joined him. Two of them were selling plaster statuettes, and were bargaining with Marshall, while the third, an undersized and emaciated man, went into the house to get, as he said, a drink of water. Marshall, even then a keen bargainer if not a connoisseur, beat the men down to five shillings for the lot, but did not like the way in which they seemed to be taking stock of the house and garden. Having purchased the statuettes, he set them up on the garden wall and proceeded to shoot at them. The third man, who had now returned, saw that he was a crack shot and asked him why he was " potting them." Marshall said, " Because there are burglars about." The three men, very impressed by the pugnacious little schoolboy's demeanour, then withdrew. That night a neighbouring house was burgled, and Marshall became for the nonce the family hero. But the story does not rest here. Marshall afterwards saw Charles Peace in the dock, and immediately recognised him as the little man who had gone into his house to get a drink of water. H. B. Irving, subsequently a great friend of Marshall's, frankly disbelieved this story on the ground that the great man always operated alone. Marshall did not rest until he had obtained evidence that Charles Peace did work in association with other burglars, and that at about the time in question he was in Sussex ; and so he continued to believe that he and his pistol had frightened away the redoubtable Charles Peace.

It is always interesting to go back over a distinguished man's life and discover what led him to follow the particular road that led him to success. Marshall's inclination to go to the Bar began when he witnessed the opening stage of a criminal *cause célèbre* before the Brighton magistrates : it was the case of Christiana Edmunds, the Brighton poisoner. The way in which the evidence for the prosecution, gathered from seemingly unrelated sources, was fitted together and made into an overwhelming case against the prisoner, by Douglas Straight, so fascinated the little boy of fourteen, taken by his father to see the proceedings before the magistrates, that from this moment he felt the call of the Bar. Since this may be regarded as the first milestone in Marshall's forensic career, it may be interesting to recall this remarkable case in outline. Christiana Edmunds was a spinster of forty-three—though even at the trial she persisted in giving her age as thirty-four—of good birth, who lived with her mother at Brighton for some years, in perfect respectability, liked by everybody who knew her. Unfortunately for her, at a critical period in her life, she fell violently in love with the doctor who attended her, a married man. She unsuccessfully attempted to poison Mrs. Beard, the doctor's wife, by a poisoned chocolate, with the result that the doctor would have nothing more to do with her. In order to clear herself of suspicion, she entered on a scheme of poisoning on a large scale. She bought in all sixty or seventy grains of strychnine from Mr. Garrett, a chemist, on the pretext that she wished to poison dogs and cats. She sent four children on separate errands to buy chocolates from Mr. Maynard's famous confectionery shop. When the children brought back the sweets she would say that they were the wrong sort, and would send them back to the shop injected with strychnine, so that they went back into stock and were bought by someone else. She would also leave in other shops packets of Mr. Maynard's sweets, poisoned with strychnine, with the result that many people felt the ill effects of the poison ; but the first and only fatality arose from a purchase of the poisoned chocolates from Mr. Maynard's shop. An uncle of a little boy named Sidney Barker, staying in Brighton, bought some of the chocolates which Miss Edmunds had tampered with and returned, and the little boy died almost at once in horrible agony.

Miss Edmunds did not neglect to send poisoned presents of food to herself, and told the coroner's jury that she herself had almost been fatally poisoned by them. This jury found the little boy had died from misadventure. Miss Edmunds did not let the matter rest here, but wrote anonymous letters, which were proved at the trial to be in her handwriting, to the little boy's father, urging him to take proceedings against Mr. Maynard. In one of these she had the effrontery to write : " Had I lost my child in such a sad way, as a parent I should feel myself in duty bound to take proceedings against the seller of the sweets."

The trial was ultimately removed from Sussex to the Old Bailey, owing to the great local prejudice and excitement which the case had aroused. Serjeant Ballantyne and Douglas Straight prosecuted, and Serjeant Parry defended. The case was hopeless from the start, except on the issue of insanity. Evidence was given which would almost certainly to-day result in a strong direction of the judge to find the prisoner "guilty but insane," but the judge, Baron Martin, did not take that view, and the trial was remarkable for the bitter arguments between Serjeant Ballantyne—who was contending for a strict construction of legal definition of insanity, as propounded in the MacNaughton case—and the doctors called for the defence. Finally she was found guilty, but she pleaded, "in order to stay execution" of her sentence, that she was enceinte, and a jury of matrons was empanelled to try that issue for the first time for many years. It was then that a bizarre incident, which Marshall often recounted, cast a ray of farce over this tragic scene. A Dr. Ryley, who was called in to assist the jury, sent out for a stethoscope; a policeman was sent to buy one from one of the shops in Ludgate Hill. After a time the officer returned, bringing a naval telescope, and apologised by saying it was the smallest he could get! When it was obvious that the poor woman's plea was groundless, her distress—she had been calm throughout the whole trial—became terrible, and the jury of matrons wept around her. "Oh, how shall I sleep to-night," she wailed. Ultimately the Home Secretary appointed two medical men to enquire into her mental condition, and she was sent to Broadmoor.

The case was one to fascinate Marshall; it contained two of the elements which aroused all his professional interest—poison and insanity—and it was a case in which he would have loved to hold the defending brief. We must picture a very handsome, sturdy little boy, with a mass of curly dark hair and a ruddy countenance, sitting by his father in the stuffy atmosphere of the Brighton police court, his beloved revolver and fishing-rod for the moment forgotten, listening spellbound as Sir Douglas Straight unravelled the evidence for the prosecution in this remarkable case, and feeling for the first time his vocation in life.

Before going to Rugby, Marshall was sent to a small school in Dorsetshire, St. Andrew's College, Chadstock. These were happy days for him, hard work and hard play, football, cricket, and paperchases for miles over the borders into Devonshire and Somersetshire amid the wonderful scenery of those lovely counties. At fifteen, Marshall had become the best cricketer and the head boy, and his father gave him the choice of moving to any of the big Public Schools. Influenced by *Tom Brown's Schooldays* and in love with the tradition of Dr. Arnold, he chose Rugby. He was placed in the Upper Middle School—a very creditable beginning—during the summer of 1874.

Marshall was at Rugby just over two years, during which time, although he won a mathematical prize, he distinguished himself most as a cricketer. Already two of the characteristics of the man were foreshadowed in the boy : his reckless defiance of authority and his passion for collecting and bartering. He held frequent auctions in his study, and sold a stamp collection in London for fifty pounds which he bought from a schoolfellow for five. According to Mr. Wellby, of the well-known Garrick Street firm, a contemporary Rugbeian, while still a schoolboy he bought a pearl for a small sum from Messrs. Wellby and resold it in Paris for a very handsome profit. He would often visit Whistler's in the Strand, and would barter revolvers and guns and jewellery during this period of his life.

One intellectual defect made the ordinary classical routine, to which all Public Schoolboys were then more or less tied, very distasteful. He could never learn lines by heart, an incapacity from which he always subsequently suffered, and which, he said, would have debarred him from success on the stage. He found the writing of Greek and Latin verse an impossible task, and was allowed as a special indulgence to do mathematical work in its place.

When Marshall was eighteen and the second boy in his house, a wave of religious emotion, which might easily have diverted him from the profession for which his gifts most suited him, swept him off his feet. His father had always destined him for the Bar, and had a real understanding of his powers and weaknesses. But the ambitions which the Edmunds trial had inspired were now forgotten, and he was set on going into the Church. His father was far from pleased, but his mother was overjoyed, and dedicated a religious acrostic to him, expressing her hopes for him in that vocation. This touching little maternal document is dedicated to him, " with the hope that he will rise to eminence in the Church of Christ," and runs as follows :

"SPEAK, LORD, FOR THY SERVANT HEARETH "

Eternal God !—To Thee I owe my life, my all ;
Devote me to " Thy work "—make plain my call.
Wean me from things below, and let Thy love
Attract my soul to " nobler things above."
Reveal to me Thy way, Thy mind, and will,
Deign, Lord, to " Speak," and let " Thy servant hear Thee still."

Hallow my life, Great God !—oh, seal me Thine
And make me in Thy Church a light to shine ;
Let " Faith, Hope, Love " each day increase in me :
Let " all my works begin, continue, and end in Thee."

His sister Ada, however, was not so enthusiastic, when " she heard from home that he had now decided what to do," and wrote to him advising him " not to choose the Church unless you feel you are really called by God, and can give your whole heart to Him." Later, even his mother began to doubt whether his temperament was suited to the Church, and writes from Brighton on January 27th, 1876, asking him to think over the future and at once " determine that if *you do not feel* that you are called of God into His service, and that it will *be a delight to you to walk with Him, and be His true servant, do not, for your own soul's sake, fix upon the Church, but arrange your studies at once according to your own choice of a profession* . . . but you must not in your choice allow any pecuniary motive to influence you." But the mother's true wishes appear in a pathetic little " Mother's Prayer," which she encloses, for her " dearest Edward " : " Help him to control his ungovernable temper, and let him not (if it is in accordance with Thy will) forsake the way he had once chosen to be Thy Minister and Steward." These old letters from mother to son enchant the reader back into the calm waters of Evangelical belief, which did so much to create the greatness of Victorian England. Marshall was very much under his mother's influence, and it was a long time before he abandoned his ambition to go into the Church. Three years later, when he was of age and in Australia, he still wished for this career. It is interesting to reflect upon the possibilities of Edward Marshall Hall as a clergyman. With his strange emotional energy and passionate eloquence, he might have made a world-wide reputation as a popular preacher, but on the whole it is a fortunate thing that circumstances sent him back to his old choice, the Law. His peculiar gifts, as his father had always seen, were far more suited for advocacy than for preaching.

Meanwhile, a feud with his housemaster, Mr. Lee-Warner, was really marring his schooldays. A great antipathy existed between the two, and Marshall was the last man to attempt to ease any such situation. He quarrelled with his housemaster as fearlessly and recklessly as he did afterwards with so many of His Majesty's judges. This gentleman used to creep noiselessly round the house in carpet slippers, a practice to which housemasters in Public Schools are much addicted, and which is universally condemned by their pupils. At the end of his third summer, Marshall was already a member of the Lower Sixth, of the " twenty-two," or second cricket eleven ; next year he would have been Captain of the House, and a member of the eleven, the ambition of most Public Schoolboys. But it was not to be. The feud with Lee-Warner was at its height, and the latter persuaded Dr. Hall that " Edward was doing no work and would only be remaining at Rugby for athletic distinction." Dr. Hall was easily persuaded, and, in the hope, perhaps, of bringing him to a more practical state of mind, made him at once a clerk in the City. Accordingly he left Rugby in 1876 for an office stool in Shepherd & Co., the well-known tea-merchants. As the youth of eighteen, condemned, as he thought, to a life of City drudgery, sat on New Year's Day, 1877, contemplating for the first time the gloomy prospect of Mincing Lane, he cursed Lee-Warner's advice and his father's decision. Indeed, deprived of the glory of a last triumphal year at Rugby, he never forgave the former, but he was on two occasions to get his own back in a manner not usually vouchsafed to hardly used schoolboys. Many years afterwards, on a fine spring morning in the later 'eighties, Mr. Edward Marshall Hall, a very promising junior, was returning from Marlborough Street, having successfully saved his client from being sent to trial. The case was of some notoriety, and Marshall stopped in Regent Street to buy an evening paper to read his own cross-examination. While he was so engaged, Mr. Lee-Warner saw him and spoke to him. " Just what I should have expected of you, Hall," he said ; " loafing about in Regent Street at 12 o'clock with nothing to do except to spot winners." Marshall had the satisfaction of handing to his old housemaster the newspaper with his own name in headlines. In still later years Mr. Lee-Warner retired to Norfolk and became a country gentleman and a justice of the peace. Marshall Hall appeared before him at Quarter Sessions, and obtained an acquittal in spite of the hostile attitude of the Bench. On this occasion Mr. Lee-Warner had the generosity to pay his now distinguished pupil a grudging compliment. " Hall has much improved," he said.

But fate was not to be denied, and did not allow him to languish in the tea-broker's office. He always said his few months there gave him a knowledge of commerce which was invaluable to him in later life. But only one incident remains on record of Marshall as a City man : the firm's entire correspondence was entrusted to him for postage one Saturday, and he, eager to be off to the country to play cricket for the Gentlemen of Sussex, fulfilled his trust by posting the letters in the dustbin ! The young clerk gave himself considerable leisure : he played for the Gentlemen of Sussex all through that summer, and there made a useful acquaintance, whom he met again, and whom he would hardly have made on the playing-fields of Rugby. His beloved jewellers' and curiosity shops saw a good deal of him during these months, and on the whole the days passed not unpleasantly till October, by which time his father had relented, and he was a freshman at St. John's College, Cambridge, with several of his fellow Rugbeians. Over these he had the advantage of " an invaluable knowledge of commerce " and a certain experience of London life. His own intentions were still to go into the Church, but his father had sent him to Cambridge to learn Law.

His career at Cambridge was, however, broken by a long

absence : he was in residence for two or three terms, and then went abroad for nearly two years. He was now, although only twenty, under another and even more common emotional stress ; but Marshall always felt things very violently, and when the course of love did not run smoothly he felt that he must go away from England. His departure from Cambridge was the first episode in the tragic story of his first marriage, which cast a shadow of grief over his whole youth, and which had so deep a bearing on his whole life and character that some account must be given of it in a later and separate chapter.

He spent a year or so, in 1878–9, in Paris, leading an amusing life with the students and artists of the Quartier Latin, and gaining, as he often said, a real knowledge of human nature. He even penetrated now and then with his Bohemian friends into the mysteries of a " life class." The brilliance and gaiety of the Second Empire still lingered on in the French capital, and Marshall's father allowed his son to spend his twenty-first year playing the part of a *flaneur* in this dangerous atmosphere, passing no examinations, it is true, but learning all the time. He supplemented the allowance made by his father by constant dealing in precious stones ; his precocious skill and eye in this business already gave him independence. He had learned what he knew about jewels as a boy in Brighton, from an old goldsmith, in whose shop he had spent very many happy and fascinating hours, watching the old man as he looked for flaws or beauties in a gem. With this knowledge he was able to buy in Paris and sell at a profit in London, and vice versa. But it is somewhat surprising that after a year of Paris he still cherished his desire to take orders.

After Paris he went on a trip to Australia. His profits in Paris and a cheque from his father gave him the fine adventure of coming of age on board a sailing vessel named the *Hydaspes*, bound for Melbourne ; she sailed from Chatham on July 30th, 1879, and made the voyage on October 18th. Marshall has left a diary of his tour, which gives a great deal of information about him at this age. He was very active, and very restless, and he occupied his time on board ship with editing a ship's newspaper, reciting at concerts, carpentering, and playing cards. But his chief employment was sport. He had taken a

gun, a rifle, and fishing-tackle on board, and he used them all
freely. His sleep was troubled by the ship's rats ; so he set to
and shot several, including one " of enormous size." At other
times he would stand on deck with his rifle waiting for prey.
His bag was very mixed, and included oyster catchers ; a
shark, which he shot in the eye after it had been caught on a
line by a piece of pork and was about to get away ; some flying
fish, hawks, Cape pigeons, Cape hens, and several mollymawks.
One day he did a terrible thing : he repeated the sin of the
Ancient Mariner. " Saturday, Sept. 20th. Did a little shooting ;
shot a large mollymawk, and an albatross measuring about
18 ft. from tip to tip." Could he, a superstitious man, have read
the weird tale of the Ancient Mariner ?

> " God save thee, ancient Mariner !
> From the fiends that plague thee thus !—
> Why look'st thou so "—With my cross-bow
> I shot the Albatross.
> " Ah, wretch ! " said they, " the bird to slay,
> That made the breeze to blow ! "

While he was in Australia he occupied his time with cricket
and shooting. His entry on November 22nd gives a good idea
of his sport : " Up early at 5.30 ; shot all day in the Karagamite ;
got wet through and then dry again. Bag : 50 brace avocet
snipe, 10 brace small ditto, 5 brace gulls, 1 kangaroo, 1 eagle,
1 grebe duck, 10 wild duck, 1 crow, 3 plover, and 10 rabbits.
The kangaroo I shot was a fine animal, with a head like a
greyhound."

He enjoyed much hospitality, and a few obviously very
fleeting flirtations. He played cricket for a team called the
Bohemians—one of the first, if not the very first, English
cricket elevens to tour Australia—in Tasmania and other places.
On one occasion he took part in a match, in some remote corner
of the continent, which was brought to a strange and premature
conclusion : a large collie dog intervened and ran away with the
ball ; it was the only cricket ball within 500 miles, and so the
game ingloriously ended.

One incident may be mentioned because it shows that Marshall
at this time was still set on a clerical future, and because it was
one of the experiences which made him superstitious. His

fortune was told by a Mr. Ellis, and he made a contemporary note of it in his diary. " Mr. Ellis told all our fortunes. Mine was : Marry in a year. New career, influenced by an elderly man for good. Bitter female enemy. My first marriage opposed by my friends, and also lady's friends, who don't think me good enough. And finally, after much travelling about, I am to settle down, lose my wife tragically, and marry again. The cards also predicted that I was never to be ordained. This I don't believe, as I hope my mind is firmly set in that direction." This forecast was, unhappily and very strangely, near to the truth.

Marshall returned by India and the Suez Canal in a steamer named the S. S. *Deccan.* He was back at Brighton in May 1880, and in the following month he encountered by a curious chance another celebrated criminal. On the evening of Monday, June 27th, 1880, he was at Brighton station, about to proceed to London, when he noticed a considerable commotion. Going to enquire the cause, he saw a man, looking very ill, who was being taken to Sussex County Hospital ; he was told that the man had been injured during his journey in the train which had just arrived from London. This man was Lefroy, the strange young fop who had just murdered Mr. Gold, a respectable London-to-Brighton season-ticket holder, in that train. He must have had hidden in his shoe, when Marshall saw him, the watch and chain of the murdered man, the presence of which was afterwards detected and led to his detention. As Marshall proceeded to London, his train must have passed over the dead body of Mr. Gold, which was lying mutilated in the Balcombe tunnel. He was naturally interested in the case, and went to the trial with his kinsman by marriage, Henry Labouchere, who criticised the tactics adopted by Montague Williams, leading counsel for the defence. Williams made a gallant attempt to materialise an unknown third person who had been in that first-class smoking-compartment and who had attacked both Gold and Lefroy. The evidence of such an individual's existence was very scanty, and Labouchere considered that the case should have been run on other lines. Curiously enough, Marshall adopted this very plan of campaign in the Yarmouth murder, when there was actually some evidence of an unknown man who had been with the murdered girl. However, in the Camden Town murder, as will be seen, the theory of the alibi and of the mysterious unknown on the scene of the murder carried the day. The junior in the Lefroy case happened to be Forrest Fulton, who did Marshall a very good turn later on.

Soon after his return to England a vital event happened to Marshall. When he had first gone up to Cambridge he had already fallen in love with the daughter of one of his father's colleagues in medical practice at Brighton ; they had been playmates as children, and had even gone to a little school together ; Marshall had always cared for her, even as a little boy, and they were destined for each other by many of their friends. The name he called her by was Ethel. She was tall and beautiful, and moved with exceptional grace. Her name suited her beauty. " She might," said a friend of Marshall's, " have been Cynthia." He was very young, and had no immediate prospects even of making a living ; his ambition was to be a clergyman ; at all events it was natural, perhaps, that a girl of seventeen should not return the ardent affection of an undergraduate. Shortly after his return from abroad, nearly two years after his early disappointment, he went to a party in London, and, by a coincidence which would be strange in fiction, almost the first lady he saw in the ballroom was Ethel. He at once went and spoke to her, and they danced together. In the course of their conversation she told him something which must have changed the whole meaning of life for him at the time.

" Edward," she said, " I might give you a different answer now to the question you asked me before you went away."

" Does that mean that you'll marry me ? " he asked.

" Yes," was the answer and a very fateful one to Marshall Hall.

Now that he was engaged to be married, Marshall seems to have abandoned his vocation to the Church, and turned his thoughts again to the Bar. He went up to St. John's again, to rush through a law course in two years. His mother and father did not approve of his engagement, and the former, although she had told her son before not to consider the worldly advantages of a lay career, did not consider Ethel quite good enough, because she had a relation engaged in trade. Ada, his sister, was especially annoyed, because that relation lived in Horsham, near her husband's place. However, these objections were " nothing beside his happiness," and Ethel was admitted to be " a perfect little lady."

Marshall seems at this time to have thought of a commercial career, so that he might have more money in his early married life, and late in 1880 his father wrote to him urging him to go to the Bar. " It would be a great comfort to me, and to those who love you, to know that the career of a gentleman is within your reach. If, however, you feel confident that such a career is foreign to your tastes, and that mercantile pursuits are more fitted to you, say so at once, and, deeply though I should feel your decision, still I will not oppose it." The old man lived till 1897, to read his son's name among the foremost juniors of the day, and, though he saw Marshall pass through great tribulation, his brave success must have been a great source of pride to him. " The career of a gentleman " and the vulgarity of commercial pursuits ! Times have indeed changed.

Marshall settled down at Cambridge, and took a pass degree in law in the summer of 1882. He was given the cricket colours of his college in 1881 by Sir Jeremiah Colman. He was a most successful racquets player, and used to indulge in pigeon-shooting matches. He made all manner of queer bets, with the odds very minutely calculated, and kept a betting book. It is interesting to see that he backed Lefroy's conviction by 7¼ to 4½. But he was cured of betting by a really heartbreaking experience. He dreamed one night in the autumn of 1881 that he heard someone saying that a horse called Foxhall had won the Cesarewitch and the Cambridgeshire. He at once took the tip, and several of his friends followed his example. They backed Foxhall, singly and in doubles, and stood to win about £6,000 between them. Foxhall brought off the double, but drove Marshall's bookmaker out of business. Indeed, the latter disappeared altogether. This disgusted Marshall Hall permanently with racing. He considered that the whole business of the Turf was one vast swindle. What was the use of a good tip straight from the Ivory Gate if bookmakers behaved in this scandalous manner ?

He had already acquired his passionate love of dogs, and this led him into another bad speculation. The keeper of a public house near Cambridge owned a retriever of remarkable skill and reputation, and Marshall coveted him. To his surprise he found the publican a willing vendor, and the dog became his for a five-pound note. He took the dog to Horsham to shoot with Arthur Labouchere, and during the shoot the dog disappeared. When Marshall returned to Cambridge, he visited the publican to tell him of his loss, and received an affectionate welcome from the dog that he thought was his, but had found its way from Horsham to its old master. Marshall was so touched and interested at the dog's intelligence and fidelity that he did not grudge the five-pound note, as other undergraduates did who were induced to part with their money by the very same means.

Before he left Cambridge he had become a member of the Hawks, a club exclusively composed of distinguished athletes. He was always devoted to his college, and was chiefly instrumental in forming the Johnian Society, a club founded to keep old members of the college in touch with each other, and of which he became president.

Thus, at the age of twenty-four, Marshall was ready to take his place in the world. He was as handsome as a young man can be ; a crack shot, and an expert in precious stones; he had some knowledge of medicine acquired from his father ; he had enjoyed some remarkable encounters with famous criminals ; and he had travelled widely. Moreover, at twenty-four, after years of waiting, he had won his heart's desire. Yet he had very little, except his gifts and his personality, with which to force his way in the world when he went down from Cambridge in June 1882, to marry his sweetheart during that same month and to seek his fortune.

Chapter II

Apprenticeship

THE Bar is, perhaps, of all professions the most speculative for a young man, without private means to enable him to wait for briefs in peace and comfort, and without influence from solicitors to give him a start. Marshall, as the youngest of a large family, had only slender private means, and little influence, and had in addition the responsibility of a beautiful young wife, when he was called to the Bar at the Inner Temple on June 6th, 1883. Just as Erskine felt on a famous occasion his little children tugging at his gown, this fact may have proved a great incentive to work, but he was already twenty-five, and there were several years to wait before he was earning a living. It is often said that a rolling stone gathers no moss, and that a young barrister should change his chambers as infrequently as possible in the early days, so as to gain a strong foothold with the clients attached to one particular set of chambers ; but Marshall was in no less than four different legal homes in his first four years at the Bar, and it will be seen that he gained something from each of them. The first year of a young barrister's life is invariably spent in apprenticeship to some busy junior, who for a fee of one hundred guineas allows his pupil to see his papers and follow him about from court to court. At his call, Marshall had already been apprenticed for some months to Mr. Tindal Atkinson (who subsequently became county court judge) at 3 Dr. Johnson's Buildings. He was at this time a busy common law junior with an all-round practice, and so suited Marshall's purpose admirably. It was Atkinson's principle thoroughly to master the facts in every case submitted for his opinion, then to write down his own opinion as to the law without recourse to the books. Then he would compare his opinion with the decisions of the judges in the reports. Whereas Marshall thoroughly mastered the first stage in his master's rigorous method, it is to be feared he never was much troubled about the second.

He had first begun to work in the Temple in October 1882, and his advent to the Bar marks the passing of an epoch. For centuries, up to December 1882, cases in the High Court had been heard in Westminster Hall, and Marshall was among the very last pupils in the Temple to go down with their master from the Temple in a penny steamer to Westminster Bridge. He was at Atkinson's side in Westminster Hall when the latter pleaded in the Exchequer Chamber, the old Court of Appeal ; and on November 23rd he went in to hear Ver Hyden's cross-examination by Hardinge Giffard in the Belt case, which was tried before Baron Huddleston, and was the last case ever to be heard at Westminster. Marshall's diary reads : " Fancy his evidence to be concocted." This action arose from an article in which *Vanity Fair* had alleged that a sculptor named Belt did not do the work that passed under his name, but that it was really performed by Ver Hyden, who acted as his " ghost." The latter gave evidence most bitterly against his old friend and colleague, and the jury agreed with Marshall, did not believe him, and gave Belt £5,000 damages. Another jury, however, at the Old Bailey, a few months afterwards, sent Belt to prison for fraud. But the days of Westminster Hall, as a palace of justice, were numbered, and on December 4th, 1882, Marshall and his wife, from the roof of Cogswell & Harrison's, watched the Queen, with " all the rest of the swells, including W. E. G.," open the new Law Courts in the Strand.

Marshall's first brief was not in any way sensational, and curiously enough its scene was set a few days after his call in the Chancery Division, in which he was hardly ever to appear again. For a consideration of a few guineas he was briefed by his brother-in-law, James Robinson, to nod his head by way of consent to a motion for an injunction against his client. This was actually the first appearance in court of the most eminent criminal advocate of the day, and it can hardly be called characteristic, either of the man or of his future practice.

His first successful case was in a county court : within a few weeks of his call he was sent to oppose an application for a new trial in a case in which another advocate had appeared before a judge who had not heard the case in the first instance. His opponent was lengthy, verbose, and indiscreet, and his application for a new trial consisted almost entirely in abuse of the absent judge. This was not well received by the Bench, and a well-tried attorney, who had had years of experience in that court and was sitting by Marshall, told him what to do. Acting on his advice and trembling with nervousness, Marshall managed to stammer out, " As my learned friend has said everything on my behalf better than I could say it myself, I will not spoil it by trying to add to its effect." He then sat down, and his opponent's application was dismissed with costs ; and, according to Marshall, this learned friend seemed to bear him a grudge for long afterwards.

So far, it can hardly be said that his mettle had been tried as an advocate, but during his first year two more briefs came for him, each marked with a fee of one guinea, the smallest which a barrister may accept. They were the only briefs received for months, and, by an unfortunate chance which seems to dog young barristers, they were both due to be fought on the same day. Marshall therefore had to employ a " devil " for the first time in his life. The friendly " devil " was sent to the Marylebone county court while he went down to the Old Bailey for the first time to defend a prisoner. Much to his disappointment, his client insisted on pleading guilty, and Marshall rushed across London to see if there was a fight for him at Marylebone. He arrived in time, and fought the case, which was quite a complicated one, to victory. Judge Stonor, who presided over that court for a quarter of a century, heard the case, and, appreciating the trouble which the eager young counsel had obviously taken, paid him one of those precious compliments which cost a judge so little and mean so much to the beginner. In this case his kindness bore immediate fruit ; for as Marshall, flushed with pleasure and triumph, rushed into the robing-room and was flinging off wig and gown preparatory to going off for lunch, a stranger touched him on the shoulder, and asked him if he would accept a brief in an action which was coming on immediately after lunch. It had been returned unexpectedly by a busy practitioner a few minutes before : it was marked with the enormous fee of eight guineas, and concerned an action for personal injuries brought against the London General Omnibus Company. So much Marshall saw, but with characteristic impulsiveness he assumed that he was

for the plaintiff. After tearing through the papers, he said to
the solicitor :

" But you haven't a leg to stand on."

" What do you mean ? " said the astonished attorney.

" Well," replied Marshall, "the plaintiff cannot win this
case."

" I am glad to hear that," rejoined the solicitor, " for I am
instructing you on behalf of the company."

So Marshall did without his lunch, and perused his third
successive brief on the same day, conscious that he was acting
for a most important client, and that much might turn on the
result. Victory did not, however, come so easily as he had at
first anticipated, but it came in the end. Indeed, Marshall lost
the case which he had rashly said the plaintiff could never win,
but he obtained a new trial and won in the second round. He
had earned ten guineas in one day, and that night he proudly
took his wife to a restaurant and a theatre.

Marshall joined the South-Eastern Circuit and the Sussex
Sessions as soon as he could after his call. Three able men, all
of them to take silk and obtain a high place in the profession,
were in the field ahead of him in Sussex—Charles Gill, H. C.
Richards, and W. P. G. Boxall, till this year Recorder of
Brighton. Gill and Richards were both first-class advocates,
and for years they overshadowed Marshall, whose fame, however, at last was so easily to outshine theirs. Marshall's first
criminal defence was a " dock " brief at Lewes Assizes. The
prisoner, in accordance with the privilege accorded to a man
on trial who has no means to employ a solicitor, but who has
one pound three shillings and sixpence in the world (one guinea
for the barrister and half-a-crown for his clerk), was no doubt
impressed by the back view of Marshall's magnificent head
and shoulders, which is the only view usually vouchsafed to the
wretched prisoner who has to choose, on the spur of the moment,
a defender of his liberty. This was before the days of the
niggardly generosity of the Poor Prisoners' Defence Act, and
this crude method was the only way in which a very poor man
could be defended, unless the judge made a special request to
a counsel in court to defend him. Marshall always railed against
the system and that of the hopeless inadequacy of the Poor

Prisoners' Defence Act in a complicated case, and wished to see a Public Defender appointed with suitable funds and organisation. On this occasion the prisoner had only fifteen shillings in the world, but, against the etiquette of the profession, Marshall undertook to defend, and secured an acquittal. Many members of the profession would have criticised him at the time had they known, and might even do so now ; but this first irregularity sat lightly on Marshall's conscience, and, in my opinion, rightly so.

It was during his first year that his association began with Sir Charles Gill, for whom he first devilled and understudied, and afterwards fought in hot but affectionate rivalry for so many years, down to the celebrated Eastbourne murder in 1920, when the older man wrested victory for the last time from his more brilliant friend and rival. He was a dozen years or so Marshall's senior, and did him the greatest service at Quarter Sessions and on circuit by giving him his devilling. In the diary which Marshall kept conscientiously from his marriage to the end of 1887, their intimacy can be seen growing. A typical entry is : " Lewes Quarter Sessions : devilled a case for Gill. Returned to Brighton —went on the pier with Gill. Quiet little supper together at the Beefsteak. Afterwards Charlie went to sleep." Gill was a striking contrast to Marshall. Although an Irishman, Gill was restrained, logical, and mature, even in his younger days. Marshall, for all his English and Scots blood, was childlike, uncontrolled, and mercurial to the end. Gill, even when the younger man was in his sixties, retained a fatherly attitude towards him, and we find him in 1918 writing to Marshall advising him solemnly not to brag ! They had many scenes together. In 1888 there was a fearful quarrel in court, and Gill swore in the hearing of others that he was done with Marshall for ever. But of course they made it up. " See that Marshall does not murder me," whispered the aged Gill long afterwards, to J. D. Cassels, Marshall's colleague in the Eastbourne murder trial. Their friendship lasted through all their association; fellow members of the Garrick, they would dine and go to a play, and come back to have supper at the club. They often spent holidays together, and for years they worked on the same staircase at Temple Gardens ; and it was to Gill that Marshall turned in the greatest sorrow of his life. It would be hard to imagine two more different methods of advocacy. Gill would have prepared a careful plan of campaign, and would advance with slow, deliberate purpose towards his goal, having, it is said, carefully worked out every conceivable reply which a witness might make, and the answer to it! The labour involved in such a method was prodigious, and, indeed, it was quite impossible where the issues were complicated and manifold, or where the case contained an element of surprise. Gill was the ideal advocate where all depended on the knocking out of one witness; he was conscious of his own limitations; and later became a confirmed settler of cases, a tendency which reacted unfavourably on his practice. He was slow of speech, somewhat ponderous in manner and appearance, and had no natural eloquence. Marshall on the other hand was so eloquent that he was the despair of the shorthand writers. He never had a plan of campaign, or, if he had, he never was faithful to it. So far from having prepared his speeches, he scarcely knew what the next sentence was going to be himself; not that Marshall did not take the greatest pains in preparing his cases, or that every relevant circumstance did not sink quickly into his consciousness. But Gill's case would be fixed in his mind like a picture in a frame, while Marshall's would shift and change, like the patterns in a kaleidoscope, into a succession of different shapes, altered as his versatile intelligence leapt from phase to phase. Charlie Gill would turn what looked like being the most scandalous and sensational cause in the list into a dry dispute as to the validity of a contract; Marshall, with his instinct and passion for drama, would transform the dullest dispute into the *cause célèbre* of the sittings.

Great generals in history do not usually meet each other in more than one pitched battle, but Charles Gill and Marshall Hall fought each other day in and day out for close on forty years, till they knew every chink in each other's armour. " I always give Marshall a bone to worry if I can," said Charlie Gill, when, at the Old Bailey, he had induced Marshall to re-examine on his quite irrelevant cross-examination; " it makes him happy and I win my case." Marshall, on the other hand, knew that if he produced an unexpected witness on an important issue he might completely upset Gill's carefully laid plan of campaign. Marshall had the advantage of the guerilla against the well-drilled army ; of an archer shooting deadly arrows in rapid succession, and often drawing his bow at a venture, against a knight clad in heavy mail and advancing slowly, with his heavy but well-balanced lance, towards his carefully explored objective.

Their association began in 1884. Marshall was attending Lewes Quarter Sessions, probably for the first time : Gill was instructed by a Mr. Evett of Brighton to defend two men for receiving stolen varnish, well knowing it to be stolen. At that time he had most of the work at Quarter Sessions, and, there being two courts at Lewes, he was engaged in the second when the receiving case came on ; fortunately he had allowed Marshall, whom he had met at Brighton, to read the brief in case of emergencies. Mr. Evett was in despair at his predicament.

" What am I to do ? " he said, wringing his hands.

" Oh, let Mr. Hall do it—he knows all about it," said Gill.

Marshall never forgot as long as he lived the look of horror that began to spread over Mr. Evett's ample features. His clients were respectable tradesmen, and the case was an important one for him. But he was kind, and a sportsman, and, seeing no doubt the heart-broken expression on Marshall's face, he at once assumed a cheerful air, and, patting him on the back said, " Come along, Mr. Hall, we will get them off."

" Well," said Marshall in reference to this incident, " I have had a good many awkward moments in my life, but never shall I forget that afternoon—the badly lighted court, the stuffy atmosphere, and the horrible accuracy of the prosecuting counsel. The prosecution called the thief as a witness against the two men, and then for the first moment I saw a gleam of daylight, for if there is one thing that a Public Schoolboy dislikes in the world more than another it is a sneak, and if ever I saw a sneak it was the lad who was called to give evidence against these two men. It is three and twenty years ago now, but I can remember, as well as I can remember anything that happened yesterday, the awfully blurred look that the jury box presented, when at last I got up to address a jury on behalf of my clients. And then, all in a moment, seated up in the far corner of that

jury box, I saw a face I knew. It was that of a man who had
known me when I played cricket for the Gentlemen of Sussex
on the County Ground. There was a friend. I knew he was a
friend ; and, oblivious of all the other eleven occupants of that
box (if indeed there were any others), I talked to that man for
all I was worth for three quarters of an hour. Poor fellow !
I feel for him even now. But the result justified the means, and
when, about an hour later, the jury returned a verdict of ' not
guilty,' I think I felt prouder then than I have ever felt before
or since."

This is Marshall's own account of his first considerable triumph
before a jury, and many a barrister will know exactly how he
felt. But how few of us have ever the luck to see an old friend
in the jury box ! Those afternoons when Marshall played truant
from Mincing Lane were, by a curious chance, after all well
spent, since by means of them he was given confidence in a very
difficult and embarrassing situation. From this experience,
Marshall learned always to pick out the most intelligent or the
most amenable member of a jury, and talk to him, to make a
particular friend among them, if there was not one there already.
If there was one of them in his favour, his keen eye was quick
to see it, and he would hammer away at the others till his
persistence and magnetism had won them too.

The cricketer on the jury was not the only colleague in the
world of sport who helped Marshall in these very early days.
An old gamekeeper of his brother-in-law's, who had loaded for
him as a boy at Stroud Park, turned poacher, and was duly put
on his trial for night poaching. Indeed, after his dismissal,
Marshall had actually accompanied him on some of his poaching
expeditions. This was of course years before the days of the
Criminal Evidence Act, and the prisoner was not allowed to go
into the witness box. The case turned upon whether the gun
abandoned by the poacher in his struggle with the gamekeepers,
from whom he had made good his escape, belonged to the
prisoner. Marshall somehow proved that it could not have been
his, so he was duly acquitted. He was not, however, satisfied.
Leaning across the rails to Marshall, he said in a raucous whisper
audible all over the court, " I say, Master Ted, what about my
gun ? " Fortunately for him, no man can be twice tried for the

same offence ; better still, the Sussex police handed back to him, like true sportsmen, his means of livelihood.

Marshall was a very keen and a very fine natural shot : in his early days at the Bar most of his week-ends in the winter were spent in shooting. Among the places where he shot was Horsted Place, the property of Francis Barchard, for many years deputy chairman of Lewes Quarter Sessions. The son of one of his outdoor servants was indicted for the murder of his wife. She was found dead on the Downs, apparently kicked to death. Mr. Barchard asked a retired solicitor, Mr. Murton-Neale, specially to prepare a brief for " young Marshall Hall," and undertook to pay him for it. Marshall succeeded in getting the charge of murder reduced to manslaughter ; this was the first of Marshall's long series of brilliant defences of prisoners for the capital offence, and it is interesting that he obtained the opportunity from an old friend.

He appears, from his diary, to have been a hard-working pupil, and often took papers home to read in the evening. He spent a good deal of time listening to *causes célèbres* in the High Court, but very little work of his own came in during the first year. Now and then he got a divorce brief from his brother-in-law, and it was perhaps the desire to fight a case on his own that sent him to the county court, like Demosthenes, as a litigant in person. On April 1st, 1884, I read in his diary : " Summons served in *Knight* v. *Self* : paid 45*s*. into court ; defended on plea of tender counterclaim for 5*s*." What had happened was this. His wife had ordered a fancy dress for a ball, and, as it did not arrive in time to suit her convenience, Marshall sent round a cab to fetch it, and deducted the price of the cab in sending his cheque. The costumiers returned the cheque and claimed the full amount. The result, I am afraid, was unfavourable to Marshall, since we read, on April 22nd : " Went to county court at Westminster, and fought action *Knight* v. *Hall*, which I lost, and had to pay costs. Such is the state of the law now."

When Marshall's first year at the Bar was over, like most young barristers at a similar time, he had to look around for permanent chambers of his own. The whole question of failure or success may depend on such a choice of one of those unofficial partnerships of free lances, which constitute a set of chambers.

Marshall had only made a few guineas during his first year, the only influence on which he could rely being that of his brother-in-law, who did what he could for him, but was chiefly a family solicitor and did not like litigation. Marshall was now twenty-six years old, and was thinking of trying his fortune elsewhere, when one of those romantic pieces of luck came to him which fortunately are not uncommon at the Bar. Quite briefless, at the end of the long vacation in 1884, wondering where he would look for chambers, he had wandered gloomily down to the Old Bailey to watch the conduct of the cases there by such men as Serjeant Ballantyne, Harry Poland, and Montague Williams. But Marshall soon got tired of hearing other men do their work, retired to the robing-room, and was sitting there doing nothing when he heard the rustle of a gown, and a busy junior in a great hurry rushed in with a large brief ; he saw Marshall, and asked him whether, if he had nothing better to do, he would make a careful note of the facts, since the brief had only just been delivered ; he had to open the case the next day, and, meanwhile, he was engaged in an important matter elsewhere.

Marshall gladly accepted one of the most tedious tasks at the Bar, that of making a carefully ordered analysis of a case for another man to use. But happily the case was one of absorbing interest, and so satisfactory was the result that Mr. Forrest Fulton, afterwards Recorder of London, obtained a junior brief for his handsome young friend, and asked him to come into his chambers in the newly built Fountain Court. It was he, too, who persuaded Marshall to join the Old Bailey Mess and the Middlesex Sessions, and to devote himself to criminal work. Undoubtedly it was owing to this meeting in the robing-room that Marshall's career shaped itself as it did, and it is very likely that he would have left the Bar altogether for a profession with quicker returns. Indeed, at about this time, Messrs. Tiffany, the American jewellers, asked him to manage the branch which they were opening in Regent Street. It is alarming to reflect upon what slender threads the destiny of a great career may depend.

The brief which Marshall noted and which gave him this opportunity was the defence of the Camberwell murderer. It was a real *cause célèbre* ; Poland Q.C. and Montague Williams were for the Crown, and it was tried on September 18th, 1884, before the celebrated Mr. Justice Hawkins, a master of our criminal law. The case concerned the murder of a brave police-constable named Cole. It bears a curious resemblance to the murder of P.C. Gutteridge two years ago ; both constables were murdered while apprehending thieves ; the identity of the murderer was for a long time a complete mystery, and was finally discovered by the ingenuity and persistence of the police investigations.

At 10.15 p.m. on a cold evening in December 1882, four shots rang out near a Baptist chapel in Camberwell. When assistance came, the dead body of a constable was found, wounded in three places ; by him lay his helmet, a cabinet-maker's wooden wedge, and a chisel on which was clearly scratched " r o c k." There were other indecipherable marks preceding these letters. A black felt " wide-awake " hat was also found near by. Enquiries were made, and it appeared that a man had been seen wearing such a hat at the corner of the street near the chapel at half-past nine. These were the only clues in the possession of the police. The constable was buried, and among the mourners who attended his funeral was a pious young Baptist carpenter of twenty-eight, named Orrock. Months passed, and it looked as if the murder would go unpunished, in spite of a reward of £200 which was offered for information.

In August 1883 the Baptist carpenter had been convicted of some offence and was serving his sentence. He was somewhat communicative, and during a discussion on " shop " among the prisoners the topic of the Camberwell mystery was raised, and to a man named Mortimer he observed, " Would you be sur-prised to know it was me ? " It was through Mortimer that Inspector Glass, the cleverest police-detective of the day, got on Orrock's tracks. The letters on the chisel were remembered ; it was sent to a handwriting expert at Somerset House, who under a microscope found two letters preceding the others, which proved to be " o " and " r." Further enquiries were made, and it was discovered that two men named Evans and Miles had been with the prisoner on the night of the crime. Orrock had expressed his intention of breaking into the chapel, where he had rented a pew, and of stealing the communion plate. The prisoner was known to have had a chisel in his possession, and also a revolver, which he had bought through an advertisement. The prisoner had also been wearing a black felt "wide-awake" hat on the night, and Miles had chaffed him with looking like a parson, and tried it on. He tried it on again at the trial and identified it. Orrock's sister remembered that her brother had returned between ten and eleven without his hat, and that he told her he had been in a street fight. He had in effect confessed to several people, and explained to one how he had broken up the revolver, and thrown it to the bottom of the river. It was not his crime, but his strange vanity and lack of discretion, that brought Orrock to the gallows. But none of his friends had given him away till the police approached them.

" Are you going to give me away for £200 ? " he asked Evans.

" I would not rat on you for £1,000," was the stout reply.

Laboriously the police traced and found the man who had sold Orrock the revolver ; the chain of evidence was now complete, and, very nearly two years after he had committed the crime, Orrock found himself in the dock on a charge of murder. All Sir Forrest Fulton's advocacy could not save him ; the jury were out for twenty minutes, and returned a verdict of "guilty," which the prisoner bore with absolute composure in spite of the judge's earnest request for him to make his peace with God.

Shortly after the Orrock case, Fulton writes to Hall : " DEAR HALL,—I am quite willing to take you on for six months ; if you like the work and think you would be willing to stick to criminal business, then I should advise you to stay on, but there is time enough to think of that : meanwhile, come when you like after October 20th. My own impression is that there is an excellent opening now at the Criminal Bar. We have had several new men lately, but they are ALL, *entre nous*, rank duffers. If you have any natural talent for advocacy you would be most useful, and I will give you a first rate start. Yours faithfully, FORREST FULTON."

Chapter III

Making his Way

So Marshall, called barely a year, had already appeared in a *cause célèbre*. He took up his quarters that autumn in Fountain Court, where Sir Forrest Fulton had acquired chambers on the second floor, moving in from Essex Court before the premises were really fit for occupation. Marshall shared the large room overlooking Essex Street with Edward Pleydell-Bouverie, who later followed him to Temple Gardens, and was a close friend of his in those days. Not long afterwards, Richard Muir, the leading prosecutor of his time, came to join him in Fountain Court. With Gill to help him in the country and Fulton in London, his feet were already set, had he known it, on the ladder of success. The latter very soon discovered that Marshall had that " natural talent for advocacy " to which he had alluded in his letter, and made him his chief lieutenant ; but, though Marshall devilled assiduously for his chief, the Bar did not as yet fill his life. He occasionally had a divorce brief in 1885, as well as work at sessions and on circuit. But when not engaged in court I fear he was often to be seen—to the great distress of his clerk—in spotless white flannels, playing tennis in the Inner Temple Gardens with Bouverie and others, while other more conventional apprentices of the law were sitting in chambers, reading law-books and waiting for work. But Marshall could never bear inactivity, and knowledge gained by study rather than experience was never attractive to him. After his tennis he would sit in chambers, quenching his thirst with large quantities of lemon squash made by himself. At times, too, the tedium of the Temple would be relieved by the bright presence of Mr. George Alexander, who was a frequent visitor at Fountain Court in those days.

But from reading Marshall's diary it is very easy to see how he won his practice, and how richly he deserved it. It was gained by determined devilling of the most persistent and strenuous kind. There can be no doubt about this, for his fee-book and diary soon begin to show the direct fruits of this method. He would devil in any court and for all manner of people. For Gill and Fulton, and later for Bargrave Deane and Sir Charles Hall, he worked in the ordinary course ; apart from them his diary shows that he worked at the Old Bailey for Montague Williams and Harry Poland, both Treasury counsel, and also for Geogeghan, that very eloquent Irish advocate who rewarded him on the first occasion " by being very rude " to him ; for H. C. Richards and Grain (the brother of his friend Corney), on circuit ; and he went down to the county courts for contemporaries like Horace Avory and Cluer (now the terror and the delight of the Jewish fraternity in his county court at Whitechapel). On June 26th, 1885, he was at the Old Bailey all day and devilled six cases ; next day, a Saturday, he devilled five more. He went down to Brighton on Sunday to read some briefs for Gill, for whom he did two cases at Brighton Sessions on the Monday. On Tuesday he is doing the same at Lewes, and Thursday finds him busy for Geogeghan at the Middlesex Sessions.

It must be remembered that work comes to counsel only through solicitors, and in estimating the former's success due credit must be given to the solicitors who discovered him and backed him. The relationship between the two branches of the profession is a most delicate one. The barrister who toadies to solicitors is rightly despised by both branches of the profession, and even friendship and relationship with an attorney will excite a sneer from brothers at the Bar.

Besides James Robinson's occasional help, among the solicitors who first supported Marshall were Rowand Harker, and J. K. Nye, of Brighton, who gave him the " Army of Lord " case described later ; Marcus Lewis, a kindly old Jewish attorney, who did a great deal of the work at Bloomsbury county court and Marlborough Street police court ; Herbert Rushton, and Henry Wilson, of Bow Street. As early as June 1885 there is to be found in his fee-book the august name of Lewis & Lewis of Ely Place. But in 1885, while Marshall was still in Fulton's chambers, he made the acquaintance of a very remarkable young attorney, Mr. Arthur Newton, who briefed him for years and gave him great opportunities again and again. Marshall always acknowledged his debt to him. He was a Cheltenham boy, who had passed into his profession with high distinction, and had much in common with Marshall. They were of an age, both

Public Schoolboys, both fine athletes, both had been wide travellers. But, if Marshall had still his name to make, Newton was already a made man. A first-class police-court advocate, his charm and ready wit made him friends everywhere, and with all manner of men and women who from time to time need the services of a clever lawyer. When Marshall was still unknown, Newton had been caricatured in *Vanity Fair* and seemed to be on the road to no ordinary success. It was perhaps natural that he should be attracted to Marshall ; at any rate he gave him a junior brief to Fulton in the case of " Ma Jefferies," a night-club queen of the 'eighties, which caused a great stir at the time. While the case was pending, Marshall went down to Brighton in the same train with her, and was amused to see her " as cool as a cucumber."

He was soon busy in the county courts, and at the end of 1886 he was beginning to refuse briefs which he could not do. He had several redoubtable opponents in these courts, and the naïve and amazed manner in which he records his failures is very charming and characteristic. In 1886 at the Marylebone county court he first met Horace Avory, who, both as an advocate and as a judge, was for over forty years to watch him so carefully. The case in question was entitled *Sylchester* v. *Fletcher* and was to be tried three times in the county court. Marshall seems to have won the first time, but lost afterwards. The last time Avory was against him, and he records in his diary : " November 23rd. Marylebone county court. *Sylchester* v. *Fletcher*—all day : again verdict for plaintiff. Horace Avory did case. Iniquitous decision." Finally, Marshall, the most persistent of men, managed to take out a summons in the High Court in connection with the same matter, but met with no greater success. " January 16th, 1887. Summons *re* Fletcher, before Master Francis : extraordinary order by Master ! " A little later, Alfred Lyttelton is his opponent at the Westminster county court ; he makes no comment except that he was " beaten easily."

It was not long before Marshall was beginning to command special fees in the county court. He was briefed by a man who wished to recover a horse, which he said had been wrongfully taken in execution. The nag was worth precisely £5, and

Marshall's brief was marked twenty guineas. This lay client came to Fountain Court and drove his astonished counsel down to the county court in a magnificent turn-out drawn by a spanking pair with glittering harness. After winning his case, Marshall asked why he had been treated so sumptuously. He was told that all the horsey men in the neighbourhood had been betting on the result of the case. There had been £700 at stake, and Marshall had been briefed by one of the rival syndicates !

At the Old Bailey, Marshall soon gained a footing. Fulton abided by his promise and did everything he could to push him. In December 1885 he led him in the very interesting case of Harry Patrick. At the very close of his career, Marshall used this case in vain as an argument for the defence, and afterwards for the reprieve, of Lock Ah Tam the Chinaman. Patrick was tried for the murder of Rachel Bailey, his sweetheart. He had taken a room for himself and his girl for the night. He went out in the morning leaving word that Rachel was to be called in two hours. She was found lying face downwards on her bed, covered with blood, her throat cut so savagely that her head was almost severed from her body. A Japanese dagger was found on the bed. Patrick meanwhile had gone straight to an aunt, confessed to having killed his girl, and dictated his will. No motive could be found to account for this extraordinary crime, and the prisoner was precluded at law from going into the witness box to make his explanation. The defence raised was that he had done it while seized with an epileptic fit. But Mr. Justice Hawkins would have none of this defence, and strongly directed the jury to convict the prisoner. They did so ; but, on hearing his sentence, the prisoner immediately had a violent attack of epilepsy, and on the morning fixed for his execution he had a succession of fits. The Home Secretary therefore respited his sentence.

Marshall once defended at the Old Bailey, without knowing it at the time, one of the most famous criminals of modern times, " Dr." Neil Cream. His method was to meet women of the unfortunate class ; he gained their confidence and prescribed remedies for them, but if they were unwise enough to take his pills they died soon afterwards in convulsions. Some years before Cream was convicted and hung, Marshall was briefed, by Mr. Harry Wilson of Bow Street, to defend a man for bigamy. When he walked into court, he was aghast to find a whole bevy of young women who claimed to have been " married " to the prisoner within the space of the last few months. The case seemed hopeless, and Marshall advised his client to plead " guilty."

" Nothing of the kind," said the prisoner indignantly ; " this is a clear case of mistaken identity. Communicate with the gaol at Sydney, Australia, and you will find that I was there at the time I am supposed to have committed these offences."

A cable was despatched with the name and full description of the prisoner, and to the amazement of all concerned, except the prisoner, a reply came immediately confirming his statement : his alibi was perfect, and Marshall left the court musing on the narrow escape from gaol of an innocent man. Some years afterwards Marshall went into court to see Neil Cream on his trial, and he was astonished to recognise his client, the alleged bigamist. The mystery was never explained, but Marshall's theory was that Neil Cream had a " double " in the underworld, and they went by the same name and used each other's terms of imprisonment as alibis for each other. There was a rumour current when Cream was executed that vengeance had at last overtaken Jack the Ripper, the celebrated murderer of women in the 'eighties. This arose from the fact that the hangman, about to send Cream to eternity, thought he heard him say, " I am Jack ——" But Marshall did not regard this as very conclusive evidence. " Vanity," he said, " is an inherent disease in murderers—and, thank God, it has hanged most of them. Therefore I say, if Neil Cream had been allowed by the hangman to complete his sentence and made a statement to the effect that he was Jack the Ripper, I should personally not have believed him. I should have regarded it as another exhibition of the murderer's vanity." As a matter of fact, this unknown criminal achieved such extraordinary fame in the 'eighties that several persons, not even in prison, actually came forward and claimed to be Jack the Ripper, without the slightest right to his title or reputation ; and Marshall himself in 1888 prosecuted in a case which concerned a letter, sent under his name to Lord

Sheffield, threatening murder to the earl and his steward on account of some supposed injustice to one of his tenants. " I should be much obliged to you," this amazing document concluded, " if you would arrange for your steward to sleep under the same roof as yourself on Monday night, October 29th, or else I shall have to bring an assistant. My knife is nice and sharp. O for a gentleman this time instead of a lady ! I am sorry for troubling you, but don't forget the 29th. I remain, yours truly, JACK THE RIPPER."

Marshall appeared, with Geogeghan, for another criminal of the same class as Cream and Jack the Ripper, under extraordinary circumstances. This man's name was Deeming, and he had murdered several women and carefully cemented their bodies under the kitchen or scullery floors, before he went out to Australia and was convicted of a similar offence. His main defence was insanity, but so great was the prejudice in Melbourne against him that the trial had to be adjourned on account of the uproar. Deeming was, however, able to address the jury, after his counsel had done so for an hour in an eloquent speech, directed to prove that he was mad ; and when he was found guilty he was sane enough to telegraph a notice of appeal to the Privy Council in London. In spite of the fact that the Privy Council will only intervene where a flagrant miscarriage of justice has occurred, the noble and learned lords actually sat to consider this appeal under the presidency of Lord Halsbury. Geogeghan and Marshall were a strange pair to appear in the quiet and august chambers of the Privy Council ; but the Lord Chancellor, one of the few Old Bailey men who have reached the Woolsack, no doubt made them feel at home. Geogeghan was one of the greatest natural orators at the Bar, but, like most such men, exceedingly hard to stop. As the Privy Council was ringing with the unaccustomed sound of his Irish brogue, an important telegram arrived, which Marshall thought his leader should see. Several times he plucked Geogeghan's gown in vain, till at last the Irishman's patience was exhausted.

" Don't dare to interrupt me when I am addressing this Court," he whispered—at the top of his voice.

Marshall then allowed him to continue his speech till the Court adjourned.

" Why did you interrupt me like that ? " said Geogeghan as they walked off to lunch.

Marshall then handed him the telegram ; it came from a prison chaplain in Australia, and read as follows. " Deeming hanged this morning " ! The colonial sheriff had indeed anticipated the decision of the Privy Council, who in due course " humbly advised " Her Majesty that the appeal should fail. Probably, at the very time that Geogeghan was pleading so eloquently, an extraordinary scene was being enacted at Melbourne : Deeming was being executed before a large crowd of spectators by two executioners, one disguised by a black and the other by a white beard. This experience of pleading with Geogeghan for the life of a dead man was a unique experience, and Marshall Hall never visited the Judicial Committee again.

Deeming, in one of his statements, openly said that he had murdered these women because they spread a vile infection. This reason has also been assigned as an explanation of the systematic crimes of Neil Cream and Jack the Ripper ; it is said that the ravages of a terrible disease had brought into their minds this terrible homicidal perversion.

Marshall once again had another rare experience, in resisting a civil claim at Lewes Assizes by a man who had been condemned to death there twenty-one years before ! Mr. John Rawlinson, afterwards Recorder of Cambridge, that great gentleman but confused advocate, appeared for the plaintiff. It appeared that he had been found guilty of murdering his wife, but sent to Broadmoor on the ground of insanity. In 1883 the Home Secretary released him on condition that a cousin looked after him ; the action concerned certain moneys entrusted to this cousin in 1886. The defence was that the cousin had spent the moneys on the care of the plaintiff, and in indulging in certain speculations in shares and horseflesh at his request ! At all events, Rawlinson and Marshall got the case into such a muddle between them that Mr. Justice Hawkins begged for mercy. " This case had better be settled, as it is now unintelligible," he cried. Ultimately the jury gave a small balance to the ex-criminal lunatic !

But it was really in his native county that Marshall won his early laurels. He had soon begun to gain a reputation in Sussex as a defender of prisoners; and having at Quarter Sessions defended a man successfully on a charge of burglary at Eastbourne, despite the fact that he was caught red-handed with a bagful of silver outside the very house which he was accused of robbing, one of the magistrates, with some lack of knowledge of the qualities which lead to the Woolsack, said, when the verdict of " not guilty " was given, " That young man will be Lord Chancellor." Like most successful young defending counsel, he began to be briefed for the prosecution; and his first appearance in the rôle of prosecutor against Charles Gill was in a terrible child murder case in the Spring Assize of 1886. Marshall only held a junior brief, and Gill obtained a verdict of " guilty, but insane."

The scene of this grievous tragedy was a small shop in the village of Polegate on Boxing Night, 1886. A widow of a grocer, Mrs. Taylor, who had in seventeen years borne eleven children, was undergoing a change of life. She was in moderately good circumstances, though worried at the time by small debts. She was given to drink, and had indulged excessively on the afternoon before the tragedy. Three of her little girls slept in one room, and her eldest little boy was awakened by a disturbance in their room, and by the voice of one of his sisters, which seemed to be saying, " Mother, you are hurting my tooth." Shortly afterwards, the eldest sister, aged fourteen, appeared on the stairway; she was holding her throat with one hand, and blood was pouring through her fingers; with the other she was pointing to her bedroom. The little boy found his mother there, holding a razor, and the two other girls dead, with their throats cut. The demented mother had killed them as they slept. The son got the razor from his mother and took her downstairs. To Kate, who died a week afterwards, the poor woman said, " You will forgive me, darling, won't you? " The dying girl replied, " Yes, mother." To her son she said, " I did it for the best."

Two years later, Marshall appeared with Gill and against Fulton in the Sabina Tilley case, which was another charge of child murder. This case aroused the deep sympathy of the public, and the readers of the *Sussex Daily News* subscribed to a " Sabina Tilley Defence Fund." These defence funds were

then rare, but are now usually raised in a criminal *cause célèbre.*
Sabina Tilley, a pretty servant girl of nineteen, admittedly
devoted to children, had paid the price of an irregular love
affair : she was delivered of twin girls at a Brighton workhouse.
A month after her confinement on a bitterly cold winter's day
she left the workhouse, her children well wrapped up in her
arms. She could not feed both of them, and they were both
found dead in a box, which Sabina left in a railway compartment
on her way to London. The defence raised was that they had
died through pueumonia in the cold air, or that the mother had
accidentally smothered them in the attempt to keep them warm.
The medical testimony conflicted, but the principal piece of
evidence against the prisoner was that of a woman who had
been sent to look after the poor distraught girl at the police
court. She took a note of a statement made by the girl : " I
was suckling my children, and I squeezed them to my breast
till they were nearly dead. They were not quite dead when I
placed them in the basket. I have not had five minutes rest
since, and every policeman I saw I felt I must give myself up."
The book, in which the note was taken, was found to have
had every page torn out previous to this entry ; Gill made tremendous play with this, and commented strongly on the
conduct of a woman who, sent to succour the girl, had the
heart to take down such a statement. Marshall's name occurs a
number of times in the report of this case, and, indeed, he argued
a point of law as to the admissibility of certain evidence. Gill's
speech for the defence was a masterly effort, and established
his reputation, as well as setting his poor little client at liberty.
That Marshall himself had been useful in this case is obvious
from a letter written to him by Mr. Infield, the editor of the
Sussex Daily News. " With regard to the Tilley case there is
nothing to thank me for. I am as much indebted to you as you
are to me in the matter—so we will call it quits. I have had a
very nice letter from Barchard about it. He strikes me as being
about as good a specimen as I have ever met of an English
gentleman, and he is a wonderful believer in you. Hope you
have been picking up a good many crumbs this week. I think
you will find before you are much older you will get hold of
good-sized bits of bread."

In these days the bulk of his work, as the local reports show, consisted of prosecutions ; but he never was at home in this class of work. He hated the rôle of prosecutor in the Vacquier and the Hayley Morris cases, though his personal feeling against both prisoners was of the strongest ; and in the very last term of his practice, while listening to a prosecution at the Old Bailey, he flung impatiently out of court and said to a colleague, " If that is the way prosecutions have to be conducted, thank God I have spent the best of my life in defending." It was the same in his early days : reading through the press cuttings of his early cases, it is impossible not to notice that Marshall, where his sympathies were aroused on behalf of a prisoner, often acted as a kind of supplementary counsel for the defence, frequently recommending that a lenient course should be taken ; and once he seems to have suppressed a most damaging piece of evidence against a prisoner. In other cases, where the nature of the crime excited his indignation, he was unable to assume that impartiality which it is the first duty of all prosecuting counsel to learn. In a case which concerned a wicked assault upon a little girl, Gill, who was defending, had occasion, as he did more than once, to comment upon " the violent, passionate, and extraordinary oratory of Mr. Marshall Hall, to which we have just listened." In the Hayley Morris case he felt the same disgust, but he conducted that case with admirable calmness and impartiality.

Mr. Cecil Whiteley, K.C., for many years prosecuting Treasury counsel, and a much younger man than Marshall, has told me that Marshall as a prosecutor was not a formidable opponent, erring as he did on the side of leniency. A letter of Marshall Hall's to this advocate, on the latter's resignation of his Treasury post in order to take silk, shows at once his chivalry and generosity to the younger men, and his real interest in them ; as well as his dislike for prosecuting and the prosecuting mentality. Whiteley had chaffingly reproached him for not congratulating him on his new silk gown ; Marshall went straight home and wrote this letter :

" *March 15th*, 1921.

" MY DEAR CECIL,—I am sorry that it was possible for you to think for a moment even that I was remiss in not writing to offer you my congratulations. You and I have been such good friends for so long that, when you asked my advice as to whether you should apply or not, I took it as a sign of both friendship and confidence, and I told you I thought you would be wise to send in your application. When a few days later, in a hurried passing whisper, you told me you had applied, I said good luck, and added that I would not write. I knew from something that you did *not* know that in your case the application was to a great extent a matter of form only, and I feel sure you have done the right thing. It tends to destroy the sentiment in one's humanity to be constantly engaged in prosecuting offenders, be those offenders ever so vile, and when many years ago, alas, I saw that I was in danger of treading that single path, I broke loose, on the advice of some of my friends, most of whom have since become judges, or worse. You have a varied practice, and in your own special line you ought to be able to do well *until you can make good all round* in the front row. Nothing you ever did proved to me more conclusively than before that you can handle big facts (aye, and complicated facts), with all the strength and lucidity that is necessary, than the opening I heard from you of that Indian extradition case. Above all things, you have earned in your position of counsel to the Treasury at the C.C.C. the reputation of being a very fair prosecutor, and a better reputation than that no man can desire. The best of all good wishes to you—good luck and success.

" Yours very sincerely,
" E. MARSHALL HALL."

Two characteristics of his advocacy are obvious from the start. The Press realised very early that they had a live wire in Marshall Hall, fighting hard in all his cases, standing up, sometimes very disrespectfully, to the Bench. According to Mr. Arthur Denman, Clerk of Assize to the South-Eastern Circuit for over forty years, he drove poor Mr. Justice Field, then old and irascible, nearly wild. Field could be very rude, and once told his under-sheriff, who came up and spoke to him in court after the high sheriff's Assize luncheon, never to address him again except by affidavit. In 1887, at Lewes Assizes, where he held nine briefs of his own, Marshall records that Field was very disagreeable, and adds, " Regular row with Field ; see daily paper." Field had accused him of unprofessional conduct, whereat Marshall turned haughtily to the jury, and said, " It seems, gentlemen, that I stand here, not only to defend my client, but myself." At Maidstone Assizes, in the same year, he held twelve briefs, and Field was " almost intolerable." It must have been in these days that his feud began with Mr. Justice, afterwards Lord Justice, Mathew, whose judgment in the Chattell case years afterwards did him considerable harm. However, in 1885, when Marshall was " junior," or secretary, to the South-Eastern Circuit, it is interesting to read that " Mathew proposed my health with that of the circuit very kindly " on Grand Night. But it did not take Mathew long to discover that he thoroughly disapproved of Marshall both as a man and an advocate. They were both in their ways great men, but utterly antipathetic. Mathew was a lawyer of the first rank and the creator of the Commercial Court, withal an exceedingly witty Irishman with a gift of dry and sarcastic humour which penetrated the chinks in Marshall's armour and wounded him deeply. Marshall once told a distinguished colleague at the Bar of a certain Assize, that he had held no less than twelve briefs before Mathew and lost them all. Finally he became very truculent, and was told by the learned judge to sit down ; he did not obey, but slowly turned round and carefully surveyed the public, sitting at the back of the court and in the gallery. " Sit down," repeated the judge, but Marshall only repeated what he had said before. Finally, thoroughly infuriated, the judge thundered out, " Sit down, Mr. Hall." " Oh, your lordship is addressing *me*," replied Marshall imperturbably ; " I thought you were addressing a lady at the back of the court. Certainly, my lord, if your lordship would prefer me to address you sitting down, I will do so."

This was not the only time that a judge told Marshall to sit down. When he was a K.C. of years' standing, the same request was made three times by Mr. Justice Grantham, who was not nearly so dynamic, but a much more explosive, occupant of the Bench. Each time the judge's tone grew louder ; after the second request Marshall said, " I will not sit down unless you withdraw what you said." After the third, " Oh, well, I suppose I must, seeing the position your lordship occupies."

Curiously enough, in his last years at the Bar, Marshall was allowed by all His Majesty's judges, for reasons of health, to address them sitting down.

But Mr. Justice Mathew rarely lost his temper, and Marshall did not always come off so well with him ; the judge's cold and hostile manner had a way of withering Marshall's expansive and exuberant nature. He was an exceedingly sensitive man, and after some years he grew tired of the chilling atmosphere of Mathew's court, and wanted to make friends. Sir Frank Lockwood undertook to put matters right, and the two of them tracked the judge to his club one evening, after the Courts had risen. It. was arranged that Lockwood should go in for a minute or two to explain what Marshall wanted, while the latter should wait outside till Lockwood came to call him in to the judge.

" I had only to wait two minutes," Marshall used to say in the charmingly aggrieved and naïve tone which he used to adopt when telling a story against himself. " In less than that time, Lockwood came tripping down the club steps, calling out to me long before he had reached me, ' It's no use, Marshall, the judge says he hates you.' "

He did not hesitate to tell the magistrates what he thought of them in those days, and on one occasion he drew a stern rebuke from his old friend, Francis Barchard. In the course of a case, Sir R. Gillespie, one of the magistrates, had asked the manager of a prosecuting company how much the defendant owed the company. The witness replied that he did not know, and that it would be impossible for him to know. Sir R. Gillespie then reprimanded him, whereupon Marshall rose in his wrath and said, " When I see members of an unpaid magistracy acting in such a way, I think it positively scandalous, and I simply blush that there are gentlemen on the bench who bully witnesses like this." On another occasion when a defence seemed quite hopeless, Marshall attacked the statute under which the prosecution was brought ! " Since," he said indignantly, " this Act was passed by an ill-advised majority of the legislature, there has been a very large increase in this kind of case brought forward by busybodies." On another occasion, when defending a builder who had contravened the provisions of the Brighton Improvement Act, he said, " A more iniquitous Act was never put upon the Statute Roll." It needs a bold advocate openly to denounce the laws, but he got his man off.

Yet again : Marshall was struggling to prevent the Bench from sending his client to trial, and the Bench seemed determined to do so and strongly criticised one of his questions.

" Mr. Hall," said the chairman, " you know that it is a most improper question to ask."

" I know," came the bold retort, " when a person has made up his mind it is not very easy to change it."

The chairman : " I do not want you to make a speech now."

Marshall : " I am going to make a speech—that is what I am paid for."

And he did make a speech and won the day.

These passages of arms showed very early the fearless quality of his advocacy. It made him bad friends on the Bench in the future, but undoubtedly his reckless courage helped to make his name in Sussex ; he was marked out as a man who would stick at nothing in defence of his client.

Another characteristic of his advocacy was also apparent at the start : his impatient and eager brain was quite unable to keep his own personal experiences out of his case—it seemed to himself the best kind of evidence, and he could not resist letting the jury have the advantage of it. He was defending a young girl of seventeen for arson ; his defence, which proved unsuccessful, was that it was an accident, and arose from the young lady's curling-tongs. Mr. Justice Mathew ridiculed the theory, but Marshall was not at a loss. " I have myself seen a fire occur like this, and have helped to put it out," he said. Further evidence elucidated the fact that some charred matches were found on the premises, and the judge remarked sardonically, " Is Mr. Marshall Hall going to suggest that the matches lit themselves ? Perhaps he knows of a match that lights when he calls to it from the bed." On another occasion, Marshall was defending the owner of a trap whose horse was accused of trotting at eighteen miles an hour. " I have been in the trap myself," he protested, " and I *know* that the horse can not go that speed ! "

Other members of the Bar who knew and understood pardoned Marshall when he did this sort of thing, where they would have been furious with a more crafty and less naïve advocate. In his last years he was against Sir Douglas Hogg, now Lord Hailsham, in a life insurance case. Relatives of a deceased man were suing on a policy ; the defence was suicide ; the answer to the defence was accident. The dead man had admittedly died from a revolver wound. Marshall was for the plaintiff, and, in order to avoid the expense of experts, asked Sir Douglas Hogg's leave to show the jury how a revolver worked, which was gladly given. Then Marshall proceeded to explain to the jury how he was the greatest expert on revolvers in the country, how he had instructed officers in revolver-shooting during the war, and how, to his personal knowledge, a young officer had died accidentally from just such a revolver in identical circumstances to the poor man in the case before the jury. " If it hadn't been dear old Marshall," said Sir Douglas, " I should never have forgiven such a thing."

But he carried this form of indiscretion to extreme in the Dennistoun case, where he cross-examined Mrs. Dennistoun on private conversations she had had with himself when he had given her advice on a previous action. Yet the whole of this tendency in Marshall can be traced to his passionate zeal for the client whom he was representing. When a client briefed him, he did not merely buy the lawyer or even the advocate in Marshall Hall, but the whole man. He had the gift of throwing the whole of his personality into the case : by the fire of his rhetoric he threw a cloak of romance and drama round the sorry figures in the dock, convincing the jury that he believed passionately in every word he said—and for the time he really did. A great friend says of him that he was a man who was without settled convictions on any subject, but who might be convinced in all sincerity of anything in the world for the moment. This made his nature bad raw material for politics, but by its very plasticity fitted him admirably for advocacy. For the nonce his case meant as much to his inflammable and emotional consciousness as it did to the prisoner, or to the plaintiff, or defendant, perhaps even more. The advocate's tears are a frequent subject for ridicule, but in Marshall's case, when they flowed, they were genuine enough. But he was fully aware of their effect upon the jury. He once wrote very modestly an account of one of his own triumphs against a very great lawyer of the time. " No counsel is allowed by the rules of the profession to express his opinion upon the guilt or innocence of an accused person, but if an advocate for the defence can legitimately, in his advocacy, convey to the jury the impression of his belief in his client's case, he has gone a long way towards securing their verdict. I well remember listening in a case to a fine speech by a man who was a great speaker without being a great advocate. The speech was perfect in composition and logic, but it left one cold, whereas the speech in reply, badly as it might read in the reports, was a human speech on the level of its audience, and it won the verdict. A few days later I happened to meet one of the jury, and asked him how they failed to be convinced by the other speech. ' Oh,' said he, ' the speech was right enough, but he didn't believe a word of it himself ; he had his tongue in his cheek all the time.' "[1] About the same antagonist, Marshall also said, " Please do not compare me with him ; he is one of the greatest intellects of the time, but," he added rather sadly, " I doubt if he has ever understood a man or a woman."

In 1887, two co-defendants, named Barker and Hughes, employed the respective services of Gill and Marshall to defend them before the Recorder of Brighton in a case which makes as strange reading as any in the reports. Gill had generously arranged that Marshall was to defend one of the defendants on his own. The case came to be known as the " Love Home " case, and concerned a sect known as the " Army of the Lord," which had established itself at Brighton under the presiding genius of one Wood. According to the evidence, he was fortunate in " converting " an old lady, who gave him £2,500, with which he fitted up a riding-school into a place of worship for the " Army of the Lord." At the time the disturbance arose, the congregation had been worked up to about a hundred persons. Meanwhile, unpleasant rumours were spreading round Brighton ;

[1] Preface to *Trial of the Wainwrights*

finally Barker and Hughes led an assault on the place, shouting,
" King Solomon, you promised to let us in to-night. King
Solomon, come out and we will fight you on your own ground."
But, when the crowd broke into the meeting place, they found
an orderly assembly listening to one of the brethren reading
from St. Mark. In due course they were prosecuted, under
a statute of 1812, for disturbing a religious meeting. Marshall
and Gill directed their cross-examination to show that the
meeting was far from being religious, and a strange story was
elicited by them step by step. It appeared that Wood himself
was known as " King Solomon " ; other leaders of the movement
were known as " King David," " King Eli," " Caleb," and
last, but not least, " Jonah." These names were given to them
by " prophetesses," poor little children passing as " Peace "
and " Love " and so forth. They " gave names " and
" prophesied," when inspired to do so by the Lord. In order to
get into a suitable state of inspiration they dressed in white,
red, and yellow dresses, and danced till they fell to the ground
in a state of exhaustion, and lay shaking and kicking on the
floor, while the congregation watched, sometimes for hours.
If they shook and kicked too much, a rug was placed over their
legs " for decency's sake " ; but it was then that the Lord
visited them, and told them to " give names," and made them
prophesy. Their prophecies seemed mostly to consist in telling
the faithful to sell their jewels for the Lord. King Solomon
would then pay a visit to the pawnshop. On one occasion the
" little one under the power of the Holy Ghost " led them to a
special sanctuary, and " distinctly " told them to take their
shoes and stockings off ! King Solomon performed cures, laid
his hands on the congregation and even kissed some of the
" sisters."

Several brethren went into the box, including King David,
but King Solomon wisely kept away. One of the brethren had
to confess that " the Kings " did not work, or do anything to
earn an honest living : they had given up everything to the
Lord. Some of the cross-examination of " Abraham " is
charming :

" I want to know how you get your living ? "—" The Lord
sends it ; that is my answer."

" I am sorry that you cannot answer."—" I am provided for by the Lord, and the Lord has sent it."

" Don't you eat and drink ? "—" Yes."

" Where do you get the money to pay for the food ? "— " The Lord has sent it."

" Where do you live ? "—" In the house."

" In the Lord's house ? "—" Yes."

" But Wood is the tenant ? "—" Yes."

" Are you all allowed to kiss a woman, or is only King Solomon ? "—" All allowed to do what we like"'

" Do you like to kiss them ? "—" I decline to answer."

" When you have the Spirit of the Lord to dance, don't you feel inclined to kiss the women ? "—" Of course I do."

" Do you kiss them ? "—" I won't answer."

" Have you, through the power of the Lord, healed anyone ? " —" Yes, a young man living in the north of Brighton."

" What was the complaint ? "—" I don't know."

This gave Marshall an opportunity to make a passionate address to the jury, who, needless to say, acquitted both defendants, almost by acclamation.

In the rough and tumble of an Old Bailey and country practice, Marshall was really learning to cross-examine. On one occasion he was appearing for an applicant for a licence to sell wines and spirits, and a pious looking gentleman appeared representing, as he said, a large number of objectors in the neighbourhood.

" Of course, you represent the majority of respectable people in the neighbourhood ? "—" I think so."

" Didn't you stand for the council here last year ? "—" Yes."

" You were defeated by a large majority ? "—" What has that to do with it ? "

" Oh, nothing," was Marshall's retort ; " it only shows you don't represent the majority of respectable people in the neighbourhood."

By 1886, Marshall Hall was beginning to find his feet, and even in those early days he made it his business to help other men not as fortunate as himself. Two years after he was called, a young man named Clavell Salter came to the Bar, without any influence to help him ; he had not been to the 'varsity, and knew very few people in London. He was almost in despair about his legal future, when one day he met in the Strand someone whom he did know, the rising young criminal advocate, Mr. Edward Marshall Hall.

" How are you getting on, Clavell," he said.

" Oh, very badly, Hall. I don't see how I shall ever get a brief."

" Never get a brief? Nonsense," said his sanguine and generous friend. " Come along with me ; *I'll* get you a brief."

He thereupon led the future judge into the chambers of H. C. Richards, who was sitting in his chair wrapped in a voluminous overcoat.

" Hullo, Richards," said Marshall ; " here's a man called Salter—wants a brief."

Then a miracle happened ; out of one of his capacious pockets Richards produced a brief and handed it to Salter : it was marked " one guinea," but it was the first that had ever come his way. " You'd better come down and support my application for a licence," he said. It was a brief on behalf of a " poor widow " who wished to ' support ' H. C. Richards's brewer ! Clavell Salter made such a successful little speech that Richards asked him to come into his chambers, where he stayed for nearly thirty years and made his fortune. Mr. Justice Salter became a close friend of Marshall's, and did much of his devilling in the early days. Marshall had a great belief in him as a lawyer, and used to rely on his notes as regards the law. When the brief was beautifully noted, Marshall would skim through it, and with the help of Salter's note would at once see the true point of law, which would have otherwise escaped him in a forest of attractive facts. " Wonderful man, Salter," he would say to his solicitor, with a *naïveté* that disarmed all criticism. " A most complicated case this, at first sight ; but, of course, the point is a simple one. Mr. Salter spotted it too, and quite agrees with me."

But, though Marshall was already earning a living, his name was becoming chiefly associated with crime. Now this branch of the profession, though it is most before the public eye, is not profitable, nor, as a rule, does it lead to the great prizes which the Law has to give. All his life, Marshall tried to escape from an exclusively criminal business, and at times he conducted a very prosperous and flourishing general practice ; but fate and circumstances proved too strong for him in the end, and it was in the Old Bailey and on circuit, where he was apprenticed, that he won his lasting fame. But in 1886 he was worried about his practice, and, now that he had some experience, he wanted to try his hand at other work. The Divorce Court gave him that opportunity. He had been doing a little business there for some time, and he had certainly made the most of these rare appearances in the High Court. " This is one of the most extraordinary cases, my lord," was his invariable beginning. A flutter of excitement would run through the court, and reporters would begin to take vigorous notes. Then followed the usual sordid story, then, as now, common form in the Divorce Court, and the Press would lay down their pens and say, " The young humbug ; there's nothing in it after all."

In 1885, Marshall had met Bargrave Deane at dinner. That learned matrimonial lawyer and future judge liked this very handsome young man and his beautiful young wife ; and, when Marshall told him that he was afraid that his practice was becoming exclusively criminal, Deane generously suggested he should come into his chambers as a pupil and learn the divorce business. Marshall consulted Fulton, and, the latter not wishing to stand in his way, reluctantly advised him to go, but continued to help his young friend long after he had gone elsewhere. So, in February 1887, Marshall moved to Deane's chambers in King's Bench Walk, as a pupil once again, and stayed there till November 1887.

Divorce did not satisfy Marshall's ambitions any more than crime did, and he was but a bird of passage in King's Bench Walk ; but his short sojourn there brought him at least one prize, a junior brief in the most celebrated case that ever came before the Divorce Court. He appeared with Sir Walter (now Lord) Phillimore and Bargrave Deane in the Queen's Proctor's historic intervention in the Crawford divorce suit. Marshall did not play an active part in court, although Lord Phillimore still remembered, last year, " a very young man who made several very useful suggestions " in the consultations which preceded the trial ; but because Marshall held strong views about this case, and since it advertised his name to the world as a practitioner in the Divorce Court, and so may be regarded as one of the foundations of his career, I will recapitulate very shortly the story of this suit.

In 1886, perhaps the most brilliant and promising young statesman in England was Charles Dilke, and had it not been for the disaster of this case he would almost certainly have been Prime Minister. Mr. Justin MacCarthy describes his fall as " that of a tower," and said that, but for this, he must have succeeded Mr. Gladstone. In 1885 he literally had the world before him, and in addition he was engaged to the noble lady who stood by him and believed in his innocence to the end. Early in 1886 a Liberal member of Parliament cited him as co-respondent. When the case was heard, the only evidence against the wife, who did not give evidence, was her unsworn confession given by her, when she was in an admittedly distressed and hysterical condition, to her husband, that she had committed adultery with Dilke. It is unlikely that such evidence would be held sufficient to-day to obtain a decree *nisi*, and of course it could never have been any legal evidence at all as against Sir Charles. Mr. Justice Butt, however, granted Mr. Crawford his decree *nisi*, but clearly ruled that there was no evidence against Dilke, and almost invited his counsel, Sir Charles Russell and Sir Henry James, not to put Dilke in the witness box to deny the wife's story on oath, and submit himself to cross-examination. At the luncheon interval, Russell and James held a consultation together in the absence of Dilke, and, falling in with Mr. Joseph Chamberlain's views, decided not to put Dilke in the witness box. Dilke acquiesced in this course, and the judge unambiguously commended it. But the result was highly paradoxical. The judge pronounced a decree *nisi* against the wife for adultery with a co-respondent, who was dismissed from the suit with costs against the petitioner. It was very strongly felt that Dilke should have gone into the witness box and denied the story. At the second trial the reasons assigned for this were two, that he had put himself unreservedly into the hands of his counsel, and that, if he were cross-examined, he would be compelled to betray the name of a lady with whom as a very young man he had carried on a love affair. The public outcry increased, and Sir Charles did not rest until he had made good his counsel's error. Had he not taken this course, the whole matter would have faded, no doubt, from the short memory of the public, and sooner or later he would have been allowed to continue his public career. But he gave the Queen's Proctor no peace until he could induce him to intervene. He would have been wiser to adopt different tactics, and, like Lord Russell, to have issued a writ or warrant for libel or slander, for the event was disastrous. When the Queen's Proctor did intervene, the nominal issue at law was whether the Court had been deceived, by Dilke's failure to give evidence, into giving a decree to Mr. Crawford to which he was not entitled ; but, in reality, Dilke was on his trial before the whole world, and the issue was whether he was an adulterer and a perjurer or was a deeply wronged man against whom a monstrous story had been concocted. There was no half-way house, and Dilke, without counsel or witnesses of his own, had to support the burden of proof. The Queen's Proctor had to establish affirmatively that the Court had been deceived on the previous occasion, and, unless he could do this, a dazzling career was hopelessly ruined. He was handicapped from the start by his failure to give evidence at the previous trial : he had neither the great advantages of a defendant in a criminal trial nor the ordinary advantages of a plaintiff in a libel action. He applied in vain to be allowed to appear as a party, so that he could employ counsel, call witnesses of his own, and cross-examine those against him. Had Sir Charles Russell been allowed to use on his behalf those matchless powers of advocacy and enquiry, it may well be that the jury would have come to a different conclusion ; but, even so, the scales were heavily weighted against him ; and, as it was, Sir Walter Phillimore was neither an experienced cross-examiner nor, as he made clear himself, did he appear for Sir Charles Dilke.

Against Dilke's denials stood the evidence of Mrs. Crawford, who now came forward to give her evidence, and to tell a far more damaging story against him than had been suggested before, a story which would make ordinary members of the public, if they believed it, turn from him in loathing. She said that the misconduct took place in the presence of a servant girl named Fanny, under circumstances which would be amazing even in a brothel. There were, however, several discrepancies in her evidence. Dilke was alleged by her to have met her on the first two guilty trysts at the house of an old servant of his ; in her original confession to her husband she had stated, according to his evidence, that they had met one morning and made the appointment for the same afternoon. Now, on that particular day, Dilke could prove that he was so busy on official and public business in the House and the Foreign Office that it was unlikely he could have been with Mrs. Crawford. In her evidence in court she said that the appointment was made for two days later. The second meeting was alleged to have taken place on a morning on which Lady Dilke, who, in defiance of public opinion, had married her husband during the pendency of the suit, went far to prove an alibi for him, for she said that Sir Charles had come to lunch with her on that day, and had arrived long before lunch-time; further, Mrs. Crawford had to admit misconduct with another man. The President, Sir James Hannen, commented very strongly on Dilke's failure to give evidence at the first trial, and refused to allow Sir Charles Russell to interpose ; moreover, he never mentioned the fact that Mr. Justice Butt had approved of the course taken. Mr. Henry Mathews, K.C., afterwards Lord Llandaff, in his address appealed strongly to the jury to free Mr. Crawford from the bitter yoke of his unhappy marriage, and they gave a verdict that the Court had not been deceived, which was virtually a decision that they did not believe Sir Charles Dilke upon his oath. It has been said fairly that in the first trial there was no legal evidence of Sir Charles's guilt, and in the second the Queen's Proctor failed to prove Sir Charles's innocence, an issue with which the Queen's Proctor was not directly concerned.

Marshall Hall was to see many another case when life and honour and liberty hung in the balance, but he was, perhaps, never to see a man who had quite so much to lose as had Sir Charles Dilke in the Crawford case. He heard the deep bass voice which said in agonised accents, " No, no," when the President described what a man of honour would have done in the first trial ; he knew that history had been made when the jury brought in their formal verdict ; and he must have longed to play a more prominent part in the proceedings. But he learned one very important lesson from this trial. Dilke always blamed his counsel, the most eminent of the day, for not putting him into the box ; and this great responsibility was undoubtedly theirs. Marshall always made it a rule never to take on himself such a responsibility. So important did he think this, that, after 1898—when a prisoner was allowed to give evidence in his own defence—he always wrote out a form : " I wish to give evidence in this case."—" I do not wish to give evidence in this case," and made his client strike out the one or the other and sign his decision. Then he would follow the course proposed by his client. He had learned from the Dilke trial how terrible the responsibility can be of the counsel who decides on his own judgment not to call his client ; it is indeed the sort of responsibility which comes back to haunt the advocate's dreams and disturb his slumbers. The wisest judgment can be mistaken, and for an innocent man to be condemned unheard, by the advice of his counsel, is a dreadful possibility. " Let a prisoner tell his story if he wants to," he said to me when I asked his advice on the point, " whatever your personal opinion." Marshall Hall's view, however, is not universally held. Lord Hailsham, for instance, considers that this supreme responsibility should not be shifted from the advocate to the client. Dilke, before he died, by his courageous and dignified attitude through the long years convinced many of his innocence, but Marshall never needed persuasion. Wherever the truth may lie, Marshall's opinion was definite. Many years afterwards he said to a friend, " *Of course* Dilke was innocent ; I have read papers which *prove* it." The documents which Marshall read may have been the statement furnished by " Fanny " on April 10th, 1886, a copy of which was found among his papers. She was the one witness who might have saved Dilke : her statement consisted in a categorical denial of any immoral relationship with him. She had been approached by a detective and frightened, and, very anxious not to be called as a witness, she disappeared. In December 1885 she married, and her husband naturally was strongly opposed to her giving evidence ; however, in April 1886 she re-appeared and made a statement in London. She then disappeared again, and the fact that she was not available as a witness must have prejudiced Dilke's case very considerably. Had the jury believed her word against Mrs. Crawford's, Dilke would have been in all probability cleared. The jury were not impressed by evidence given on his behalf by others in his service, and very probably they would not have believed her denials. But Fanny's absence was perhaps more deadly to Dilke than any cross-examination of her would have been. She said in her statement, which of course, in her absence, could not be given in evidence, " I never heard of Mrs. Crawford till the commencement of this case, and I should not know her if I saw her. The reason why I decline to say where I was during part of 1883 and 1884 has nothing to do with Mrs. Crawford or Sir Charles Dilke. The detective told me that I knew I had seen Mrs. Crawford at Sir Charles Dilke's house. I told him it was not true, but he told me that he did not believe me, and that if I did not admit it I should be prosecuted. I told Mr. Humbert (Sir Charles's solicitor) this, and that I was too frightened to go into the witness box, and felt I could not stop at home after what the detective had said, but should go away somewhere. My husband was very anxious that I should not be a witness ; we agreed not to let anyone know where we were."

It must be remembered that Marshall was always a strong and sanguine partisan ; but the personal opinion of so great and experienced an advocate, who actually appeared in the case, should be of great public interest ; and, at all events, some may regret that the public lost so great a public servant, because he himself chose a tribunal and a procedure which demanded the criterion which Cæsar set up for his wife, whereas the meanest felon is not convicted until his guilt is proved beyond reasonable doubt.

It must not, however, be thought that Marshall believed in every client for whom he appeared, or that he considered it any part of an advocate's duty to do so. His view was that the lawyer, like the doctor and the cab driver, is on the rank, and any person who engages them is entitled to the benefit of their talents. It is true that Marshall entered enthusiastically into his cases, and usually persuaded himself that his client was in the right, but there were exceptions. Only twice in his career was he tempted to refuse a brief, and on the first occasion he so disbelieved his client's story that he went to consult the then

Attorney-General, afterwards Lord Alverstone. " If you were a doctor," said Sir Richard Webster, " would you refuse your aid to a poor Magdalen dying of a horrible disease ? " Marshall thereupon took the brief, and when he had gone more deeply into the evidence he satisfied himself, and afterwards the jury, of his client's innocence. " That taught me a lesson," said Marshall, " which I never forgot." The second brief which Marshall wished to refuse was offered to him by a Nonconformist minister against whom a terrible charge of immorality had been brought. He did not like the case, and he did not like the man, but he remembered Webster's words and his previous experience. However, he did his very best to make it impossible for him to appear, by instructing his clerk to demand an exorbitant fee. The only answer was a cheque for the amount, and he went down and did the case. From ten o'clock in the morning till seven at night he was fighting with all his might for this man, about whose real history he had formed a strong opinion. He succeeded in demonstrating that the chief witness against the prisoner was not a strict adherent to the truth, and from this succeeded in persuading the magistrates that it was unsafe to convict on the evidence of this witness. When he was leaving for London, after he had won, his reverend client came up and thanked him. " I told you I was innocent," he said, " and now you have proved it." " I have proved nothing of the kind," was Marshall's stern reply ; " I have only induced the Bench to say you are not proved guilty." The man then put out his hand for his counsel to shake. " No," said Marshall, as he turned on his heel, " that is not included in the etiquette of the Bar or in the brief-fee."

Yet again : when he had fought a case desperately hard for prisoners in whom he did not believe, against a hostile judge, the latter sarcastically asked him, after the verdict of " guilty " had been returned :

" Well, Mr. Marshall Hall, do you consider it your duty to say anything on behalf of your clients ? "

" Thank you, my lord," he said ; " I think I have more than discharged my duty to them, and to you."

During his eighteen months in Deane's chambers, Marshall was quite constantly briefed by the Queen's Proctor, and in one of these had the good fortune to attract the fancy of Sir Charles Hall, Q.C., a namesake, but no relation, who was the tenant of chambers on the first floor of 3 Temple Gardens, and carried on a fashionable general practice. He met Marshall and liked him at once, and asked him to come and help him in his chambers ; this invitation was accepted. Marshall was now in chambers which might lead him beyond the limits of crime and divorce into a more general practice. Sir Charles was a man after Marshall's own heart ; he was a bachelor, man of fashion, fine gentleman, and collector. He was Attorney-General to King Edward, when Prince of Wales, and on intimate terms of friendship with him. Indeed the Prince used frequently to come down to the Temple to have a friendly chat with his Attorney-General in the room afterwards occupied by Marshall. It is said that Sir Charles first won the royal favour by his marvellous skill in sleight of hand. He preceded Forrest Fulton as Recorder of London, and won golden opinions whilst holding that office. Marshall went into his chambers in November 1888, took them over on Sir Charles's appointment as recorder in 1892, and remained there as tenant till he died. In these beautiful rooms most of his life's work was done, and much of his life's happiness was enjoyed. He had at last found anchorage, and he always had unmixed affection and pride in what he called " the little coterie of Temple Gardens." He considered that the choice of suitable chambers was the most vital necessity for the young practitioner, and was extremely grateful for his own good fortune. " My dear Edward," he wrote to me in the last year of his life, with that kindness and anxiety which he always showed to a young man who came to him for advice ; " the great and important thing is to get into a congenial atmosphere, where you will be liked and trusted, and vice versa : otherwise, however successful, you will not get the best out of your profession ; and for the thirty-nine years I have been in these chambers we have had the most delightful lot of young fellows, and now that I am growing old I esteem it a great compliment that the young men still want to come."

In these chambers he found Harvey Murphy, afterwards to take silk, and to become famous for sound advocacy, but still more for his enormous bulk, which became the subject matter for caricature by any young counsel on the South-Eastern Circuit clever with a pencil. Nor did he in the least resent such caricatures. The kindliest of men, he was for many years "Nestor" of the Divorce Court, giving advice from his great knowledge to all and sundry, from the judge to the youngest barrister with an undefended petition. One of his visits to the Chief Justice's Court, as a silk, was celebrated by a rare witticism: "Do you move, Mr. Murphy?" said the Chief. "With difficulty, my lord," was Murphy's truthful answer. Ashton, too, was in these chambers, also to become a King's counsel and a recorder, whose charming reminiscences, *As I went on my Way*, came out a year or two ago. Marshall survived these, and his fame far surpassed theirs, but their close friendship and frequent counsel were an important part of his professional life and brought him much happiness. Among the "delightful young fellows" were C. K. Francis, an Oxford cricketing blue, till his death a Metropolitan magistrate; R. E. Moore, Marshall's first devil and now a county court judge; Sir Guy Stephenson, now Assistant Public Prosecutor; Wellesley Orr, now a magistrate at Manchester, who noted some of his most famous briefs; Francis Barchard, the nephew of Marshall's old host and patron; Rupert Gwynne, dashing rider and bold debater, whose promising career in the House was cut short by death; Spiro Mavrojani, whose Hellenic wit once led him to make a grim jest. Armstrong, the murderer, was his solicitor in the country, and it was his duty to sit on the Bench which committed their own clerk to trial for murder. Mavrojani, being rebuked by a fellow magistrate for a kindly word spoken to the prisoner, said, "We lawyers and married men must hang together." There were also Max Labouchere, Marshall's beloved and brilliant nephew, whose death in the war brought him such deep sorrow, and Norman Birkett, one of the greatest leaders of the present day, whose rise to fame Marshall so materially assisted. Nor must his clerks be forgotten: A. E. Bowker and Ernest Harvey served him for over a quarter of a century, and were not only his servants, but his close personal friends; the latter dealt with his most confidential affairs; for hundreds of people came to consult him whose names never appeared in his fee-books or in the law reports, but to whom he was most generous in giving them his counsel gratuitously. So much did he trust Harvey that he became executor and trustee under his employer's will.

Thus it will be seen that Marshall had in four years seen work in four sets of chambers. In the sound common law chambers of Tindal Atkinson he had become acquainted with the rough and tumble of the county court ; with Forrest Fulton he learnt every corner of the Old Bailey ; with Bargrave Deane he was initiated into the mysteries of a purely matrimonial practice ; and finally he emerged into the distinguished atmosphere of Temple Gardens, presided over by Sir Charles Hall. He had served, therefore, a varied and useful apprenticeship before he really began to practise in the greatest and most profitable of all tribunals, the High Court of Justice, King's Bench Division. He was now in his thirtieth year ; already the Press was beginning to take notice of him, and a Sussex daily could remark proudly, " It cannot have been overlooked that this popular member of the Sussex Bar has been greatly in demand in the courts lately. Nature has been very bountiful in her gifts to him. He has a fine presence, an admirable voice, and a great flow of words. One may readily be forgiven for predicting for him an exceptionally brilliant future." He was already knocking at the door of fame.

CHAPTER IV

Tragedy

AT the time of which I am speaking, Marshall Hall was working as perhaps only ambitious young barristers can work ; he had the constant responsibility of other men's lives and troubles upon him, and the work of a young barrister just beginning to make his way is often as responsible as that of the most fashionable leader of the day. He is, perhaps, briefed at the last minute to defend the man in the dock, with a guinea or two to spend on his defence ; or he has to appear in the county court for a manager of a small business who has been wrongfully dismissed, and to whom the loss of his small action will mean the bailiffs in his home, and no funds to pay the rent of his cottage ; or, again, for a poor woman maimed in a street accident who will spend the rest of her days in the workhouse if she loses her case.

It is often said that a man who has to battle in the world must have peace at home; the greatness and heroism of Marshall Hall was that, with the most bitter domestic misery always present to his mind, he continued on his way with a courage and determination too high for praise. This was perhaps the bravest part of his very brave life, and, painful as it is, no biography could be complete without some account of it. When tragedy spread wings, and seemed to overshadow his whole life till there seemed no chance that happiness could return for him in his former surroundings and associations, he clenched his teeth and, smiling before the world, continued the old battle, unshaken and undaunted, till his tragedy was forgotten by the public, and indeed would scarcely have been believed by anyone who saw his cheerful bearing and knew his optimistic nature. " Open the ledger account with Life," he once said in a speech to young people at Southport, " and take good care to put in big letters everything to the credit side, and in as small letters as you can that which has to be placed on the debtor side, because it is not by the contemplation of unhappy things that you can make life happier." How faithfully the preacher had followed the lesson of his sermon that audience did not know.

It is to be supposed that he had looked forward to the day of his marriage as one of great happiness ; he was twenty-four and very much in love, but on that day itself all joy was taken away. While they were still in the carriage that drove them away from the church, his bride told him that she had never cared, and could not care, for him as he cared for her.

How much this must have meant to a sensitive and emotional man like Marshall Hall it is difficult to appreciate. The meaning of these experiences can only be known by the sufferer. Certainly the future must have appeared very black and threatening. But it was now too late to turn back, and he went off to Paris for a honeymoon with a wife who could not love him, but whom he loved passionately. This story is the great personal event, tragic as it is, in Marshall's life, and the writer approaches it with some hesitation. But he desires in this book to show the character of this brave man, and without this story of his first marriage no one could guess either at the tenderness or the courage that was in him. I have before me his personal diary of the first six years of his married life and of his career at the Bar, and it is one of the most touching documents I ever read. Ethel was one of those neurotic women who should probably never be married, unless to men who can completely dominate them. This Marshall never was able to do ; he always threw all his cards on the table and kept nothing back—this was not the way to interest a wayward girl like Ethel. Two days after the marriage he writes, " Ethel had terrible fit of low spirits ; she said some very cruel things. But resolved to take no notice and try and make her love me by kindness. She is a dear little thing."

They went to Paris and stayed at the Hôtel Domenice. Ethel's nerves became worse, and, on June 24th, " Ethel told me she would be just as happy without me as with me, which is not altogether a cheering prospect " ; so the poor young bridegroom went out by himself and " wandered about all over the old part of Paris, and bought some little ornaments for Ethel, which seemed to please her much." But he makes a heart-rending addition, " Poor little child, how I wish I could make her happy. She does not seem to care for me much, and I *cannot* make any difference. Spent a wretched evening." On the next day her nerves reached a climax, and he writes, " She said she did not love me at all now. I went down to breakfast, and meanwhile E. went out without my seeing her. I then went out to shop and bought her a ring, but, as there were no signs of Ethel at 4 o'clock, I started out all over Paris looking for her. As I did not see her, the agony I endured was something awful, but at last, when I was quite in despair, I saw her in the Rue Castiglione. I induced her to have some dinner and then pacified her grief a little, but I fear her love is almost gone for ever. I wish I were dead. Words can never tell my grief." " *Wednesday, June 28th.* In some measure things got a little better, and finally Ethel said she would try and love me, and I felt so happy I did not seem to know where I was. A weight seems lifted off my mind, and a cloud that had been so long between us since our wedding was dissipated. We went for a long walk all through the Rue de Rivoli."

It is hard to imagine a more poignant and pathetic figure than the young bridegroom searching Paris distractedly for his bride in the first month of his marriage, thinking he had lost her for ever ; and yet the grief " which no words could tell " was the merest prelude to the tragedy that was ultimately to come to him through her during the eight years that succeeded. Indeed, it would have been far better for him if he had not found her in the Rue Castiglione.

After these sad days, however, there follow a few weeks when he was almost happy ; clearly, he is very much in love, and his love quickens his sense of the beauty of Paris and the French countryside in wonderful early summer. They " go for a glorious drive for two hours, all through the Bois to Longchamp and Neuilly. The smell of the hay and the fresh air in the moonlight was lovely." They visit Fontainebleau and Versailles and go for a trip in a steamer down the Seine ; they disembark and eat cherries together in a wood. Back again in Paris, they stay at home after dinner. That night they had " a very slight quarrel, which soon passed away." The next day he " spent a very happy day."

On going back to London they took rooms in Seymour Street, where they were to stay until September 1886. They settled down to a very unhappy married life. Ethel was often ill and miserable, and the tragic mistake of his marriage became clearer every day. He began to be very impatient with his wife, and obviously he was under great nervous strain. But he was quick to blame himself. In December he writes " Perhaps, if I am more attentive, things may come round again, though I much doubt it at present." However, there are still reconciliations ; " Ethel was very cross and excitable, but a very good child after and seemed very sorry indeed." He still tries to please her by buying presents, and his exquisite taste in these matters ought to have charmed her ; he buys " a diamond star for her at Whistler's, but she did not seem at all pleased with it." His mother's influence is still very strong, and he goes to church regularly every Sunday, either to the Temple to hear Boyd Carpenter or to Quebec Chapel. Later his religious views are changing, and he begins to go down to Westminster to hear Cardinal Manning. One Sunday the fog prevented him from going to church as usual, so he " read the service in the afternoon with Ethel." He goes for long walks with her in the Park, picks wild flowers with her in the country, and takes her to a great many theatres. He does not like it when she goes to stay with her people, and is " very glad to have her back."

During the summer after their marriage they went for a tour abroad to the south of France, to Italy, Switzerland, and Germany. This seems to have been his only really happy time with Ethel, and even so it was marred by her continual ill-health. He went bathing and fishing with her, and his diary shows an appreciation of natural beauty which will surprise many who knew him only as an advocate. "*August 9th*. We went fishing, and only managed to catch one small trout, but we were rewarded for our trouble by seeing one of the finest sunset effects I ever saw. The change of colour was something marvellous, from red to light pink, from darkest, deepest violet to black." Later in August they were in Milan : " After dinner I went for a little stroll alone, as Ethel was again ailing, and after listening to some music at a café and walking through the garden I suddenly came upon the cathedral, like a ghost, with its lovely spire bathed in the full moonlight, and I shall never forget the sight."

But on his return to England, and as he became busier at the Bar, matters became much worse. To be married to a young and struggling barrister without comfortable private means is not an easy task, even for a woman who is devoted to her husband ; he is away all day, and very likely will have to sit late at night doing other people's work. Marshall certainly did so, and in addition, being a circuit man, he was away in the country for weeks at a time. Then there is the uncertainty of the remuneration ; briefs will at first be few, the fees very small and not recoverable at law—solicitors are sometimes inconsiderate in sending in fees to young counsel. For a young woman who believes in the man she has married, and is eager for his success, the struggle may be transformed into the most romantic adventure ; but Marshall did not in those early days possess the priceless boon of such a co-adventurer, and his first battles were fought single-handed.

In addition to his exacting profession he had two passions which his wife did not share, and resented bitterly. He found it difficult to keep away from the cricket-field during the summer, and his love of shooting at any kind of game can only be described as a passion. In the close season he would take out his gun and shoot at bats in the dusk, and at pike in the pond at his sister's place. He went for shooting-parties all over Sussex : with Francis Barchard at Horsted, with his brother-in-law at Stroud Park, with Stuart Oxley at Fen Place, with Lord Leconfield at Petworth, and with many others. In August 1884 he joined a party of five or six guns, mostly old Cambridge friends, at Hunthill in Forfarshire, and, according to the newspaper reports, in twelve days they shot 1,305½ brace of grouse and 200 various. He had held a brief for Montague Williams, and won that veteran's affection so quickly that we find him constantly shooting with him at Farnham Royal and contributing very handsomely to the bag. Perhaps his domestic unhappiness filled him with an insatiable desire to do something, and the wonder grows, as the diary is read, that he could really have crammed all these activities into his time. He was a clubman from the first ; when he first came to London he joined the

Union, and in 1887 he joined the Garrick and the Beefsteak. In this way he was introduced to an amusing theatrical circle. Yardley, a fellow Rugbeian, the great cricketer and minor playwright, is often calling on him; Charles Wyndham and George Alexander visit him; Ethel gives little at homes and " looks very pretty " at them. They go out to Corney Grain's parties, and meet Bancroft and Pinero, both to be among Marshall's most chosen friends. One night, Miss Ellen Terry comes to have supper with them. He is often taking Ethel to theatres and dances; he debates every week at the Mansfield Debating Society; during entire week-ends, when he has no work to do, he carpenters, making things " for Ethel," though some sympathy must be felt for her during the noisy progress of this work. He is overdrawn at the bank all through these early years, and he supplements his earnings by dealing in precious stones. In April 1884 he is calling on Wellby's, Whistler's, and Boucheron's, selling them rubies, emeralds, and a valuable pearl necklace, presumably on commission, buying stones at auctions and re-selling them quickly. These deals were probably very useful to him. Mr. Parsons of Tessiers says of him, " He never made a loss in all my experience of him."

Altogether it is not surprising that this very attractive, neurotic girl Ethel was not able to be happy with the restless, sensitive, and much occupied man whom she had married, but whom she had never loved. He was so occupied with his profession that she must perforce have been left much alone, and she began to make friendships of which her husband disapproved. One very stormy Christmas, in 1885, when they were staying together at Ada Labouchere's, they quarrelled so violently that a permanent separation nearly followed. Ethel had been as usual very poorly, and her husband refused to let her go to a ball at a neighbouring country house because of the snow. She became exasperated and said she would leave him for ever, and she actually left for her parents' house the next day. Marshall followed her to the station, begging her to reconsider her decision, but she replied that " she was quite determined, and had decided." However, she did come back to Seymour Street a month or so later, and there she underwent an important operation. " Poor little Ethel," he wrote, " is rather dreading to-morrow, and so am I. Pray heaven it may go all right." The operation was performed successfully by a Dr. Phillips, but thereafter their married life becomes more unhappy still. It is pitiful to think of this overworked young barrister returning home night after night to the wretchedness of his home. Towards the end of 1886 they moved to Wynnestay Gardens in Kensington, and Marshall was only too glad to leave the house in Seymour Street, where nearly four years of misery had been spent. But a change of scene made no improvement, and early in 1887 " things are really getting desperate." In the autumn, Ethel went by herself to stay " with the old people " at 8 Mont Ephraim, Tunbridge Wells, and his mother, who was naturally a strong partisan of her son, wrote him a very sad letter about her daughter-in-law. The old lady's letter is that of a very sad and wise woman, who is convinced against her will that two well-loved lives are entangled in an almost hopeless net by the force of circumstances and their own personalities. She clearly felt that she could do practically nothing to make the situation better for either of them; there was only one resource which was left to her, that of prayer ; and she really seems to have had some sense of premonition as to the coming tragedy. In December 1887 Marshall was so miserable that he was unable to attend to his cases, and entrusted them to " devils." The Bar is a great fraternity, then as now, and his unhappiness was not unknown to his colleagues. Among those who wrote and offered to help him with his work, if he should be unable to do it, was Sir Archibald Bodkin, with whom he was always to be on the terms of closest friendship. Marshall was touched, and very grateful, and the great defender wrote the future Public Prosecutor a charming letter expressing his gratitude for his timely offer of assistance. The last entry in his diary is, in view of the dreadful sequel, full of sadness and pathos, revealing as it does the nature of his patient courage and optimism. " *December 31st.* I saw the old year out and the new year in. Home very tired indeed. So ends the old year. May the new just beginning be a happier one for all of us. I fear the domestic horizon seems more cloudy than ever, but what begins in misery often ends in happiness."

But it was not to be : in 1888 the end came between them.

. . . .

Marshall was heart-broken, and for a time was determined to go abroad. A letter from Charles Gill to his brother Arthur shows that he was desperately anxious to obtain a colonial appointment at this time.

" Garrick Club,
" <i>Thursday, February</i> 23rd, 1888.

" Marshall is sending in an application to the Colonial Office, with his testimonials, for a colonial appointment. I think he would very likely get one—Attorney-General of Jamaica or something like that—but I don't think it is a good thing for him to do, as he is so much accustomed to civilisation ; but he says he would have a very good time."

Gill, however, persuaded him to stay at the Bar, at any rate for the present. His wife went away to Australia ; and, perhaps because he hoped that she might one day come back to him, no divorce proceedings were taken. Indeed, when, as he had anticipated, she returned a year later, he agreed to give her a large proportion of his professional earnings, which were then not more than seven or eight hundred a year, although she had £400 a year of her own. He must still have cared for her very much. A separation deed was drawn, and Marshall never saw his wife again.

But Ethel, cursed by delicate beauty and a wayward nature, shortly after her return from abroad met a young officer who fell in love with her ; they became lovers, and began to live together. The poor girl—she was only twenty-seven—was terrified of having a baby, thinking that a confinement would kill her. She made the acquaintance of a woman with whom she visited in Pimlico one of the greatest villains and impostors who ever disgraced the practice of medicine. He was a certain " Dr." Albert Laermann, forger and drug fiend, who purported to hold a Belgian medical qualification. He also passed himself off in Society as the " Vicomte de Larma," and subsequently he complained querulously that his arrest had prevented his marriage to a lady of great fortune. It was in this scoundrel's consulting-room that an operation was performed on Mrs. Marshall Hall. Before it was done Laermann gave a quantity of wine both to her and her companion ; the operation caused her the most excruciating agony, and, according to evidence given at the inquest, Laermann played the piano and the woman sang loudly to drown the patient's screams. She was taken home to her house in Duke Street, Manchester Square. Her lover became alarmed at her prostrate condition, and sent for Laermann, who gave her a poisonous injection that ultimately killed her. During the inquest which followed, Mr. Pepper, the expert whom Marshall was later to cross-examine on many occasions, said that there had been an injection of " corrosive mercurial poison " used with great negligence or ignorance. Her condition soon became desperate, and an urgent telegram was sent to Laermann. He, however, had now been arrested for forgery, and was found to be in such a helpless state from morphia that he had to be carried into the dock, and his case had therefore to be adjourned.

Ethel's regular medical attendant was now called in, but it was too late. By a cruel irony, she had just received a letter from Marshall begging her to return to him. As the poor young lady lay dying, she began to be tortured by remorse, and asked pitifully for her husband, expressing the deepest repentance for the past. He was in Paris, and in answer to a telegram came over at once to London, but she died before he could reach her side. He could not even bear to go in and see her for the last time, although the doctor told him that she looked most beautiful and serene, at peace at last after all the misery and suffering of her short life.

Her lover was beside himself with grief, and actually tried to see Marshall in Temple Gardens ; but the latter's friends there knew his excitable nature and the depths to which it had been moved, and, understanding how dangerous such a meeting would be, mercifully prevented it ; otherwise the tragedy might well have been even greater than it was. He sat grief stricken and unapproachable in his chambers, saying again and again that he must get away somewhere, or he might lose his reason.

A prosecution followed at the Old Bailey, and Laermann was sent to fifteen years penal servitude. Thus, in the court which he knew so well and which was so often to be the scene of his great triumphs, was enacted the aftermath of his own terrible tragedy. No wonder the atmosphere of that grim old building was hateful to him for ever afterwards, till it was pulled down and succeeded by the present edifice.

Gradually, with his wonderful buoyancy, he was able to pick up the threads and interests of his profession, and to find in hard work some sort of solace for the past. " I used to wonder," writes Edward Bouverie, " if even that grand physique would stand the racket of his emotional and excitable nature." But in the end his giant's strength and hero's courage pulled him through. The old wounds healed but were never obliterated. He never forgot ; he endured in silence many unjust and cruel criticisms, and, whenever he spoke of his wife to someone who had known her, it was always with pity and tenderness; nor did his tragedy make him cynical. " The one thing worth living for," he wrote, in the last year of his life, in a beautiful letter, " is that perfect understanding between two human beings of different sex. It is so rare, that many do not believe in its existence, but those who have been there, know that it not only is, but IS." Now and then he would show a close friend a miniature portrait of a fair-haired girl with an exquisite face marred by an expression at once sad and hard ; and thirty-seven years after her death, when he too was dying, she was still in his thoughts.

But, even with this terrible ending to marriage and first love, he could still be an optimist ; even now he could not believe that the whole story was told, or that so deep a tragedy could be the real end ; and it was partly for this reason that in later years he went to the Spiritualists in the hope of discovering from them that in some way the bitterness and unhappiness engendered in this life between those who ought to be everything to each other would in some way be redressed and explained. We do not know the reason for these things, any more than Marshall did. Nor is it possible to apportion blame ; these two young people were caught up in a hopeless situation from the very beginning. When once, perhaps impressed by his ardent love for her and convinced that it alone was enough to carry them both through, she had consented to marry him, the circumstances already contained all the seeds of tragedy, and proved too strong for them. A heart cannot be ordered or disciplined into an affection from which it instinctively rebels.

It is hard to see reason or justice in such a catastrophe as befell Marshall Hall at the very threshold of his career; yet it can at any rate be said that it is doubtful whether, without this heartrending experience, he could have had that vivid power of compassion which made other men's tragedies his own, and himself the greatest counsel for the defence of his time. He had to go through the fire as few men have done, and in the end he emerged, unconquered by fate, with his invincible nature strengthened and enriched, and without any bitterness in his heart. Such men are rightly deemed to be great.

Very few realised the depth of his feeling; he did not mention it even to intimate friends; only sometimes, when in the Divorce Court or at the Old Bailey, while telling the story of some other man's life and unhappiness, his own memories would come flooding into his mind and prove too strong for his composure. "Marriage," he burst out once in his last years, "can be one of the most immoral relationships in the world." There were some of his colleagues who used to sneer at him for these outbursts, but they did not know what was behind them.

For he never gave himself away; he appeared to be a man without a care in the world; outwardly very determined to get on, a hard fighter, rather impatient, quarrelsome, and sometimes truculent. The great strain of the experience through which he had passed accounts very largely for the scenes which he had in court with anyone who disagreed with him, and his quick temper with everyone. In his later years he became the charming and gentle companion whom everybody liked; he had incurred many enmities and disarmed them all. But in those days there seemed to be a devil of restlessness in him; he could not bear to be inactive for a moment. When there was no legal work for him to do, he would turn carpenter and go round his chambers with chisel and hammer, mending the furniture or the window-blind with immense energy and much noise, till he drove his colleagues nearly mad. But the most pathetic picture—for which I am indebted to a correspondent—of

Marshall about this time shows him captaining a famous club's cricket eleven, making no runs and putting himself on to bowl for hours on end, very erratically and with little success.

> Now in Maytime, at the wicket,
>   Out I march with bat and pad.
> See the son of grief at cricket,
>   Trying to be glad.

CHAPTER V

Making a Name

" THERE comes a tide in the affairs of men, which taken at
the flood leads on to fortune." In no walk of life is this more
true and more obvious than at the Bar. All barristers begin as
understudies : they may soon begin to play leading parts in
the county courts and at Sessions, but it will be a long time
before they control a case which excites the interest of the
public at large. Beginners appear by luck or favour in *causes
célèbres* as very small fry, as Marshall did at the Orrock and
Dilke trials, or obtain sometimes an honestly earned junior
brief with a few lines to say, as he did in the Tilley case. But
sooner or later the greater opportunity arrives, and the limelight is thrown on a rising junior fighting a big battle single-
handed ; then success on this one occasion may bring fame and
fortune, and failure may mean long years of waiting and in-
definite postponement of the front row and the silk gown, till
the Fates forgive, and grant another chance. For such a leap
into fame the circumstances of the Criminal Bar are most
auspicious. The calendar of the Old Bailey is the history of
poverty, as well as the history of crime ; and poverty drives
men and women into dreadful situations, and leaves them there
unprotected. Here, then, is the chance of the young advocate
who is given a short cut to fortune as well as the few paltry
guineas marked upon his brief.

There had always been indications that Marshall was not
always prepared to take a back seat or always to adopt the
course advised by his leaders, and one incident bears almost
the true Nelson touch. Arthur Newton had briefed him as a
junior to Gill and the celebrated wit, Sir Frank Lockwood,
Q.C., in a breach of promise case. The defendant was an eccentric
old Welsh millionaire of untarnished reputation, whose chief
foible was to preach the gospel at street corners from the
eminence of a tub. It is related of him that he once took as his
text, " A little while ye shall see me, and then again a little
while and ye shall not see me " ; as he spoke the last words the
tub gave way and he disappeared into it. To make comedy

complete, a small boy, perched on his father's shoulders to get a better view of the proceedings, called out in a loud shrill voice, " Oh, you lie, I can see you ; you are in the bottom of the tub." It will be understood that it was most important to protect the old gentleman from all scandal, when, somehow or other, he became involved with a lady, who did him little credit, and who brought an action for breach of promise. Lockwood advised a settlement, with which view Gill, already an inveterate settler, agreed. But Marshall and Newton wanted a fight. The terms offered by the lady were so exorbitant that the case came on, and the poor old merchant had to be practically dragged into court. The leaders on each side immediately began " to put their heads together." But their conference was interrupted by a loud conversation between Marshall and Newton, who were carrying on a little sideshow on their own. They kept up a running fire of observations, audible all over the court, about " proceedings for conspiracy and blackmail," with the result that the plaintiff and her leading counsel, Willis Q.C., a truculent old leader, withdrew the action. To have daunted Willis was no mean achievement ; he was well known for his ferocity, and the proverbial " Barkis is willin'" was transposed for him by some legal wit into " Willis is barkin'."

In another breach of promise, in which a solicitor was the defendant, he effected an even greater coup. This legal Lothario had sent to his fiancée, who was visiting in India, a cable announcing his own death, in order to escape from his amatory entanglement. This farcical end to romance was rendered the more ludicrous by the fact that, when she had first accepted him, he had written, " If I had not received the joyful news you might have had a black-edged card." In proposing to her he had written, " Many men marry without the means ; I have the cage but no bird inside." Marshall's commentary on the letter in opening the case was, " So far as I know, the cage is still empty, but the bird is in court." When the defendant was cross-examined, he was unwilling to admit that he had sent the telegram at all. But Marshall had already prepared a form with the words of the original written on it : " Poor nephew died very suddenly at Bristol on December 15th of blood poisoning.—PRICE." Marshall waved this document in the air, as he read the tragic words, and asked sternly :

" Now, sir, do you mean to say you did not write this telegram ? "

The witness turned pale, and, probably thinking that Marshall had in his possession the original form, admitted that he had sent it, a fact which could not otherwise have been proved, as the period of three months, during which the Post Office keeps the manuscripts of telegrams, had long elapsed.

This very resourceful young advocate was now thirty-six years old, and, though he had a good business, he had never handled as yet a *cause célèbre* on his own. The opportunity came to him through Mr. Arthur Newton. During March 1894, in Grafton Street, Tottenham Court Road, a poor destitute woman of forty-three, who was known to the police as a harlot, had been committed on a charge of murder. There was very little money in the case, and Arthur Newton, who would otherwise have gone to one of the big leaders on account of the great public interest aroused, instructed Marshall, with a fee of ten guineas, to conduct her defence.

Here was his great opportunity. On the evening of March 15th, 1894, at about eleven o'clock, a young girl named Louise Hutchins was dressing for a ball on the second floor of No. 51 Grafton Street, when she was disturbed by loud noises from the floor below.

" Oh, I expect it's nothing," said her mother ; " it's only the old lady downstairs scrapping with her husband."

Now, on the floor below, there had come to live a middle-aged Austrian lady, who said that she was a music teacher, and that her husband came to see her from time to time. Her name was Marie Hermann. In fact she had been a governess, but had become a very pitiful, but not uncommon, product of modern city life. She had had three children, one of whom was blind, and had taken to prostitution as a method of gaining a living. At first she had been successful, and was known in Piccadilly as " the duchess," because of her grand airs and generosity, but now her beauty was fading into a set and ill-favoured middle age. She was a small, emaciated woman with beady grey eyes and thin compressed lips, with a pointed chin and the worn, hard, dissipated look of her kind. Altogether her appearance seems to have told in the clearest way a long story of sordid tragedy and suffering.

After the first noises, Louise went out upon the landing to listen, and now she had real cause to be alarmed.

There was a loud crash, and she heard a man's voice say in a low moaning tone, " Murder, murder, murder."

The young lady went out to her dance, but her mother went down to speak to the landlady, and while on the stairs she heard a man repeating :

" My five pounds, give me that five pounds."

Then came a woman's answer in a foreign accent, " I give you account of the five pounds presently." Mrs. Hutchins heard the sound of washing, and the woman spoke again : " I'll get you brandy, you'll soon be better. I'll *make* you better." Marie Hermann then went to a public house opposite, and came back with a bottle of brandy. Afterwards, at about 12.30, a terrific crash was heard, and the woman's voice said, " Did you hurt yourself, dear ? . . . Speak ! speak ! speak ! " The repetition of the word was louder each time, the last being almost a shriek. At about 3.30, Mrs. Hutchins heard another great crash and a noise as of wood being broken. Next morning she found blood in the sink which was used in common by all the tenants, and this was cleaned up by a Mrs. Bricknell, another middle-aged lady, who lived on the ground floor. Later that morning, Mrs. Hermann met Mrs. Hutchins on the stairs and announced the fact that she was leaving, and a large trunk was seen ready corded among her effects. The next day, Mrs. Hermann called at a furniture shop and bought some furniture, and instructed the firm to remove her things from Grafton Street to 56 Upper Marylebone Street, where she had already paid a deposit for new lodgings. Mrs. Hutchins, however, kept a close watch on the " removal," and noticed two men carrying away with difficulty the large trunk. Mrs. Hermann was heard to observe, " Take great care of that box ; it contains treasures of mine." Mrs. Hutchins followed the cortège to Upper Marylebone Street, and then reported the matter at once to the police. Sergeant Kane, who knew Mrs. Hermann of old, was sent to investigate. After a short search, he saw the box, and asked if there was anything in it. " Yes, I should think so," was the significant retort. When the trunk was forced open, it was found to contain the body of an elderly man, weighing sixteen stone, huddled into a sitting position. The box was soaked with blood, and the body had seven or eight wounds upon the head, notably a particularly brutal one just above the right ear.

The woman immediately made a statement : " I know you, Mr. Kane," she said ; " why should I lie to you ? I will not do it." She went on to explain that she had picked up the old man in Euston Road, that he had no money, and that that was the beginning of the trouble. He had told her to undress, and she had refused to do so " without her present." Thereupon a struggle took place : he seized her by the neck, then he took hold of the poker : he was drunk, and she got the poker from him and hit him with it three or four times. Later (which was subsequently proved by independent evidence) she had gone out to buy brandy for him and bandages for his head. He had been alive at seven in the morning, and then had passed into a sleep from which he had not wakened. Before he went off, she claimed that he had said, " You are very good to me—I shall not say a word against you." She also said that Mrs. Bricknell had helped her to get the body into the box, and had, from some strange superstition, thrown in a thimble. Enquiries were made, and it was found that a retired cab-owner of over seventy years of age, named Henry Stephens, had disappeared from a house in Albany Street on the Thursday night. The body in the box was identified by his son. The matter had now attracted wide public attention, and so great was the crowd at this poor old man's funeral that the police had to make special arrangements for traffic.

These, in brief, were the facts which faced Marshall in the first great case which he fought on his own. He had an uphill task. First, the man was cruelly wounded in seven or eight places ; the character of the prisoner was notorious and deplorable. The evidence of the girl who had heard the old man say " murder," and her mother's statement as to the argument about the £5, were deadly. But this was not the worst of it. On March 15th, Marie Hermann was hard up and pawning her possessions ; on the 16th and 17th she seemed to be flush, spending money freely, paying her debts, changing her abode. Witnesses deposed to seeing notes and gold in her purse. The dead man's son said that his father always carried money on him, and shortly before the murder had drawn £50 out of the bank. Mrs. Bricknell indignantly denied that she had helped the prisoner to dispose of the body. This was also deadly for the prisoner ; how could she, a frail woman of nine stone, lift a man of sixteen stone into a tall box ? If she had an accomplice, the case against her was blacker than ever. The case was, long before the trial, described by the Press as " The Most Terrible Murder of the Age," and a rule *nisi* for contempt of court was obtained against several newspapers. The great Mr. Pepper had sworn at the inquest that death must have followed very soon after the infliction of the blows, and that it was in the last degree unlikely that the old man could have lived till 7 o'clock a.m., as the prisoner said. Lastly there were the loathsome devices by which she had sought to conceal his death. No one was more convinced of her fate than the prisoner herself. " I shall be hung," she moaned, when her solicitor came to see her in gaol ; " I shall be hung."

Only two pieces of evidence were discovered on the scene of the tragedy which might tell in her favour : a piece of hair was found in some clotted blood on the mantelpiece, and the prison physician, Dr. Walker, found on her neck twelve bruises.

Marshall had thus a very difficult case to fight, and he had two most formidable opponents, Mr. Charles Mathews and Mr. Archibald Bodkin, both subsequently to be Directors of Public Prosecutions. Charles Mathews, usually known as " Willie Mathews," was one of the last advocates who were not afraid to use real eloquence at the Bar. The son of a distinguished actress, he was, like Marshall himself, very dramatic in his advocacy. But his effects, unlike those of Marshall Hall and like those of an actor on the stage, were carefully rehearsed and prepared. His voice was high and thin, and his face somewhat feminine in appearance ; but a jury soon became accustomed to these peculiarities, and, indeed, they increased the effectiveness of his questions and speeches. It was impossible not to listen to him. In prosecutions, at any rate, his histrionic style would nowadays be thought out of date, but in his time it was most effective. He had a great gift of moving the sympathy of the Court from the prisoner to the prosecution, and would sweep juries off their feet by the pathos he could put into a single sentence. When he had described Dr. Laerman's playing of the piano there was scarcely one composed face in court. In him Marshall had an opponent worthy of his steel, an advocate of equal histrionic and oratorical powers, and far greater experience. In physique, indeed, Marshall had a great advantage, the little " feminine " prosecutor contrasting strangely with the heroic build and handsome face of the counsel for the defence.

Against this doughty opponent, Marshall had to establish, at the very least, that the blows had been delivered in a scuffle, and that no robbery had been intended or perpetrated. To do this he had to discredit a great deal of evidence, expert and otherwise, and reproduce the terrible scene in the jury's mind according to his interpretation of the evidence, without being able to call the prisoner, the sole surviving participator in it. The main witnesses with whom he had to deal were : the son of the murdered man, who gave his father an excellent character, and said that he must have had a lot of money on him at the time of his death ; Mrs. Hutchins and her daughter, who had overheard that grim conversation ; Mrs. Bricknell, who denied the prisoner's story about the disposal of the body ; last and most formidable, Mr. Pepper, the great medical expert called by the Crown, who swore that the mortal blow had been delivered from above, and that the dead man could not have survived it long.

Marshall had no difficulty in discrediting Mr. Henry Stephens, junior, who described himself as a horse trainer. Marshall put it to him that his father was a man of abnormal physical strength, that he was of violent temper, and had been known to throw women about. He further elicited the fact that, actually, the £50 had been spent pretty quickly, and that the house in Albany Street was really a disorderly house. Stephens was really a very easy witness.

" Was not this house a disorderly one managed by your mother ? "—" It might have been or it might not have been."

"Don't you live with one of the women at Albany Street ?"— " No."

" Don't you live with Amy Chase ? "—" No."

" Will you swear that ? "—" Am I bound to answer that question ? "

Mr. Justice Wills : " Yes, I think you must answer."

The witness : " No. I was not living with her, she was living with me."

" How many times have you been convicted ? "—" Two or three times."

" Seven times, I put it to you, since 1892 ? "—" I cannot say, I have got a bad memory."

Miss Louise Hutchins was a nice young lady, and had to be handled more delicately, but she had to admit that she could not be sure the word she first heard was " murder " ; " it was so very faint and indistinct." From Mrs. Hutchins he elicited that she regarded the prisoner with loathing and abhorrence, and was able to pour scorn on her suggestion that the words " Speak, speak, speak " were spoken in an argumentative and angry voice. The impression made was that she was prejudiced against the prisoner on account of what she was. Mrs. Bricknell had to admit that she had accepted presents from Mrs. Hermann when she left, and had drunk with her during the night. Finally he produced the thimble, and Mrs. Bricknell thought she had scored by saying at once, " It does not fit."

" It is very easy," said Marshall Hall, " to say it does not fit. Do you apprehend the reason why I ask these questions ? It is not to suggest that you knew anything as to the way in which this man met his death, but for the purpose of establishing the truth of what this woman has said. You stand there in the box as a witness of truth. Now, on your oath before God, did you not help to put that body in the box ? "

Though the witness still denied having done so, Marshall's cross-examination had had its effect. The most interesting duels of all, however—between Marshall and two medical men, Dr. Lloyd and Mr. Pepper—were yet to come. He had already cross-examined, in a friendly manner and with great effect, Dr. Taylor. First he had asked him about the bruises on Mrs. Hermann's neck. The doctor had put his own hands on the woman's throat, and found that his thumbs exactly covered the bruises. Then Marshall put with admirable pithiness the vital question : " Do you believe that an old man of seventy-one years of age, after he had been struck seven times in rapid succession with a crowbar, which inflicted wounds sufficient to cause death, would have the strength left to have inflicted those bruises on her throat ? "

" No, I do not."

So far so good ; then the old man must have seized her by the throat, from in front, *before* the blows were delivered. Now this disposed of the theory of Dr. Lloyd who gave evidence that the blows over the right ear were delivered from behind. If this had been so, the whole case for self-defence or misadventure arising from a scuffle fell to the ground. But Dr. Taylor had already proved from the bruises on the throat that at some time before the blows were delivered the man and woman must have been face to face. How had she got behind him to deliver the fatal blows ? Now, the man had a contusion on his left elbow, and Marshall made Dr. Lloyd admit that the left arm was probably so hurt when used to ward off a blow directed at the right side of the head. But this would have been impossible if the blow had come from behind. The only possible arm to use for this purpose would be the right. But Marshall had another hypothesis to explain the contusion on the man's left arm. He had fallen heavily on the woman and had bruised his elbow on the floor, thus pinioning the woman's right arm. The woman had then reached out with her left and only free hand for the poker and hit the old man six times in rapid succession. Further, the wounds were not " clean " ones. They were obviously wild and random blows, such as might naturally be delivered " by the imperfect power and directive force of the left hand." The further Marshall pressed his hypothesis the more convincing it became. More formidable than Dr. Lloyd was Mr. Pepper. The latter's hypothesis was slightly different. Whereas Dr. Lloyd said that the head must have been above the level of the woman's hand when she struck, Mr. Pepper said the man was sitting down, and the woman was standing on his right side and delivered the blows from above. The experts for the prosecution were thus disagreeing on a vital detail. Marshall made Mr. Pepper admit that it was possible that the blows might have been delivered with the left hand.

By his cross-examination of the medical witnesses he had
already won over the jury. Rarely has a hypothesis for the
defence in a capital case more perfectly fitted the case. " Strange
are the coincidences of truth," as Lord Hewart is fond of saying,
and there is little doubt that in this case Marshall, with his
advocate's flair, discovered the truth.

But Charles Mathews still persisted in the murder charge,
and made such a powerful speech in support of it that Marshall
had to win the jury back again by his final speech for the
prisoner. The hypothesis was put in terms which were crystal
clear : " The deceased, who was drunk, forced the prisoner down
on to the ground and seized her with both his hands round the
throat. The prisoner then, in her frenzy, with her right arm
pinned beneath the man, stretched out her left hand, and,
seizing the poker, delivered six blows in rapid succession on the
right side of the head in self-defence." To prove this he stressed
two main points ; the first was the conflict of medical evidence
as to whether the blows were struck from behind or in front.
" If you convict this woman of murder," he said, " it will be
on the opinion of one medical man." Then he made a tremendous
effort with his interpretation of the words " Speak, speak,
speak." Were these words spoken in argument and anger, or in
pity and despair ? Could there be any doubt ? " Is there a person
who would believe that a woman who had inflicted such terrible
injuries, and had awakened to the consciousness of what she
had done, could speak in terms of passion to her victim ? My
explanation of this incident is that her poor disordered mind had
seized on the fact that the man was dead, and, prompted by
womanly instinct, was endeavouring to do what she could to
succour him." Then came the peroration, in which he appealed
to the jury to cast away the obvious prejudice. " Let them
remember," he said, the tears pouring down his cheeks, " that
these women are what men make them ; even this woman was
at one time a beautiful and innocent child." At this moment
the prisoner's feelings became quite uncontrolled, and it was
possible that some really decent feeling was passing through
her consciousness ; she had once been a well-educated woman,
and had taught little children. Had she not first taken to the
streets to support her own ? But Marshall seemed to be

concluding on a note, not of pathos or entreaty, but of defiance. " Gentlemen," he said slowly, " on the evidence before you I almost dare you to find a verdict of murder." Marshall paused as if he had finished, but before he sat down he caught sight of the wretched little prisoner, hideous, huddled, weeping, in the dock, the very flotsam of humanity. Pointing to her, he said, his voice full of the pity of this last appeal, " Look at her, gentlemen of the jury. Look at her. God never gave her a chance—won't you ? "

The Old Bailey rang with applause as he sat down ; he had fought the case like a lion for three whole days ; he had spoken for three hours with a speed that amazed his hearers ; only once he stopped, apparently overcome by the atmosphere of the place ; perhaps his feelings were too strong for him. He apologised, and resumed, " This court is utterly unfitted for the administration of justice," he said, " and is a disgrace to the richest municipality in the world."

He had won over the judge, who had first been rather against him. Mr. Justice Wills was never afraid to change his mind. On one occasion, after he had delivered judgment and before it was formally recorded, he found out that he was wrong and that his mistake could not be put right on appeal. He summoned the parties together and gave judgment to the opposite effect. After Marshall's speech he summed up strongly in favour of a verdict of manslaughter, which the jury found after only fifteen minutes, adding a strong recommendation to mercy. However, Mr. Justice Wills hardly gave effect to this, for he sent her to six years' penal servitude. He could not put out of his mind her ghastly method on disposing of the body. Marie Hermann expressed the deepest gratitude to her counsel and solicitors, both at the time and in letters from prison, calling them " her saviours," but the sequel is a curious commentary on the gratitude and mercenary nature of such persons. When she was released she employed an attorney to write to Arthur Newton demanding an account of moneys spent on her defence, to which she had not contributed. The reply was short and to the point : " DEAR SIR,—We saved your client from the gallows. Yours sincerely, ARTHUR NEWTON."

Marshall Hall's career at the Bar had in his early years been cruelly interrupted by personal unhappiness, but peace of mind was returning to him, and with it he was beginning to feel his strength. The chance had been rather late in coming, but it had come at last, and Marshall had made the most of it. His name had been proclaimed all over Britain, and wider still. The great London papers took note of his triumph. " He has for some time been coming to the front as a criminal advocate. But his defence of Marie Hermann brings him out conspicuously as a made man. Still young, with a capital presence, a resonant voice, wonderful vigour in the cut and thrust of cross-examination, Mr. Marshall Hall will, unless we are grievously mistaken, go very far indeed in his profession." He was not to take silk till four years later, but henceforth he was to be to all effects a leader. A flood of work, both criminal and common law, came into Temple Gardens as a result of his triumph. Marshall was never very much of a lawyer, and found the opinions and pleadings which his advertisement brought too much for him. By a happy chance he met, in a county court, a very learned young apprentice of the law, R. E. Moore ; and Marshall asked him to sit in his room in Temple Gardens to act as his devil with the paper work.

Marshall Hall learned a great lesson in the Hermann case, the slender thread upon which failure or success may depend. His dramatisation of the death scene had undoubtedly done much to convince the jury ; he performed the first of those wonderful physical demonstrations which were to be a feature in so many of his great defences. Without this vivid theatrical performance the jury, and even the judge, might never have seen the picture of that sordid drama as he saw it : the frail, aging, foreign harlot determined to make her bargain ; the mean, powerful, lustful old libertine ; the struggle that ensued ; the frenzied retaliation of the pinioned woman ; her horror when she realised the truth. His interpretation of the words " Speak, speak, speak," by slightly changing the tone and accent given by the witness, was probably the turning point of the case. The *nuance* of a change of accent, which can alter the whole meaning of a sentence and make the whole difference between innocence and guilt, was once more in Marshall's voice, and before the same wise and gentle judge, to save a woman from the gallows.

. . . .

Now for practical purposes a leader, his commanding personality was henceforth to charge with electricity nearly every case in which he appeared. He was always anxious to help younger men, especially those who worked for him, and he obtained a junior brief for R. E. Moore in the defence of G. E. Brock, Jabez Balfour's chief of staff. These men, who had juggled with millions, were practically penniless when they stood on their trial. They could not afford to brief a leader, and John O'Connor, an Irish member of Parliament who had known and liked Jabez in the House, undertook his defence at a nominal fee, and Brock briefed Marshall and Moore, also at a very low fee. Brock made a strange contrast to his chief; he was a giant of a man, with a fair beard and blue eyes; Jabez was only tall enough not to be called a dwarf, enormously fat and had a short satyr's beard and little sparkling eyes. Altogether his appearance was extraordinary; some found it comic, others repulsive. But he had great personal magnetism, and his optimism was highly infectious. The collapse of the Balfour companies had fallen on the small-investing public as an unforeseen calamity. For over a score of years, Balfour, with his specious puritanism and marvellous genius for financial conjuring tricks, had deceived, not only the humble investor, but expert opinion in the City. He was a shining light in the Nonconformist world, a fine platform speaker; as Liberal member for Burnley he frequently intervened in debate in the House of Commons, and was even talked of in the Liberal party as a possible candidate for ministerial office. Moore and Marshall, perhaps with the natural bias of defending advocates, took a lenient view of Jabez; in time, with the enormous increase in values, things might have come round, and, if Jabez's capital had come from big business instead of from the savings of the poor, it is just possible that he would not have had to resort to those ingenious devices to pay dividends, in order to keep his shareholders quiet, which brought him to ruin. Undoubtedly he got hold of valuable properties, but his frauds at the very outset were a heavy charge on any profit accruing in the future, and in all his transactions there was only one instance of genuine profit, amounting to £2,500. The facts unfolded in the long opening of the case by Sir Richard Webster are very hard to resist, and it is difficult not to conclude that Balfour's system was rotten to the core and that he knew it ; his only reasonable ambition could have been to die as he had lived (a piece of good fortune that fell to the lot of several of his lieutenants), a man of wealth and position, universally respected and admired. Indeed, in 1890, J. S. Balfour, M.P., J.P., first Mayor of Croydon, occupied a unique position before the public ; not only could he make money for himself, and pay a safe eight per cent. on their money to the many thousands of his humble investors throughout England, but he could achieve this remarkable result from a concern based upon philanthropy. For what were the building societies from which his whole system sprang but an enlightened and profitable philanthropy ? Every Englishman likes to live in his own house : J. S. Balfour had come forward to make this practicable for every working man in England. It was a far cry indeed from the artisans' dwelling-houses which his early schemes covered, to Whitehall Court, the Victoria Hotel, and the Hotel Cecil, the site of which one of his companies bought from Lord Salisbury for £200,000, and with which his gigantic frauds culminated. There they stand to-day, three massive reminders of the greatest thief of the nineteenth century, monuments indeed of which a Roman emperor or an Egyptian Pharaoh might well be envious. But, for a quarter of a century, he kept the snowball rolling, till one fine morning the hot sun came out and melted it in a day.

Balfour, with his infectious optimism, had no difficulty in surrounding himself with able lieutenants who followed him blindly, men whose natures were naturally honest and whose keen intelligences should have told them that the whole vast business was a swindle. Such a man was Mr. George Brock. Balfour's scheme was masterly in its simplicity ; he was weary of his business as election agent, and began to see the great possibilities which, owing to the enormous increase of population, speculative building offered to a man of capital. He had no capital, but he soon showed that it could easily be raised. In 1868, the Liberator Building Society was formed " to make advances on building-agreements to purchasers of the company's lands "; working men were to be " freed " from the tyranny of landlords. The shares were hawked all over England, and the intermediaries used were Dissenting ministers, who, owing to their positions, had the means of influencing the small investor ; indeed, the whole scheme was religious in tone from the start. As much as 8s. 9d. was given as commission to these agents for placing each £10 share, and altogether £13,000 was expended in this way. Brock came into the scheme very early in the story ; he had been a humble insurance clerk, but Balfour was quick to see that he had a wonderful head for figures, and first made him secretary, then a director, of the company. But in order to develop his scheme, for reasons that will appear plainly, Balfour had to use more than one company. Almost simultaneously the Lands Allotment Company was formed to work in co-operation with the Liberator. Afterwards the companies came thick and fast, and the public eagerly devoured their shares ; in 1875, the House and Land Investment Trust was formed ; in 1882, came the London and General Bank ; in 1884, the Building Securities Company ; in 1885, Hobbs & Co. was incorporated ; in 1886, George Newman & Co. came into being ; finally, in 1888, the Real Estates Company was founded with a capital of a few hundred pounds. All these companies were under the direction of Balfour or his creatures, and most of them had offices situated in the same building in Budge Row. The directors worked so hard in running so many companies at once that they were given exceptional privileges ; they took a large proportion of the surplus profits ; this was an inducement to these excellent directors to make profits, and was conceived to be in the best interests of the shareholders. They were also allowed to make contracts with their companies.

The " contracts " were the first source of real prosperity to Jabez; he, or one of his nominees, would introduce properties and sell them at a price far above their real value, and pay himself out of the money subscribed by the shareholders of one of his companies. It was necessary for him to justify the exorbitant price paid to himself in the balance sheets, so he hit upon the happy idea of the purchasing company reselling to one of his other companies at an even higher price. This transaction would be celebrated by an exchange of cheques which cancelled each other, and not a penny would pass. But the inflated price at which the second company had *nominally* bought would be written up in the first company's books as sovereigns in the till, and divided among the shareholders as dividend at eight per cent. ; due proportion of the surplus would of course be paid to the directors. Another device to increase " profits " was to increase the *book* value of properties held by the company by improvements which were purely imaginary. This finance can aptly be described in a single phrase ; dividends were not paid out of profits, but profits were declared to make dividends. To keep this system going it was essential for Balfour to form new companies and apply to the public again and again and " offer " them a new issue of shares. His companies paid eight per cent. year after year, and nobody but the directors guessed that the dividends of the old shareholders were being paid out of the subscriptions of the new ones. As his needs increased he found that he could keep pace with them. His wonderful personality attracted to him knaves and dupes who were willing to do his bidding. The companies needed a solicitor ; they got one in the person of Granville Wright, a rogue who introduced many of the properties, and served later a long sentence for forgery. It was essential that they should have a valuer to place inflated values on their properties ; they got hold of a reputable valuer named Bird, who was probably a dupe and was fortunate enough to die before retribution came. They needed a builder ; J. W. Hobbs, later to turn himself into J. W. Hobbs & Co., a thorough rogue and speculative builder, came forward, and later went to penal servitude. They needed a surveyor, and Newman, later George Newman & Co., stepped forward to fill the vacancy and his own pockets. Hobbs and Newman were both insolvent when they became connected with Balfour, but they bought vast properties at hugely inflated prices from the Balfour companies to " make profits " for them, their cheques to the company being cancelled by corresponding cheques from another of the companies, given to them by way of loan. For these " loans " they would nominally pay a high premium, which again would be put down as money in the till of the lending company, though not a penny ever passed. By the end,

Newman owed the companies £600,000. The companies also needed an auditor, and they found one in Theobald, whose eyes were opened in 1887 ; he thereupon severed his connection with Balfour, but had nevertheless to stand his trial by his side. Lastly, the Balfour companies needed a bank to store the subscribers' money, and to clear their fraudulent cheques, so in 1882 the London and General Bank was founded. It started business with a fine clientele, for all the companies banked there, and every material cheque passed through its parlours.

Thus it will be seen that, if one company fell, the whole of them fell. Their one hope was the continued subscriptions of the public, and between 1890 and 1892 enormous sums were subscribed. At the end the net loss to the public amounted to something over eight millions sterling. As was to be expected, the bank fell first ; in September 1892 the General Bank stopped payment, and the collapse of all the companies was only a matter of time. Balfour left his beautiful Oxfordshire mansion and his cellars of wonderful champagne ; with his pockets full of unimpeachable bonds, he fled to South America, and vanished for a time ; but soon after his disappearance a retired Civil Servant of independent means, named Samuel Butler, began to take up his residence at Salta in South America ; his astonishing resemblance to Jabez was noticed by a chance traveller, and this led up to his arrest. Samuel Butler and Jabez Balfour were indeed one and the same ; but his strange attraction had found him many friends in his new domicile, whose fortunes doubtless he was about to make. At all events, friendly caballeros galloped their horses in front of the train in which Jabez sat under arrest, in the hopes of stopping it and rescuing him by force. After lengthy extradition proceedings, which he fought every inch of the way, he was brought back to England to stand his trial. Meanwhile, the fall of his companies had become almost a national disaster. *The Times* called it a great national calamity, and a relief fund, which ultimately reached the figure of £114,000, was opened for the sufferers. The wide results of his frauds may be judged by the fact that no less than four members of the jury empanelled to try him obtained exemption from service on the ground that, in one way or another, they were interested in his companies. Hobbs and Granville Wright had been tried and sent to penal servitude in 1893, but it was not until October 1895 that Balfour sat in a Queen's Bench Court with three of his dupes and associates by his side. Much of the public indignation had died down, and the court had all the atmosphere of a civil case ; and the formal charge against the defendants was that of " preparing false balance sheets and falsification of accounts." It was the first prosecution of its kind under the Companies Act, and many doubted whether the criminal law would cover Jabez's gigantic operations. A galaxy of talent was arrayed for the prosecution. A future Chief Justice, Sir Richard Webster, led for the Crown ; he was supported by a future Lord Chancellor, Sir Robert Reid, by a future Public Prosecutor, Charles Mathews, by Sir Charles Gill, and by the greatest living master of our criminal law, Mr. Horace Avory. Literally, cartloads of documents had to be perused and sifted to bring home the prosecution. The case was tried before Mr. Justice Bruce, a kindly old gentleman who was wont to drink a frequent cup of tea on the Bench. The arch-criminal himself was defended by Mr. John O'Connor, who had a hopeless task. The lieutenant, Brock, was brilliantly defended by Marshall. He had appeared for him throughout lengthy bankruptcy and liquidation proceedings, and had acquired a great affection for and belief in him. The man was evidently under the spell of Balfour ; he owed him every position he had held ; perhaps he believed what he wished to believe, but, at any rate, there can be no doubt that he did not dream that the companies would crash so suddenly. He invested the whole of his wife's settlement in the bank, and in August 1892, a few days before the end, he paid £3,500 into that bank on deposit. Marshall did not cross-examine to prove that the amazing manipulation could possibly be considered wise finance, but his questions were directed to the very human personal issue—here was George Edward Brock, a man of ability and honour, who was so deeply in the debt and under the spell of his chief that he had actually assisted him in his frauds for years, and at the same time had not been afraid at the eleventh hour to put all his savings into the very concern which his intimate knowledge of its affairs ought to have told him was rotten to the core. These arguments did not avail to alter the verdict, but his speech in mitigation is a model of what this very difficult task should be. It visibly moved the judge, who gave Brock a sentence of only nine months, a small sentence in comparison with Balfour's fourteen years. " Mr. Marshall Hall followed," said a daily paper, " with the speech of the day, eloquent in words, judicious in tone, sincere in manner and altogether admirable under the circumstances." This speech was an instance of Marshall's inability to keep his personal opinion out of his advocacy. " I have known Brock personally," he said, "during the last three years, and I believe firmly, from personal observation of him, in the honour and integrity of my client. He has lost everything ; it is only by the kindness of his friends that he is defended at all. It is common knowledge that men will and do, in their excessive regard for other men, trust them blindly and implicitly, and make no effort to exercise an independent judgment." In another remarkable passage in this speech, Marshall expressed Brock's feelings of remorse for leading his co-defendant Theobald, the accountant, into disaster, and his desire to take the whole blame for this on his shoulders. His whole conduct of this difficult case won Marshall Hall the sincere admiration and staunch friendship of his antagonist the Attorney-General. During his cross-examination of the liquidator, one of his questions had misfired, and Marshall for once did not persist. " I am sorry, my lord," he said ; " I see there is no point in my question." " Then it's the only question my friend has asked of which that could be said," said Sir Richard Webster. When Marshall sat down after his plea in mitigation, Webster passed him along a special note of congratulation which said that, " both in form and substance, I have never heard anything better." More generally it was said at the time that this speech saved Brock from years of penal servitude. This very difficult part of the advocate's business was one in which Marshall Hall excelled, and for which he was frequently retained. One of the saddest and most poignant of these speeches was made some years later on behalf of a personal friend, a contemporary Rugbeian and one of his first clients, with whom he had often played cricket. As a solicitor to Lord Orkney's trust this man had embezzled moneys to pursue speculations of his own. Marshall did not avail to change the judge's mind as he had done with Brock.

Mr. Justice Bruce's words were very severe against Balfour, but his tone was gentle towards Brock. "It has been suggested," he said to Balfour, " that, if times had been more auspicious, your operations might have been successful. Better times might have covered, but could not have lessened, the fraud. I am sure that no small part of your punishment will be the remorse you must feel at having darkened many a humble home. No prison bars can shut out from your ears the cry of the widow and orphan whom you have ruined." Turning to Brock, he said, " You have stood by Balfour to the last, and have participated in his fall. No doubt you owed much to him, and you were compelled by an almost irresistible impulse to support your benefactor. But you should have remembered that it is never honourable to be dishonest."

Mrs. Brock sent a pitiful little present of china to Marshall Hall and Moore, as an acknowledgment of their services. Poor Brock found some small employment as an accountant, but did not survive his imprisonment long, whereas Balfour survived his fourteen years and started afresh. Finally, I am informed, he was given a really good appointment in North Wales, and died—on his way to take it up—as some say, of joy !

.   .   .   .

Very shortly after the Jabez Balfour case another crisis took place in Marshall Hall's life and career. The strain of this case and many others during that Michaelmas term had told upon his vitality, and after a long day's shooting with the late Lord Burnham, whom he had met through Montagu Williams, he contracted double pneumonia. For many weeks he lay between life and death at the house of his old friend Sir Douglas Straight, whose opening of the Edmunds case at Brighton had first inspired him to go to the Bar so many years before. He went down to Brighton to recuperate, and had to be wheeled along the familiar streets of his native town in a bath-chair, his aged father tramping by his side. A serious illness hits a barrister very hard, and a return to the Temple may mean almost a fresh start. Old clients make the acquaintance of new counsel, and, unless they are personal friends, are often hard to win back. Fortunately his faithful friend and devil, Judge Moore, did his work during his long absence, and it was owing to him that Marshall found his practice alive at all when he returned to Temple Gardens late in 1896 after nearly a year's absence. But his practice had been even more individual to himself than that of most barristers. His personal charm and magnetism had won him much of his work, as Foote of the Western Circuit, an extremely able advocate, found out to his cost. The latter had served an attorney with great success and efficiency, and wondered why his old client's work was going elsewhere. The attorney met him in the Temple one day, and felt it his duty to make some explanation of his faithlessness. " Mr. Foote," he said, " I have no complaint to make about the way you did our work for us, but the fact is, when I brief Mr. Marshall Hall, and point him out to my clients in court and say ' that's your counsel,' they always seem so pleased ! " Fortunately Foote, who was an extremely ill-favoured man, had a sense of humour, and went straight to Marshall with the tale.

But Marshall did not only return to the Bar with much legal ground to recover, he had lost his wonderful health, and he never threw off the effects of that critical illness in 1895. The varicose veins, which compelled him in later years to go about in a suit of medical armour, were a consequence of the pneumonia, as was his tendency to colds and coughs. He had needed in the past all the strength of his grand physique to establish him in his most exacting profession despite fortune's brutal slings and arrows ; henceforward, with impaired health, he had to draw still further on his courage to carry him on to fame and fortune. Misery and illness and hard work might break his health, but they never broke his spirit. Another personal event must necessarily be mentioned here : when he returned to the Bar he was no longer alone. He had married Henriette Kroeger, the daughter of a Hamburg shipowner, a lady whom he had known for some years.

It has been said that much of his practice had vanished because, in the first instance, it was so peculiarly the reward of his personal qualities ; it is obvious that he could with good fortune regain his position by the same means. He was financially in low water at the date of his second marriage, as a result of his illness, and his father came to his assistance with a generous loan. His name had disappeared for many months from the law reports, and he needed the advertisement of a big case to bring him again before the public. Arthur Newton again came to his assistance with a brief for the defence in the Russell—Scott case. This suit was the culmination of the warfare which Lady Scott had compelled her son-in-law, Earl Russell, to wage for many years, and it excited enormous public interest. Never had dirty linen been washed in public at such length and so thoroughly. There can be no concealing that Marshall Hall was on the wrong side in this case ; but that does not in the least detract from the credit due to him in his long fight, against a hostile judge, and for a hopeless cause. It is right and proper, as Marshall often said, that anybody, however black circumstances may appear against him, can have at his command a courageous and competent advocate. He fought every inch of the ground, and, as a result of the case, his name once more was before the public, and his reputation justified the Lord Chancellor in granting him a silk gown. This case was memorable for his frequent duels with Mr. Justice Hawkins, in which that famous judge more than once received as good as he gave. Very shortly, the story which occupied the attention of many judges and several courts throughout the 'nineties was as follows. Lord Russell, a brilliant young nobleman, rather alone in the world, had left Oxford early, and amused himself by sailing his own small yacht. While on one of these expeditions he made the acquaintance of a Lady Scott, who lived with her daughter Mabel by the side of the Thames. She was an extravagant woman, with little money to support her extravagance ; she had a quick feminine gift of sympathy, and soon won Lord Russell's close affection, and letters passed between them of the most affectionate nature. He married her pretty daughter in February 1890. The marriage was a failure from the very start, and, in May, Lady Russell left her husband, and never lived with him again. A woman friend seems to have poisoned her mind, and she believed rumours repeated about him ; she objected to one of her husband's friendships, and filed a petition for judicial separation from him on these grounds. Her case broke down completely, and her counsel apologised for his client's allegations in open court. Lady Scott, however, after the case was over, repeated the charges with aggravation in an interview published in 1892 by a sensational paper called *The Hawk*. The next stage in the remarkable history was when Lady Russell, having in 1891 petitioned for judicial separation, now, goaded by her mother, asked the Court for a restitution of her conjugal rights ! She said in the box that it was her wish to return to her husband, whom she now knew to be " pure and innocent." He, however, cross-petitioned for a judicial separation on the grounds of her " cruelty " in the broadcasting of vile charges of immorality against him. The jury found that the charges were untrue and made maliciously, and amounted to " cruelty " ; they therefore gave him a judicial separation. But, like Wellington's soldiers, Lady Scott did not know when she was beaten ; moreover, she had always played a double game. At the same time that she sent her son-in-law a Christmas card inscribed " God grant that this time next year you will be with people who love you, and that all will be forgotten," she was writing to a man named Dickinson, one of the many detectives in her employ, " Have you any news to send ? How strange if you are the person to bring the proper person to justice ! I am sure you have the wrong man ; but any man who proves anything will not only get my thanks, but enough to set him up for life. We have now enough evidence to hang any ordinary man, but it is not enough for us."

The charges which implicated Lord Russell's friend were now again remembered and broadcast by Lady Scott and her daughter, and he had to bring an action to vindicate his character. Lady Russell made the completest apology in court, but to pay the costs of this action the bailiffs had to be put into her house. Lady Scott was now determined on her revenge ; she remembered that Lord Russell had sailed his own little yacht, as a young man of twenty-one, and her detectives discovered the whereabouts of three members of the crew, named Cockerton, Aylott, and Kast. The last named she purchased out of his regiment stationed in India, entertained him royally in Bombay, and brought him back in triumph to England. She concocted a statement of the most defamatory kind, which she got them to sign ; she printed the document and circulated it to the members of the Lords, Commons, to officers in the army, and to many others. The only possible course was for Lord Russell to prosecute her for criminal libel, with her hired associates. It was a brave thing to do, with the Wilde case fresh in the public memory, but the only course open. George Santayana, the famous writer and philosopher, came forward to give evidence on his friend's behalf. Frank Lockwood, Charles Mathews, and Travers Humphreys appeared for the prosecution ; Lawson Walton for Lady Scott ; and Marshall Hall for the three men. The defence set up was justification. The case occupied twelve whole days in the Old Bailey and was adjourned over Christmas owing to the illness of the principal witness for the defence, Kast. A most unusual thing then happened : this prisoner died before the case recommenced, and, with their chief witness dead, it was now hopeless for the defence to establish a justification for the whole libel, which, having justified it *in toto*, they were legally bound to do to secure an acquittal. So Marshall cleverly seized the opportunity which offered itself and pleaded " guilty," in spite of the wily offers of Mr. Justice Hawkins that he should be allowed to amend his plea so that he should only have to prove so much of the justification as the other witnesses could speak to. But no bald account of the case can show to its proper advantage Marshall's brilliant attempt to make bricks without straw. Mr. Justice Hawkins refused at the outset his application for bail, though he granted it to Lady Scott. " The police," observed Marshall meekly, " raise no objection."

" I don't care a farthing for the police," was the judge's hot reply ; " they are not superior to myself at present."

" Not even, I believe, in their own estimation," murmured the unruffled advocate.

But the judge was not the only opponent with whom Marshall crossed swords in this action. His friend Sir Frank Lockwood, usually the wittiest and most urbane of men, found his patience very nearly exhausted during this long and trying case. " Absurd," he said audibly, at one of Marshall's questions put in cross-examination. The latter hotly asked for the protection of the judge. " Coming from such a source, such an observation is unpardonable," he said. " Very well," said Hawkins, " don't pardon it " ; and the honours were with the judge this time.

After Christmas the contest was resumed : as Kast lay dying, counsel had attended to take down his dying deposition, which under statute would have been admissible in evidence. But the doctors had certified that the dying man could not have stood cross-examination, and so no deposition was taken. The evidence of Kast was of course vital to the defence, and Marshall was rightly determined to extract as evidence the exact circumstances under which the deposition had been refused. He maintained that the dying man was perfectly fit for cross-examination at reasonable length, but that the doctors had certified that he was unfit, simply because the prosecution had stated that they must cross-examine for hours. " That is a very simple method," he argued, " to avoid the statute whereby the deposition of a dying man can become evidence. No dying man, *ex hypothesi*, can stand cross-examination for hours." Mr. Justice Hawkins was, however, not impressed, and said that Mr. Marshall Hall was only pursuing this line of question for prejudice.

" Justice, my lord, not prejudice," said the advocate.

" Prejudice," retorted the judge.

" Justice, *not* prejudice," repeated the advocate, and there the matter was allowed to rest.

On the last day before sentence was given, Hawkins sent for the counsel for the defence, complimented them all, especially Marshall, on their conduct of the defence, and told them that if the defendants would withdraw their statements and apologise he would bind them over. Lady Scott's attitude made such a course impossible, and at the very last moment she stated in court that she believed in every word of the libel. The other defendants did not instruct their counsel to apologise, and a sentence of imprisonment was therefore unavoidable. Finally, when all was over but the sentence, Marshall made an undoubted score against the judge. In his plea in mitigation, he made much of the fact that his clients had at any rate believed the statements of Kast, who had died and left them unprotected. About to sentence them, the judge, turning to Cockerton and Aylott, said, " Before the magistrate, when you were asked for the defence which you had, each of you, to the charge, you had an opportunity, if you thought fit, to state what that defence was."

Mr. Marshall Hall : " My lord, I do protest. I tell your lordship, the magistrate declined to allow three persons to go into the box."

On the judge stating baldly, " I do not believe that," Marshall, quick to take affront and thinking that his personal honour was being assailed, began ostentatiously to gather up his papers and made as if to leave the court, his face flushed with anger. " I cannot take any further part in these proceedings," he said, " and shall therefore retire from the court." The judge thereupon apologised, and said he had not meant the matter personally. Mr. Lawson Walton came to his colleague's assistance, and established the fact that the sworn evidence of the defendants had been offered at the police court, and that the magistrate had in fact refused to hear them. The judge got over his mistake with very little grace ; " I will pass the matter over," he said. But the sentence was a light one, eight months for each of the prisoners ; and it may well be that Marshall's shrewd blow in the last round had some effect on it. The judge had made a false point, and it had been shown to be false. Lady Scott persisted in her allegations to the end, and interrupted the judge's summing up again and again by offensive comments. When sentence was pronounced, Countess Russell uttered a loud shriek, audible even outside the court. So ended this famous prosecution for criminal libel in a victory for Lord Russell : unhappily it was not the last legal episode in the history of this miserable marriage, but with the rest of it the biographer of Marshall Hall is not concerned. The case is an important milestone in his forensic career, because as a result of it he decided to apply for a silk gown.

One of his last cases on circuit as a junior was the celebrated prosecution of the " Monk " by Canon Deedes. Richards prosecuted and Marshall defended a peculiar young man, named Alfred Rose, for stealing certain valuable books, but behind this simple charge there lurked a bitter ecclesiastical feud. " Behind this prosecution," said Marshall Hall, " is one of the bitterest pieces of religious persecution heard of for many years. I shall show that Canon Deedes was the involuntary instrument forced by others to bring this prosecution." The facts were shortly these : Alfred Rose, who was admittedly very learned on the subject of monumental brasses, was introduced by an invalid clergyman called Douglas to Canon Deedes, who owned a wonderful ecclesiastical library. Rose was a member of a brotherhood living in a monastery situated on the Isle of Dogs. These monks were of the extreme High Church faction and believed " that the vice of private ownership was to be cut off by the roots " ; like the early Christians, they practised a rigid communism. Rose, dressed in the monkish attire of his order, where he was known as Brother Oswald, gained access to Canon Deedes's valuable library, and cut out certain pages of a rare book ; and other valuable books belonging to Canon Deedes were subsequently traced to him. Meanwhile, Douglas, an intimate friend of Canon Deedes, died, and Rose told Canon Deedes, when the latter asked him about the lost books, that he had been given the books by Douglas, and thus attempted to shift the blame of his theft to a dead man. Though, of course, there was no defence in law, the prosecution would in fact never have been instituted for this petty theft had it not been for wider considerations. Certain members of the monastery at the Isle of Dogs belonged to a secret association known as the Society of the Holy Cross. This society, which to some extent was protected by the High-Church English Church Union, had incurred the disapproval of the Archbishop of Canterbury, owing to the private printing of a book known as *The Priest in Absolution*. While Rose was a member of the monastery, the Church Association, who did not approve of the Catholic tendencies of the Society of the Holy Cross, wrote him a letter offering him twenty-five shillings for a report of the transactions of the Society of the Holy Cross, and, in fact, through his agency a list of its members was published in the *Church Intelligence*. While Rose was away, two brethren, named Green and Drake, suspecting him of owning private property, searched his cell and found, not only the incriminating letter, but the books belonging to Canon Deedes. They said at once, " We have a traitor in the camp." Rose then, it was alleged, under the advice of the Church Association, issued a writ against the two brethren who had broken into his cell and detained the books and papers found therein. As a result of this writ, the prosecution against Rose for the theft of the books followed. Canon Deedes, who had traced the whereabouts of his books, received a letter from the monastery that they could not return the books, and that if he wanted them he must take action. Cross-examined by Marshall Hall, the Canon admitted that the writ against Green and Drake had led to the prosecution. The only line Marshall had for a defence was thus one of prejudice. There was really no doubt that Rose had stolen the books ; on the other hand it seemed improbable that the Canon would ever have prosecuted if it had not been for the determination of the members of the Society of the Holy Cross to punish the " traitor in the camp." It really looked as if the prosecution had become a contest between the Church Association and the English Church Union. Marshall succeeded in making Brother Drake somewhat ridiculous by asking him, " But a traitor in what camp did you mean ? You see, you have so many." He then read out a long list of societies with very Romish titles, such as the Confraternity of the Blessed Sacrament, the Society of the Holy Rosary, the Guild of All Souls, and the Order of Saint Benedict, in which the witness admitted membership. The communism of his order was also an easy target for ridicule.

" Do you suggest no member has any individual right to property at all ? "—" Not if he is fully professed."

" Not even a pen ? "—" That may be so."

" Is your pocket-handkerchief your own ? "—" No."

" I only want to know how far the doctrine went."

But however successful he was in this line, this case was certainly one of his failures. Mr. Justice Grantham gave the book-thief, aged only twenty-two, and of uncertain mental balance, a sentence of three years' penal servitude. But Marshall's observations in his speech in mitigation was, to say the least, unconventional. Referring to the prisoner's defence that the late Mr. Douglas had given him the books, he said, " I think it my duty to say that I saw the prisoner personally before the case came on, and I pointed out to him, in my view, the defence was untenable. The prisoner, however, insisted upon it." These observations appear at first sight very unlike Marshall, who usually acquired such a passionate belief in his client. When his wife once teasingly asked him how many murderers he had got off in his life, he answered hotly, " Not a single one."

But he had known Mr. Douglas, and he had loathed the duty laid upon him of suggesting dishonest conduct on the part of this blameless clergyman ; so, when the curtain was rung down, and the case was badly lost after a dogged struggle, he felt it his duty in honour to make his position clear. It is often said that an advocate will not scruple to throw mud at innocent persons if it will help his case, and sometimes it is an advocate's duty to discredit other people in order to save his client ; but, on the whole, the wide privileges of the Bar are not abused, and Marshall Hall on this occasion hastened to make amends.

.   .   .   .

Usually the decision to " take silk " is a great risk and crisis in a barrister's career. The work of a busy junior is very different from that of a leader ; he is concerned with the preliminaries and technicalities of a lawsuit, and, though he may seem to his client to be taking very little part in the actual trial to earn his fee, the craft or lapse of a junior may have made victory or defeat certain or probable long before the case ever came into court. It does not follow, by any means, that a good junior will make a successful leader. Marshall, however, stood to gain much by becoming a Queen's counsel ; he was never good at plodding junior work ; he was always by nature a leader, and had been bred in the criminal school of advocacy, where the youngest junior may have at any time to play a leader's part.

One of the very last cases in which he appeared in a stuff gown was in an action for libel by W. S. Gilbert ; Lawson Walton and Marshall appeared for the famous rhymester, and Carson for the defendants, a widely read theatrical journal called the *Era*. It was a veritable " trial by jury," and the court never lost the atmosphere of comic opera. The case arose out of a very similar situation to that which nearly thirty years afterwards brought Lady Terrington into the witness box, to burst into tears under cross-examination by Marshall. Gilbert, to say the least, was very sensitive to criticism. He had recently written a play called *The Fortune Hunter*, which several London theatres had refused. It was then put on with moderate success at Birmingham and Edinburgh ; during the production he gave an interview to a Scots newspaper, out of which all the trouble arose. When the interview appeared, Gilbert was reported to have called Mr. Sidney Grundy, the well-known playwright, " a mere adapter," and to have compared the English very unfavourably with the French Stage ; English poetic drama, it also appeared, was doomed to failure, because no English actor, including Tree, Irving, Wyndham, Hare, and Alexander, could make a thirty-line speech at all interesting. Sir Henry Irving made an angry speech about Gilbert, and the stage people generally were furious. An article appeared in the *Era*, accusing him of unbearable conceit, and ingratitude to the artists who had made his fortune. " Mr. Gilbert's self-esteem has with advancing years developed into a malady. In his own estimation he is a kind of Grand Lama or Sacred Elephant of dramatic literature. His good nature has become obscured by the abnormal protuberance of self-esteem. That this—what's his name ?— Grundy should have written successful original works, while he, the great Gilbert, has met with failure after failure in modern drama is preposterous and not to be borne."

Gilbert—though, as a barrister, he should have known better—lost his temper and sued for libel. He recovered it sufficiently at the trial to make some very good fun with Carson. The defence had pleaded that the article was fair comment on a matter of public interest. As for *The Fortune Hunter*, Gilbert was ready to admit " that it was a very bad play," but he confessed he did not like the critics saying so ; he had never said that Tree and the rest had a dull method of delivery ; he had merely been attacking the fashionable blank verse of the time, thirty lines of which could not be made interesting by anyone. Carson's not very difficult task was to show that Gilbert detested criticism, and was touchy to a degree ; the latter would not admit the notorious fact of his breach with Sullivan, but he had to admit feuds with D'Oyly Carte and John Hare, " with whom he was not then on speaking terms." He confessed to cutting short a lifelong friendship with Mr. Clement Scott, because of a severe criticism of one of his plays. Had he said, asked Carson, at the interview that he was going to write no more plays ? " I did say," he replied, " that it was no longer necessary for me to be a cock-shy for a herd of low-class critics." The many compliments paid him by the *Era* in the past left him cold. " I never read favourable criticisms," he said ; " I prefer reading unfavourable ones. I know how good I am, but I do *not* know how bad I am." He denied that he had ever offered a poetic drama to Irving and been refused.

There was now only needed Sir Arthur Sullivan and the Savoy orchestra to turn Mr. Justice Day's court into one of the best scenes of comic opera, and Carson happily concluded, to the delight of the jury, by putting to the witness a passage out of Gilbert's own *Rosencrantz and Guilderstein.*

> The Acts were five—though by five acts too long,
> I wrote an act by way of epilogue,
> An Act by which the penalty of death
> Was meted out to all who sneered at it.
> The play was not good, but the punishment
> Of those who laughed at it was capital.

But Gilbert was not at a loss at the Irishman quoting scripture. " Those were the words of Claudius of Denmark," he retorted, " not of myself. I wrote them, but I do not hold myself responsible for anything King Claudius says."

Irving made a lightning appearance in the box to swear that Gilbert had, in fact, offered him a play in verse for the Lyceum ; but, as this was all Carson intended him to say, when Mr. Justice Day, in true Gilbertian fashion, ruled the evidence inadmissible directly after he had said it, Carson, well satisfied with its effect upon the jury, sent him away without more ado.

During Carson's speech, Gilbert again lost his temper and walked indignantly out of court. Moreover, when years afterwards they met at Bancroft's for dinner, Gilbert turned his back on Carson and refused to speak to him ; some months later, at another dinner, he repeated the same pantomime. The judge summed up against Gilbert, but the jury's affections were divided between him and Carson, and, after two and a half hours' absence, they came back to tell the judge that there was no prospect of their being able to decide between the two favourites. So ended in laughter Marshall's last *cause célèbre* as a junior.

But, when a junior takes silk, some relics of his junior work always remain to be completed, and in one very sensational case he acted both as a leader and a junior at different stages. The junior drafts and signs the " pleadings," or preliminary abstract of the issues of the case ; and Marshall had early

in 1898 signed his name at the foot of a statement of claim, in
which a Dr. Kingsbury of Blackpool claimed £30,000 under
the will of a deceased patient. When the case came for trial
before Mr. Justice Gorell Barnes, Marshall had already taken
silk, and he went into court in his first big case as a leader by
the side of two great veterans, Inderwick and Edward Clarke,
R. E. Moore being taken in as a junior. So, curiously enough,
Marshall, who, as a junior, had so many times played the part
of a leader, in his first case as a leader was relegated to a junior
rôle. But the subject matter of this case was enthralling to
Marshall, as a man interested in medicine. The defendant, the
eldest son of the testatrix, relied on a will made in the previous
year, and contended that the later will, under which Dr. Kingsbury claimed as residuary legatee, was signed by the old lady
while under the plaintiff's hypnotic influence. Dr. Kingsbury,
who had acquired her affection owing to his resemblance to a
favourite son who died in 1886, was, in fact, a young Irish
physician who had made himself a considerable authority on
hypnotism. He had attended the testatrix very often indeed
before she died, and had attempted to hypnotise her by way of
treatment, at her request, a number of times without success,
by the instrumentality of a silver matchbox. Three very interesting issues were discussed by expert witnesses on both sides :
whether hypnotism had a deleterious influence on the patient's
character ; whether the patient could perform an act, when
freed from hypnotic influence, which had been suggested to her
while in a hypnotic trance ; and whether hypnotism could be
effective at all against the patient's will. Carson Q.C. strenuously
cross-examined the doctor on these issues, and the two Irish-
men had more than one amusing passage of arms. Carson asked
him if he could hypnotise people of strong as well as those of
weak intellect. " Some of my best experiments," rejoined the
doctor, " have been on members of the Manchester Bar." Then
he began to take the great advocate into his confidence. " If
you and I, Mr. Carson, were making experiments——" he said.
" No," interrupted Carson, with his slow smile, " please leave
me out of it. I shall want to make a speech about you later, and
you may stop me."

The defendant, it appeared, had been far from dutiful to his mother during her lifetime : he had tried to make her pay rent for her dower-house, and she had been much upset by the enlargement of the family grave during her last illness. In the result, despite all Carson's eloquence, the jury found without hesitation in favour of Dr. Kingsbury on all the issues. Many years afterwards he came to the Bar, where his great medical knowledge made him a useful advocate in all cases where medical issues were involved.

Seven other juniors took silk with Marshall in 1898 ; among them was H. C. Richards, his old colleague at the Sussex Sessions, whose three years start of him he had more than overtaken ; Rufus Isaacs, now Marquess of Reading, who was to run neck and neck with him in his first highly successful years as a silk ; Sir Thomas Hughes, a distinguished veteran still practising in the Court of Chancery, who, as doyen of the profession, is now the president of the Bar Council. It was not till the next year that Charles Gill, and the greatest orator of them all, Henry Duke, now Lord Merrivale, took the same decisive step.

Marshall Hall's promotion to the rank of leading counsel almost exactly coincided in date with a revolution in criminal practice. By the Criminal Evidence Act, which passed into law in August 1898, all prisoners were allowed to give evidence in their own defence. The privilege was used cautiously at first by defending counsel, but, before Marshall died, it had become a two-edged sword, to such an extent that some old-fashioned advocates say that the old fundamental doctrine that a man is innocent until he has been proved guilty has been seriously impaired. A prisoner's neglect to go into the box to explain his conduct is usually heavily commented upon by modern judges, so that defending counsel have to choose between exposing their client to the deadly effect of this almost certain comment or to the even more deadly ordeal of cross-examination both from the prosecution and the Bench. The Act has certainly worked mercifully in some instances : on the one hand, the judge expressly stated in the Lawrence case that the witness box had probably saved the prisoner, and the view is strongly taken by Mr. Wellesley Orr that it saved Wood ; on the other hand, Seddon's demeanour, when he gave his evidence, probably sent him to the gallows. The Act has undoubtedly made it

harder for a guilty man to be acquitted. Marshall Hall regarded
it as a mixed blessing, and, as a great defender, thought the
practice of comment from the Bench on the prisoner's refusal
to go into the box not in accordance with the purpose of the
Act. " The Act was intended," he said to me, " to confer a
privilege, not impose an obligation." But if the Act had never
been passed, Marshall's great cases would have missed some
of their most dramatic moments and might well have had
different results.

Thus, at the age of thirty-nine, Marshall Hall threw aside
his stuff gown, and took his place in the front row. He was no
longer the young Hercules he had been, but he was already
known as " the Apollo of the Bar." Behind his youthful appearance he hid a great experience of advocacy and of life. " He is
the most mercurial of counsel," wrote a contemporary observer
of the courts. " He has a mobile countenance, over which varying shades of expression are constantly flickering. Generally
speaking, he strikes one as a man with an immense fund of
nervous energy, which he expends lavishly in his client's case.
For Mr. Hall is not a trifler ; far from it. He doeth everything
with his might." The journalist's chance praise was strangely
appropriate to him, as his favourite motto always was, " Whatsoever thy hand findeth to do, do it with all thy might."

A few weeks before he officially became a leading counsel,
his only child was born. He adored children, and began writing
letters to his little daughter when she was barely a month old.
The quotation that follows may come as a surprise and a relief
to the reader, who has been concerned more with the indomitable
advocate than with the affectionate and gentle man who could
write this tender little first letter to his only child.

" MY DEAR LITTLE DAUGHTER,—I am writing this very
first letter to you. I suppose it ought to be a very serious
letter, but I am afraid it will not be so, as I do not feel at all
serious. I hope that you are behaving yourself well, even
though you are no longer under your father's hard, cruel eye.
I trust also that you are doing your duty to your mother
and allowing both her and your dear friend Mrs. Sanders to
get some small amount of sleep at night. I suppose you will

soon be taken out to see more of the world, for, strange as it may appear to you, there is some place outside the most charming rooms in which you have hitherto spent your life. Why you ever came to the place at all I know not, but I presume you had some good purpose in so doing, and I heartily pray that you may not find the world in which you now are all a delusion and a snare. You looked wondrous wise when I talked to you the other day, but I was much pained that you did not answer me when I asked you so many questions. . . . And now I dare say you would like to know what your father has been doing. The ship was full of great people ; there was Dr. Jameson and others from South Africa, and beautiful ladies, and one Paderewski, who travelled to Paris with your father, and they made great friends—he is coming to see you and your father in London, and perhaps talk German with your mother. Give my love to your mother, and tell her there are lots of beautiful ladies here, and they must be real ladies, because they wear all the colours of the rainbow at once and their faces are whitened with all sorts of white things, like tombstones. Please also give my kindest regards to Mrs. Sanders. With my love to you,

" Your ever affectionate,

" Father."

CHAPTER VI

Fame and Fortune

AFTER taking silk, Marshall experienced a few years of great success. Rufus Isaacs and he ran neck and neck as young leaders in the special-jury courts. He still, of course, appeared in important criminal cases, and, indeed, this phase in his career culminated in his brilliant defence of the Yarmouth murderer ; nevertheless, any student of *The Times* newspaper of the period would be struck by the frequency of the appearances of his name in the civil reports, and the consistent success which attended it ; in the end it was a too great success which proved his undoing. At the time, political position, for which he appeared admirably equipped, seemed the one thing lacking to make the highest success in the profession certain. There, too, fortune was to lead him, and it was his own fault that he did not take the opportunity so generously held out to him. For no one ever entered the House of Commons at a more auspicious moment for himself. Still a young man, of commanding presence and great talents, with a name on every man's tongue, the winner of a seat which had been regarded almost as a forlorn hope, he seemed marked out for political favour and advancement.

In one of his earliest cases he made a real friend from the witness box. A newspaper known as *Society* had blundered, as all journals which subsist on gossip must do sooner or later : a lady named Mrs. Keighley and her husband had set up in Bond Street as palmists, under the picturesque names of " Saturn and Satanella." They separated, but the husband stayed on in Bond Street with a new lady assistant ; the latter had at one time been connected with a man who had been concerned in an attempted murder, and who had an unfortunate reputation for performing the well-known " husband trick " on guileless young men of the 'nineties. *Society* quickly scented material for a paragraph, and wrote up " The Notorious Satanella." Mrs. Keighley, the wronged wife, still practising palmistry under that name, sued for libel. The defendants pleaded that their words had not referred to Mrs. Keighley, but to her successor ;

and one of the witnesses called to prove that the words *were* generally understood to refer to Mrs. Keighley was Count Hamon, better known as " Cheiro," the celebrated palmist. This profession always savours of illegality to a lawyer. For, though every lawyer earns his pay by advising as to the past and future of his clients, he knows very well that under the old Witchcraft Act, still in force, and other Acts, the law forbids the telling of the future for money. Marshall tried to discredit Cheiro by showing that he professed to tell the future for reward, but he found his task not an easy one. Cheiro, to the question, " Can you tell the future ? " answered that, so far as the tendencies of persons were concerned, he could ; he even broadly hinted that he could tell Marshall's future from his tendencies ! At any rate, the cross-examination was a failure. Vainly Marshall pleaded that Mrs. Keighley had had a rare advertisement out of the case, and that the character of a lady " who was running a side-show at a twopenny waxworks " could have suffered little damage ; the jury gave her £1,000 damages. That night, Marshall met Cheiro by chance at the Carlton Hotel : he went up to him and congratulated him on his skill as a witness. A day or two afterwards he paid Cheiro a visit, and the latter took an impression of his hand and cast his horoscope.

Years afterwards, in November 1924, Marshall found the notes of this interview and wrote to Hamon : " DEAR CHEIRO,— It may interest you to know that I have just been re-reading the deductions you drew from my hand in August 1899, and I find that they have proved to be wonderfully true." Those interested in palmistry may read with interest the original notes of that interview. " The left hand, which denotes the inherited qualities, does not give nearly as much promise as the indications given by the right, which shows the development of the individual. Judge, therefore, that by your own efforts and determination you have carved out your own career, and must stand out as the one really distinguished member of your family. The commencement of your line of destiny being so uncertain, as it starts from the wrist, shows that in early life you were very undecided as to the career you should adopt. . . . There is no sign of any success whatever until . . . your twenty-fifth year. . . . From . . . thirty years of age to the last moment of your life, your success will be steadily on the increase until . . . you are fated to become one of the most prominent men in your profession. Your line of head indicates that you are endowed with more eloquence than logic. . . . The worst feature of your hand has to do with the affectionate side of your character. The line of heart under the base of the fingers shows that you will be singularly unlucky in connection with such matters. You will be idolised by women, but they will bring you little happiness. There are two marriages distinctly indicated ; the first will cause you to pass through some bitter ordeal that will affect the whole of your life. . . . In length of life you will reach the average span. You will die in harness at the very zenith of your career." Marshall's note at the end of the interview reads as follows : " Cheiro then said, ' I see something so vividly that I feel bound to tell you of it, though at the same time it seems to be of such small importance, and so impossible, that I hesitate.' I asked him to tell me what he saw, and he replied, ' I see you standing on the balcony of what looks like a large country house with a big garden below and big trees all in front. But the strange thing is that the grounds seem lighted up with a very vivid electric light, and even the trees are lighted up with coloured lamps ; what makes it still stranger is that there are thousands of people trampling down the flower beds, and looking up to the balcony, and you are apparently trying to speak or actually speaking. There are several people on the balcony, men and women, and the faces of the crowd are very white in the strong light. Beside you, on the left, is a woman, much shorter than you are, waving a white handkerchief in her left hand, and the people below are shouting. That is what I see, but what it means is more than I can tell you.' "

Shortly afterwards, the lawyer received a return visit from the palmist, who in turn came to consult him as to his immediate future ; he had been cited as a co-respondent by the husband of one of his clients. " Guilty, of course ? " said Marshall, with his most aggressive cheerfulness, as he listened to the distracted man's story. However, he advised him to go to some reliable firm of solicitors, and undertook to appear for him gratuitously. But things never came to that; the trouble had all arisen from the fact that two women had chosen the same Oriental costume at a Covent Garden ball, and out of this situation had arisen a comedy of errors in the course of which poor Cheiro was cited as a co-respondent!

Marshall later consulted Cheiro on many occasions. He had already leanings towards spiritualism. He certainly believed that he received messages from those for whom he had cared. " I am only too thankful," he wrote in 1926, " that on occasions I have been permitted to receive messages from the other world through the intervention of another. I believe in my heart in the truth of what I state, and to me it has always been a source of great happiness in circumstances of great difficulty." The experience which first convinced him that in some unknown way there may be a channel of communication between the living and the dead made a deep impression upon him. On March 10th, 1894, he was staying with his sister at Hampton. Mrs. Labouchere had been for some time an intimate friend of Miss Wingfield. On this occasion the latter was answering, by automatic writing, questions put to her. Marshall was sceptical, and it occurred to him that he had the means of testing her powers. He had in his pocket a most unpleasant letter, received a day or two before from his elder brother. John Cressy Hall was much older than Marshall, and had long since fallen, from high prosperity as a merchant, into poverty; in 1894, he was living in South Africa on remittances sent him by Marshall. For his own protection, the money was sent through a certain Archdeacon Gaul: this was strongly resented, and the letter in Marshall's pocket was the culmination of a very offensive correspondence on the subject, and was dated February 1894. Marshall had said nothing about this unpleasant letter to his sister, and decided to ask Miss Wingfield as to the authorship of it; he sealed it in a blank envelope, and handed it to Miss Wingfield. After some delay a message was spelt out: " The writer of this letter is dead." To the question, " When and where did the writer die ? " the answer came, " *He* died yesterday in South Africa."

The séance made only a temporary impression on Marshall's mind. However, on March 27th, he received a letter from

Archdeacon Gaul, with a Kimberley postmark of March 5th. This letter gave an account of moneys received and expended on Cressy Hall, but asked that, owing to his character, his allowance should thenceforth be paid through the Standard Bank of South Africa. Accordingly, on March 29th, not without misgiving, Marshall wrote a long letter to the Archdeacon, complying with his request. On April 2nd, 1894, he received a second letter from Gaul, bearing a Kimberley postmark of March 8th, to the following effect : " DEAR SIR,—I little thought when I wrote last week that I should have this week the melancholy duty laid on me of informing you of the death of your brother, which occurred yesterday." Poor Cressy Hall had, indeed, been found on March 8th dead in his bed. The message received through Miss Wingfield on March 10th had stated that the writer of the letter had died in South Africa " yesterday "—that is, March 9th. But, even with this slight discrepancy, it was a very strange experience.

. . . .

In July 1899 Marshall Hall successfully appeared for a medical respondent in an interesting matrimonial suit, involving the Scots law of marriage. The wife brought a suit against her husband, Dr. MacCormac. She alleged that he had already contracted a previous marriage, in Scots form, to a girl called Maggie Kay, and that therefore her own marriage was void. The girl Maggie came forward to give evidence for her, and swore that the doctor had treated her as his wife before witnesses, and that he was therefore her lawful husband. Marshall put to this girl a curious letter she had written to MacCormac at the date of his marriage to the petitioner. " I have done you harm," she wrote, " but I have had my punishment. You can have no pity for a girl who has treated you so badly, but it will gratify you to know that I am about as bad a specimen as there is in London. The life is all very well, plenty of pleasure and excitement, but when one is alone and thinks—oh, it nearly sends one raving mad. . . . I do not want to compromise you in any way. I know what your wife would think if she knew." But the real question was one of law : a Scots lawyer was called, but Marshall Hall merely put to him an amusing poem by Lord

Neaves on the Scots marriage law, entitled " The Tourist's
Matrimonial Guide through Scotland : "

> Suppose the man only has spoken,
>   The woman just given a nod,
> They're spliced by the very same token,
>   Till one of them's under the sod.
> Though words would be bolder and blunter,
>   The want of them isn't a flaw,
> For *nutu signisque loquuntur*
>   Is good consistorial law :
>   Woo'd and married and a'.
>
> If people are drunk or delirious,
>   The marriage of course will be bad,
> Or if they're not sober or serious,
>   But acting a play or charade.
> It's bad if it's only a cover
>   For cloaking a scandal or sin,
> Or talking a landlady over
>   To let the folks lodge at her inn.
>
> A third way of tying the tether,
>   Which sometimes may happen to suit,
> Is living a good while together,
>   And getting a married repute.
> But you, who are here as a stranger,
>   And don't mean to stay with us long,
> Are little exposed to that danger,
>   So here I may finish my song :
>   Woo'd and married and a'.

The grave Scots lawyer had perforce to agree that these
frivolous verses were a correct exposition of the marriage laws
north of the Tweed, and Mr. Justice Barnes ruled that the
second verse exactly governed the case, and dismissed the case
against Marshall's client with costs. In a later suit, Marshall
won him his freedom from the wife who had charged him with
bigamy.

In the Michaelmas term of 1899, Marshall Hall appeared in
one of the longest cases in which he ever took part ; it lasted
fifteen full days at the Old Bailey, and concerned the formation
of a bogus discount bank. The master mind was that of Edward
Beall, known in the City as the " Black Prince." Every business
day, for many a long year a magnificent coach drawn by four
princely blacks would take him to and from the City by way of
the Embankment ; but in the end he, and three of his associates,
Singleton, Wain, and Lambert, sat in the dock on their trial
before Mr. Justice Channel. Compared with Balfour, the Black
Prince was small fry, and, indeed, the London and Scottish

Banking and Discount Corporation (Limited), with the aid of puffs in a tame paper managed in his interest, only obtained £30,000 from the public; on the other hand, the assets amounted to only £336, and did not pay the costs of the liquidation. Like Balfour, Beall faked "profits" to declare dividends. He was defended by Rufus Isaacs, while Lambert was represented by Marshall. The latter's defence was run on very much the same lines as Brock's had been. A part of the assets of the bank which the directors had valued very highly, and in which Lambert firmly believed, were the shares in a process for dust-destruction, which would also produce electricity in some wonderful way. Marshall made a great deal out of this invention, and argued that it was only due to the scepticism of vestry boards that this scheme had not been adopted all over England by local authorities, with immense profits resultant to the patentees. The surveyor to the Westminster vestry was called, and gave high praise to the invention. He said that it had not been adopted all over England owing to the " *conservatism* " of the vestrymen, but that the city of Mexico was shortly going to adopt it ! " Oh," said Sir Robert Finlay, the Solicitor-General, who prosecuted, " are they more enlightened than we are ? " " No," said the witness, " but they soon will be ! " Marshall then re-examined the witty surveyor. " You find," he said, " that the vestrymen are more *sceptical* than a Liberal-Unionist Solicitor-General ? " As the witness had stressed the word " conservative," and as the Conservative and Liberal-Unionist alliance was yet young, the joke put everybody in court in a good humour. This case is the first important one in which Marshall Hall put his client into the box under the Criminal Evidence Act to tell his own story. Only Singleton, of the four defendants, preferred the safety of the dock to the unknown terrors of the witness-box ; the only one of them to be acquitted was Marshall Hall's client. The learned judge's summing up is interesting because of its great fairness in distinguishing between those prisoners who had given evidence and the one who had not. " Three of the defendants," he said to the jury, " have availed themselves of a recent Act of Parliament, and have given evidence, but the other has not. You must not put that too strongly against Singleton, but I do not say that you must not take it into account at all. You must recollect that the recent alteration to the law is a privilege to defendants, of which they are entitled, if they like, to avail themselves. It does not alter the law that a case has to be proved against an accused person, and that the accused has not to prove his innocence. You must not draw too much inference against Singleton in respect of his not going into the witness box." In this case Lambert offered very gamely to Marshall to " plead ' guilty ' if it would help the rest." This was not the only instance of this kind of generosity which he had seen : years before at Lewes a man was on his trial for a serious assault and for night poaching ; he had been identified by his boots ; some suspicion had fallen on his brother, but he insisted on pleading " guilty." " He's a married man," he said, as he went to serve his sentence. The fact was that on the night of the assault his brother had borrowed his boots. Marshall described this as the most impressive scene that he ever saw in court.

In his first two capital cases as a Queen's counsel, the prisoners did not go into the box ; just as in the Hermann case the guilt or innocence of the accused depended on the construction of a few sentences spoken by them. The first is, in my opinion, one of the most pathetic and interesting of all Marshall Hall's defences. A young working girl with a lovely face, named Annie Dyer, had been seduced by a married man, who was in a higher station of life. Knowing that she was to become a mother, she went into a different locality, and obtained employment as a laundress. She went to lodge with a Mrs. Favell, representing herself as a married woman. Very soon afterwards, on September 7th, her baby was born ; according to the prosecution, at the time of its birth she told the monthly nurse " not to mind about the baby, but to attend to her " ; ten days afterwards the young mother was sitting with the nurse and her baby, and said, " How can anyone get rid of a baby ? " Shortly afterwards she took the baby up to bed, and the child was never seen again alive. The girl left the next day to stay with her married sister at Hornsey, and said nothing there about a baby ; she was traced, and a police-inspector took a statement from her ; according to the latter she said, " I will tell you the truth. I killed it—I did not know what to do with it—I put it in a box ;

you will find it there." The body was subsequently found, and, according to Inspector Upfold's evidence when he charged her with the " wilful murder " of her child, the prisoner admitted it. Before the merciful Infanticide Act passed in 1922, under which a mother who kills her newly born baby before she has " fully recovered " from the effects of childbirth is not guilty of murder, many poor women whose disordered minds led them into this dreadful situation were necessarily indicted for murder ; and in this case the prosecution, represented by M. R. Wilkinson and by Mr. Ernest Pollock, the present Master of the Rolls, opened the case as one of murder. The question, " How can anyone get rid of a baby ? " just before the baby must have died, together with her flight and apparent admission to the police officer, justified this line of action. The defence was as subtle as it was surprising. The very words relied upon for the prosecution, by a slight change of accent and punctuation, constituted a conclusive defence. Marshall called no evidence, and his entire defence was elicited by cross-examination. Two nurses who assisted at the prosecution admitted, when questioned by Marshall, that the accent fell upon the word " can," and that the actual words used by the girl were " How *can* anyone get rid of a little baby like this ! " This, together with the admission that the mother was kissing and feeding her child when she said this, completely contradicted the sense suggested by the prosecution ; so far from indicating a deliberate plan, the words, as stressed by Marshall Hall, showed the very opposite. As to the words " I killed it. I did not know what to do with it ; I put it in a box," the whole meaning of the statement is changed by making the middle sentence go with the last, and not with the first. As to the alleged admission to the charge of " wilful murder," under cross-examination the inspector, after referring to his notebook, admitted that he had made a mistake ; he had never charged her with the " wilful murder " of her child, merely with " causing the death " of it. The defence was now complete, and Marshall Hall made a wonderful and very logical appeal to the jury ; his own dreadful tragedy, now nine years old, came flooding back to his mind, and the listeners in the quaint old Assize court at Guildford were held spellbound by his eloquence. But nobody in that court except his junior,

Max Labouchere, and perhaps the judge, Mr. Justice Wills, knew why he spoke so bitterly and passionately. " The laws of nature," he said, " press unfairly on a woman in matters of this kind. The act is the act of both, but the punishment is the punishment of one. I first felt almost inclined to call evidence to prove where the man now is who had robbed the prisoner of her virtue ; but I have decided to spare him and the woman he has married, and leave the prisoner to bear the burden and support the result alone. . . . Her remark at the confinement is accounted for by the fact that she had not seen the child, and that her maternal instincts had not been aroused. It is impossible to believe that a woman kissing and fondling her child the night before, and actually—as the doctor's evidence showed—feeding it from her breast, would deliberately have murdered it. As to her admission to the police-inspector, sup-posing the child had been accidentally killed by overlaying, is it not the most probable thing she would do ? On the other hand, if she had made up her mind to kill the child wilfully, is it not the most improbable thing ? " Mr. Justice Wills was deeply impressed with the defence by Marshall Hall. " There is no doubt," he said, " that the prisoner was fond of her child. In the whole of my experience I have never known a case where accent had greater significance. I confess that when I read the depositions taken at the inquest I thought the girl's words were meant as an enquiry, but what Mrs. Deaker said before the magistrates was exactly consistent with what she said this morning, namely, ' How *can* anyone get rid of a baby like this ! ' with the accent on the ' can.' This puts an entirely different complexion on the matter. With regard to the prisoner's admis-sion to the police-inspector, that is a very serious illustration of the difference punctuation may make to the meaning of words. ' I killed it—I did not know what to do with it.' If you make a pause there, and then go on, ' I put it in a box,' the phrase is an ugly one, inasmuch as it is perfectly consistent with, ' I killed it *because* I did not know what to do with it.' If, however, you pause after, ' I killed it,' and proceed, ' I did not know what to do with it, and I put it in a box,' the import of the phrase is not nearly so serious."

The jury, without retiring, returned a verdict of " not

Iн

guilty," and such a scene of enthusiasm followed as has rarely
been seen in the old Guildford court. As the judge, who sternly
rebuked the crowd, said, it resembled a scene in a theatre rather
than a court of justice. Curiously enough, the Guildford court,
when the Assizes are not in progress, is dismantled and used as a
place of entertainment.

The next capital case in which Marshall Hall appeared was
one before Mr. Justice Mathew in July 1900. A young publican's
wife, named Lucy Packham, had died one night from injuries
after a drunken brawl with her husband at their inn, the
Marlborough Hotel, Brighton. The fatal scene had not been
witnessed by anyone, but the conversation between the two
had been overheard by several persons. Both husband and
wife were alcoholic subjects, and had spent a most wretched
married life, but the man still cared for the woman, and was
madly jealous concerning her. On the night of the 1st–2nd of
March they were both drunk, and had been quarrelling more
violently than ever. Their voices were overheard in loud altercation by two policemen outside. " You wants killing, you
——— " the prisoner was heard to say. Some time afterwards his
wife's voice was heard to plead several times, " Don't, Tom."
Later the man said, " You are a lazy woman. Will you get
up ? Wake up old girl, and let's get to bed." Two of his servants
heard him say with deep compassion in his voice, " Lucy, I
forgive you. What have I done ? Oh, Luce, Luce, come back
to me." At four o'clock in the morning he fetched one of these
servants, who found the young woman dead and cold upon
the ground ; her husband seemed utterly dazed, and his clothes
were covered with blood. The prosecution alleged that the man
in a jealous and drunken fury had brutally assaulted his wife
again and again, and that by her words, " Don't, Tom, don't,"
she was entreating him to spare her. Marshall's answer was that
the woman was hopelessly drunk, that the fatal wound on her
head was caused by an accidental fall and that the words,
" Don't, Tom," did not imply ill-treatment by the prisoner,
but rather that " he was endeavouring to get her up, and that
the pain when he moved her caused her to ejaculate these
words." Further, that " the idea running through the man's
mind all the evening was to endeavour to arouse the woman

out of her drunken stupor and get her to bed." " It may be," he said, " that, in his efforts to get the deceased up, the prisoner, who was in drink himself, let her fall once or twice, and that the very injuries to which the doctor attributed death were caused in that way." The woman had been terribly bruised all over her body, but the doctor had admitted that a woman given to alcoholism " bruised " very easily, and the blood on the prisoner could be explained by the fact that he had held the dying woman in his arms.

After a short absence of twenty minutes, the jury found a verdict of " manslaughter," but added a strong recommendation to mercy ; and thus Marshall had saved another unfortunate from the gallows.

In 1900, Marshall Hall first appeared for a man who was to be his client consistently for over twenty years till the collapse of a certain prosecution for libel at the Old Bailey. Mr. Horatio Bottomley was sued in 1900 as the guarantor of a Stock Exchange account, and even then he was hardly unknown to the British public. Mr. Justice Ridley took an instant dislike to him. " I cannot believe this man's evidence," he said. Marshall very properly protested. " There is no reason why your lordship should not believe this gentleman just as much as the plaintiff," he said. Whereupon, Mr. Justice Ridley, the most learned of scholars, but the most inconsequent of judges, observed, " I never heard of this man before in my life." This, for a first in " Greats " at Oxford, was an almost perfect *non sequitur*, and Bottomley replied in a famous open letter to the judge, in which he concluded to the effect that, if the letter made him guilty of a " contempt of court," that was precisely the attitude from which he regarded Mr. Justice Ridley's court ! At any rate Sir Edward Ridley was the last of His Majesty's judges for many a long year to refuse to take judicial notice of Mr. Horatio Bottomley.

Shortly afterwards, Bottomley's paper, the *Sun*, was in trouble for its " lucky spot " competitions. The reader who was fortunate enough to buy a copy containing a certain " spot " won a money prize. Muir, for the prosecution, contended that the prizes depended on mere chance, and contained no element of skill, which was of course obvious. Bottomley and Marshall now for the first time adopted a plan of campaign which was to prove invincible on many occasions during the succeeding years : the prosecutors were anxious that neither Bottomley, as editor, nor the publishers should slip through their fingers, and proceeded against both. Marshall Hall said, " There's only one counsel in England who'll do you justice in this case." " Who's he ? Let's have his name," said Bottomley, interested. " Yourself," said Marshall. This plan had many advantages. Bottomley appeared in person for himself, and Marshall for the publisher ; the result was that Bottomley enjoyed to the full the licence always allowed to a litigant in person, and at the same time had the advantage of all his great advocate's professional skill and experience. Plaintiffs in libel actions invariably made the same mistake that Muir had made, until a certain young junior named Douglas Hogg, who had seen that deadly team in combination, began issuing writs against the publishers alone, and Bottomley, except as a witness, was muzzled. But when the plan was still working, Marshall used to address the jury after Bottomley. " Following as I do," he would begin, " after my unlearned leader——" In this particular case, Bottomley secured a complete victory for himself. For the publisher, Marshall contended that the " Winning Spot " was a mere advertisement for the paper, and was not " in law " a lottery. " But what, then, is a lottery in law ? " asked the Lord Mayor. " Marriage," said Marshall readily, " is a lottery, and a very bad lottery sometimes ; and so, too, is the purchase of a ham or a cheese ; but none of these are lotteries in law." " Mr. Marshall Hall," said the Lord Mayor, " you ignore the skill of the purchaser in these instances." In the end the publisher of the *Sun* escaped with a fine of £25, and a good advertisement.

Shortly after the Brighton murder case, Marshall Hall, worn out by a most exhausting year of prosperity, was looking forward to the long vacation : he had arranged to spend it at Marienbad with his old friend Charles Gill. Before leaving, he had gone down to spend a few days with his wife and little daughter at Ellen Terry's cottage at Winchelsea, which he had taken for the summer. On the morning on which he was starting for Marienbad, his groom came riding towards him with a telegram ; it was a message from Sir Edward Carson asking him to come to London to meet Lord Derby. The meeting took place, and Marshall was asked to contest Southport in the Conservative interest. The seat was a fickle one ; Lord Curzon had won it for the Tories, but the sitting member was Sir George Pilkington, a very popular local magnate, and a Liberal; the General Election was fixed for the autumn, and the seat was now regarded as all but a forlorn hope. Marshall Hall had been approached several times by the other side, but politics, in spite of his oratorical gifts, never really appealed to him. Mr. Samuel Brighouse, the local chairman, came to see him, and after a short interview said, " If you'll stand, sir, we'll win Southport." Marshall cancelled his Marienbad plans, and paid a visit to Southport. So little did he then know about politics that the local Tory chieftains, assembled on the platform to meet him, were horrified to see their prospective candidate wearing a tie of blazing red, the local Radical colour.

Marshall Hall did not come to an immediate decision, but by September he had already made up his mind that the political road to fame was not one which he would take. The General Election was imminent ; it was the 1st of September, and the little brown birds seemed far more attractive to him than the fickle electors of Southport. After a wonderful day's shooting with Lord Devonport on the " First " at Marlow, he had accepted another invitation to shoot at Leicester. He had already made up his mind to telegraph a definite refusal to Sam Brighouse when he reached Liverpool Street ; but the train was almost on the move when he reached the station, and he only just got himself and his guns into the train in time. He was tired and sleepy. " Then," he writes, " a strange thing happened. I fell asleep in my corner, and woke up to find what seemed an endless line of trucks moving on a parallel line in the same direction as we were going. Fast as we were going, it took a long time to overtake them. Eventually we ran abreast of the engine, and there in big gold letters was the name ' Southport.' It struck me as very curious that this name should be on a G.E.R. engine. It seemed to me a direct omen, and, when I got to Leicester, I stopped at the telegraph office and sent a wire to say I would stand for the constituency."

How like Marshall to let a chance omen change his mind, on a matter vital to his career !

A few days later, he was in Temple Gardens, hard at work with R. E. Moore on an election address. " I hope you will read my address," he was saying to the Southport Conservative Club a week later ; " I have put into it a good many hours' very hard work. I did not buy it by the yard. With the assistance of my friend Mr. Moore, who is an authority on English grammar, I wrote it myself." Marshall's ingenuous pride in the fact that he had written his own address " with assistance " was the subject of an amusing Radical cartoon.

On September 22nd he went down to Southport to be adopted and open his campaign ; he had a difficult task. At the previous election, Lord Skelmersdale, who had strong local influence, had lost by six hundred votes ; Marshall had nineteen days in which to make his impression, and he took the town by storm. He was laughed at by the Radicals as a carpet-bagger, a mere pawn in the political game. " At any rate," was his retort, " that is better than being a knight, like Sir George Pilkington, because a pawn can at least move straight, whereas a knight cannot." His opponent himself was rash enough to say in one of his speeches, " Who is this Mr. Marshall Hall ? He hasn't even an address ! " Marshall's answer to this was received with delight. " If Sir George will have patience," he said, "for three short weeks, he will find that my permanent address is ' House of Commons, Westminster.' " When he had first arrived at Southport, he had impressed his supporters by his physical resemblance to Lord Curzon. " A second Curzon," was the Conservative Club's verdict upon him on his first introduction. It is possible to see what was meant ; but, though in the two proud, handsome faces there was no doubt some superficial resemblance, never were there two more dissimilar beings. George Curzon was essentially an aristocratic figure, whereas Marshall Hall was essentially a democratic one ; the masses loved him, but the warmest feeling that Curzon ever inspired in a popular audience was admiration. " We praise him, but our eyes are dry," wrote even an Etonian poet when Curzon died ; and the huge crowd that stood outside a Marylebone church to see the great defender's funeral pass was perhaps more impressive than

Curzon's stately obsequies. At Southport, Marshall charmed everybody by his lightning repartees, his torrential eloquence, and his versatile accomplishment. At a Conservative bazaar he exhibited his skill as a shot by shooting cigarettes and playing-cards held by his wife between her teeth for him to aim at. His speeches were great popular successes. R. E. Moore, who was at his side throughout the election, tried, not only to teach him grammar, but political science ; realising how important it is for every politician to show some kind of consistency, he drew up careful notes to which he urged the candidate to be faithful. But Marshall, with no judge to restrain him, could keep to no plan of campaign ; though his utterances aroused the greatest popular enthusiasm at the time, the leader writers of the *Southport Guardian* had no difficulty in finding, when the shorthand notes came in, contradictions and glaring incon-sistencies in a single speech ; while the *Southport Visitor* was sometimes hard put to it to defend him. But, after all, it was the meetings that mattered, and there he was irresistible. In one of the first, Marshall had raised a laugh against an inter-rupter named Mr. Scarlett, but, when he was told that the latter was blind, he was so gentle and charming that the interrupter confessed himself almost won over by the candidate. But his favourite method of dealing with noisy interrupters was to entice them on to the platform. The first victim to suffer this was unwise enough when he got upon the platform to mutter some uncomplimentary observation to the candidate. " What did he say ? " asked the crowd. " Oh," said Marshall, " he only said that he hoped I should be his member." Another of these victims, having been led on to the platform, saw the trap into which he had fallen. " I am led like a lamb to the slaughter," he said. " Is this your Unionist way of treating gentlemen ? I am really astonished. It is not Christian. I discard you." Thereupon, with the boast that " he was as good a man as Marshall Hall," he left the meeting amid roars of laughter. On the eve of the poll, the enthusiasm for this brilliant candidate was exceptional, and Marshall, always quick to respond to popularity, surpassed himself as a platform orator. " You could do anything to-night," said his wife to him proudly, as they went home.

On the polling-day, October 11th, Marshall Hall drove all over his wide constituency in a coach and four, and so the campaign ended. The general opinion was now that, if Marshall Hall had another week, he would win the seat. " No candidate," said Mr. F. A. Greer, now Lord Justice, who spoke for him, " has ever become more popular than Mr. Marshall Hall in so short a time." Another young politician who spoke for him was Mr. F. E. Smith, announced as a Fellow of Merton and ex-President of the Oxford Union. Yet another of his helpers was his own little three-year-old daughter, Elna, who went about wearing a placard bearing the following legend :

> Every youngster born alive
> Is either Liberal or Conservative.
> I'm a Conservative, not very tall,
> So vote for my daddy, Marshall Hall.

The counting took place at the town hall that night, and the excitement grew as it became obvious that the contest was a very close one ; the blue clips and the red clips, containing fifty votes each, were almost equal in number. At length his agent told Marshall Hall that he had been beaten by about three hundred votes ; but his supporters insisted on a recount, and it was found that four blue clips had been accidentally placed among the red and counted for Sir George Pilkington. This made a decisive difference, and Marshall was in by 209, after a campaign of nineteen days. The voting was 5,552 to 5,343.

The returning officer then made a request before announcing the result to the crowd below ; it had been the custom in the past for a lady supporter of the winning candidate to wave a red or blue handkerchief and so anticipate the formal announcement of the returning officer ; this he asked should not be done. Marshall then went out with his wife and supporters on to a low balcony. With the great elation of political triumph in his mind, he looked down and saw a great multitude of people, their faces very white under the bright lights ; the trees behind were illuminated with coloured lamps. " Where have I seen all this before ? " he thought, and then he remembered Cheiro's prophecy. The scene recorded in the note of his interview with Cheiro sixteen months before was exactly reproduced. Then he looked down at his wife, standing by his side, and saw that she

" SOUTHPORT " (Cartoon of Marshall Hall by " Spy ")

was waving a *white* handkerchief. She had taken the returning officer's request very literally, and had thought that, whereas a red or a blue handkerchief was forbidden, there could be no objection to a white one. Thus the last detail of Cheiro's " prevision " was exactly reproduced in fact.

Lord Curzon, on hearing of Marshall Hall's triumph, wrote from the Viceroy's Camp, Delhi, a long and truly Curzonian letter advising the new member, with whom he was not personally acquainted, how to keep the seat he had so boldly won, discussing in detail the position of almost every ward in the constituency.

> " Viceroy's Camp,
> *October* 31*st*, 1900.

" MY DEAR SIR,—Will you allow me to write you a letter of very warm congratulation upon your recovery of my old seat ? I know so well the difficulties both of winning and holding it that your triumph under recent conditions seems to me a testimony to what must be remarkable abilities and powers of speech. Now that you have secured the seat you are of course safe for five or six years, but you want to make it safe for a lifetime. Will you allow me to give you a few tips ? . . . In the first place, Southport is Radical. . . . Except in times of imperial crisis it unquestionably inclines to the Radical side. Therefore you cannot take too much trouble about it. Go to all the small ward clubs. Make yourself known and liked in the suburbs as well as in Cambridge Hall. Show an interest in their domestic joys and sorrows. Subscribe to their local concerns. Kick off at their football matches. . . . You will find the land question a great nuisance. But don't be tempted by its local prominence into dallying with Socialism. . . . Banks[1] is quite hopeless. For twelve years I laboured at that place. I visited every house in it over and over again. I tramped along those roads and along those muddy flats all to no purpose. I got fewer votes there in my last election than in my first. I should not waste much time there. . . . The place in which to strike out and to build up your future majority is in the Radical suburbs of Southport.

[1] One of the wards.

Get the women and the young men there on your side, and you can afford to disregard the soured Radicals of middle life. . . . The constituency is exacting in petty demands, and placed a great strain upon my correspondence. In larger matters it was singularly lenient. It never cost me more than £250 a year during the twelve years that I represented it, except in election years.

" I hope that these few hints may not be considered by you ill-timed or impertinent. They are only offered in the hope that they may assist you to retain the seat that you have so brilliantly won, and which I hope will open to you the paths of political fame.

" Yours faithfully,
" Curzon."

Marshall Hall replied to Curzon in a long letter describing his campaign. The conclusion of the letter makes a very generous offer. " When you come back to this country, if you want a seat, I shall be only too pleased to make way for you in your old constituency, and if, as I anticipate, when you do come back you occupy a very high position here, you will find in me an enthusiastic and, I hope, a useful supporter." Curzon in a second letter thanked Marshall Hall for his " singularly magnanimous offer," but refused it on the grounds that " the seat must be held by the man who won it after it had twice gone astray, and who is probably the only man who could succeed in retaining it."

The electors of Southport had chosen a member whose name was to be very soon famous throughout Britain as counsel for the defence in the most sensational case of the new century. Marshall Hall had impressed many people in his early days in Sussex in the police courts and the county courts. To young Mr. Edward Elvey Robb, a solicitor's clerk at Tunbridge Wells, Marshall, with his wonderful looks, his eloquent tongue, and his beautiful linen, had become a hero, even in the 'eighties. It was young Robb's early ambition to brief Marshall Hall in a really big murder case ; he got his articles, and soon was making a name for himself. He once obtained a judgment against Mr. Bottomley, and recovered from him all but £50. Driving down to his office on an omnibus, he saw a huge poster emblazoned, " Mr. Bottomley's advice to the Chancellor of the Exchequer. How to raise £50,000,000 sterling." He went straight to his office, and wrote to Mr. Bottomley : " DEAR SIR,—I see you are about to raise £50,000,000 sterling for the Exchequer : in the magnitude of your financial operations it may have escaped your memory that you still owe my client £50, for which I shall be glad to receive a cheque forthwith." To his surprise he received an immediate reply : " DEAR SIR,—Your argument is irresistible : please acknowledge my cheque for £50."

Mr. Robb had already briefed Marshall Hall on a number of occasions, notably in a complicated company case, in which his hero signed his name to a learned opinion, no doubt written by Judge Moore, which ultimately prevailed against an even more learned opinion by Lord Buckmaster. In consequence the delighted plaintiff always thought Marshall the greatest lawyer in England. By 1900 Robb was already in good practice, and, very soon after Marshall's return to London from Southport, he was sent a retainer by Robb for the defence in the Yarmouth murder. The young clerk's ambition was thus an accomplished fact.

On the very night of September 22nd when Marshall had gone down to Southport to open his campaign at about eleven o'clock, a young fellow named Mason, at another watering place, had taken his sweetheart to a secluded part of the beach to enjoy her company. About thirty yards away they noticed another couple, who seemed to be talking to each other in loud tones ; they then heard the woman cry, " Mercy, mercy ! " The two young people then got up, and walked unconcernedly past the scene without lifting a finger to help the young woman, whose cries they had heard, and who was now lying beneath a man in a dark suit, who moved his head to look at them as they passed within five yards. The night, however, was too dark for them to notice his features. This behaviour was afterwards described by the Lord Chief Justice as " miserable cowardice " ; but of course they completely misunderstood what was happening, and did not think it their business to interfere. In the place where these two had seen the struggling couple, next morning at about six o'clock a workman found the body of a young woman, her skirt pulled above her knees ; she had been strangled by a knotted mohair bootlace tied so tightly round her neck that the flesh had closed over it ; the bootlace was skilfully tied by a reef-knot. The woman proved to be a " Mrs. Hood " who, with her baby, had been staying since September 15th at a lodging-house in the Rows kept by a Mrs. Rudrum. On the same morning, Mason saw a young man, wearing a blue suit and a cap, walking up and down the beach in the neighbourhood of the scene of the murder, in a state of agitation and apparently searching for something. Mason, however, lost touch with him. The woman had no mark of identification except the laundry mark " 599 " found on her baby's underclothing ; the landlady could add nothing useful, except that a watch and chain, which the dead woman had been wearing, was missing ; but her daughter, Alice Rudrum, said that on Friday night she had seen Mrs. Hood standing outside the house under an arch. A man's voice said, " You understand, don't you ? I am placed in an awkward position just now." Then she had distinctly heard through the open window the " sound of a kiss." Suspicion suggested that the murderer might have been a seafaring man, because of the reef-knot, but, of course, this was mere conjecture. The police all over England were busy finding innumerable clues from laundry marks " number 599," but of course, over so large a field, these could lead to nothing. Weeks passed, and on November 4th, at Stepney, a respectable young draughtsman from Woolwich Arsenal, aged twenty-one, was taking tea with his betrothed, Miss Alice Meadows, at her mother's house ; they were to be married at Christmas, and he had just given her " a pick and shovel " brooch, and some expensive clothes towards her trousseau. He was an enterprising young man, and had thoughts of going to America. Alice's sister was there, reading a Sunday newspaper. " Strange," she said, " isn't it, that nothing has yet been heard of the Yarmouth murderer ? They never caught Jack the Ripper either." " Oh," said the young man, " didn't they ? I rather fancied he had been caught in America." He then held out his cup for another lump of sugar. Alice did not care for discussing murders, and was so innocent that she had not heard of the Yarmouth murder up to that moment. They went on chatting pleasantly of river trips which they had taken together that summer, till it was time for Alice to put on her hat and to take out her young man for a happy evening with her.

Meanwhile, at Yarmouth, on October 29th, a coroner's jury had returned a verdict of " murder of a woman unknown by a man unknown," and little else was talked of in the town except the murder; indeed, all over England the interest of the "khaki" election was eclipsed by this unsolved mystery. Naturally the Rudrums talked over everything connected with their ill-starred lodger, and went again and again over that eventful week which she had spent with them before her death, searching their memories for any incident that might prove important. Both Mrs. Rudrum and her daughter remembered that she had talked of a jealous brother-in-law, and that a letter had arrived for Mrs. Hood, a day or two before her death, in a blue envelope. Mrs. Hood had been out at the time, and Mrs. Rudrum had examined the postmark, which she remembered was "Woolwich." This did not seem of any importance to them, but, when the police heard of it, they were at once interested. They verified the story, and determined to narrow their enquiries with regard to the laundry mark to the region of Woolwich : in this comparatively narrow area it might lead to something. The police were right ; the mark was traced to a Woolwich laundry, and the mark was used for the clothes of a Mrs. Bennett, who had recently lived at No. 1 Glencoe Villas, Bexley Heath ; she had come to live there in July 1900. She had been ill in August, and a telegram had been sent for her husband; he had come to see her, and periodically letters arrived for him addressed to " J. H. Bartlett." She had packed her things and left with her baby on September 15th, but had never been seen again ; afterwards Bennett had come and fetched away their little dog which had been left behind. The police had traced the laundry mark, through the postmark, on November 5th ; by the 6th, Inspector Leach had all this information, and set about to find the bereaved husband : he found him through a shop-assistant named Allen, who had a grievance against Bennett, and Leach discovered from this man some interesting facts. In June, Bennett had told Allen that his wife was an accomplished pianist ; in October he sold Allen a bicycle, and took him to Glencoe Villas to see a piano which was for sale. Allen had asked him where his wife was, and Bennett told him he had no wife, but that he was soon to be married. Allen paid him a deposit on the piano, but afterwards thought that Bennett had cheated him, and bitter words passed between them. Inspector Leach asked Allen to put him in touch with Bennett. On November 6th, the day after " Mrs. Hood's " identity was discovered, Leach, in plain clothes, was " introduced " by Allen to Bennett, whom he promptly arrested in the name of the law. He charged him with the murder of " a woman named Hood " at Yarmouth. Bennett, taken completely by surprise, gave a very curious answer. " I don't understand what you mean," he said ; " I have never been to Yarmouth. I have never lived with my wife since January, as I found a lot of letters in her pocket from another man."

Enquiries made immediately afterwards seemed to justify the inspired arrest made by Inspector Leach, which was certainly supported at the time by very slender evidence. Bennett had been first a newspaper lad, then a grocer's assistant. At the age of seventeen, against the wish of his parents, he had married Mary Clarke, a young woman two years his senior, who was pregnant by him. She was an accomplished pianist ; he was musical, and they had met as mistress and pupil. In 1898 a baby was born : in February 1900 he opened a grocery shop at Westgate ; soon afterwards it was burnt down, and Bennett recovered over £200 from an insurance company. This young grocer was very extravagant ; had a banking account and drew out large sums of money. The husband and wife made some, at any rate, of this money by fraudulently selling violins through a trade journal. The South African war was still continuing, and Bennett had paid a mysterious trip to South Africa, but not in khaki, with his wife, staying only four days at the Cape before his return in May. On coming back, they took rooms at Plumstead at the house of a Mrs. Elliston. Mrs. Elliston said that the wife was always crying, and that Bennett was always ill-treating her. On one occasion he said he would leave her, and go away for good. She then said, " Herbert, I shall follow you for the sake of the child, and if you are not careful I will get you fifteen years." Bennett retorted that " he wished she was dead, and that, if she did not look out, she soon would be." At the end of June they separated ; the wife took the house at Glencoe Villas, and Bennett went to lodge at Union Street, Woolwich, with a Mrs. Pankhurst near the Arsenal, where he had now obtained employment. Another young man who lodged there, named Stevens, had a sweetheart who was a West End cook, and she introduced to Bennett a pretty parlour-maid named Meadows ; he paid court to her, and she began to fall in love with him. He was now involved in a double life, and, knowing that he had no chance with Alice if he disclosed that he was married, he kept his marriage an absolute secret from her, and explained his visits to his wife by saying that he had a " cousin " who lived in Bexley. He seems to have behaved very well to this girl : he was always gentle and considerate, and never took advantage of her. She trusted him so much that she was prepared to go to Yarmouth for a week-end with him. Through a recommendation from Stevens's sweetheart, he wrote a letter to a Mrs. Rudrum of No. 3, Row 114, Yarmouth, applying for lodgings for the bank holiday week-end : he used his usual notepaper of a greyish blue, and posted it from Wool-wich. On Mrs. Rudrum replying that her rooms were engaged, he and Alice went down first class to Yarmouth on bank holiday, and took rooms at the " Crown and Anchor " ; they occupied separate bedrooms, and were attended by a waiter called Reade. At the end of August Bennett was absent on holiday from the Arsenal, and used his leisure to take Miss Meadows for a tour in Ireland. Here he spent money freely, and Alice promised to marry him, and received a ruby and diamond ring. They returned on September 11th, and on the 14th Bennett visited his wife; the next day she left Glencoe Villas with her baby and had not been heard of since.

Now, according to Mrs. Rudrum, " Mrs. Hood " had received a letter from Woolwich ; but, when information reached the police that the man who had come down with the girl in August to the " Crown and Anchor " had also come down on September 15th and gone away early next morning, the net was already closing round Bennett. A man had arrived at about 11.45 at the " Crown and Anchor " on the night of September 22nd, out of breath and saying he had missed the train, but he was not recognised as the man who had been there on the two former occasions ; he had a thicker moustache ; he was wearing a light suit and a dark trilby hat ; he had left by the early Sunday morning train, and a newsagent had noticed him at the station, the only other passengers being a departing theatrical company. Was Bennett the man who had been at the " Crown and Anchor" on September 15th or September 22nd ? Could he establish an alibi ? His own landlady said he was not at home on those nights ; on September 14th he had told Alice Meadows that he could not see her the next day as he had to go down to Gravesend on account of his grandfather's illness ; this was a lie. At twelve o'clock on Sunday the 15th he was at Mrs. Meadows's house in York Road, Stepney. The 7.20 from Yarmouth had arrived at 11.47. On Saturday the 22nd, Mrs. Pankhurst had seen Bennett with a time-table, at 3 p.m., as if about to take a journey. But, on Sunday the 23rd, Mrs. Lensen, a widow who lived with Mrs. Meadows, said she remembered Bennett being at Stepney at 11.30 a.m., that is, shortly before the 7.20 from Yarmouth was steaming into Liverpool Street. At about 12.50 he met Miss Meadows, apparently by chance, in Hyde Park ; she was hurt and surprised to see him, as he had told her that he was to be at his grandfather's. Later he told her that his grandfather had died, and he wore mourning for him. According to enquiries made, Bennett told several people who had known his wife that she had died in South Africa, and he gave one a photograph of her ; to the landlord of Glencoe Villas he said she was away ill ; to Miss Meadows he said that a cousin who lived at Bexley and had been a nuisance to him had gone to South Africa, and that he had bought this woman's furniture, so that they would soon be able to set up house. He certainly gave Alice a quantity of trinkets and finery, afterwards identified as belonging to Mrs. Bennett.

When Bennett was arrested, his keys were taken from him ; the lodgings at Mrs. Pankhurst's were searched, and in his portmanteau were found a receipt from the " Crown and Anchor " at Yarmouth, a revolver, a false moustache, wigs for a man and a woman, a much dented watch with a long, gold, link chain. Bennett on his arrest at once stated that two young men named Parritt and Cameron could prove that he was at

Rose's Distillery, Woolwich, on the night of September 22nd. These young men denied this; they had met him there on September 29th, but not on the 22nd. Thus his first alibi broke down.

It will be seen that a most damaging chain of circumstantial evidence had already gathered round Bennett. His double life and his lies had already prejudiced him with public opinion. But the rope was being drawn tighter round his neck day by day. The discovery of the watch and chain in his box was almost conclusive evidence of his guilt; for it seemed that this watch and chain had been left to Mary Bennett by her grandmother, and that she had been photographed wearing it round her neck at Yarmouth a few days before her death. Moreover, fresh witnesses came forward to prove his presence in Yarmouth on September 22nd. A publican named Birking now identified Bennett as a man who had come into his house in a light-grey suit with a " clerical cut " waistcoat, with a woman whom he identified by a photograph as being the murdered woman. The waiter and the " boots " at the " Crown and Anchor," and the newsagent at the station, all recognised Bennett at " identification parades " as the man whom they had seen at Yarmouth during the week-end on the 22nd–23rd.

There now began a newspaper campaign against Bennett which marks an epoch; it is often thought that sensationalism is a product of the twentieth century, but in fact it is a relic · of a more brutal age, and modern journalism is much fairer to-day in this respect than it was thirty years ago. When at the beginning of the nineteenth century, Thurtell murdered Mr. Weare, lurid accounts of the crime and broadsheets reviling the prisoner were circulated all round London before he was tried, and the story of the murder was dramatised and played at a leading theatre nightly, even while the trial was proceeding. Marie Hermann had suffered from a similar newspaper agitation. As Bennett was conveyed through the streets of Yarmouth to appear before the magistrates he was the subject of bitter and hostile demonstrations, and had been hooted by the crowd. This feeling had been fostered by a series of articles in the local Press, presupposing the prisoner's guilt, and copies of scurrilous verses which had been widely circulated throughout the county of Norfolk. A thick moustache had been added to a photograph of Bennett published in one local newspaper, because it was known that witnesses were saying that the man seen at Yarmouth on the 22nd had one. An application was made to the King's Bench for a rule to remove the trial from Norfolk to the Central Criminal Court on the ground of local prejudice. This was obtained without difficulty, Mr. Justice Phillimore observing " that there was a grave probability that a fair trial would not be had in Norfolk." But the Press went further ; representatives were sent to individuals who had known Bennett, and their statements were taken and published before the trial by journalistic "crimes investigators " who represented themselves as " detectives."

Marshall Hall had thus a seemingly hopeless task when Mr. Elvey Robb delivered his brief for the defence ; it was marked fifty guineas. Charles Gill was retained by the Treasury, with the fee of a hundred guineas, almost unprecedented at the time, with Muir as his junior. The evidence against the prisoner was overwhelming, and the general opinion in the Temple was that Marshall Hall could make nothing of it. The young men in his chambers spent their whole time in puzzling over the case, and working out every conceivable defence, but the more they worked at it the more hopeless it seemed. " This case is dead," said Max Labouchere. The defence knew well that Bennett's first alibi had broken down. Marshall at first shared that view, but, after his first interview with the prisoner, completely changed his mind. Later, Elvey Robb and his junior counsel, Mr. Thorn Drury, had returned from a depressing day at Lewes Assizes, where a poor girl whom they had been defending for child murder had been sentenced to death, to interview Bennett in prison. He impressed them both deeply on that occasion, and Drury said, " My God, I believe that man's innocent " Robb had never held that view until this moment. They were both so convinced by the interview that they went at once to consult with Marshall : they found him at the House of Commons. " I believe Bennett's an innocent man," repeated Thorn Drury. " Of course he is innocent," said Marshall coldly. The fact that Bennett had told so many lies did not shake the faith of his leading counsel. He saw at once that Bennett was a man who could not tell the truth ; the defence must therefore come from the facts themselves : these could not prove that he had done it ; they could only prove that he *must* have done it. Obviously it was very dangerous to call the prisoner himself ; the defence had largely to depend on cross-examination. Now the most deadly links in the chain of circumstantial evidence against Bennett were as follows : the evidence which went to show Bennett had ill-used his wife and threatened to kill her ; his infatuation for Alice Meadows. This evidence showed motive and intention. There was Bennett's presence in Yarmouth during September, as attested by many witnesses ; there was the evidence of Allen and the others to whom he had lied about his wife after her death ; there was Bennett's fatal slip when Inspector Leach arrested him on a charge of murdering " Mrs. Hood " ; his answer, " I have not lived with my wife since January," was, as it stood, only consistent with guilt ; finally, there was his possession of the watch and chain, which had been photographed round his wife's neck at Yarmouth—if the prosecution could bring this home, the defence was at an end. In answer to all this there seemed to be only one weapon ready to Marshall's hand : that Bennett's fair trial had been grossly prejudiced in advance by the Press ; this was in itself a good point of prejudice, but nothing else. But it will be seen that there was not one link in this strong chain of evidence which Marshall Hall did not assail until opinion began to veer round and a disagreement at the least was expected.

First, as to the watch and chain : it was a link chain, and Mrs. Bennett's father was called to prove that it was a gift of her grandmother. Mrs. Elliston, her former landlady in London, had seen it ; Mrs. Rudrum had seen it at Yarmouth ; it had been actually photographed at Yarmouth. But Marshall Hall's eyes, keen for any kind of jewellery, at once saw something very interesting. He went round to his old friends Messrs. Wellby, and one of the firm, who was also an amateur photographer and whom Marshall afterwards called for the defence, confirmed his view, and told him that the chain in the beach photograph was a rope chain, of the " Prince of Wales " pattern, and that the chain found in Bennett's possession was a *link* chain of an old-fashioned kind, not made nowadays. Directly he rose to

cross-examine Conyers, the beach photographer, he put this
to him. The photographer, no doubt anxious to defend his
work, agreed that the chain in the photograph was a rope chain,
and that the chain found in the defendant's box could not be
photographed in such a way as to give a rope effect, and the
first point was scored for the defence. Marshall's old friend, the
new Lord Chief Justice, trying his first murder case, saw the
importance of this point, and said that the chain appeared to
be out of focus. Another Yarmouth photographer said the rope
effect might have been achieved by the woman's breathing.
All through the case this controversy raged ; the police photographed the chain in an attempt to obtain the same effect ;
jewellers and photographers were called on both sides ; and in the
end it may be said that Marshall Hall had, even before he had
called his own evidence, disposed of that part of the case which
was based upon the chain. This is a curious instance of how a
connoisseur's quick eye, and expert knowledge on a seemingly
unrelated field of knowledge, can be used to save a man from
the gallows. Next came the witnesses called to prove that
Bennett was in Yarmouth. Mrs. Rudrum was here the most
interesting ; it was her chance memory of the Woolwich postmark and the " blue envelope " which had led to the arrest
of Bennett. Here again Marshall scored a point : at the police
court she had said that the letter was on blue-grey paper ; at
the trial she now said that it was blue ; she said nothing about
simple blue before the magistrates. Nettled by Marshall's
questions, she said, " I did not say it was dark blue." This gave
Marshall an opportunity for his favourite gambit. " I did not
suggest you said dark blue. Do not trifle with me. This man's
life is at stake." At first, Mrs. Rudrum saw differences between
the chain in the photograph and the one produced, but she
later became positive. She was certain that " Mrs. Hood "
wore a link chain. This was another opportunity.

" Though you had doubts before, now that you have been
cross-examined you are positive ? "—" Yes, I am."

" What made you doubtful when you first went into the
box ? "—" It was the light."

" But the photograph has made you certain ? "—" Yes."

" Are you as sure of that as of everything else ? "—" Yes."

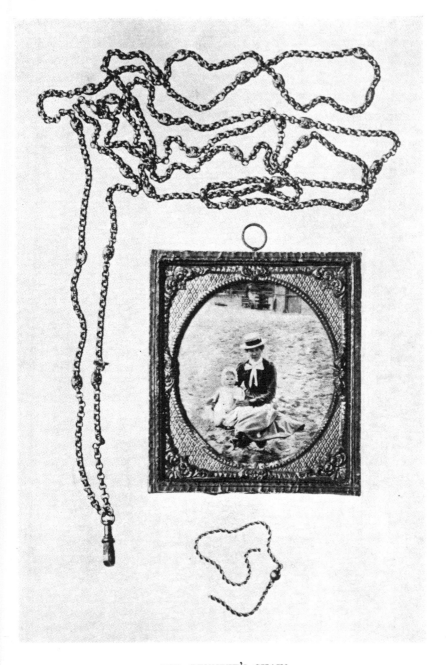

MRS. BENNETT'S CHAIN

The big chain was found in Bennett's possession in London. If Mrs. Bennett is wearing that chain in the above photograph, Bennett must have been guilty, and his "alibi" false. Marshall Hall maintained that she is wearing a chain of the type represented below the photograph, which would have been consistent with Bennett's "alibi."

" As sure as you are of the handwriting ? "—" Yes."

The suggestion was now open to the jury that this very positive woman had been mistaken. Bennett had undoubtedly written to her in July for lodgings ; she confessed that she had read the name Bennett for the first time in connection with the murder, and, when she had, she searched for and found his application for lodgings in July. Might not her memory have played her a trick ? But there was one further line of attack against this witness : at the date of the committal, the identification of " Mrs. Hood " as Mrs. Bennett rested entirely on photographs ; the police had searched high and low for some mark which would identify her. Just before the trial, on January 16th, a most vital garment was discovered in Mrs. Rudrum's house ; it was a petticoat, marked " Bennet "; the ink with which it was marked had run. Marshall suggested that the name was not written in marking ink at all. Mrs. Rudrum was recalled and cross-examined closely as to her spelling of the name.

" How did Mrs. Bennett spell her name ? "—" How should I know ? She never spelt it."

" How would you spell it ? "—" B-e-n-n-e-t " (and then after a pause) "-t."

" You said one ' t ' first, then two ; which is it ? "—" Two."

" Will you write it down ? "—" I cannot, unless you tell me how to spell it."

The effect of this line of cross-examination was obvious, and the defence had scored again. Each point had been one of detail which might easily have escaped a less vigilant advocate, and others were to follow. The man at the bar, Borking, who said that Bennett was in the bar at 9.45 on September 23rd, remembered him because he had a " heavy moustache," a clerical, or square cut, waistcoat, and a steel-grey suit. The prisoner, in fact, had a youth's incipient moustache, and his steel-grey suit, which, according to the prosecution, he must have been wearing, had an ordinary waistcoat. Mrs. Gibson, who was also at the bar, recognised him because he was twirling his moustache. " I have never seen a man," she added innocently, " do that before." It was urged later that Bennett must have been wearing a false moustache ; but it would be rash, to say

the least, to " twirl " a false moustache. William Reade, the
waiter of the " Crown and Anchor," made a most important
admission. Bennett, according to him, had stayed at the hotel
on August 4th, September 15th, and September 22nd. He
recognised the man who came on September 15th as the man
who had stayed on August 4th, but when he came on the 22nd,
late at night, he did not recognise him as the man who had
stayed twice before ; he was wearing a heavier moustache. He
had only identified him after arrest, when the newspapers were
full of the story. All this went to take away the effect of the
evidence for the prosecution, but there were elements in their
evidence which positively told in his favour. Alice Rudrum had
heard a man kiss Mrs. Bennett on Friday night, when the
time-sheets of the Arsenal showed conclusively that Bennett
was at work at Woolwich. Mason and his girl had said that
the man lying on the murdered woman was in a dark suit, and
Bennett's one dark suit was proved to be at the tailor's. Next
morning he had seen a man in a blue suit on the scene of the
murder, after Bennett must, according to the prosecution,
have left by the early train for London. Lastly, there was the
evidence, called later for the defence, of Mrs. Lensen, who said
that Bennett was in Stepney at 11.30 on the Sunday morning,
which made it quite impossible for Bennett to have come to
London by the 7.20 train. Besides all this, there was the very
deadly weapon, used skilfully by Marshall, that the whole of the
witnesses had been subconsciously influenced by newspaper
articles, which had appeared before they ever made statements.
Mrs. Elliston, the landlady who had heard Bennett threaten his
wife, was attacked strenuously on account of an interview she
had given to a reporter. She defended herself by saying that the
newspaper had put in much that she had never said. Marshall
read this article out, and the Chief Justice said, " Everyone
will agree that such articles are wicked and monstrous. I think,
having read the article, there is a considerable amount she
could not have been responsible for." One witness especially
was open to attack on the grounds of prejudice : this was Allen,
who had been instrumental in arresting Bennett, and who was
quarrelling bitterly with him over the affair of the piano and
the bicycle, which he still held, though he had only paid a small

deposit on them. " I do not know what is to be done with them yet," he said. With poor Alice Meadows, one of the principal witnesses for the prosecution, a pathetic little figure, Marshall naturally dealt gently. Bennett had been attracted to her at once : " He was kind and gentle, and we gradually got more fond of each other." Directly he was arrested he had sent for her ; she had kept all his letters, and some of them were very charming.

Bennett explained his statement at his arrest in the following way : the officer had asked him if he knew " Mrs. Hood " ; he said, " No," whereupon Leach had said, " Why, the poor woman was your wife."

When the case for the prosecution ended, the result of the trial was no longer a foregone conclusion : even as it was, all the important links in the chain had been assailed with great success. But, as things went better and better, the anxiety in Marshall's mind, unknown to any except his colleagues in the defence, became greater. A most terrible responsibility was weighing on his mind. Should he, as the case was going so well, simply call his experts, jewellers and photographers, and just one witness, Mrs. Cato, who had lodged the Bennetts in her house in 1899, and who gave a very different account of their life together from the witnesses for the prosecution, and said that Mrs. Bennett had had two watches and two chains ? Should he leave it at that, a good negative defence, or should he take quite another line and try to establish Bennett's innocence positively ? It was the most perplexing tactical decision which he ever had to make in his professional career.

On the fifth day of the trial he opened the defence. He began with a fierce attack on the Press. " The greatest difficulty with which the defence has had to contend has been the Press of the United Kingdom, the behaviour of some parts of which has been a disgrace and a scandal. As a consequence of this, any enquiries instituted on behalf of the prisoner have had to be conducted with the utmost secrecy." Then, most dramatically, and to the surprise of everybody in court, he disclosed something which had been kept an absolute secret from everybody except the prisoner's advisers. " I shall call before you a witness, absolutely independent and respectable, who will say that it was impossible for this man to have murdered his wife on September 22nd last, because so late as seven o'clock in the evening of Saturday, September 22nd, he was in Bennett's company. The last train for Yarmouth left at 5 p.m."

Marshall spoke confidently, as if he was playing his trump card, but only after the greatest deliberation had he decided to take this course. In January, long after the police court proceedings, one Douglas Sholto Douglas, a manufacturer of fancy goods, in the London Fancy Box Company, had come to Mr. Robb with a very remarkable statement. On September 22nd he was taking a long walk near Bexley ; at about 5.15 p.m. he had met a man wearing a grey suit and a black bowler hat ; this man said he was a traveller, had recently been in Ireland, and was now a draughtsman in Woolwich. Douglas had not been anxious for his company, but the stranger walked along with him, and at length induced him to have a drink. As they came out, the man said, pointing to a signboard over a barber's shop, which is still there, " By the way, a namesake of mine lives there." The name over the signboard was " F. K. Bennett." After seeing the photographs in the papers, Douglas was convinced that the man he had met was the prisoner. If his recollection was accurate, Bennett was an innocent man. Douglas gave as his reason for not coming forward before the fact that he was negotiating a certain partnership, and he did not at the time wish anything to interfere with it. Douglas was taken down to see Bennett in prison, and they saw each other alone ; there were no witnesses of their conversation, but it is clear that they recognised each other as companions on that Saturday walk. At first, Marshall, with his characteristic impulsiveness, regarded Douglas's evidence as "the intervention of Providence." But the strangest mistakes are made about identity, and coincidences are inexhaustible, and Marshall soon began to doubt the wisdom of using Douglas's evidence. Bennett had told Alice Meadows that his foot was bad at the time, and this would make a long country walk improbable. Not a word had been said to hint at such an alibi by Bennett up to the time of Douglas's intervention. An alibi, if established, is a perfect defence to a whole case, but an alibi which fails almost certainly mars the effect of any other points which the defence may have made. Moreover,

Bennett was a man so wholly unreliable that it would be most hazardous to put him into the witness box to corroborate the story. Now the cross-examination of the Crown witnesses had gone very well; there was more than a suggestion of another man in the case, so was it worth while to call Douglas and risk the questions of the deadliest cross-examiner at the Criminal Bar? Just as Marshall had, with some success, tried to make everything turn on the identity of the chain, at first the strongest then the weakest link in the prosecution's evidence, might not Gill turn the tables on Marshall and hang Bennett on an exposed alibi? There was, indeed, this advantage: no one knew of Douglas's evidence, and Gill would not have time to prepare an unanswerable series of questions overnight. He would at all events be taken by surprise. If Douglas was called, this prevented Marshall from putting forward what he now thought was the true defence. The case had gone so well that, in his opinion, if only Bennett would go into the witness box and make a clean breast of his past, and of his presence in Yarmouth on September 15th and 22nd, he was sure of victory. When the case for the prosecution was in its closing stages, before the Court met on Friday, Marshall had a long conference with Bennett alone in the cells. What passed between them as regards Bennett giving evidence himself is best described in a letter by the advocate himself to Sir Arthur Pinero in answer to a criticism by the latter.

"House of Commons,
"*March 7th.*

"My Dear Pinero,—I have had no time to write. When I saw that wretched man Bennett on Friday morning ALONE, I said to him this: 'If you will only go into the box and admit *everything* except the actual murder, I can get a verdict, but of course you must admit that when you saw the papers the day after the murder you *knew* it was your wife, but that you were afraid to communicate for fear of losing Alice Meadows.'

"His reply was: 'I cannot say that, because I was not at Yarmouth on the 22nd, and I never knew that the murdered woman was my wife till I was arrested.' I pointed out that this was hopeless, and he declined to give evidence at all.

"So you see great minds coincide, and the deadly thing from the tactical point of view was the advent of Sholto Douglas, who was absolutely honest, and who, in spite of a long cross-examination by me, stuck to his story, and would not allow me to suggest that he was mistaken.

"Yours always,

"MARSHALL HALL."

The question remained, was Douglas to be called ? Marshall explained to Bennett how vital the decision was, how dangerous a defence an alibi was, and then asked him dramatically if, before God, he had taken that walk with Douglas on that afternoon. Bennett replied gravely that he had. Marshall took the view that, if Bennett persisted in this attitude, he must call Douglas : he could not ignore an independent witness whose story made a complete defence. But he dreaded Gill's questions, and was not satisfied yet. "Now, Bennett," he said, "I'm going to leave you for two hours with this piece of paper : on it is written, 'I wish Douglas called' and 'I do not wish Douglas called'; strike out one, and send it to me by the warder. But consider the matter fully, and don't send it to me for two hours. Remember that you never said a word to suggest this alibi before Douglas turned up, and you have declined to go into the witness box to corroborate." In due course, Bennett returned him the paper signed, with the latter alternative struck out.

Accordingly, Marshall made his dramatic announcement in opening the defence, to the surprise of everybody in court, not least that of Charles Gill, although outwardly his features never moved a muscle. There was a great sensation and every newspaper ran its special editions all over England. Sketches appeared widely of "the man who may save Bennett." Douglas gave his evidence well, but, as Marshall had anticipated, by the time Gill had sat down, much of the effect of his evidence was gone. Without suggesting that Douglas was giving false evidence in any way, Gill showed the jury that Douglas had obtained no information about Bennett which he could not have gathered from the newspapers ; that he had come forward very late in the day, after the case had been fully canvassed in the Press ; and, above all, there was absolutely no corroboration for his story, which rested on his word and recollection alone. The entire absence of corroboration in this story contrasted very unfavourably with the mass of corroboration on which the case for the prosecution was built up. Douglas's evidence had shown up the nakedness of the land.

After Douglas, Marshall called Mrs. Cato ; her account of the Bennett household in its earlier days contradicted that of Mrs. Elliston, the later landlady. Whereas Mrs. Elliston said she had never seen Bennett do a kind thing for his wife, Mrs. Cato said that Bennett was a very good husband and that Mrs. Bennett was a very bad wife ; and, above all, that she had possessed two watches and two chains. She was very certain as to the watches, because, when one was damaged, Mrs. Bennett had said, " As soon as one gets mended, the other goes wrong." Mrs. Bennett had bought an " imitation " chain, for second best, which was more " snaky-like " than the gold one ; thus Marshall's " rope " theory, based on the photograph, was corroborated by a landlady's picturesque phrase. This witness was cross-examined by Gill as to a "life of Bennett" which she had written to the papers, and which omitted any reference to the two watches and chains. But she said that the gentleman who had interviewed her about the Bennetts for the *Evening News* had told her that there was a tale of two chains, but that it was discredited, and that she had thought it better to leave that out. Lastly, Mrs. Lensen was called to prove that Bennett was at Stepney at 11.30 a.m. on the 23rd, and the case for the defence closed. On the afternoon of the fifth day, Marshall began to make his final speech for the defence ; he again began by vigorously attacking the representatives of the Press who had approached witnesses and tried to convince them that Bennett was convicted. They were like " ghouls revelling in the blood of their fellow victims." He suggested that the man who had kissed Mrs. Bennett was the murderer ; that it was unlikely in the extreme that Bennett would go down after he had committed the murder to the very hotel where he was known. As to the petticoat marked " Bennet," he said, " Have you any doubt that the name—with one ' t '—was written to establish the identity of the deceased with Mrs. Bennett of Bexley Heath ? "

The Court adjourned before Marshall concluded his speech, and it really looked as if this remarkable case was drawing to a close. But a new surprise was in store for the jury. When the Court met the next day, Marshall announced that he had received a telegram from a newsagent at Lowestoft, named O'Driscoll, the day before. The telegram read : " Have Lowestoft police made report if not communicate at once most important." Now, it appeared that O'Driscoll had reported that on Wednesday the 26th, four days after the murder, a man had entered his shop and asked for the " best account of the Yarmouth murder." The man had scratches on his face, was wearing a dark suit, and had a thick dark moustache. One of his shoes lacked a bootlace ; the other had one made of " mohair." For a short while he stood excitedly reading the paper, " groaning as he read." " While he was reading the paper, he mumbled, and he turned round and caught me looking at him, whereupon he clutched the paper in both hands and hurried out." He was corroborated in all he said, except as to the bootlace, by his assistant. The police had ignored this report, and O'Driscoll chose this dramatic moment to intervene. This was the last of a series of surprises which Marshall provided for the jury. So dramatically did he use this fresh development that no one in court saw how little further the case ought to be taken by it ; and Charles Gill perhaps added to its effect by recalling the doctors to say that no skin was found in the woman's finger-nails, which would have been there had she scratched her assailant. Marshall, in cross-examination, made the doctor admit that, if the woman had clutched the sand as she was strangled, this would have removed any traces of skin. Thanks to Marshall's wonderful advocacy, it was only after the trial was over that the ludicrous nature of this evidence was perceived. " That the man who murdered Mrs. Bennett," said the *Standard*, " should be roaming about stationers' shops four days after his crime in such a guise, and with the mohair bootlace with which the woman was strangled still unreplaced, was one of the wildest, most irresponsible hypotheses that a jury was ever invited to accept " ; and the *Morning Post* dismissed " O'Driscoll with the tribute of a smile." But nobody smiled when Marshall first produced him. Doubtless he had received this mysterious visitant ; indeed, a rumour reached Marshall that he was a sailor just returned from a long voyage who was anxious to read, like many people in England at the time, the best account of the murder.

Marshall Hall then rose for the third time to address the jury ; he stressed especially the evidence of Mrs. Lensen ; referring to O'Driscoll, he said, " It is as if the hand of Providence had been stretched over this utterly wórthless man— immoral, and a forger, with more than a suspicion of arson against him : this man has been utterly worthless in the past, but there is no man so utterly worthless in the eyes of God that there may not be an opportunity for reform. It seems that in Mr. O'Driscoll there has come the hand of Providence at the last moment to protect this man, *tried as he has been by his journalistic peers and found guilty.*" Bennett's previous crimes and dishonesty accounted for his changes of name. As to the evidence of his presence at Yarmouth in September, Marshall said, " The evidence of identification with regard to September 15th has broken down, and that with regard to September 22nd was of the weakest possible character. If this man kept his wife's watch and chain after committing the murder, he ought to be sent to a lunatic asylum, not to the gallows." He then made a supreme effort to make the jury decide the case on the question of the chain alone, on which it would be manifestly unsafe to convict. He concluded his speech with a skilful apology for his own shortcomings. " I have done this case very im- perfectly," he said, " but the physical strain of doing a case in the atmosphere of this court is very great. Seven years ago I complained that the atmosphere of the court was a scandal, and I say the same to-day. In these circumstances it is almost impossible that I should not have missed some point. I only wish a man like Sir Edward Clarke had had the chance of doing what I have so imperfectly done. . . . When you remem- ber how the matter of the chain has been pressed by the Crown, I think you must see that such are the improbabilities of the case that you dare not honestly say you are satisfied beyond reasonable doubt of his guilt. But, gentlemen, I think you ought also to say that the positive evidence is so overwhelming that you are satisfied that the prisoner was never at Yarmouth on that Saturday. I pray that you may come to a right conclusion in the matter, and that God will give you grace and power to come to a just and righteous decision."

Marshall sank back exhausted into his seat. It was the sixth day of the trial and Bennett had watched the proceedings with the greatest coolness throughout, more like a critic listening to a dramatic performance than a man on trial for his life. His advocate said he had never met a cooler man. He would constantly stroke his face and chin; when the Lord Chief Justice made a point, he gave a frank boyish laugh; at one time, when the evidence was purely technical, he ceased to listen, and, plainly bored by it all, he looked out through the window at a couple of sparrows who were twittering on an adjacent wall; indeed, he would frequently appear bored, and towards luncheon he had yawned and looked round at the clock; once or twice his cheeks had flushed, notably when his sweetheart and grandfather had been in the box. When the luncheon interval came he had once looked round for a friend, nodded, and made a signal of recognition. An observer of him during the trial said that the peculiar thing about him was that, whereas in profile he looked capable of anything, in full face he had a decidedly kindly expression. He saw without concern the garments of his dead wife spread out before him, and, a few minutes after the bootlace, with the murderous knots still in it, had passed from the hands of his advocate just below him, he was laughing merrily at a remark made by a witness : he seems to have been altogether an abnormal and extraordinary man.

In his final speech, Marshall was in a far worse position, owing to the Criminal Evidence Act, than he would otherwise have been. As the Lord Chief Justice said, " If the evidence of Douglas is accepted, there is an end of the case for the Crown." But the accused, who had not at first mentioned the incident at all, did not go into the box to corroborate ; Marshall was reduced to excusing him on the ground that he was too unreliable to put in the witness box, but from his abstention an overwhelming inference was drawn. Had the trial taken place a few years before, instead of the lame excuse which he was

compelled to make, with what force would Marshall Hall have
urged that the prisoner's mouth was shut, and that, if only the
law allowed, he would go into the box to corroborate. Such
a powerful argument might well have caused the jury to doubt,
and Bennett might have escaped.

However, even as it stood, Marshall's speech was powerful
enough to make Gill rise to address the jury, which he had not
intended to do. " Owing to Mr. Hall's speech," he said, " it
appears to be necessary, in answer, to bring your minds back
to the case presented on behalf of the prosecution." Gill's
speech was a masterly summary of the facts of the case, exposed
in his most careful and impartial manner. In answer to Marshall's
contention as to the unlikelihood that the murderer would keep
the watch and chain, he said, " If men did not make such
mistakes they would not stand in the dock." The studied
moderation of his almost halting speech gave the impression
that, though he was saying much, he could say a great deal
more.

The Lord Chief Justice then summed up decidedly against
the prisoner, but he did pay some attention to the O'Driscoll
evidence, and told the jury not to let the beach photographs
tell against the prisoner. The summing up of the judge lasted
just over two hours. From 4.30, when he began to speak, the
light began to fail, the shadows deepened, the gloom surrounding
the dock increased ; then, as the old fashioned gas-lamps lighted
up the old Court of Tragedies, a strange shadow was cast
against the neck of the prisoner ; it was like the shadow of a
rope.

But Bennett was troubled by none of these things ; when the
jury had filed out there arose that impressive hum of a crowd,
moved, excited, expectant. Bennett beckoned to his solicitor,
and Robb and Marshall Hall went over to the dock to speak to
him. " Robb," he said, as cool as ever, " you might ask the
usher to close that window. I'm feeling the draught terribly."
Marshall then spoke to his client. " Bennett," he said, " I don't
know what the result of all this is going to be ; but I want you
to know we've done our best ; and I think you ought to be very
grateful to Mr. Robb for the great trouble he has taken for
you."

" Yes," said Bennett, " I'm very well pleased with both of you—up to now."

The jury had retired at 6.35, and came back thirty-five minutes later " agreed upon their verdict " ; it was " guilty." But Bennett behaved with absolute composure ; this, however, could not be said of the Chief Justice of England, wearing the black cap for the first time. " I can only say that after the evidence," he said, his voice unsteady with emotion, " that the jury could not possibly have returned any other verdict. I can hold out no hope for you, and I implore you to make your peace with your Maker."

Bennett left the dock with his head high, and was executed in due course at Norwich. Except Seddon, he was the coolest and cleverest man whom Marshall ever defended on the capital charge. Marshall was convinced that his visit to South Africa, his employment at Woolwich, and his tour in Ireland, together with the revolver and the disguises found in his possession, were only consistent with his having been employed as a Boer spy. In Marshall Hall's opinion he was far too clever to kill a woman in that clumsy way and walk off with the tell-tale watch and chain. Besides, why should Bennett, who was tired of his wife, have made a sexual assault upon her, with which medical evidence was at least consistent ? Marshall considered that the real murderer escaped scot free, and was a brutal sadist like Jack the Ripper. He wrote to his old friend Pinero, on the Sunday after the verdict :

" MY DEAR PINERO,—Many thanks for your very kind letter. I am afraid, however, much of the credit of my defence is taken away when you know that personally I am convinced that he did *not* murder his wife. He is much too clever a criminal to have done such a deed in such an appallingly bungling way. As I said at your house *months* ago, I am confident that the murder was done by some erotic maniac, and the extraordinary story told by that man, yesterday morning, of the Lowestoft incident confirmed me in this view. The judge and Gill, being absolutely convinced that *the* chain found was the one the woman wore the night of the murder, were quite incompetent to weigh impartially the

probabilities and the improbabilities of this most extraordinary
case, and, although both tried to be absolutely fair, it was
a fairness tinged unconsciously by the conviction that he
was actually found in possession of the convicting chain.
The jury disbelieved the chain theory, but were entirely led
away by the deadly summing up, which, though perfectly
fair, was all one way *really*. The best thing for society is that
a born criminal like Bennett should be hanged, and I should
not be surprised if it were proved against him that he had
committed six murders hitherto undiscovered, but he never
murdered his wife on Yarmouth beach on September 22nd,
1900, unless I am sadly deceived.

" Yours always,
" E. MARSHALL HALL."

Owing to his certainty as to Bennett's innocence, he gave
himself no rest until he had tried every legitimate step to secure
a reprieve. He wrote to his old chief, Sir Forrest Fulton, now
Recorder of London, asking him for help, and his great anxiety
is obvious in every line of his letter :

" House of Commons,
" *March* 11th.

" MY DEAR FULTON,—I am much concerned about that
man Bennett, worthless scoundrel tho' no doubt he is. The
more I think of it the more convinced I am that he never
murdered that woman. That he got her down to Yarmouth,
meaning to take all her goods and chattels from Bexley
Heath, I have no manner of doubt, but I cannot believe he
murdered her. You see, it was absolutely impossible to try
him fairly, as the evidence of the ' chain,' unless destroyed,
was conclusive *against* him, and, although the jury were
satisfied the chain found in the prisoner's possession was not
the same as the one photographed on the dead woman, yet
both the Chief Justice and Gill were satisfied that it *was* the
same chain, and, being satisfied of that, it was a physical
impossibility for the Crown mind to be absolutely impartial.
. . . Then, again, there cannot be the slightest doubt that
the evidence for the Crown was tampered with, so far at any

rate as the production of that petticoat marked ' Bennet '
four months after the murder was committed—and, if that
was tampered with, why not the rest ? The identification,
too—when the papers publish a photograph of the accused
person, in the town where identification is to take place, and
print into the photograph a moustache which does not exist
in the original plate. Then, too, the highly unsatisfactory
character of the hotel evidence—where nothing was known
by the waiters on enquiry by the police the morning of the
murder, but every detail remembered six weeks later, *after*
Bennett is arrested and the chain found in his box. My object
in writing to you is to discharge what I feel is a duty I owe.
Personally, I cannot see any better fate for a man of that
criminal nature than a painless and easy death, but that is
not the question, you know very well ; and I am not the sort
of man to worry unnecessarily about anything, least of all
about a worthless life like that, but, honestly and solemnly,
I do not and cannot believe that he murdered his wife. My
own theory of it is that he *did* go to Yarmouth, that he *did*
write the letter, and he *did* take his wife out that night, and
gave her drink, and that he went to the hotel, leaving her
about 10.30 or 10.45 near to the Rudrums' house, and that
some prowling scoundrel saw her golden hair and golden
chain, and beguiling her to the beach for sexual purposes,
she resisting, there was a struggle, an attempted rape and
murder. . . . As to the prisoner's conduct after the
murder, it is absolutely consistent with the theory that,
having wished her dead, over and over again, and having
been at Yarmouth, he was afraid to admit that he
recognised by the description in the papers that it was his
wife who had been murdered—and this for two reasons, as,
first, he was bound to be accused of murder, and, secondly,
he would have to claim the body, and so have let Alice
Meadows, whom he meant to marry, know that he had a dead
wife and a living child. As to the alibi—Sholto Douglas was
absolutely positive : I cross-examined him for an hour and
so did Gill, but we never touched him—he was undoubtedly
honest. Personally, I believe he was mistaken in the date.
And now I will not bother you further, but I want you to see

Ritchie[1] and tell him that, tho' as an advocate I am debarred from expressing any *opinion* in court, yet as a man, after the trial is over, I say this : that I would not personally, knowing all I do know, take the responsibility of hanging that man. . . . The chain found was not *the* chain, and I will prove that to anyone in five minutes with the beach photograph and a strong microscope. I am up to my eyes in work, but I must satisfy my conscience by stating my firm belief . . . and that of one of the ablest men of the day, who heard the trial from beginning to end, and starting with the certainty that the man was guilty, is now equally certain of his innocence. I, too, started with a certain conviction of his guilt, and have come now to the contrary opinion. . . . I know it detracts from any credit due to me for the conduct of the case, for, tho' it may be a matter of great merit to make a fine defence on behalf of a guilty man, it is discreditable to have been unable to convince the jury of the innocence of a man you yourself believe to be innocent.

> " Yours always,
> " E. MARSHALL HALL."

He also wrote to the Lord Chief Justice himself, asking for an interview ; but, from the following courteous but discouraging reply, it is obvious that he did not take Lord Alverstone into his confidence in the same way.

> " Hornton Lodge,
> " *March* 17th, 1901.

" DEAR MARSHALL HALL,—My warm thanks for your very kind enquiry and your letter. You have nothing with which to reproach yourself. No man could have been more ably defended. I think you have let yourself regard the details too much, in your last letter, without considering the broad facts, which have to be dealt with. If Bennett could have given *any* account of where he was on the nights of the 15th and the 22nd which would bear investigation, the case would be different. Or if he could bring anything to corroborate your theory that he did not know his wife had gone to Yarmouth.

[1] The Home Secretary.

You see, the statements which were not evidence and were properly excluded, but which I think should be examined if they tell in favour of a prisoner, do not help him. If it is any comfort to you to come and see me, do so. I shall be quite free from two till four. Do exactly as you like.

"Very truly yours,
"ALVERSTONE."

Marshall saw both Mr. Ritchie, the Home Secretary, and the Lord Chief Justice, and then knew that all was in vain. He was the most persistent advocate that ever lived, and would continue his advocacy, even after verdict and black cap, with the same passionate zeal. When he knew that he could do nothing further, even then his thoughts went out to the poor condemned wretch in Yarmouth gaol, and he wrote him this last letter, faithful and thoughtful unto the very end.

"3 Temple Gardens,
"*March* 19th, 1901.

"*Mr. H. J. Bennett.*

"DEAR SIR,—I should not like you to think that my interest in your case ceased with the verdict. Relying upon your repeated assurance of your innocence, I was able to do what I did at the trial on your behalf, and I have since felt it my duty to a fellow creature to see both the Home Secretary and the Lord Chief Justice, so that they should know all that you told me. As you have been informed, there is no hope for you, and the sentence of the law is to be carried out. If there is anything that you would wish to tell, or anything that you would desire done after your death, write me a few lines and any reasonable request that you may make I will endeavour to carry out. May God in his great mercy grant you peace in the world to come.

"I am, faithfully yours,
"E. MARSHALL HALL."

During the case he received two strange missives, one from Yarmouth and the other from Victoria Docks, of a kind very well known to defenders, but all the more curious for their frequency. They serve as specimens of the many similar ones he received in his career.

" Yarmouth,
" *March 4th,* 1901.

" SIR,—Bennett is not guilty. I committed that murder and have written the judge by this post to say I did it. They will hang the wrong man. Signed—

" GUILTY.

" *To Mr. Marshall Hall, K.C.*"

" Victoria Docks,
" *March 4th,* 1901.

" MY DEAR SIR,—I write to tell you that I was in the court and heard what Mr. O'Driscoll said about me on the night of September 26 at 9.15. I went into Mr. O'Driscoll's shop at Lowestoft, and to buy a paper about the murder, and when I saw Mr. O'Driscoll looking at me, I ran out of the shop, and the next morning I took train for Newcastle, and got a ship for London, and I have been in London ever since Oct. 3, 1900. I have been in court every day since the trial has been on. The reason I confess to the murder of Mrs. Bennett is that the time you get this letter I will be out of the way, and all what Mr. O'Driscoll said is true. No one knew me in Court, as I was in disguise, for I had a false Beard on to cover the scratches on my face. Sir, I hope you will do all you can for the man Bennett, for if he dies I will never rest ; for he is not guilty of the murder. Sir, all what I write hear is true. For it was me that murder the woman. I am five foot 8½ inches in high, and I am a greaser, and my age is 27. I think I have told you all I have to tell you now—

" I have know the woman 3 weeks before the murder— reason I did the murder was I wanted her to let me have something and she would not let me do it, and then I over-power her and outrage her and murder her afterwards. it was at 11.30 at night I did it. This is all I have to say,

" C. P."

Alice Meadows, loyal and generous throughout, could not bring herself to think Bennett guilty. She fainted when she heard the verdict. " I shall always have a doubt," she said, " about Bennett having murdered his wife. Sometimes everything seems so plain and straightforward that I feel half inclined to believe him guilty, and then I grow so bewildered and puzzled that I don't know what to think. There are so many mysteries about the whole case still unexplained that I cannot feel thoroughly convinced of his guilt. If Bennett dies without confessing, I shall go through life with a grave doubt. Who was the mysterious man who kissed Mrs. Bennett, and said ' good night ' to her, on the night she was murdered ? If Mr. Sholto Douglas is mistaken, where is the real person he had the conversation with ? Why does he not come forward ? All this is not explained." Poor girl, she showed herself a true lover to the end. I wonder what has become of her, and of the baby, Ruby Bennett, who was made a ward of court to receive the sum raised by Mr. Bottomley on her behalf, both innocent and pathetic actresses in the sordid story of Herbert Bennett.

Did Bennett confess ? He certainly saw the prison chaplain, and the Bishop of Norwich, and received the Sacrament ; it was rumoured that he said, as the white cap was put over his face, " it is just," but this story has never been verified. But, at all events, as the black flag was being hauled up to announce that all was over, the flagstaff fell from its socket, an accident which led many to believe in Bennett's innocence who had remained unconvinced by Marshall's masterly defence. However, the better opinion must always be that the jury were right. It is, however, an interesting fact that throughout the case the prosecution had put forward as a motive Bennett's infatuation for Alice Meadows ; it seems probable that they were wrong. Bennett was a cold-blooded brute, and to elevate this sordid character to the rôle of a man carried forward by emotion to a kind of premeditated *crime passionel* would be to pay him, innocent or guilty, too great a compliment. It will be remembered that Bennett was a man who had crammed many crimes into his short life, possibly not the least of which was that of being a traitor. " I can get you fifteen years," poor Mary Bennett, who knew everything, had said. She paid with her

Bennett

Beach murderer.

old Bailey

20th Feb 1901

Leslie Ward

DRAWING OF BENNETT

Made by "Spy" in Court

life for these words. Bennett would not have stopped short at bigamy : with Mary Bennett alive or dead, he would have " married " Alice, as he could not take her ; but with the former still alive, and " following him for the sake of the child," he would never be safe. Perhaps he went down to Yarmouth to make terms with her, and, finding her obdurate, killed her in a fit of rage and fear. It may be taken as certain that he did not do murder to legalise his union with the girl he loved, but, rather, to silence the tongue which could at any time get him fifteen years.

But turning from the question as to whether Bennett may really have been innocent, to a mere point of tactics, was Marshall Hall right to call Douglas ? In later years he always thought he had made a mistake. Douglas's evidence must always be a mystery. His honesty was not questioned throughout the proceedings. It was only at his recollection and the absence of corroboration for his story that Gill directed his deadly cross-examination. Afterwards he and his firm were much annoyed by communications addressed to them as the " London Fancy Box and Alibi Manufacturing Company " ; however, Douglas had the satisfaction of receiving a letter from the Lord Chief Justice, saying that he had no doubt that his evidence was given honestly, and Marshall's own opinion was that he had really met Bennett, but on a different Saturday. But the coincidences of life are amazing, and it may be that Douglas met a man named Bennett on September 22nd, of appearance similar enough to the prisoner to deceive Douglas, when they met, into a mistaken recognition.

It would, at any rate, not be a stranger coincidence than the one which occurred to three of the principal characters in the Bennett trial. It so happened, in 1916, that Marshall Hall was retained to defend a man named Lawson against whom a prosecution for fraud had been launched by his partner, Douglas Sholto Douglas. They ran a fancy box manufacturing business, which now brought in thousands a year. Marshall at once identified the prosecuting partner as the Douglas of the Bennett trial, and by a strange coincidence it was the original negotiation of this very partnership in 1900 which, according to Douglas, had prevented him coming forward earlier to give evidence for

Bennett. This case was, according to Marshall, one of the most remarkable of all his triumphs. By another strange chance, Muir, who had been Gill's junior in 1901, was again prosecuting in this case. The trouble had largely arisen out of each partner drawing on the partnership account for private purchases, in order to get a trade discount on the latter from the wholesale merchants. One of the invoices appeared to have A. T. L. written upon it : this meant that the whole explanation of the accounts given by the defendant was thrown out, and that he would very probably be found guilty. The prisoner was positive that originally the document had also D. S. D., Douglas's initials, on it, which would have made matters right. At first, Marshall thought Lawson had acted irregularly, but on going into the case in the greatest detail he felt quite sure of his innocence. When he saw the original of the initialled document, the jury saw joy and surprise written all over his countenance. He turned round to Sir George Jones, his junior, and said, " Look at it— there it is—plain as anything." Sir George looked at the document and pretended to understand what his leader meant, but saw nothing but what appeared to be a tea-stain. Then Marshall sent his clerk for his beloved microscope, and his junior said, " I hope you're right about this, Marshall ; if we fail on this, now you've raised it, it may be very serious." When the microscope arrived, Marshall was quite sure he was right, and that there were traces of the initials D. S. D. on the paper, just as his client had said. He demanded that an enlarged photograph should be taken, and there, surely enough, were traces of the letter ' D.' Mr. Lawson was acquitted. This was an amazing instance of Marshall's wonderful eye, which saw things to which an ordinary eye is blind. Just as he saw at once a flaw in a diamond and the distinction between the two chains in the Bennett case, so he saw the traces of that dim letter, and probably saved his client's liberty thereby. The case lasted eight days, and Marshall cross-examined Douglas closely and at great length, among other matters, as to the Yarmouth murder. Douglas re-asserted with the same positiveness, fifteen years after the trial, that he had been with Bennett on the afternoon of Saturday, September 22nd, 1900. He had this advantage over Marshall, that the latter had called him as a witness to truth. " My evidence," he said,

" was given honestly, and no one knows it better than you."
Marshall retorted, " The point I am on is this, that you would not
admit the possibility of mistake then any more than you will
admit the possibility of mistake here." Later, Douglas took the
offensive, and began to cross-examine Marshall, till the latter
told him frankly, " I think it would have been better not to have
put you in the witness box with a man's reputation at stake upon
it. I am not entitled to say more." A truly remarkable encounter
as strange as any that has happened in the courts. In itself it
contains a most typical and dramatic triumph of Marshall
Hall's ; owing to this, and to the reunion of Marshall Hall,
Douglas, and Muir at the Old Bailey, its interpolation in this
chapter is perhaps justified. The sequel was an action for the
dissolution of the partnership, brought by Mr. Lawson: this
landed Marshall Hall once more in the academic atmosphere
of the Chancery Courts, where he had received his first brief.
The facts were again fully investigated, and after what Mr.
Justice Younger described as " one of the most remarkable cases
ever brought before a court of equity," the partnership was
dissolved on the ground that Mr. Douglas had wrongfully brought
the charges against Mr. Lawson.

   The Bennett case was probably the most dramatic trial of
the century, and it was the last occasion in which it can be said
in England that a prisoner " had been tried by the Press." In
no other case have the witnesses been so peculiarly an object
for attack, on this and other grounds. The witness who shunned
giving evidence for fear of " being dragged into a murder trial,"
the witness who allowed himself to be photographed as the man
who had " recognised Bennett," the witness who heard a woman
moaning and groaning " about thirty yards away, and never
moved to help her," have happily not often reappeared ; nor,
nowadays, are witnesses examined in advance by newspaper
reporters ; nor is the guilt or innocence of the accused canvassed
in advance in the Press. For this humaner practice, prisoners
on their trial owe considerable thanks to Marshall Hall on
account of his impassioned protest in this case. Indeed, he went
beyond the bounds of accuracy and discretion, and indicted
the whole Press ; he was carried away altogether by his
enthusiasm and anxiety for his client, for no one knew better

than he the power of the Press. During the trial an article appeared which described Marshall as having had " scenes " with the Chief Justice and the prosecuting counsel. As a matter of fact, this was quite inaccurate ; both Alverstone and Gill were his dear friends and really loved Marshall Hall. Never was a case fought to the bitter end with more fire and determination or in a more friendly atmosphere. " Cannot you and I," said the Chief, " afford to disregard what they say about us in the Press, Mr. Marshall Hall ? " " *You* may be able to do so, but I cannot," said Marshall, unconsoled. His words were prophetic.

However, his brilliant conduct of the case raised him to a very high place in the profession. Congratulations poured in from every class of person ; one fair lady wrote and asked him for a photograph of the " most brilliant and handsome man at the Bar " ; Marshall promptly sent her back a portrait of Rufus Isaacs ! Nearly every English newspaper, with characteristic generosity, gave him ungrudging praise, and when he went down to the House after the trial he was easily the best-known and the most observed of all the new members. More was expected of him than any other man, and the maiden speech of the magician who had come near to saving Bennett was eagerly awaited.

.   .   .   .

On March 21st, 1901, the day on which Bennett was executed, Marshall returned two lucrative briefs, and went down to the House at mid-day to catch the Speaker's eye for his maiden speech. The occasion was the second reading of the Children's Temperance Bill, a private member's measure designed to prevent little children being sent to fetch drinks at public houses. A little girl of twelve, named Cissy Silversides, had written to Marshall from Southport, and begged for his allegiance to the measure. He was touched, and wrote back to her : " DEAR LITTLE CISSY,—I have received your letter, and I will look after the children's interests. No one can be fonder of children than I am, and I will do anything I can for them. I am afraid we shall not be able to get all you want at once, but we must get a little at a time. Yours sincerely, E. MARSHALL HALL." Very characteristically, he had been persuaded by this little girl's letter to make his maiden speech on a private member's bill, when it would have been far more useful for his political future to have chosen a much more important occasion. He was called on shortly before five o'clock, the last to speak before the division, and he had to compress his speech into a few minutes, a discipline to which he was not accustomed. Apart from an unfortunate mistake of the Speaker's, who called on him as Mr. Wilson, he began well, and his quick mind was rapidly finding the atmosphere of the House when something very unfortunate happened. Some member sitting behind Marshall said contemptuously, " Why not deliver the beer round like milk, in milk-cans ? " The picturesque idea struck Marshall's impulsive mind, and without seeing its ludicrous aspect, he solemnly put it forward as a suggestion that the difficulty should be got over in this way. The House, one and all, rocked with laughter : at first they were laughing *with* him, thinking that he had made a joke, and a rather good one ; but when he flushed up, and angrily said he did not care for their ridicule, they laughed *at* him. The speech was a failure, and its results went far beyond the mere failure of a maiden speech. He was no Disraeli, and never forgave the House of Commons or tried to make a position for himself in it, which he could easily have done ; indeed, he affected to despise it. " It is all repetition without variation there," he used to say. In return, the House regarded him with affection and amusement, but never as a serious politician. The milk-can business followed him relentlessly for years, and did him real harm ; not only was he laughed at, but the suggestion was made that he had been bought by the brewers, and that, while pretending to advocate temperance, he had really been serving " the trade." Probably this speech cost him those few precious votes which lost him the seat at the next election. Although he was a member of the House altogether for eleven years, on no single occasion did he make a speech of any importance. Another disappointment finally discouraged him. This time he had heavily prepared a speech on the Irish question, and, though he sat right through the debate, and rose again and again, he was never called on ; so he went home, woke up his wife, and made the speech to her, because, as he said, " it seemed such a pity to waste it." His abstention was a real loss to Parliament ; he was not, indeed, at all interested in party politics, although he was wonderfully skilful in discovering the popular prejudice of the time, and hitting it off, from the party's point of view, in a magnificent platform speech. In this capacity he was a great asset to the Conservative party. But there were great public causes which were really near to his heart, and for these he would have made a wonderful spokesman. He believed, for instance, that drastic changes were necessary in our criminal law and procedure, such as the modification of capital punishment and the foundation of an office for a Public Defender. He longed passionately for a reform in our marriage laws ; yet he never spoke in the House on those subjects on which his experience would have given him a unique authority. The prevention of cruelty to animals and the protection of young children were causes for which he would speak anywhere but in the Commons. There was real work to be done by him in the House ; but he failed to take a great opportunity ; indeed, after an initial failure which he could easily have repaired he wilfully threw it away.

But, of course, his practice at the Bar did not suffer from his failure in Parliament : his consistent success in the courts gave him supreme confidence, and he won many unexpected victories. One of the most amazing of his verdicts was obtained in July 1900, against the *Daily Mail*, recently acquired by Alfred Harmsworth. Two young and popular actresses of the day were Miss Hettie Chattell and Miss Rosie Boote. They were both under thirty years of age, and the latter was engaged to be married to Lord Headfort, and was the subject of many paragraphs. The *Daily Mail* published one under the heading of " Green Room Gossip " which stated that " Miss Rosie Boote, whose name is frequently before the public just now, is the daughter of Hettie Chattell, the principal ' boy ' in the Hippodrome pantomime." Now, Miss Chattell was only twenty-eight ; she was therefore furious, and at once issued a writ against the *Daily Mail* ; the newspaper at once published a paragraph, apologising for " their obvious mistake," concluding, " There are many well-known married actresses who perform under their maiden names, but the many friends and admirers of Miss Chattell are aware that she is an unmarried lady, and we offer her our sincere apologies." Now the paragraph did not mention the one thing which would perhaps have satisfied Miss Chattell, viz. that she was twenty-eight. She considered that a very offensive inference might be drawn from the original paragraph and the apology read together. The solicitor for the *Daily Mail*, after the apology confessing an " obvious mistake " had been published, asked for three weeks in which to deliver a defence. In the end, none was delivered, and the case went to an under-sheriff's jury for assessment of damages. The plaintiff claimed £1,000 on her writ. Marshall and Montague Lush appeared for the plaintiff, and Avory K.C. and Arthur Gill for the defendants. Marshall Hall was, as usual, absolutely fearless when once launched on the case ; without considering the dangers of further antagonising the Press, and thinking only of Hettie Chattell and her wrongs, he argued that the apology was an aggravation of the libel : further, he suggested that the *Daily Mail*, as they had already confessed their mistake, had asked for the three weeks in which to deliver a defence in order to make enquiries all over England concerning the young lady ; but that nothing against her had been found, and so there was no defence. The *Daily Mail* had been asked for the name of the contributor who had supplied the information, and it had been refused. " My client may have to work for her living," he said, " but her reputation is entitled to the same consideration as that of any lady in the land, including Mrs. Alfred Harmsworth." Marshall could put great force and bitterness into his voice, and no doubt he used all his power when he spoke this sentence. He asked for heavy damages, and commented bitterly on the gossip paragraphs of the Press. " Had the slightest trouble been taken to investigate the report, it would have easily been discovered that it was not only inaccurate, but utterly impossible for the allegations to be true." The jury gave a verdict for £2,500, being £1,500 more than was claimed on the writ ; moreover, the foreman improved the occasion by adding, " We only wish it was a criminal offence to take a person's character away without giving the name of the informant." A memorable victory indeed, for the libel, though the result of negligence, was not to the ordinary sensible reader a damaging one, and the plaintiff had admitted to **Mr.**

Avory that her grievance was really only that her age had been misrepresented. Thus, for what must have appeared to the majority of readers a piece of false tittle-tattle, the plaintiff obtained £2,500.

This great confidence in himself, his rapid success and the enthusiasm which made him reckless in attacking anybody whose conduct and interest seemed to be opposed to his clients, had been making him many enemies ; no doubt to many who did not know him he seemed arrogant and even spoiled by success, but letters to his baby daughter during this very year show how very simple and unspoiled he was at heart. By August his wife and child had gone abroad, but he was still in London for House of Commons business. He writes from the House in August :

" MY DARLING,—Your welcome telegram arrived this afternoon about four o'clock, and I was glad to get it. Tell Mumsie I hope she is not very tired, and that I hope also that you slept well all the night. I had such dreams about the trains rushing along whistling all the time, and I wondered if you were awake, but, as I did not get away from the House of Commons till nearly four o'clock, I hadn't much time to dream about anything. It looks as if we shall be very late to-night too. I went home to dinner all by myself and put all the silver and things away, and had a little talk with the King and Queen and Pickles and all the rest of the animals [her toys]. I wonder if Alice is still being asked if you can see his ears and whiskers !—and I wonder what you think of Switzerland and the bears. You would find it much too hot to be loved, if they squeezed you, I can tell you. Bears *do* squeeze so hard, and are so stupid they won't leave off when they are told. And now I must say ' good night,' so bye-bye, Baba—take care of your Mummy and Nannie and don't let them spoil you before I join the party.

" Your own loving
" GAGGIE."

In September, he was, as usual, shooting partridges in Norfolk, and he wrote again to his daughter, telling her all his news, in this charming letter, in which there are still some crushed violets :

"My Darling,—I was so glad to get Mummy's telegram and to hear that you had arrived all safely. We have had some very good shooting—but yesterday it blew as it used to blow at Seaford, and the birds were in such a hurry they forgot to stop when I shot at them ; and they were up so high sometimes that they looked like starlings more than partridges. Never mind, we managed to get 164 of them and that was pretty good. I expect we shall do better next week and the wind may get less. I have been a walk this morning in such a lovely old garden, oh, how you would have loved it—full of flowers. I picked you some violets which I am sending you and there was a dear old doggie who wouldn't quite make friends, and a Persian cat who followed *me* about everywhere, and jumped on to the railings and ran along, and then jumped on to my back and began to purr, but just at this moment a pheasant jumped up out of the grass and the pussy got very excited indeed, and rushed off after it, but it had gone too far. I hope you found Grandmama quite well. Give her my love. And now good-night, my darling ; God bless you.
" Your loving
" Gaggie."

In the autumn he was very busy as a counsel " specially " engaged on the Northern Circuit, and he could not get away to see his daughter by the time he had promised. He writes :

"My dearest Baba,—I am so very sorry, my darling, but the naughty people here won't let Gaggie go away, and he has got to work, work, work, which will keep him in Liverpool till next Wednesday. He is so angry, and is stamping about and saying such dreadful naughty words, and making noises like Baba does when she is angry. But it's all no use—the naughty judges won't make haste, and so Gaggie will be kept here. . . . Gaggie got Baba's letter all right. It was a wonderful letter and so bootifully written. Gaggie hopes Nannie is quite well, and

has not got lost in the mountains. . . . Dr. Porter has just been
to send his love to the ' Princess,' and everybody asks after her
and Mummie.

" Your loving

" Gaggie."

His connection with Southport brought him a considerable
amount of work in Lancashire ; and in particular he was
briefed by the brewers at an enormous fee to apply for the
renewal of a number of licences before the justices. In these cases
he came into personal contact with a young man who had
spoken for him at the election, Mr. F. E. Smith. They made
friends at once, and were greatly impressed with one another.
" No one could have been as wonderful," Lord Birkenhead has
written, " as Marshall Hall then looked." The young man made
an even greater impression on his leader. " I have just been
leading the cleverest young fellow I ever met in all my life,"
he said to the Attorney-General on his return to London ; " his
name's Smith—you ought to send him some Treasury briefs."

Marshall and F. E. had the first of their many consultations at
the old Adelphi Hotel ; the latter informed his leader that it was
the determined policy of the Liverpool justices at that time to
reduce the number of licensed premises, and that Demosthenes
himself could not change it. But Marshall, on the crest of the
wave of his great success, felt sure that his advocacy would
prevail over the justices. Next day he found out his mistake.
" When half his cases were finished—and he had failed in every
one—he rather dramatically announced that it was useless for
an advocate to proceed confronted by a travesty of justice ; that
he did not propose to continue taking part in pre-arranged farce,
and that he had advised his clients to carry the matter to
Quarter Sessions. . . . I have always thought that the incident
illustrated very clearly the impetuosity of the man."[1] His
departure from court excited considerable hostility. A headline
ran, " Mr. Marshall Hall retires from business." However, his
policy proved to be merely *reculer pour mieux sauter*, for at
Quarter Sessions he obtained a reversal of several of the decisions,
and this in spite of the prophecy of so wise a junior as Lord

[1] Lord Birkenhead, *Law, Life, and Letters.*

Birkenhead, who knew so well the local conditions. "Demosthenes himself could do nothing with them." But Marshall Hall had done something. These appeals were heard in November 1901, and Marshall Hall may be forgiven if in those days he sometimes appeared to consider himself invincible. It really seemed sometimes as if he could not lose a case. Early in December he appeared with Mr. A. H. Bremner, that learned lawyer and fine gentleman (still practising, and the doyen of the junior Bar), for the South Eastern Railway in four successive accident cases, always difficult for the defendant to win. His clients luckily gave him a model signal-box to demonstrate with ; he could do wonders when any such toy was put into his hand, and in all four cases the juries found in favour of the defendants. He was on the crest of the wave, perhaps the most fashionable and successful of all the younger leaders, and was making nearly five thousand a year, a very large professional income for those days. This was only his third year as a silk, and it looked as if he would almost certainly double or treble that figure in the succeeding years. Moreover, a law officership, even after the failure of his maiden speech, seemed well within the grasp of that vigorous and masterful hand.

CHAPTER VII

Setback

BUT Marshall Hall had been making very powerful enemies. When he had returned in triumph from the sheriff's court after his heavy verdict against the *Daily Mail,* an angry consultation had taken place between Alfred Harmsworth and the latter's advisers. This was the second time in one year in which Marshall Hall had violently attacked one of his important newspapers. The prestige of the *Evening News* must have received considerable harm as a result of Marshall's onslaught upon it in the Bennett case ; for onslaught it was. He had made just another such an attack on the *Daily Mail* in the Chattell case, when there was far less provocation. But, as is already obvious, Marshall Hall was absolutely fearless and respected no man's interests, not even his own, when his client's life, fortune, or reputation was at stake. Like the famous Roman advocate, he would be ill with nervousness and anxiety before he went into court, but, once there, all his anxiety would vanish, and he would literally hurl himself into the fray, and live only for the victory which he was determined to wrest. Harmsworth was like many great men, a good hater : this even his best friends would probably admit ; nor was he the man to let Marshall's unrestrained attacks on his papers go victorious and unchallenged, until he had used every legitimate weapon against him. Yet, if it had not been for one observation made by Marshall Hall, the element of personal bitterness would probably have never been introduced, for Harmsworth respected a brave fighter as much as any man. But he did not lightly forgive what he considered to be a personal insult. He went at once to Essex Court to consult a great counsel, Sir Edward Clarke. He explained in no uncertain terms that he wished an attack made in the appeal on Marshall Hall's conduct of the case, and to teach him a lesson, once and for all. For the appeal he briefed no fewer than five counsel, Clarke, Avory, Charles Gill, Arthur Gill, and Walter Frampton ; it was heard on December 13th, an unlucky day indeed for Marshall Hall. Sir Edward Clarke put as his main ground for a new trial that the jury had been inflamed by the violent address of leading counsel, and had given absurdly excessive damages in consequence. " It is a matter of wonder," he said, " how this immense verdict was obtained." Then he came to the point on which the appeal was to turn ; Marshall Hall, he said, had put it to the jury that the *Daily Mail* had asked for three weeks in which to consider their defence, in order that they might ransack all England to find something against Miss Chattell.

Now, the Court which was hearing the case was composed of the Master of the Rolls (Sir Richard Henn-Collins) and the Lords Justices Stirling and Mathew. It is difficult not to agree with Lord Birkenhead's opinion that it would have been fairer if the last named Lord Justice had not sat at all on this particular occasion. It was notorious that he disliked Marshall Hall, both personally and professionally ; he had long thought his methods of advocacy offensive and unfair, and many complaints had reached him to this effect ; and it is hard to resist the conclusion that on this occasion he and the other members of the Court made it their business to teach him a lesson. Marshall went further, and attributed the antipathy of the Lord Justice to him to his own violently expressed Unionist speeches, Mathew being an Irishman and a Home-Ruler ; but here, as one who had suffered considerably at Mathew's hands, he was attributing a motive quite alien to a man of the latter's quality ; for, after all, in spite of one historic encounter, Lord Justice Mathew and Sir Edward Carson himself became close friends. But there was a story current in the Temple that Marshall had been very offensive and unfair to a very young and inexperienced opponent. If this was so, it may have contributed to the dislike ˙which Mathew undoubtedly entertained for Marshall Hall. But, at all events, it must be better, when a counsel's personal conduct and honour is to be questioned, that his tribunal should not contain a judge already strongly prejudiced against him ; nor should a general reputation, or complaints received of conduct in other cases, be allowed to influence any Court in their censure of a counsel on a particular occasion. This implies no criticism whatever of the sincerity of the particular judge whose language on this occasion was the strongest ; he thought, as many thought, that Marshall Hall had exceeded the privileges of an advocate in this and other cases, and he expressed his views faithfully in no uncertain voice.

If Marshall Hall had, to the Lord Justice's knowledge, treated a beginner unfairly, it must have been almost a solitary instance, for he liked nothing better than to help the young men. Any young junior who had the privilege of attending one of those wonderful consultations in Temple Gardens will testify as to his thoughtfulness and generosity in this respect. The junior would come with his solicitor, rather bashfully, into the great man's room ; he would receive a hearty welcome ; whoever he was, Marshall would know something about him, and show that he knew it. " I've just been looking at the depositions in this case," he would say, looking searchingly at the solicitor ; " did *you* cross-examine at the police court ? " " No, Sir Edward, junior counsel cross-examined." " Ah," Marshall would rejoin, " I could see that it was done by a person of ability." And so the consultation would progress, interrupted by observations as to a recent purchase of a snuff-box or an eighteenth-century print, and punctuated by a telephone call from a stockbroker or a lady, or an urgent note which had to be read at once, delivered by hand from Mr. Alfred de Rothschild. When it had somehow come to an end, Marshall would ask the junior to stay behind and have a chat " on an important aspect of the case." Then would follow a flow of stories and anecdotes, in which any reference to the case in hand would be irretrievably lost. But the young man would leave Temple Gardens—perhaps with the promise of a " red bag "—not only encouraged as he had perhaps never been before, but really helped by the notice which had been given to him in the solicitor's presence. Indeed, it may be said Marshall Hall never neglected an opportunity, in court or out of it, to help a young man.

When he rose to answer Sir Edward Clarke, it was obvious that, as he had said in an early case, he had not merely to appear for his client, but to defend himself : his personal honour, and perhaps his whole future at the Bar, were at stake. But Lord Justice Mathew, who at the outset had said of the libel that " a more offensive kind of statement could hardly be imagined," engaged in a long and bitter altercation with Marshall, in the course of which the latter's attitude become more and more uncompromising, and plunged him further and further into difficulties. Finally, a reference to the solicitors for the defence brought the *dénouement*. A less obstinate and courageous, or even a wiser, advocate would have extricated himself by a tactful apology ; but this, Marshall—goaded by the Lord Justice's epithets—could not or would not do. With regard to his suggestion as to the use to which the defendants intended to put their three weeks' adjournment, Lord Justice Mathew said, " It is a most shocking imputation to make, and it is without foundation of any sort."

Mr. Marshall Hall : " I submit there was foundation."

Lord Justice Mathew (severely) : " None."

Mr. Marshall Hall : " The jury thought so . . . there must have been some reason in the delay."

Lord Justice Mathew : " It is one thing or the other. Either you make the imputation or you don't."

Marshall Hall : " I put it as a suggestion."

Lord Justice Mathew : " And what is the meaning of that ? "

Marshall Hall : " The defendants could have called the solicitors to say there was no truth whatever in the suggestion."

Lord Justice Mathew : " What next ? It was a disgraceful imputation that was made upon them."

Marshall Hall : " I resent the word disgraceful."

Lord Justice Mathew : " You make a *disgraceful* imputation against the solicitors, and you suggest that they should have been put in the box."

Marshall Hall : " I must accept your lordship's comment when you say that my conduct was disgraceful, but I submit with respect that it was perfectly legitimate advocacy to say, ' Here are the facts. I suggest that the inference is so and so.' "

The temper of the Court was now obvious ; Marshall was never at home in the Court of Appeal, and, stung by what was said to him, and by his own vital personal interest in the matter, he had put his case very clumsily ; the mention of the solicitors, newly imported into the argument, was his final mistake. It was not a pleasant task for a junior to follow his leader in the heated atmosphere of that court. But Mr. Montague Lush was fortunately the most courageous of men : on another occasion he was presented with a silver trophy for " fearless advocacy " in a case in which one of the members of the Court was actually a party. Montague Lush had argued against him. In the Chattell case he boldly defended every word which his leader had said in the court below, though Lord Justice Mathew intervened and almost invited him to withdraw his support.

" Now, Mr. Lush," he said, " are you going to defend the imputation that was made against the solicitors for the defendants that they had been employing an individual to go about making enquiries with a view to disparaging the character of a perfectly blameless lady ? "

Mr. Lush then announced slowly and deliberately, " I do defend what Mr. Marshall Hall said. I say it was perfectly legitimate."

He continued unabashed to argue, and his loyalty and courage on this occasion upheld the finest traditions of the English Bar. He was interrupted again and again by Lord Justice Mathew.

" It was a treacherous thing," said the latter, " to imply at the time that the solicitors might go about making enquiries so as to disparage the woman. That is the charge which has been made. The defendants had absolutely satisfied themselves, when they made the apology, that there was no ground for the assertion contained in the paragraph. Do you suppose that after they had committed themselves to that view that this disgusting conduct ought fairly to be attributed to the solicitors ? It was a very difficult position that the defendants were placed in—whether to go to the court above or to permit the case to be dealt with by the under-sheriff, and I can well understand there being considerable perplexity to this case."

Mr. Lush : " On the other hand, the defendants' solicitors might have spent their time in ascertaining how much ought to have been paid into court."

Lord Justice Mathew : " The sooner you stop the better, Mr. Lush."

However, Mr. Lush did not stop, until he had said all he had intended to say. When the judgments came to be delivered, the Master of the Rolls said that, while he had no sympathy with the class of literature complained of, which pandered to the unhealthy taste of the public, while the anecdote was " false in fact and a very grave libel," it did not appear that the plaintiff herself regarded it as conveying an imputation against her moral character ; and, while " the apology was open to some suggestion of inadequacy," there was no suggestion (presumably by the plaintiff) that it was not complete. As to Marshall Hall's inference, he said, " I have no doubt that the speech of Mr. Marshall Hall had a very serious effect in inflaming the damages, which in this case are immoderate and out of proportion to the facts. It was suggested that the solicitors sent all over the country to find some facts to justify the libel against this lady and to enable them to throw further imputations upon her character. . . . For counsel to suggest that the solicitors and advisers who shaped the course of the defence up to that point, and had debarred themselves from anything like a justification by reason of the apology, which tied them to the admission that there was no foundation for the statement in the paragraph —to suggest that they had utilised the time in order to enable them to set up a case inconsistent with the apology—I say it is a monstrous imputation to make. The charge was made without a shadow of foundation for it. I say that a verdict that was procured by such means cannot stand, and ought not to be allowed to stand." Lord Justice Stirling agreed, and Lord Justice Mathew, who had been the dominating judge through-out the argument, " desired once more, in as moderate language as he could use, to express his entire concurrence with the views expressed by the Master of the Rolls as to the unfortunate course that was taken before the under-sheriff." " I regret," he said, " that it should have been done. I regret that it should have been attempted to defend it before us." It may have been noticed that the " most moderate language " which the Lord Justice could use had already almost exhausted the ordinary armoury of vituperation. The epithets, " shocking," " disgrace-ful," " treacherous," and " monstrous " had all been freely used.

The effect of these judgments was very serious for Marshall Hall ; it destroyed his confidence, and, taken with other related circumstances, wellnigh ruined his practice. Every newspaper took notice of it ; even *The Times* used the headlines, " Counsel

censured : verdict obtained by such means cannot stand."
Other papers referred to " Mr. Marshall Hall's shocking suggestion " and to the " severe judicial reprimand " which he had
received. *The Times*, in a leading article, put the matter most
moderately of all. " The leading counsel of the plaintiff, making
a point of this application [for three weeks' delay], suggested to
the jury that time had been asked for to make enquiries to find
out matters which might be prejudicial to the lady. In the heat
of forensic strife an advocate might inadvertently let fall such a
remark. But what is surprising is that counsel defended it when
the Court of Appeal found fault with it. ' I made the suggestion
in my opening speech to the jury so that evidence might be
called by the defendants to rebut it.' This is a naïve confession
of a curious conception of counsel's licence. An offensive suggestion—' a disgraceful imputation ' is one of the Lord Justices'
description of it—is put forward without a particle of evidence
to support it. A bolt is shot at a venture, and the excuse for this
is that it gives the person who is held up to odium an opportunity
of contradicting the statement." But, in comparison to the
comments of other newspapers, *The Times* was moderate.
Even the *Law Times*, a paper published exclusively for lawyers,
said, " Advocacy such as this [Mr. Marshall Hall's] does much to
tarnish the honour of the Bar, and we do not think that the
strictures of the Court of Appeal—' a shocking suggestion ' and
' a monstrous charge '—were one whit too strong." The *Law
Journal*, however, the most widely read of all the legal papers,
published an article strongly criticising the Lord Justice's
suggestion to Mr. Lush that he should not support his leader, and
clearly indicating the view that he was unjustified in his censure
on Marshall Hall.

His wife was abroad at this time, and Marshall wrote at once
to tell her of his misfortune. " My dear little woman," he wrote,
" I have had very serious trouble while you have been away,
about a case I did before Mathew in which he grossly insulted me.
The Times, however, wrote a leading article going against me
most strongly, and the matter has caused great excitement. I
was absolutely right, and the judge and the newspapers wrong,
but I fear the matter cannot rest there."

" Few people," writes Mr. S. Mavrojani, " knew how sensitive

he was." He was grief-stricken : he went round to Paper Buildings, for advice and consolation, to A. M. Bremner, with whom
he had won that series of victories a few days before. A libel
action against a judge for observations made in a judicial
proceeding was, of course, impossible. He wanted to resign his
seat and challenge Mathew to prove his allegations at a re-
election. Bremner calmed him down, and told him that the whole
thing would blow over if he would only remain quiet. How hard
it was for Marshall Hall to do this appears in a letter which he
wrote to Lord Edmund Talbot in 1917, when he finally retired
from politics. In this he refers to Lord Justice Mathew's dislike
of him. " In 1901, when I was at the top of the tree . . . he made
a violent and absolutely unjustifiable attack upon me and my
personal honour.   The present Mr. Justice Lush was my junior
in the case, and in open court protested against the unjustifiable
attack that Mathew made upon me. The position was very
serious for me professionally and financially, for in consequence
my income dropped from thousands to hundreds. The only thing
for me to do was to resign my seat and challenge Mathew
publicly to prove his allegations at a re-election. I consulted the
Whips, A. J. B., and Finlay, and I was asked not to resign, as
by that time the seat was very unsafe. I most reluctantly
agreed, and had to labour under the stigma, supported only by
the knowledge that it was absolutely unjust, and also, I am
thankful to say, by the kindly help of my colleagues at the Bar.
Ask Rawlinson, Pollock, Salter, Hohler, anyone you like, and
they will tell you this is the absolute truth. Well, I fought my
way back through a second attack by Mathew, and, by sacri-
ficing my collection of silver and other things, I was enabled to
pull through these years of persecution, and, by 1905, things
were going well again."
   The judgment in the Chattell case had so great an effect on
Marshall's career, as he felt the charges made against him so
deeply, that it has been the duty of his biographer to go into it at
some length. The rights of it depend on a somewhat technical
point of legal practice. Under the circumstances of that case,
was Marshall's suggestion justifiable or excusable ? Now, the
Lord Justices certainly agreed with Marshall Hall that the
paragraph was a very grave libel, and the Master of the Rolls

admitted that the apology might be considered inadequate. That apology, which under the circumstances might very well have been a handsome one, omitted the fact that Miss Chattell was twenty-eight, and that therefore it would have been impossible for her to have a grown-up daughter. The reason given, in fact, for their mistake was that " there are many well-known actresses who perform under their maiden names." The *Yorkshire Post*, which had copied the original paragraph from the *Daily Mail*, had inserted in its apology that Miss Chattell was twenty-eight, and no proceedings were taken against it. Now, by itself, without any offensive innuendo, the libel that an actress is the mother of a woman of her own age, followed by an apology that the mistake is one which might be made any day, was a damaging one. All women are inclined to be sensitive on the question of age, but, to an actress of musical comedy, youth is literally golden, and of supreme importance ; and a libel on her youth is in itself the most damaging trade libel that can be made against her. Under the circumstances, it was no wonder that Miss Chattell continued her action after this apology : the defendants had had their opportunity, and the plaintiff could hardly be expected to demand a further one. She was entitled to go on with her action. As far as can be seen from the report of the judgments, the Lord Justices did not appreciate this aspect of the case. The defendants had apologised, they said ; therefore they had made it impossible to defend the action. But the story that Miss Boote was Miss Chattell's daughter was manifestly untrue, and it would never have been defended for a moment. Therefore there was no merit or generosity in the apology. But, under the Law of Libel Amendment Act, a defendant, although he does not defend the claim, may serve a notice on the plaintiff that he intends to prove facts to show the bad reputation of the plaintiff. If such facts are substantially proved, the plaintiff will, in all probability, receive only small, or nominal damages ; this is an extension of the principle that no man is entitled to receive damages for injury to a reputation which he has no right to possess. Further, Lord Justice Mathew did not seem on this occasion to have appreciated that, whenever a writ for libel is issued against a great newspaper, enquiries, sometimes very exhaustive, are made concerning the person advancing the claim, and individuals are legitimately employed to make them. This fact is notorious, and a very proper protection for the Press ; it would be a monstrous thing if a man of straw and of bad repute could at his will take advantage of an error in a great newspaper, with all its multitudinous news columns, and recover substantial damages ; it was and is common sense that these enquiries should be made ; and, indeed, a solicitor employed to protect a great newspaper from claims for defamation would be failing in his duty if he did not make adequate enquiries concerning individuals who make these claims. Thus Marshall Hall was not, in suggesting that exhaustive enquiries had been made, really making any " monstrous " charge against the solicitors at all, but inferring that they had utilised the three weeks in performing a perfectly legitimate duty for the defence in an action for defamation. Marshall spoke, no doubt, in eloquent and rhetorical language, but there is no rule at the Bar that counsel may not make full use of their rhetoric on their clients' behalf. The facts, recapitulated again very shortly, were these. The newspapers had published what the Lord Justices defined as a very grave libel : they had followed it up with an apology which the Master of the Rolls thought " was open to some suggestion of inadequacy " ; the action went on, and, in spite of their apology which admitted an " obvious error," the defendants asked for three weeks to consider their defence. No defence materialised. The explanation of this procedure, in the absence of evidence by the defendants, was surely a matter for inference —and argument. It being notorious that defendants do make these enquiries, Marshall used the following argument : " After an apology for an obvious error, they asked for three weeks to consider a defence, and then delivered none. For what did they need those three weeks ? Having admitted the libel, their only line of defence was to mitigate the damages. To do this, evidence would have to be called, and for this purpose enquiries would have to be made. But nothing resulted from any such enquiries ; for they have made no suggestion against Miss Chattell." The alternative explanation was put forward by Lord Justice Mathew, that the defendants were in a state of perplexity as to whether the action was to be brought in the High Court or the sheriff's court ; this was also a matter of inference, and would seem to offer a less probable solution. However, the chief point in the indictment against Marshall Hall was his suggestion that, *after an apology*, the defendants had " made enquiries." Marshall Hall's whole point was that it was the defective terms of that very apology which led him to the natural inference that such a course was taken.

Whatever were the rights or wrongs of this celebrated scene between Bench and counsel, there can be no doubt that the reprimand could hardly have been severer. Only £1,000 had been claimed, and the jury had awarded £2,500. The Court of Appeal could perfectly well have granted a new trial on this technical point alone, without any animadversion on counsel's behaviour, and the justice of the case would have been met. But they felt it their duty to censure counsel in the strongest terms, knowing full well how great a blow their censure would be to his practice. To account for this policy they must have taken a very decided view of their duty, and also altogether mistaken the character of the man : whatever wrong Marshall did, he did in the heat of the moment, in his enthusiasm for his client, without fear or favour ; and it was no wonder that a man of his character, courageous, quick to anger, without finesse, under the lash of Lord Justice Mathew's epithets, should have been stung into further indiscretion. " I have no doubt," writes Lord Birkenhead, " that the Court of Appeal, on this occasion, was guilty of a great injustice. He was treated as a conscious delinquent. He never was one."

It is also interesting to know that the leader of the Bar took at the time the same view. Marshall Hall went to Lord Finlay, then Attorney-General, for advice. Mr. Attorney took pains to look into the whole matter, and formed a strong view that the censure was out of all proportion to the justice of the case. As a mark of confidence, he sent to Marshall Hall the most important Treasury prosecution at the next Lewes Assizes.

The Chattell case was a disaster to Marshall Hall. The figures speak for themselves. In 1901, his third year as a silk, he actually received 4,420 guineas ; in 1902, his total receipts were 2,099 guineas, of which the greater part was arrears owing from the previous year. By August 1902, he was in serious financial difficulties. His old friend and rival, Rufus Isaacs, knew of this, and, greatly daring, offered the proud man financial assistance. So generous and courteous was the offer that Marshall Hall did not refuse indignantly, as Rufus Isaacs had perhaps expected, but suggested that he should give his favourite pearl pin as a security for a loan of £500. Although the loan ultimately fell through owing to Marshall's pride, the two letters written by Lord Reading on the matter reflect on both parties the highest credit, and record a notable instance of the chivalry of the Bar. Marshall Hall told many people in after years of his friend's sympathy and generosity at this difficult time.

> " 24 Palace Court, W.,
> " *August 9th,* 1902.

" MY DEAR MARSHALL,—I have not enquired of anyone as to the value of the pin, and from my point of view it is quite unnecessary. I have no desire to purchase such a pin. . . . But I have a great desire to assist you, whilst placing you under the minimum sense of obligation possible under such circumstances. Substantially I agree to what you write. That is, that I buy the pin for £500, you agreeing to repurchase it within twelve months at that price. I cannot purchase it to keep, for the reason given. I cannot purchase it outright to sell, as under no circumstances could I make a profit out of such a transaction with a friend. If I have an opportunity of selling it at more than £500 I shall submit the offer to you, and, if you approve, accept it and hand you the proceeds after deducting the £500. Therefore you see it is unnecessary for me to submit the pin to an expert. The only difference between your proposal and mine is that, instead of exercising my option in twelve months, I do so now, and, further, that I cannot make any profit and will not receive any interest. I agree with your views as to conducting this transaction on business lines, if by that you mean, as I do, that we should be clear, precise, and definite as to what we agree ; but, except for that, it is not with me a business transaction. I know what value you have always set upon this pearl, and could not under any circumstances deprive you of any value above £500 it might fetch. I send you the cheque for £500 upon the terms above stated.

" As we are now separating for the vacation, let me wish you a very speedy return of the prosperity you used to enjoy—come it will again assuredly, and, when it does, none will rejoice more than

" Yours very sincerely,
" RUFUS D. ISAACS.

" Good luck and all good wishes to you ! "

" 1 Garden Court, Temple, London,
" *August* 12*th*, 1902.

" MY DEAR MARSHALL HALL,—As you will not have the cheque, I have destroyed it, and now return your pearl. I understand your views and respect them deeply. At the same time I cannot forbear repeating to you that you can count on me in need, while I hope it will not happen. But, if it did, you and I are friends, and need not waste more words about it than these. I am ready when called upon. Good-bye, my dear friend, for the present. Your dash and courage will stand you in good stead now, as always, in fighting the battle of life, and when we return to these haunts I hope you will be quite restored in health and spirits—professionally I am quite sure you have *had* your bad times.

" Yours very sincerely,
" RUFUS D. ISAACS."

All hopes that he might step into the first place in the special jury courts were for the time gone, and his practice really only kept alive in the criminal courts, where no blow to his prestige could blind solicitors and prisoners to those brilliant talents. Not only his prestige, but his efficiency also, was affected. For the time, his confidence in himself was gone ; yet he contrived to conceal this under a mask of recklessness. If he had lacked judgment before, he seemed now to lack ordinary self-control. Very quick to take affront, he was now convinced that all the judges on the bench wished to ruin him, a pack of Erinues, inspired by the *Daily Mail*, under the presidency of Mathew ! His sufferings at the hands of the last-named he was able to visit on judges of lesser calibre, such as Ridley and Grantham ; but such scenes were not dignified or edifying and grieved

Marshall's best friends. Most painful of all was a scene with Lord Mersey, who has the highest opinion of Marshall's advocacy. He, as a great commercial lawyer, was chosen to sit in the famous Liverpool Bank forgery case, which, from some aspects, was the most astonishing case of fraud in recent history. A young Scot named Goudie had come down to Liverpool from Shetland, with a blameless past and a promising future. He obtained employment as a clerk with the Bank of Liverpool at £150 a year. He was given a responsible post as a ledger clerk for customers accounts, H—K. He took lodgings with a respectable relation of his own in Liverpool at £1 a week, and in all respects, save one, lived modestly. He acquired a passion for horse-racing, and, unfortunately for him, was at first very successful, winning as much as £800 in one week. But of course bad times soon came, and bookmakers began to press him for a debt of honour amounting to £100. He could not pay, and exposure meant certain dismissal. To save himself, he forged a cheque in the name of a millionaire, Mr. Hudson of soap fame, whose account he checked with the ledger. The forged cheque was expressed to be payable to " T. P. Scott," and Goudie endorsed it in that name. When the cheque returned to the bank to be paid, a clerk in the clearing office entered it in his journal, and then handed cheque and journal in the ordinary course to Goudie so that they might be checked in the ledger. Goudie did not enter the cheque in Mr. Hudson's account, nor enter it in the ledger, but ticked off the entry in the journal as if it had been compared with the ledger. Then, instead of filing the cheque, he destroyed it. The first cheque forged was only for £100, but, by this simple method, Goudie was to steal £160,000 from the bank in the space of a few weeks, and hardly enjoy one sovereign's worth of that vast sum for himself. " In the whole history of crime," observed Mr. F. E. Smith, in his masterly speech in mitigation, " there is not a case in which a man enjoyed himself so little as the result of his crime as Goudie has." With the £100 first stolen, the fatal step was taken. *Facilis descensus Averni.* A comparison, by a third party, of the journal with the ledger would have meant instant detection ; to escape it he had to make good the deficiency ; his only resource was the Turf. He was now frequently attending meetings, and in October 1901 he was at Newmarket. In the train to London he was unfortunate in falling in with an unsuccessful " turf accountant " named Kelly, and his even more unsuccessful " runner," one Styles. They enticed Goudie into a game of cards, and found that a young man had fallen into their hands who possessed a really extraordinary capacity for believing anything. Finding how remarkable his powers of credulity were, they were not anxious to part company with him. They unfolded to him a pretty tale. Styles, the runner, was a man of enormous wealth, and Kelly was the fortunate but sagacious expert selected to do his betting. " Telling the tale " is a common fraud which consists in telling a man that bets have been made for him, and that he has lost, and then bringing pressure on him to pay his alleged losses. Goudie, on the other hand, whose appearance was pathetically ingenuous, told them that he was in a position to command money, and agreed to make his bets through Kelly, and, as a great favour, he would be allowed to " follow " Styles. In the space of a week or two, Kelly had put Goudie on to so many good things that he had to use Mr. Hudson's name to draw £64,947 from the coffers of the Bank of Liverpool, of which Kelly took £29,615, and Styles £35,332. Poor Goudie was plunging into hundreds of thousands to cover up the original theft of £100. But worse was yet to come. There appears to be a regular detective organisation in the limbo of the Turf, and two persons, more dangerous even than Styles and Kelly, learned and grew envious of their good fortune. These gentlemen were three *chevaliers d'industrie,* named Marks, a bankrupt bookmaker, Mances, of no occupation, and Burge, a pugilist who had made as much as £30,000 by his fights over six years, but was now on the rocks. These men intercepted telegrams to the racecourse from Goudie to Kelly, and made enquiries as to the philanthropist who was giving away such enormous sums ; Burge was so anxious to know this benevolent personage that he took a train to Liverpool forthwith, on purpose to meet him. He identified Goudie in a post office, accosted him, and told him that he knew all about him. " You are a clerk in the Bank of Liverpool," he said menacingly, " and are in a position where you can command money." He then said that he was not a detective, but was out to make his fortune ; he knew a rider named Ballard, whose information was infallible, and all he needed was capital; he knew a bookmaker named Marks who would do all the betting. In a few weeks, Goudie, by the old device, had drawn £91,000 more out of the bank, of which Marks took £15,000, Burge £38,500, and Mances £36,750. The bets were, of course, never made in fact. "Ballard's" horses always lost, and, when Goudie himself spotted a winner and stood to win £25,000 as a result of his bet, Marks was most unfortunately ill and had been unable to put the money on. On November 21st, barely a month after Goudie had met Burge, the fraud was discovered on a comparison of the journal with the ledger. Goudie then disappeared, and a few weeks afterwards was found, at no great distance from the bank, in abject poverty. Mances, with commendable forethought, had invested his windfall in Consols and had to leave £33,000, thus invested, in London when he fled to the Continent with a few thousand odd and escaped arrest. Marks made an attempt to do the same; but only his bag was found in the Channel steamer in which he had embarked, and it was presumed that he had jumped overboard. Burge, Kelly, and Styles were all arrested. Ultimately, about £100,000 out of £160,000 was traced and restored to the bank: Goudie pleaded guilty, and gladly, it must be thought, turned King's evidence against the gang who had ruined him. Burge pleaded not guilty; but his pugilistic past did not prevent him from bursting into tears under Gill's cross-examination: he was duly convicted and went to prison for ten years; so also did Goudie, in spite of his advocate's brilliant speech in mitigation. "I do not know," said Lord Mersey in passing sentence, "whether to marvel more at the folly of his wickedness or the wickedness of his folly." Many years afterwards, Lord Mersey was enjoying a Turkish bath, and, himself very much in dishabille, was accosted by a man still more scantily attired. "Judge," said the latter, "you don't recognise me."

"No," said Lord Mersey, "I don't."

"But I recognise *you*, judge: last time we met, you gave me ten years." The stranger was Burge. Rarely can judge and prisoner have met under such unique circumstances!

Owing to some difficulties of evidence, the judge accepted a plea of guilty by Kelly and Styles on a minor count, that of

NH

conspiring to defraud, for which the maximum punishment is only two years. Marshall Hall appeared for Styles, but the judge had not been greatly impressed by his speech in mitigation and Marshall tried to supplement it on the following day.

" How many more speeches am I to hear ? " asked the judge. " I heard you on Thursday."

Marshall flushed with anger ; it was in vain that Rufus Isaacs (defending Kelly), who had been much grieved at Marshall's misfortune in the Chattell case, tugged the latter's gown and said, " Remember that *he* is sitting there, and *we* are sitting here."

" I don't think your lordship did hear me," said Marshall ; " your lordship did not *wish* to hear me."

Everyone in court caught their breath, and wondered what would happen next. For it might have been possible to make some such observation under great provocation to other judges, but not to Bigham.

" You have no right to say such a thing, Mr. Hall," said the judge ; " it is a most indecent observation for you to make. I cannot allow it. You meant to be offensive, and you must not be offensive."

But there was really a reason for Marshall's persistence : he wished to account for the small amount which his client was able to restore to the bank out of the plunder, in comparison to the other prisoners. He had already repented for the loss of his temper. " You can say anything you like," the judge generously said.

At the conclusion of his speech, Marshall asked for forgiveness. " I hope your lordship will now acquit me of any attempt to annoy you."

" Yes, I do," said the judge, and so the affair passed off better than most of Marshall's scenes with the Bench.

Marshall was always grateful to Lord Mersey for his generosity, and, when the latter was confined to his house as an invalid, used to visit him often, and sit with him. " Marshall," he once said, " you come to me like a breath of fresh air."

Even when Marshall Hall undoubtedly distinguished himself, he was the subject of ignorant criticism, which damaged his prestige, especially in his constituency. He was briefed by

Mr. Pitt Hardacre, in his celebrated action for defamation which
cast a terrible light on the sordid side of life in a great modern
city. Mr. Hardacre had been for many years the lessee of the
Comedy Theatre, Manchester ; during the 'nineties it appeared
that the police authorities had been lax in enforcing the licensing
regulations ; but there followed on their laxity a grave police
scandal, and a new régime was inaugurated. Mr. Hardacre's
theatre was the first target for their reforming zeal, and the
Watch Committee opposed the renewal of his licence. Owing
to Marshall's advocacy, it was renewed, but on certain conditions, until a slander action brought by Hardacre against Mr.
Holt, a councillor, should be decided. Mr. Holt in a speech in
the council had, in effect, said that the management of the
theatre was a scandal. He agreed to waive the unassailable
defence of privilege—that he had spoken as a public official in
the course of his duty—and to fight the action out on its merits.
The case was difficult to fight, owing to the great public prejudice aroused against Mr. Hardacre, and to a mass of evidence
adduced by the police, to the effect that chorus girls had been
compelled to purchase their contracts with their virtue, that
unfortunates were allowed to ply their trade in the theatre, and
that no attempt was made to comply with the licensing regulations. The defendant " justified " his libel by many folios of
" particulars." Marshall did this case magnificently, discrediting
much of the police evidence by cross-examination, and finally,
by his concluding speech of five and a half hours, to which no
less than sixty members of the Bar came in to listen, almost
winning the case for the plaintiff. After an absence of three
hours the jury returned with a qualified verdict for the defendant,
adding that they had not been influenced by the evidence of
certain girls who had brought personal charges against Mr.
Hardacre, and who had admitted coming to the theatre for
immoral purposes. When the jury first retired, five of the
members wished to find for Mr. Hardacre, while seven voted for
the defence. A long discussion followed, as a result of which
only one juryman held out for Mr. Hardacre. According to his
own account, he finally only gave in " because his head was
reeling round from sheer exhaustion."

Marshall's achievement was a magnificent forensic effort.

He was complimented by the judge, and surrounded after the case by members of the Bar, who were glad to congratulate the much criticised advocate on his magnificent speech. This was just the chance that he had needed to recover his old position, but even this was not allowed to pass without criticism. Mr. J. M. Astbury, K.C., an equity leader who had recently been against Marshall in a chancery action, had lately been adopted as the Liberal candidate for Southport. At one of his first meetings a certain Nonconformist clergyman, the Rev. W. Reid, proposed the health of the " future member," of whom " he was proud as a Manchester man." " In Manchester," he said, " we had a little thrill of surprise, and a little shame, that the member for a religious town like Southport should be the advocate for the man in the ' Comedy ' case, which was one of the worst ever brought up in Manchester. Our present candidate will never soil his hands with disgraceful cases like that." Mr. Astbury afterwards " sincerely thanked Mr. Reid for his eloquent and inspiring speech." Now, the reverend gentleman's observations were calculated to prejudice Marshall Hall, and were inspired by the deepest ignorance of the duties and honour of the Bar. Where, indeed, would justice be if a man round whom a cloud of deadly circumstances had gathered could not employ an upright and honourable advocate ? Marshall did not hesitate to reply in vigorous language. " Barristers are public servants," he said, " and may be called upon just as a doctor may be called upon to operate on a man suffering from a loathsome complaint." He then quite legitimately told the story, recounted in a former chapter, about the gentleman, " who by the merest accident happened to be a Nonconformist minister," whose acquittal on a serious charge he had secured, but with whom afterwards he had refused to shake hands ; moreover, he added that, if the Reverend W. Reid at any time stood in need of his services, he should be willing to appear on his behalf for a proper fee ! " I belong to a great and honourable profession," he said. " So far as the ' Comedy ' action of Mr. Pitt Hardacre is concerned, I am convinced that several of the charges brought against him were not only exaggerated, but absolutely and entirely false. I did my very best for my client ; I was not successful. I appeared for a man whose character did not commend itself to the gentleman who made this attack ; but that is no argument why my constituents should be insulted by the suggestion that they have sent to Westminster a man of improper character. If Mr. Astbury had had the courage to deal with this matter, he should have asked the reverend gentleman to withdraw his remarks, or he should have left the room, as I would have done."

Before brighter times came there was another scene in the Court of Appeal which brought Marshall's practice to its lowest ebb, and in this instance it is impossible to defend his course according to modern rules of advocacy, although those who knew him well will understand exactly how he came to make the mistake into which he fell. What was done was inspired by an impulse in the heat of forensic strife ; it could only be defended on other grounds by a theory of advocacy which happily was out of date. It is not generally appreciated how rapidly and recently the modern rules of moderation and fair play in advocacy have grown up. Three centuries ago, in an age of gallantry and chivalry, Coke could denounce the greatest gentleman of the day as a " scurvy knave " and urge on his judges allegations of which there was no semblance of proof. Even a hundred years ago, Erskine repeatedly did things, in his conduct of a case, for which a modern counsel would be summoned before the Benchers of his Inn, and perhaps disbarred. In the 'eighties, Sir Charles Russell himself had been widely and vigorously attacked for the licence with which he had conducted a certain cross-examination, and from this time began a gentler and more restrained use of this powerful weapon. Now, in March 1903, Marshall Hall had been sent a brief which certainly did not appear attractive. He at first wished to refuse it ; but the pleadings set out a legal claim, and he remembered Lord Alverstone's advice to him on a former occasion. So, unfortunately for him, he accepted this ill-omened brief. The action was brought against the American widow of an English baronet ; the statement of claim alleged that she had employed the plaintiff, her late husband's secretary, to watch her husband with regard to his attachment for another lady ; the plaintiff alleged that in consideration of such a service she had promised to make him " independent for life." He duly performed the offices of a detective on the movements of his own master, who, however, died before any useful information could be gleaned concerning him. Certain rumours then were circulated in connection with his death, and the widow stated to her new secretary that the plaintiff was a disreputable person and was attempting to blackmail her. Thereupon the plaintiff brought an action against her, claiming £5,000 in respect of remuneration as a detective, and £5,000 damages for defamation. Marshall appeared with Mr. Low, K.C., and George Elliot, together a distinguished team, to support this unsavoury claim, which was resisted by Sir Edward Clarke and Lawson Walton. Now, Marshall's instructions contained certain suggestions about the defendant and her sister which it was conceived would be very useful in cross-examining the former if she went into the witness box. But it appeared later that Sir Edward Clarke was determined never to call her, and wrote to the Court of Appeal that he would immediately have returned his brief if the calling of the defendant had been a condition in his instructions. From the first it seemed improbable that she would be called ; Judge Moore, remembering the disaster of the Chattell case, begged Marshall Hall to be cautious, and implored him at any rate not to refer in his opening to the scandalous information which he could not possibly prove except by cross-examination. Marshall promised that he would say nothing about the matter ; but, when he was actually in court with the pleadings before him containing the allegation that his own client was a blackmailer, he forgot the promise exacted in his own interests, and was carried away into taking the opposite course. Indeed, as has been stated before, he could never be faithful to a plan of campaign : the glance or smile of a juryman would encourage him into abandoning an entire scheme, carefully worked out in consultation with his junior, and into embarking on an absolutely new line. While it was amazing how often his quick eye and imagination justified such a course, for his juniors, always less mercurial than himself, his conduct would sometimes be bewildering in the extreme.

Lord Hailsham tells a story of another case in which Marshall behaved very much as he did in that about to be discussed. One of two lines was open to him on this occassion : the case might be

argued as a simple question of contract, or it might become a *cause
célèbre* adorned by scandalous issues of the most sensational kind.
But the latter course was beset by difficulties and dangers.
Hogg urged that this second line should be avoided at all costs,
and Marshall gave him his assurance in consultation to keep
clear of it. Relying on this assurance after formally " opening
the pleadings," Hogg left his leader to open the case and went
to another court. He had only been engaged there a few minutes,
when the solicitor instructing himself and Marshall Hall came
round to him in great distress. " Oh, do come back, Mr. Hogg,
at once," he said ; " Marshall Hall's in the thick of it." He was
indeed, but there was nothing to be done. Marshall was well
launched, and could not now be stopped by tugs at his gown
or any other method. The jury was hostile, the judge contemp-
tuous, Marshall himself flushed and angry. Indeed, the case
seemed lost beyond hope of recovery. But Marshall, after
plunging further and further into the mire, somehow emerged
on the other side, and won a miraculous verdict.

This same quality in his temperament, at once his weakness
and his strength, betrayed him into a fateful blunder in the
case of the secretary-detective. Since it was a case of defamation,
with Sir Edward Clarke there on the other side to remind him
of Miss Hettie Chattell, with R. E. Moore's previous warning,
it is perhaps surprising that he was unable to restrain himself.
Yet, after reading the words complained of, which were an
accusation of blackmail against the plaintiff, he said that this
might have very considerable weight with the jury, " because
she could not for one moment say that she did not know what it
was to be accused of blackmail herself." But he went further :
" I may afterwards, gentlemen, have an opportunity of asking
her some questions with regard to her views on this particular
subject. But be that as it may, she is a woman who knows exactly
what she means by the word ' blackmail,' and she cannot
possibly read all the American Press, dealing with her and her
sister, without knowing what an accusation of blackmail really
means." The plaintiff was called, and was subjected to a gruelling
cross-examination by Sir Edward Clarke ; but, when the turn
came for the defence, the latter called no evidence, but made
a strong attack on Marshall Hall's opening. Sir Edward protested

that his learned friend had no right whatever to make statements about the defendant which were supported by no evidence whatever. " It is, I think, rather sad," he concluded, " that the plaintiff is able to find a mouthpiece in court, and in the row of this court which I occupy, to make such statements, with the object of inducing the defendant to give way, and pay the plaintiff something rather than fight the matter out." Marshall replied by a vigorous counter-attack. " Sir Edward," he said, " could not attack the plaintiff more than he has done, and he dared not put his client in the box : and so he looked about for someone else to attack, and fixed upon myself. Sir Edward has thought fit to call this action a blackmailing one, though he has called no evidence." Fired with indignation, he asked for substantial damages. Now, according to *The Times*' report, Sir Edward's words meant that his opponent had deliberately, by making scandalous suggestions, attempted to bring about a settlement to a blackmailing action. This was, of course, tantamount to accusing him of being a party to blackmail himself. Nothing could be further from the facts. There was no deliberation in Marshall's action. The statement was made on the spur of the moment, contrary to the plan which had been arranged ; and, so far from wishing to effect a settlement and preventing the defendant from going into the box, Marshall was longing for the fray ; he was never more keen for any cross-examination in his life. But he knew that Sir Edward was far too wary an advocate to put his client in the box, and either thought that it was unjust that she should escape, without comment, this ordeal or wished to force her into the box. If the latter was his object, his policy was remarkably successful, for Sir Edward Clarke only kept her out of it with difficulty. Lord Alverstone, of course, knew Marshall Hall well enough to understand exactly how the matter had arisen, and generously came to his assistance in his summing up. " In opening this case on his instructions," he said, " Mr. Hall referred to matters which probably, when we know what the case is, ought to have been left out ; but I do not think that you ought in any way to consider, as affecting the plaintiff's rights, that anything has been done which ought in any way to be visited on him. . . . Now, gentlemen, looking back upon the matter, it certainly is a matter which need not have been brought into the case at all. One certainly does not see what should have induced the plaintiff to tell his learned counsel to use it ; but possibly counsel think, in opening the case, that a person is going to be called, and they indicate that they have certain matters that they will ask him about. . . . It is a matter in which general observations of the kind are sometimes made by counsel in opening their case : ' If the defendant dares to go into the witness box, I shall ask him this or I shall ask him that.' It is better that these observations should not be made, but, at the same time, one does not blame counsel for making them. . . . But having called attention to them, and rather concurring in the view that some of them had better have been omitted, there is really nothing in them which I think need affect your minds when you are dealing with the real questions you have to decide." Further, Lord Alverstone told the jury that they were entitled to take into consideration in assessing the damages the fact that the defendant, through her counsel, had reiterated the charge of blackmail against the plaintiff. Thereupon the jury, though it would have been far better for Marshall Hall had they not been persuaded by his rhetoric, awarded the plaintiff £50 for the services rendered and £500 for the defamation of his character. The defendant, who had bitterly resented the fact that she had not been called, received the verdict with loud cries of expostulation addressed to the learned judge. She demanded to be allowed to go into the witness box ; and, as she continued to talk and gesticulate, and refused to desist, the attendants forcibly removed her from the court. An application for a new trial followed, and the protagonists on each side dropped out— Marshall because he was advised that it would be extremely unwise for him to be involved in another wrangle with the Court of Appeal in a case where his own personal conduct was to be called in question ; and Sir Edward Clarke because one of the appellant's grounds of appeal was his misconduct in not calling her into the witness box, contrary to specific instructions. This ground of appeal failed, because the Court held that Sir Edward had undoubtedly exercised a legitimate discretion in the matter. But, as to the other ground of appeal, Marshall Hall's introduction of irrelevant and scandalous matter, they were unanimous ; they held that on the face of it the action was a blackmailing one. " The jury had awarded £500 damages for slander to a blackmailer, and they awarded it to him because the slander charged him with being a blackmailer." Certain documents, unknown to Marshall and not preduced at the trial, were allowed by the Lord Justices to be read on the appeal " to show the general course of the proceedings." These certainly lent colour to their harsh view of the claim. The Master of the Rolls (Sir Richard Henn Collins) also referred to the difficulty of limiting the discretion of counsel in opening a case, and condemned the course which Marshall Hall had taken. " One cannot appreciate what effect this had upon the jury. The Lord Chief Justice dealt with it and no doubt modified it. . . . But the Lord Chief Justice did not seem to have completely realised how far this departure from the ordinary practice at the English Bar might influence the jury." With this judgment, Lord Justices Mathew and Cozens-Hardy concurred. Full publicity was of course again given to Marshall Hall with reference to these judgments, the reports of which differed in one very material particular. Whereas *The Times*, which gave the fullest report, omitted any reference to a motive, other reports, notably in the *Standard*, the *Globe*, and the *Daily Mail*, reported the Master of the Rolls as imputing a very improper motive to him for his conduct of the case. " If," ran the *Standard's* report of the Master of the Rolls' judgment, " Mr. Marshall Hall had made these statements during the hearing of the case, counsel for the defendant would have objected, and would have taken the judge's ruling thereon. But he knew this, and also that, if he put them to the defendant, he would have to abide by the answers she gave. Therefore he decided to get his thrust at her in his opening speech, when he was not likely to be called to book. . . . " Both the *Standard* and the *Daily Mail* reported the Master of the Rolls as adding that he (Mr. Marshall Hall) had told the jury, though he knew the action was brought under a threat of exposure, that the defendant's husband met his death by violence. Now, these reports imputed a very improper and sinister plan to Marshall Hall in his conduct of the case : the mistake, as the Lord Chief Justice had seen, was a result of impulse, irresponsible and blameworthy perhaps, but not of deliberation ; and, as reported in the last-mentioned reports, the Lord Justices had again mistakenly treated him as a " conscious delinquent." But no motive was, as I have said, imputed to him in *The Times'* reports. Headlines once more appeared, such as " English Bar's Honour—Appeal Lord's Criticism of Counsel's Honour," " Mr. Marshall Hall, K.C.—Strong Rebuke by the Master of the Rolls " ; he at once wrote to the Master of the Rolls, enclosing the reports which had attributed to him a motive in pursuing the course which he had taken, commenting upon the fact that *The Times* omitted any such imputation. Sir Richard Henn Collins replied that " the report in *The Times* is as nearly as possible a verbatim report of what I said, as far as I can recollect. I attributed no statements to you that I did not read verbatim from the shorthand notes of your speech . . . and the other reports, so far as they differ from *The Times'* report, do not agree with my recollection." Marshall made use of this correspondence in a letter sent to the Press. " I agree," he wrote in this letter, " that if the reports in some of the daily papers, other than *The Times,* were correct, such remarks would involve an attack on the honour of the Bar, and that it ought not to be allowed to rest there. The Court of Appeal has held that certain statements made by me in the course of my speeches in the case were irregular, and, although it was an irregularity for which I had ample precedent, I am not concerned to defend it. But I do most categorically deny that they were ever made by me with any discreditable or dishonourable motive. It is always dangerous to impute motives to any man in regard to anything he says or does. It would have been unjustifiable for the Court of Appeal to take upon themselves to impute to me motives of a dishonourable kind in the conduct of a case without inviting me to explain what my real motives were. I was not present at the hearing in the Court of Appeal, but, when I read the reports, I at once wrote a letter to the Master of the Rolls. . . . On the hearing of the appeal, certain documents were referred to, which, although they had been in possession of Sir E. Clarke at the trial, had not been used by him to cross-examine the plaintiff, and had never been read to the jury, and the existence of which up to that moment was absolutely unknown to me. The Court of Appeal expressed an opinion that the contents of these documents put a serious complexion on part of the case. . . . But I did not know of them, and I am sure that no judge would attempt to affect me with the knowledge of these documents and their contents, and on the basis of such assumption accuse me of having done something dishonourable. If the Court of Appeal had intended to impute to me any such dishonourable conduct, I would take any steps in my power to refute such an imputation. My style of advocacy may be pugnacious. . . but I hope it is, at any rate, fearless and honest." Marshall continued to think that he was even in theory justified in his conduct of this case, and quoted Lord Russell of Killowen as having frequently adopted the same tactics ; he also brought forward a comparison, rather nearer home, with reference to Lawson Walton, the very opponent who, in the Court of Appeal, had successfully upset this verdict. " I have nothing to be ashamed of," he said. " At the most, I was guilty of a slight irregularity ; I suggested in my opening that I should cross-examine the defendant on certain matters, and that is a course for which I have many precedents. . . . A notable instance was given by Mr. Lawson Walton in the Hartopp divorce case a little while ago, in his references to Lord Cowley in his opening speech." At all events, whatever the precedent, the practice was a relic of the bad old times of advocacy, and could only have been excused as an error committed in the heat of legal strife ; and Marshall's persistence in defending what he should certainly have admitted as a mistake, certainly lent colour, in the eyes of those who did not know him well, to the impression that he really did these things of set purpose.

These strictures upon him, coming after the Chattell case, appeared very like a decisive blow to his practice. What was the use of briefing Marshall Hall in a civil case ? However signal his victory before a jury in the court below, it seemed almost a rule that these verdicts would be set aside in the Court of Appeal ; and this was more disastrous than initial failure. Many solicitors who still admired and were personally fond of Marshall felt themselves unable in their clients' interests to send him briefs. With crime it was different ; there was no

Court of Appeal to interfere with the verdicts obtained by his daring rhetoric. The worst that could happen would be a " stern judicial reprimand," which might very likely be turned by him into an advantage with the jury. In 1904 his income dropped to 1,990 guineas, and in 1905 to 1,743 guineas, so that the statement in his letter to Lord Edmund Talbot, that his income had been reduced from " thousands to hundreds " is hardly an exaggeration. His position may have been affected to some extent by the attitude of the Harmsworth Press. He had not been forgiven, and Mr. Thomas Marlowe, editor of the *Daily Mail* for a quarter of a century, has informed me that the feeling of the Chief was still hostile to him. Marshall Hall himself was certainly under the impression that he was being " persecuted " : he complained that, if he won a case, his name was not mentioned, or he was referred to as Mr. Hall ; if he lost a case, his full name was inserted, or even " starred," in headlines. Certainly in one case where he appeared for a builder, who had taken a shooting in Sussex for £100, and, killing very little game, felt himself to have been swindled, this was so. The action arose out of a prosecution instituted by the builder against the landowner, which failed, and a letter addressed by the former to a third party. " DEAR SIR,—I am sorry to inform you that the shoot is a swindle. Our bag shooting the woods, guns nine —beaters 12, were 2 pheasant, seven rabbits, one pidgeon— We have a special keeper, and netted in all three weeks 14 rabbits. He has only seen 4 pheasants in the woods. I have given instruction to my solicitor to make an applacation to the police court for a summunds against him to answer the charge of optaining money under false pretences." The landowner brought action for malicious prosecution and libel. The defendant was amusingly cross-examined by Henry Duke. On one occasion the sporting builder had gone out with six guns, and shot eight pheasants (four of which were let out of a pit), one partridge, twenty-four rabbits, of which twenty-two had been caught beforehand. Two of the pheasants were such skeletons that his wife gave them to the dog. He honestly believed he had been swindled. The plaintiff was, he said, very sharp. " He had that ability, he done me." The jury awarded the plaintiff £25 damages, not a large verdict in a case for malicious prosecution. But

Marshall Hall was annoyed to see the headlines over the *Daily Mail* report of the case : " A Bit of a Mug—Mr. Marshall Hall's Client Loses his Case." Probably Marshall Hall exaggerated both the persecution and its effect ; but his own feelings on the matter appear in a letter to Charles Gill in which he asked his friend to intercede for him with Harmsworth. This letter was written after another rebuke, by Mr. Justice Bucknill, which he received during the hearing of a most distressing divorce petition. It was indeed a very sad case. Marshall was appearing for a young wife, who had been, and was still, devoted to her husband ; but she had met a young man on the hunting-field, and had been seen everywhere with him. She would not give him up, and her husband petitioned for a divorce. She was deeply distressed, and longed to return to her husband ; indeed, she was so broken-hearted that her medical advisers feared for her life. A most pathetic letter to the husband from her old nurse and companion was read, begging him to forgive his wife. " It is heart-breaking to see her and hear her longing for you every day, wishing she might die. She loves you so faithfully, and would sooner die than be without you. She seems to have no future or interest in life, and if she did not care for you so devotedly she would not trouble so. She is always hoping to catch a glimpse of you as you pass by. She has passed through more than enough, and how young to have had it to bear ; but you would not even hear a reproach. . . . Take her once more to your breast—she is your little treasure—for which you would be rewarded tenfold. I do hope I have not made this appeal in vain. I shall pray each night for your reunion. Neither would regret it : each would be all the dearer and sweeter to the other after this bitter separation. Think deeply, and don't ask others. Be your own judge. Do please return, and God in His glory will look down and prosper your noble deeds. Affectionately yours, MARY." Evidence was given by a series of Peeping Toms, and it was a case which deeply moved Marshall's very sentimental heart. One police officer had watched the young wife and her lover together, and Marshall asked him why he had troubled to watch them, and if he had sent in his bill for private enquiries. " No," he said, " I am a detective pure and simple." " I doubt," retorted Marshall, " about the ' pure and simple.' "

The case lasted six days, and aroused the greatest interest in the local papers, but a very unpleasant medical issue, which had been necessarily investigated in great detail, had been generously omitted from these reports. A great deal of very unpleasant evidence, however, had been given by the Peeping Toms who had kept a watch and observation on the lovers. Marshall Hall was carried away by emotion for his client when he came to make his speech for the respondent. He said that on their verdict her very life, perhaps, depended. He thought only for the poor distracted girl, his client, and as usual every other consideration counted as nothing. He believed passionately in her innocence, and said that her very courage in coming to prove it, in spite of the columns and columns of filthy details which were appearing daily in the local Press concerning the case, told tremendously in her favour. The matter had been, indeed, very fully reported. The next day, when the Court met, a reporter handed up to the judge a note to the effect that Marshall had said that " column after column " of the filthy details of this case had been published in the Nottingham papers. The judge took this to mean that Marshall had said that the terrible medical evidence had been reported. As the newspapers had had the good taste and mercy to forbear altogether with regard to this issue, he called Marshall Hall's attention to the matter, and was given an explanation. This was the most undeserved of all his troubles. He had used an argument which, until the recent Act curtailing publicity in divorce, was perfectly legitimate for an advocate to urge on behalf of any respondent, especially when she was a very young lady. There was a risk of the very greatest publicity, and, as it was, only this one aspect of the case was omitted. Marshall never meant for a moment that it had been reported, nor was he concerned to attack the Press at all. He was only concerned with the poor girl's courage in coming forward to face the glare of publicity which was inevitable if the case was fought. But the incredible speed with which he had spoken made it difficult at all times to report, and the tone of passion which he had used might well have given the wrong impression. With certain newspapers it was, " Mr. Marshall Hall again " ; and the *Liverpool Evening News* commented on what had happened.

" Mr. Justice Bucknill deserves the thanks of the Press for his interposition during the remarks of Mr. Marshall Hall, K.C. . . . Mr. Hall made the statement that column after column of filthy details had been published in the Nottingham papers, and the judge, after reading the papers, decided that the charge was quite unjustified. Mr. Hall then withdrew his remarks, and apologised for them, and with that apology the papers which he has libelled must rest content."

It was after this incident that Marshall wrote to Gill in the following terms :

" MY DEAR CHARLIE,— . . . . A few days ago I had a most difficult and most disagreeable divorce case before Bucknill, which lasted several days, and, during the case and at the end of it, the judge went out of his way, not only to say how well I had done the case, but he actually wrote me a letter to the same effect. I began my speech on the Monday evening, speaking for two hours that evening (to a jury who had intimated that they had made up their minds against me some days previously), and I concluded my speech on the Tuesday morning, the 24th of November. It appears that one of the reporters handed up to the judge a slip of paper to say that I had said that ' column after column of the filthy details of the case had appeared in the Nottingham papers,' and so Bucknill called my attention to it, thinking that I had said it, and that I had meant that the medical details . . . had been reported. I at once said that I had not meant to say anything of the kind, and that what I had said was in commenting on one of the respondent's letters, where she had implored the petitioner not to subject her to all the scandal and disgrace of such a trial. ' Is it likely, gentlemen,' I said, ' that a guilty woman would willingly allow all the details of this case to be made public, as, through the columns of the local Press the filthy and loathsome details of this case have flooded her little world of Nottingham ? ' I was alluding to the details as to adultery . . . which had been alleged against her. Now, the point is this : the judge never found the smallest fault with me, nor, to quote his own words, was there the smallest justification for the suggestion of any friction between him and me—and yet, the very next day, the *Daily Mail* comes out with a paragraph headed in big type, ' Mr. Marshall Hall again,' disseminates this throughout the country, proceeding to comment on the judge's rebuke and my apology.

" I know, of course, that the hostility of the editor is due to the fact that I said in the Chattell case that, but for bad editing, those untrue personal paragraphs would not have found their way into print, and I *believe* that the editor was hauled over the coals for his carelessness. Can you help me to stop this persecution, which, though it does not matter much professionally, causes me immense annoyance politically. . . . I can, of course, go to Chamberlain and tell him and get him to help politically ; but I don't want to do this if I can avoid it. I thought you would do something for me with Harmsworth, who, I believe, belongs to the Beefsteak Club. Sorry to worry you, but I thought you wouldn't mind.

" Yours always,
" E. M. H."

Marshall was obviously in an excited and indignant frame of mind when he wrote this letter, and he was quite wrong as to the source of the trouble, which did not come from the editor at all.

But, if Gill made any efforts at a *rapprochement* as a result of this letter, they came to nothing ; and it was not until Marshall had himself approached, at a later date, the editor himself that the real cause of Northcliffe's personal feeling against him was discovered by Marshall, and matters were put right between them. Courageously as he was facing the situation, and optimistic as he might seem to his colleagues, he was well aware of the meaning of the diminishing returns shown in his fee-book. His income had sunk in three years from nearly five thousand to a little over fifteen hundred a year. Instead of being regarded as a certain success, he was beginning to be looked on almost as a failure. He began to be talked of as " poor Marshall " in the Temple ; for his unpopularity at the Bar had gone as had his prosperity, and envy and dislike gave way to admiration and sympathy. Even on the Press he was beginning to have his

Oᴴ

defenders. " It is to be regretted," said one newspaper, " that
the Master of the Rolls should have found it necessary to rebuke
Mr. Marshall Hall. To the layman it seems incredible that the
member for Southport should not be *persona grata* with the
Bench. Except with the judges, he is the most popular of men,
and in appearance he is more like the ideal advocate of the lady
novelist than the real practitioner in the King's Bench Division.
His marvellous zeal on behalf of his clients has earned for him
the title of the ' Maître Labori of the English Bar ' : in fearless-
ness and persistence in fighting uphill cases he may be justly
compared with the brilliant defender of Dreyfus." In September
1903, just after the second reprimand by the Court of Appeal,
Vanity Fair paid him the timely compliment of an article and
a cartoon. " He may not be a great lawyer," wrote " Jehu
Junior," " but he is a good advocate, who has always successfully
weathered the judicial storms that his ready speech has brought
upon his head ; and he seems likely to weather many more of
them. For he has a very taking way with him, and, although
some of those who know him regard him as aggressive, he is
naturally a kind-hearted, rather nervous fellow, who hides his
modesty under a bushel of assertiveness. The British jury
believes in him, and the British public admires him ; but Lord
Justice Mathew is supposed not to love him." And who could
not but admire the man, known to be bitterly disappointed,
and really hard put to it for money, who never repined or
allowed misfortune to embitter that boyish and enthusiastic
spirit ? He had had troubles before, and he knew how to bear
like a man far deeper unhappiness than comes from professional
reverses and financial anxiety. Day after day he would come
into Inner Temple Hall for lunch " surrounded by the young
men in his chambers, apparently in the highest spirits of them
all, gay and full of delightful anecdote." [1] And, curiously enough,
it was at this time, when there was hardly a judge on the King's
Bench with whom he had not quarrelled in court and with whom
he was not fully prepared to quarrel again on the slightest
provocation, that his great popularity with his colleagues began.
The Bar began to be proud of this picturesque and indomitable
personality.

Lord Birkenhead, *Law, Life, and Letters.*

Wellesley Orr, who came into Temple Gardens as his devil, when his legal fortunes were at their lowest ebb, testifies to his high spirits and cheerful personality, which was so expansive that no single room seemed able to contain him and his many interests : he would overflow into the smaller room occupied by Moore and Orr. He still kept up his old interests of collecting every kind of curiosity. One afternoon the sound of a big man coming up the stairs was heard ; then followed a crash on the door, and a shout for " Ernest." Marshall came in with a huge parcel wrapped in a newspaper under his arm ; he then sat down at Orr's desk, sweeping away any papers of his that were there. " Come, look here, Orr," he said. " I'll show you something wonderful." The newspaper was then opened, and the multi-form parts of an exceedingly old clock were found to be the contents of the parcel. " Wonderful old Nuremberg clock, this, Orr," he said. " Probably the first clock that ever kept time in Germany—bought it for a song. You don't mind if I sit here, Orr, and just put it together ? " His skilful hands then got busy, and the " first clock that ever kept time in Germany " began to do so again in Temple Gardens. Another day he brought in another huge parcel, which, on being opened, turned out to contain a litter of Pekinese puppies that began running about all over Orr's room, and misbehaving themselves. They had been bought for his daughter Elna, and of course they had come straight from the most sacred of the Dowager Empress's kennels : there was something superlative about all Marshall's purchases. Later, he brought in a silver revolver, which had the " lightest trigger " ever attached to a lethal weapon. " Just picked it up—don't know if it is loaded at all. Might go off at any moment. Just look at it, wonderful work, isn't it, Orr ? " Truly the business of being devil to Marshall Hall was not without interest.

There are times in a man's career when there seems to be an ebb all along the line. Early in 1905—the year in which his professional fortunes had fallen to their lowest—his beloved sister, Mrs. Labouchere, died, and for weeks he cancelled all but professional engagements. " I had the good fortune," he wrote in 1923, " to be brought up by this sister, and between her and myself existed a bond of affection which I fear is very rare, but than which I believe there can be none more perfect. There was between us a telepathic sympathy that was independent of separation, and I could record many instances where we both have known what was happening to the other far away."[1]

But the year 1905 had at least one piece of good fortune in store for him ; his peace was made with the *Daily Mail*. He was, with years, becoming wiser, and experience had taught him that it was foolish to make enemies by some reckless gesture induced on the spur of the moment by thoughtlessness or some real or fancied grievance. He was firmly convinced that the " *Daily Mail* people " were on the watch to report any defeat or reprimand from the Bench that he might suffer, and to ignore his successes. He did not understand the reason for their dislike of him, but he was determined to come to an understanding with them. In March 1905, Marshall appeared in a libel action against the *Daily Chronicle*. An article appeared in that newspaper giving an account of how a young woman named Mary Davis had "kidnapped" a baby: as a fact the baby was her own. Marshall Hall won £800 for the plaintiff ; it was a difficult case, and the verdict was a handsome one. When Marshall read the account in the *Daily Mail*, he found he was referred to as " Mr. M   Hall." A blank space had been left which would have been filled exactly by the name " (M)arshall," and he considered that, because he had been successful, the first name, originally inserted, had been deliberately cut out. The editor of the *Daily Mail*, Mr. Thomas Marlowe, was a fellow member of the Garrick : though they were not acquainted, Marshall wrote from Knowsley the following letter :

" *February* 4*th*, 1905.

" DEAR SIR,—I have had my attention called to the report, in your issue of February 3rd, of the libel action against the *Daily Chronicle* by Miss Davis, in which the jury awarded her £800 damages. I notice that, for some reason known only to yourselves, my name has been altered, after the type had been set and spaced, from Mr. Marshall Hall, K.C., to Mr. M Hall, K.C. For myself it matters not whether you print my name properly or not at all, but what does matter is that

---

[1] Introduction to *Guidance from Beyond*, by K. Wingfield.

this careful sub-editing lends colour to what I have been told is a fact, viz. that some member of your staff has a personal grievance against me. I have been loth to believe it, but I must say that a good deal of colour is lent to the statement by the way your paper has treated me during the past three years. A straw shows which way the wind blows, and that anyone on the staff should have taken the trouble to alter Marshall into M, but leave the valuable spacing, shows that an amount of care and attention is lavished on my name in your reports which is far in excess of my deserts. The curious coincidence is that if by any manner of means the report of a case in which I have been engaged can be made to seem to reflect upon me in the smallest degree, the sub-editing is all the other way. The value of space is nothing, the ' Marshall ' is put into capitals, and it is thought worthy of a full capital headline for you to print, ' MR. MARSHALL HALL AGAIN.'

" Yours very truly,

" E. MARSHALL HALL."

The two men met at the Garrick Club a day or two later, and Marshall went straight to the point. " Why is it," he said, " that you and Harmsworth have got this down on me ? I don't like to squeal, but the thing's been going on for years, and I'm being driven out of business. Surely it can't still be the Chattell case ? You got your own way then."

" But didn't you say something in that case about his wife ? " said Marlowe. " He hasn't forgotten it."

What Marshall said in the heat of the moment was soon forgotten by him, and he had not remembered that he had mentioned the name of Mrs. Alfred Harmsworth with all the bitterness of his rhetoric at full flood. But his words now came back to him : " My client may have to work for her living, but her reputation is entitled to the same consideration as that of any lady in the land—including Mrs. Alfred Harmsworth." Harmsworth had taken these words as a deliberate insult to his wife.

Now this was a grievance which Marshall Hall could understand. Though years had passed, he was really contrite that any words of his should have been construed into an insult against a lady who was in no way connected with the case.

" What had I better do ? " he said.

" Well, a gentleman can always apologise," said the editor.

" But would an apology be accepted ? " asked Marshall, his proud spirit perhaps afraid of another humiliation.

" That would depend on the terms of the apology."

Marshall then and there sat down and drafted a letter. " DEAR SIR ALFRED HARMSWORTH," he wrote—" I have just been told that you are under the impression that something I said three years ago, in opening the case as counsel for the plaintiff in *Chattell* v. *The ' Daily Mail,'* was intended to cast some reflection upon your wife. I take the earliest opportunity of expressing my deep regret that anything I said should have been so understood. I had not the smallest intention of making an aspersion or reflection upon anyone, still less upon a member of your family. But now that my attention has been called to it, I quite feel that the remark was an unfortunate one to make, and that it would have been better left unsaid." A personal interview followed, in which the apology was accepted and the two men became friends. Indeed, two years later he was asked by the *Daily Mail* to make a special request for them to Lord Alverstone with regard to the reprieve of Rayner, the youthful assassin of William Whiteley ; and, before his death, Lord Northcliffe briefed Marshall in several important cases of libel and slander, notably the " Red Cross " litigation, where medical knowledge as well as forensic skill were needed in the advocate.

In 1904 and 1905 he had made repeated attempts to induce Lord Curzon to fight his old seat. Lord Curzon at first seemed disposed to do so. But it appeared that the Southport Conservatives now wanted the much criticised advocate more than the illustrious proconsul. " As you know," Curzon wrote in July 1904, " they won't *have* me at Southport now." So depressed was Marshall that he took steps to obtain some colonial appointment before the Balfour administration went out, and he interviewed Sir Edward Carson for that purpose. This other great advocate wrote :

" My Dear Marshall,—I cannot tell you how miserable I felt after your interview to-day. I am sure I did not show the sympathy I felt. . . . I saw the A.-G. at once, and nothing could have been nicer than the way he received what I had to say, and I am sure he will try and further your wishes in any way. . . . I think you are right to try and get an appointment whilst the present Government is in power, and, indeed, you fully deserve it—much as I regret the cause of your anxiety to leave the profession.

" I merely write this line that you may understand that I fully appreciate the situation, and that I have an earnest wish that something should be done.

" Yours very sincerely,
" Edward Carson."

But, fortunately, Marshall Hall took no irrevocable step, and, after another attempt to persuade Lord Curzon to take his place, he faced the electors of Southport a second time. The full tide of public opinion had turned against Conservatism, chiefly owing to the Tariff Reform policy of the Chamberlain group, which now dominated the Tory councils. Marshall was a whole-hearted disciple of Mr. Joseph Chamberlain, and the full force of the " dear food " cry was available against him. Besides this—the real issue of the election—the Government had been very unpopular for other reasons. The Licensing Bill had been received with execration by temperance enthusiasts, and lost Marshall many of his keenest supporters. The Liberals had also made much capital out of the so-called " Chinese slavery " question. Indentured Chinese labour had been imported upon the Rand, owing to the impossibility of obtaining sufficient white or native labour for mining purposes. But there were also personal grievances against the member. His maiden speech had been a real failure ; his attendance at divisions had not been good ; he had never spoken on any really important question, and his occasional interventions in debate had not been fortunate. He had expressed himself as being in favour of a tax on bachelors, and Henry Labouchere, in an article in *Truth,* parodied the idea by proposing that both bachelors and spinsters should be taxed, exemption being granted to a female " on making a statutory declaration that she had never had an offer," and to men on production of three certificates, such a certificate to be given by a girl when she " refused a *bona fide* proposal." A few days later, Marshall Hall's reference in a speech on the Licensing Bill to Henry Labouchere's " impudent buffoonery " was not at all well received by a House which had long since taken to its heart that wonderful old comedian, by birth and right a direct descendant of Molière. Further, quite apart from political considerations, the severe strictures made on Marshall Hall by the Court of Appeal had, of course, been given a wide publicity in his constituency.

But, against all this, his democratic and breezy personality had made him friends in every quarter at Southport, and his first-class platform ability went far to induce his constituents to forget his shortcomings at Westminster. He had been used as a platform orator in most of the by-elections. " What about oats ? " a stolid elector in the Forest of Dean had said. Marshall asked him to stand up so that he could see him better. " I understand," he said gravely, when this was done, " and I beg your pardon. I couldn't see your legs. I thought you had only two." On occasions, it is true, these ready sallies recoiled on him, as when he offered " three acres and a cow " to an insistent interrupter if the latter could milk the cow and till the land, and next day received a number of letters from competent farmers accepting the offer and claiming to have been the interrupter ! But usually he contrived to get the last word. In his very close fight with Mr. Astbury at the General Election in January 1906, he was at the height of his form. " What price Thibet ? " shouted an interrupter, referring to an unpopular British expedition into Thibet for which Marshall had voted. " Oh," he said, " I was not aware that Thibet was for sale." Then, when this retort was received with delight, he added in a confidential tone, " As a matter of fact, I paid him half a crown to ask that question." But he made a much better score with regard to " Chinese slavery." He read out from a document before him a number of clauses dealing with conditions of employment for coloured labour, which the audiences assumed to be those applying to Chinese labour on the Rand. " Is that slavery ? " he repeated, as he read each clause. Every time, he was greeted with yells of " Yes." " Well," he rejoined, " I am glad to hear it ; for I have reading from the British Guiana ordinance, sanctioned by the Radical Government." Again, he was very fortunate in one heckler, whom he promised to answer if only he would put an intelligible question. " What is the difference between Fiscal Trade and Free Policy ? " was the question finally elicited. One epigram in a speech of Marshall's on the fiscal question was very successful. " England expects," he said, " that every foreigner will pay his duty." His personal popularity seemed to increase every day, but, in his heart, on the eve of the poll he knew that he was beaten. He was particularly hurt at the defection of a personal friend, Dr. Porter, whose name has been mentioned in a letter on a previous page. He was Vicar of All Saints' Church, and had been one of his strongest supporters in 1900. Now he was antagonised by the fiscal and licensing policy of the Government, and actually preached a sermon in his own church on " How to vote and whom to vote for," in which he gave his congregation a clear indication of his views : he said that, in his view, the Licensing Act had given security of tenure to publicans, and that drink was the curse of the country ; and that Protection was morally selfish. " If," said this pulpit politician, " selfishness was detestable in a man, what is it in a people ? " His exhortation was greeted with cries of " Hear, hear," like a political speech, and once a cry of " Vote for Astbury " was raised. Unfortunately this election was, in other respects, not free from personalities on either side. The Liberals had named their candidate " Honest Jack Astbury." The Tories eliminated the last two syllables, and sent a donkey, caparisoned in red, round the town with a placard attached behind, on which was written, " Brothers, vote for Astbury." Marshall could not understand Dr. Porter's attitude, and, in his speech after the poll, attributed his defeat to his influence. But, with all his disadvantages, he came very near to victory. Southport polled almost last of the constituencies, and before their polling day came it was abundantly clear to the Southport voters that the Conservatives had suffered such a defeat as they had not known since the Reform Bill. Seats which had been regarded as strongholds, with majorities of thousands, had turned Radical, with four-figure majorities.

This did not prosper the Conservative cause at Southport. In this general landslide, when Southport finally voted 6,607 for Astbury to 6,367 for Marshall Hall, the contest must be regarded, if as a political defeat, also as a personal triumph. Nor did that small majority of 240 make itself known in the great crowd awaiting the result outside the town hall. The announcement of the result was lost in the great noise below, and, when Mr. Astbury tried to speak, his voice was drowned by loud cheers and boos. The only articulate words which the pressmen heard were the reiterated shouts of the Conservative crowd for " Marshall Hall," and the bewildered reporters had to go in and get the figures from the counters themselves. Finally, Marshall obeyed the persistent calls for him, and went forward to address the crowd ; but his speech was surely the shortest ever made by him. He called for " three cheers for Astbury."

He took his defeat with great cheerfulness ; but he had made up his mind to retire from politics in the event of defeat. He was in low water financially, and the election had been very expensive. A day or two after the poll he left Southport by the early morning train with a very sad heart. He had tried to keep his departure a secret, but a large crowd had gathered to bid him farewell and sing " Auld Lang Syne " to him on the platform. As the train steamed out, he shouted words of encouragement to Sam Brighouse and the rest, and waved a blue scarf to his enthusiastic supporters—who had seen him, on his first visit, wearing a necktie of Radical red—but, under his gaiety and apparent optimism, he was a sad and disappointed man. First, in youth, had come to him bitter personal sorrow ; then the promise of a great career at the Bar ruined by what seemed to him a great injustice ; now, to crown it all, political defeat. This closed his chance of preferment by reason of parliamentary services to the party ; had a few votes gone the other way, Marshall Hall, as an old parliamentary hand, would have been one among the small band who kept the Unionist flag flying in Parliament till 1910. At this game of opposition there would have been ample scope for Marshall's recklessness in attack and repartee, which would have been better employed against a Liberal Treasury Bench than His Majesty's judges. As it was, the place in the party which he might have made his own was earned and richly deserved by his young junior in the Liverpool licensing cases, who lately had written to him asking for his help in obtaining a recordership, describing himself with uncharacteristic humility as an " abominable nuisance." It must have seemed to Marshall Hall on his journey back to London that, with all his gifts, his life had indeed been a failure. The future must have appeared to him very uncertain, and the past full of disappointment. Indeed, a tinge of pessimism invaded his optimistic spirit, and he began to talk of himself as a failure to his friends. But, sensitive and vain as he was, Marshall Hall was one of those rare men who have the courage to fight their own secret conviction that they are failures and prove it to be utterly false.

CHAPTER VIII

Recovery

MARSHALL HALL returned from Southport with the determination to devote all his talents in future to the Bar, and to the recovery of his lost position there, and now that peace had been made with his powerful antagonist he could look forward to the future with greater confidence; but there was one sacrifice which he had to make to tide him over his financial difficulties. He had made up his mind to part with his treasures, and, to a man who loved so well the business of collecting and the possession of things collected, this must have seemed like losing a great part of himself. In May 1907 there came under the hammer at Christie's one of the rarest collections of silver and antiquities ever amassed by the taste of a man of only moderate means; it was a monument of his versatile and accurate judgment in these matters. Altogether the sale realised £5,971 15s. 1d. The gem of this collection was a complete toilette service of a Restoration beauty, engraved with Chinese figures, trees, and birds, half of it made by the craftsman " B." in 1677, and the other half by " I. L." in 1682. This service was a reminder of the exquisite, if elaborate, silver age of Charles II, which arose in all its gaiety and splendour after the depredations and coining of the Civil War and the solemnity of the Commonwealth. £1,000 was bid for this service. With it went many weighty tankards, flagons, and porringers; among them, the darling of Marshall's collection, a Commonwealth plain porringer (1655, maker's mark " R. W."), was sold at 580 shillings an ounce.

Many stories could be told of Marshall Hall's wonderful eye for jewels and silver. Once he was walking with Charles Gill in the Rue de la Paix, and saw in a shop window hundreds of single diamonds, set out in velvet in the shape of a star, at 100 francs apiece. He at once went in and chose seven or eight, tendering the advertised price. " No," said the diamond merchant, " I don't sell *one* to you, monsieur; you know too much." All the stones which Marshall had chosen were worth much more than 100 francs: those which he had left were worth far less. Again, he was selling a pearl necklace in London: he took it to a famous jeweller, and told him that the price was £3,000. " Three thousand pounds, Sir Edward ? " said the jeweller ; " you must be joking. Why," he added, producing another obviously far finer necklace, " we are only asking three thousand five hundred pounds for this one." Up went Marshall's famous microscope into his eye. " Well, will you give me an hour to consider the matter ? " he asked. Marshall went away and came back in an hour with £3,500 in notes. " I'll give your price for that necklace," he said. It was, of course, worth far more than the price he paid for it.

. . . .

Only a day or two after his return from Southport, Marshall had a good beginning in an amusing special jury case. It was the second trial of an action brought by a young actress against Messrs. Gatti for wrongful dismissal. She was engaged as a " Gibson girl " in a piece called *The Catch of the Season*. She had two lines to say : " I'm a perfect wonder at hugging widowers—I hardly ever lose a breach " and " Dear old Hyde Park." The question for the jury was whether she was an actress, and entitled to be employed for the run of the piece when once engaged, or whether she was a " show girl," or player engaged because of her beauty, or a mere chorus girl, in which case she was only entitled to a fortnight's notice. The jury in the first trial, before Mr. Justice Darling, disagreed, and Marshall was taken in to lead for the plaintiff against Eldon Bankes in the second trial, before Mr. Justice Ridley. Between ragging the witnesses and teasing the judge, Marshall had the time of his life. Mr. Seymour Hicks, part author of the play, said, " If one line makes an actress, I do not know where we shall end." Marshall raised loud laughter by saying, " I only want to know where you begin." The peppery judge then made his usual protest that he would not have his court turned into a theatre. Marshall asked another witness if he considered the part of the second murderer in *Macbeth* a part, or if the man who comes in and says " My lord, the carriage waits " is an actor. Mr. Augustus Merne, then in the box, said that to say that line without getting a laugh the man would have to be a very great actor ! After further breezes with Marshall, the judge summed up, and the jury could not agree as to whether Miss Thomas, the plaintiff, had been engaged as an actress or not. Speaking that night at the Playgoers' Club dinner, Marshall said, " During the week I have been trying to find out when an actress is not an actress. Some might also enquire, ' When is a judge not a judge ? ' " The case came on for the third time, before Mr. Justice Grantham, when the jury found for the plaintiff on all points and gave her £200. This judge certainly made the case as amusing as ever. He told counsel that he could well understand their being nervous about the question " What is an actress ? " because " it was now the third time of asking." Miss Thomas in her evidence said she was now married. " Ah," said the gallant judge, " the Catch of the Season ! " Sir Charles Wyndham came up to support her, and said that a chorus girl became an actress if she had a single line to speak. By this time the original coarseness of her first line had become bowdlerised in the reports and she now gave it as " I am a perfect wonder at spotting winners and hardly ever lose at bridge." But the most amusing duel took place between Marshall and Mr. James Glover, musical director of Drury Lane. " Because she happens to be given a single line," the latter said, " I do not agree that she becomes, *ipso facto,* an actress. When the chorus is engaged there is a general battue for lines." " Who drives ? " retorted the advocate, amid loud laughter.

Altogether the year 1906 shows a decided improvement : Marshall was in a variety of other cases, several of them of that unusual kind which he found and made so interesting. There was the gamekeeper whom he defended unsuccessfully, who was charged with stealing 20,000 of Sir Walter Gilbey's pheasants' eggs. There was the old gentleman with religious mania who left his money to one Godley because he was " fully convinced that the free spirit which dwelt in the Lord Jesus in the days of His flesh does work in such proportion as God sees fit in Godley." There was also a poor mad woman whom he prosecuted for killing a child in a nursing-home because, as she said, " the Devil tempted me. I thought that if I did something dreadful in this world it would be easier for me in the next." She, of course, was found " guilty but insane," and detained during His Majesty's pleasure. He was in one strange matrimonial suit where a husband, who had pursued his wife's liner in a little tug out of the harbour in order to be quite sure her lover did not join her, petitioned for damages from the co-respondent, but not for a divorce.

But another great trial suited to his conspicuous and versatile advocacy was needed to bring him back to his old position at the Bar ; and very soon the opportunity came from the same firm of solicitors which had first brought his name into eminence. In November 1907, Mr. Arthur Newton revisited Temple Gardens, and held a long conversation with Marshall Hall, after which the latter came into Wellesley Orr's room in a great state of excitement. " I want you to concentrate on this case entirely for the next three weeks," he said, throwing a mass of documents upon his table. " This is the greatest case I've ever had in my life. If you have an idea, however remote or far-fetched, come in and tell me. The man's innocent, and a chance idea may mean life or death to him."

The papers flung on Orr's table were the depositions in the Camden Town murder case ; and it was on the wings of the prestige which Marshall Hall's conduct of this great trial brought him that he was to rise once more to take his place among the leading advocates of the day. On the morning of Thursday, September 12th, a young man named Bertram Shaw, employed as cook on the Midland Railway, returned from his night duty to his flat at 29 St. Paul's Road, Camden Town, in order to meet his mother and introduce her to the girl who was about to become his wife. Her name was Emily Dimmock, but she was always known as " Phyllis." He had taken her, as he thought, from the life of the streets to marry her. She was already known as Mrs. Bertram Shaw. When he returned on that Thursday morning, he found his door locked ; letting himself in by a borrowed key, he found poor Phyllis lying quite naked on her bed, her throat cut from ear to ear, so skilfully and savagely, that her head was only attached to her body by a few muscles. Otherwise, she was lying peacefully in an attitude of repose ; expert medical opinion said she had died in her sleep at about 3 a.m. Only a few articles of trifling value were removed, and some other motive than robbery had to be found to account for the crime.

The murder became the sensation of the time, and, as in the

Bennett case, for weeks no arrest was made, and it seemed as if the whole affair would remain a complete mystery. But the Criminal Investigation Department of the Yard, under Inspector Neill, were busily making enquiries. It was discovered that, up to the time of her death, Phyllis could not keep away from her old mode of life. Unknown to Shaw, she was frequenting public houses and taking men home. The "husband's" nights on his dining-car gave her both temptation and opportunity. As late as 11.30 on the Wednesday night she had been seen with a young man of "shabby genteel" appearance at the "Eagle" public house, and reports reached the police that she had been seen at a later time with another man, smarter and better built. Further enquiries showed that on Monday night and Friday night she had been seen, with the same young man with whom she had been at the "Eagle" on Wednesday, at a neighbouring house called the "Rising Sun." The information as to the "shabby genteel" young man came from a young ship's cook, who almost at once came forward and frankly confessed that he had slept at 29 St. Paul's Road on the three nights before the fatal one : for the night in question the ship's cook could establish an alibi. His information about the other young man was corroborated by other girls of easy virtue ; but, considering the number of men who had been her chance lovers, the discovery of the murderer among them seemed a hopeless task. As Robert Wood, a young artist of twenty-eight, employed by the Sand and Blast Manufacturing Company of Gray's Inn Road to paint delicate designs on glass, said to one of his colleagues, "It is not surprising. These women never know whom they're taking home."

The police, however, had one important clue : well concealed in a drawer in Phyllis's room they found a post-card ; on one side was a rather decorative picture of a woman with her child, on the other side was writing which appeared to be a message of rendezvous from one woman to another for Monday night. It was received by her on the Monday morning. "PHYLLIS DARLING," it ran—"If it pleases you, meet me at 8.15 at the [here followed a little sketch of the rising sun]. Yours to a cinder, ALICE." It was addressed to "Mrs. B. Shaw, 29 St. Paul's Road, Camden Town." Now, when the police had first

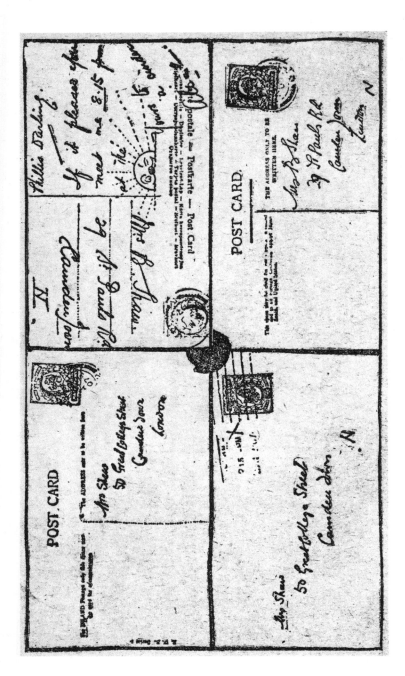

CAMDEN TOWN CASE

The fateful post-card

[*By courtesy of the "Sunday Dispatch"*]

come they found a post-card album lying on the floor ; several post-cards had been taken out, and some lay scattered on the floor. Altogether, it looked as if the murderer had been interested in looking for a post-card before he went. Further, the police found in her room fragments of what appeared to be a torn and charred letter, and the writing appeared to be the same as that on the card of assignation for Monday. The ship's cook said that Phyllis had shown him both, that they were in the same hand-writing, and that Phyllis had put the post-card in a drawer. It was therefore naturally considered that if the writer of these documents could be discovered an arrest would be justified. Inspector Neill remembered the postmark and the laundry mark of the Bennett case. They therefore decided to use the newspapers and to give the post-card in facsimile the widest publicity.

In the ordinary course, a few words on a post-card reproduced in facsimile would be very hard to identify as the writing of any one person. But suppose that a young woman has received long and frequent love-letters from a man over a period of years, so that she knows every sport and trick of his hand ; suppose, further, that her lover is an artist and has a habit of embellish-ing his love-letters with little sketches—it might then well be that a girl would immediately recognise her lover's hand in a a few words on a post-card, reproduced in facsimile in her Sunday newspaper ; and so it was. Ruby Young, a delicate-looking girl of refined beauty of the Rossetti type, with dark hair, pale face, and deep-blue eyes, was an artist's model. She had been a nurse, and had been seduced by a medical man ; shortly afterwards she made the acquaintance of Robert Wood, a young artist, in whose work the great William Morris had shown a kindly interest. Wood fell in love with her, and she with him. He belonged to a very respectable middle-class Scots family living in London : he was of a very gentle and lovable nature, but his general popularity with everyone, men and women, had made him spoilt and vain ; and, whereas respect-ability was a fetish with him, a strange vanity made him seek the acquaintance and pay court to attractive women of the streets. He himself said that this was only a foolish whim of his in his curiosity to know all sorts of people. Probably he and

PH

Ruby would have married, if she had not told him of her former misfortune. He gave her his mother's ring, became her devoted lover and constant companion, but never married her. He was poor, and she began to receive financial assistance from other men. Wood's discovery of this did not terminate their friendship, and she much resented any attentions paid by him to other women. Her jealousy had lately caused a serious breach between them. Then, on Sunday, September 29th, she saw the " rising sun " post-card in her Sunday newspaper, and recognised the writing at once as being that of her lover. She then recalled that he had been very strange in his behaviour lately. Up to September 13th, they had only met once, and then by chance, since the quarrel in July. But on that day she received a telegram from him asking her to meet him at a shop. They went to a restaurant, and Wood said to her, " Ruby, if any questions are put to you, will you say you always saw me on Mondays and Wednesdays ? " She asked him why, but he merely pressed her till she promised. Afterwards they met several times, and he reminded her each time of her promise. Then, on Sunday, the 29th, came the publication of the post-card. Ruby had clipped out the cutting and put it in a letter to Wood which was lying on her table, when he himself called on her. He was in great distress : " Ruby," he said, " I am in trouble." " Yes," she answered, " I know you are—that is your handwriting." He then said, " Be patient, and I will explain all." He said that he had met Phyllis Dimmock in the " Rising Sun " on the Friday before the murder. A little boy came in to sell picture post-cards. She collected them and was going to buy one. Wood advised her not to, as they were " not artistic." He then pro-duced some that he had brought back from Bruges, and she liked the one of the woman with the child. " There," she said, " that's a pretty one—write something nice on it for me." Wood had been showing Phyllis his sketches, and he then scribbled the words of assignation on the post-card, and signed it " Alice " at Phyllis's request, because " the governor might cut up rough," if he signed a man's name. He told her he would post it to her. Next day he met her again in the street, and she said, " You have not sent me my post-card." He did post it to her on Junday night. On Monday he met her again in the

" Rising Sun " ; she was with a lame man whom she said " she hated." Wood told Ruby he had never seen her again after that night, and that he had spent Tuesday with his brother ; on Wednesday he had been out walking alone, but he could not prove it. She asked him if he had written again to Phyllis, and he said he had scribbled and sketched for her in the " Rising Sun," and she might have kept something in his handwriting.

Ruby and Robert then made a careful plan of where they would say they had been on the Wednesday. They arranged to say that they had parted at Brompton Oratory at 10.30, she to go home to Earl's Court, he to King's Cross. Ruby then began to be nervous about this conspiracy. " Your word and my word will stand against the world," said her lover, in his histrionic way. He left her happily, confident that she would stand by him. They met again several times, and she went to see Charles Wood, a brother. He explained to her that it might be important for Robert to prove his whereabouts during the week of the murder. " I can answer for Wednesday, anyway," she said. Robert had confided in his brother Charles, just as he had done with Ruby. After anxious discussion, Charles had advised him to send the following letter addressed to Charles at a poste restante, which was duly done. It was signed by Charles Wood, Bessie his wife, and Robert, and was expressed thus. " We are jointly anxious to assist the police, but we are very anxious to avoid the publicity and personal inconvenience of present communication. Being satisfied of his *bona fides*, we think it wise to await the result of the inquest. We are determined that if the necessity arises after the inquest that Robert Wood shall make his avowal to the authorities immediately." Meanwhile, the thing was getting on Ruby's nerves. Robert kept on worrying her " to be true," and she replied, " I will be true, but don't bother me." But she was a woman, very much alone in the world and frightened. She went to another friend, and put her predicament in a hypothetical way. " What ought a girl to do who is in that position ? " she said. Of course her friend guessed the truth and told her that unless she told the truth he would do so for her. This frightened her, and she was introduced by her friend to a journalist, who obtained the whole story from her. This man in turn caused her to meet Inspector

Neill outside Piccadilly Tube Station. Poor Ruby was now in a most unenviable position. She loved Robert Wood, and surely cannot have wished to give him away ; but through her own indiscretion she was now almost compelled to help the police. Accordingly, on October 4th, she met Robert Wood in Gray's Inn Road. She greeted him with a kiss ; he had an uneasy feeling that he was being watched. " I believe that man is a detective," he said. Ruby bade him pay no attention. But very soon Inspector Neill came up to him, and explained to him that he would have to detain him, as he had reason to believe that he had written certain post-cards to Phyllis Dimmock. Wood replied that he had only written one, and, as he got into a cab with the inspector, and saw Ruby crying hysterically, he, still confident of her loyalty, said in his pathetic theatrical manner, " Don't cry, girlie, I have to go with these gentlemen. If England wants me, she must have me. Be true." " Be brave," answered Ruby, " and leave that to me." Well might Ruby cry ; it was perhaps now dawning upon her that she had really caused her lover to be arrested for murder, an eventuality which she had not first considered possible. Trusting entirely in Ruby, as well he might, he made a long statement to the police, making the alibi which she had concocted with him the main point of a protest for being detained at all. This false statement was to bring him close to the gallows. Other investigations concerning him were not favourable to him. A young bookseller named Lambert had seen him with Phyllis in the " Eagle " as late as 10.30 on the Wednesday night. Wood had telephoned him the very next day, and begged him to say nothing about having seen him with a girl.

When Wood was arrested, the inquest on Phyllis Dimmock was already in progress, and it became necessary for his friends to be busy about his defence at once. His employers ridiculed the idea of his being a murderer, and for the sake of abundant caution retained Arthur Newton. Wood, they said, was gentle and amiable to a fault ; and really the evidence against him was so slender that the clever solicitor at first thought the task before him was an easy one. But he was soon to have a rude awakening. When he applied for bail, Inspector Neill made the dramatic disclosure that Wood had been identified as a man who had left 29 St. Paul's Road at about five o'clock on the morning of the murder. The witness of this fact turned out to be a man described as a " carman," and as such I shall describe him throughout the trial. As he was going " to look for work," shortly before five on the morning of September 12th, he had seen a man with broad shoulders coming out of 29 St. Paul's Road, where Phyllis Dimmock lived, and walk away in the opposite direction. An electric lamp in the street had clearly lighted up his figure ; he was wearing a long dark overcoat and a bowler hat, but the carman had identified him by a peculiarity in his walk. He had his left hand in his overcoat pocket, and he walked with his right shoulder advanced, swinging his right arm. Poor Robert Wood, during the progress of that much ad-journed inquest, had to attend many identification parades, and at one of these the carman had identified him by his " peculiar " walk. Just after he had touched Wood, a woman called " May," a friend of Phyllis, had identified him by his face. But the real tragedy to Wood was the evidence of Ruby Young. The police, perfectly properly, in the course of their duty had, step by step, wrung the whole truth from her. This was not a pleasant or, indeed, an easy task. Inspector Neill himself said to me, " All through, the poor girl was a most difficult witness, and most distressing to handle. There is no doubt that she loved him passionately." But in the end when she gave evidence, breaking down again and again, she told " the truth, the whole truth, and nothing but the truth " as regards the prisoner's conspiracy with her to manufacture the alibi. She went further, and, after Newton had poured scorn and contempt on the evidence of the " carman," she said that he had a peculiar walk, " such as no one could copy ; he puts his left hand in his pocket, and jerks his right shoulder forward." When pressed by Newton, she said that if his sixty-five fellow employees came forward to say that he had no peculiarity in his walk she would still say that he had. Why she said this must always be open to doubt ; she must have known that it would be a deadly piece of evidence against her lover ; indeed, if implicitly believed, it was sufficient to hang him. Perhaps, when closely examined, she had said it inadvertently, not realising its full import. It is difficult to believe that the reason of this was the mere

vindictiveness which Newton and Marshall Hall quite legitimately, on behalf of their client, ascribed to her. The fact that
she broke down so pitifully when she described her last parting
with Wood was inconsistent with vindictiveness. Besides, to his
chosen mistress every man has a peculiarity in his walk, just
as he has in his handwriting. But to Wood's sensitive mind,
Ruby's betrayal of him must have come as a grievous blow.
Two of the remarkable sketches executed by him in prison
reveal something of what he felt. In one a girl in her nightdress
is kneeling by her bed, her face hidden in her left hand and by
her long, black hair, while her right hand holds a letter. Love
lies drowsing at her feet, while in the background a man's
figure hangs limply from the gallows. In another of these
sketches, Arthur Newton and a police officer are playing poker
for the artist's life, represented by a little chained puppet in the
centre of the table, while Love whispers the secrets of the cards
into the officer's ear. The officer is given a tail and conceals a
secret store of cards beneath the table !

The evidence of these two witnesses, powerful as it was when
taken together, was severely impeached before they left the
witness box at the police court. The carman was, I am assured
by Inspector Neill, a perfectly honest witness who had come
forward with the genuine conviction that he had identified the
prisoner. But how much his evidence was worth is shown by the
many inconsistencies in his evidence when it was probed by Arthur
Newton. Again and again his confident testimony was impeached,
and it became obvious that much more than this man's evidence was necessary to identify Wood with the murderer. A
witness who may be swearing a man's life away by his evidence
must be accurate, and this man's memory was shown to be
inaccurate in very material particulars. Dominated by the clever
solicitor, the witness adopted Newton's suggestion that it was
a drizzly, foggy morning. The answer, which was contrary to
the truth, was accepted for a good reason ; and Newton continued, " But of course you were able to see him quite clearly
by the light of the arc lamp opposite ? " " Yes," said the
carman, " I saw it, positively." " And, as it was a dark morning,
if the light had been out, you could not have seen the man ? "
" Any fool could tell you that," was the answer. Then came

the surprise : Newton had long ago realised the value of detail in criminal defence. When he had put his cunning questions, he had in his pocket a lighting-chart from the electric lighting authority, stating that the current was switched off at 4.37, a quarter of an hour before the witness had seen the alleged murderer pass beneath its glare. The carman could hardly go back on his word, for he had sworn that he had heard a clock striking five. Now a witness, who remembers a light when there was no light, may perhaps be mistaken as to a man whom he claims to have encountered at a particular place at a particular time. Here exact time and place were all important. The witness was becoming very unpopular, and Newton pressed home his advantage by a ruthless cross-examination as to credit.

No such preparation was needed for the cross-examination of Ruby Young. Her immoral life and the fact that she was, wilfully or no, betraying her lover, made her an easy object for attack. But, as to Wood's conspiracy for an alibi, she was obviously telling the truth, however bitterly the " kiss of Judas " was charged to her account. All Newton's questions and eloquence did not save Wood from being committed to trial for murder. It was all very well for Newton to say " the case for the prosecution rests on two prejudiced witnesses and a silly statement made by Wood to avoid publicity " ; Wood was nevertheless in great peril. Yet, by his cross-examination of the sweetheart and the " impartial " witness, Newton had already excited deep sympathy for Wood in the public from whom his twelve judges were to be drawn.

Meanwhile, the faithful devil, Wellesley Orr, had been poring and puzzling over the documents in this baffling case. Wood had been identified by the carman as a man who had been at 29 St. Paul's Road in the early hours of Thursday morning : by the ship's cook, who had identified Wood as having been with Phyllis at the " Rising Sun " on the 9th ; it was he who had sworn to the letter of assignation received on the Wednesday morning for the meeting at the " Eagle " ; he said the same handwriting appeared on the post-card making an assignation for the Monday, admittedly the prisoner's. Altogether, he was a witness who had to be dealt with very carefully, and very efficiently ; he had several witnesses to prove an alibi for himself on the night of the murder. There was also the girl named May, who identified Wood as a man, called " Scotch Bob," who had known Phyllis for some time and who threatened and ill-treated her. Now Wood spoke with a slight Scots accent, and his name was Robert. She said that she had seen Phyllis with Wood late on the night of the murder, and that Phyllis was very frightened of him. The statement of this girl was, on the face of it, contradictory and impossible ; she was not called at the police court proceedings, but her statement was, according to the custom then prevailing, supplied to the defence. In her statement to the police she said that Phyllis had told her at four o'clock on the Wednesday that she had had a letter to meet a gentleman friend that night, and that she was afraid to go, and afraid not to go, as it was " Scotch Bob," who had a terrible grievance against her. Phyllis had also shown a part of the letter to a sailor who had spent the Tuesday night with her, and had then burnt it. Now May could not have seen Phyllis at four o'clock, as she was then with her " husband," Bertram Shaw, and, indeed, it was unlikely that they had met at all that day. Who then had told her about the incident at all ? The only other person could have been the ship's cook. A sudden inspiration flashed across Orr's mind. The ship's cook and Wood—what a contrast they made ! The one a brawny sailor man, the other a weedy little artist, exceptionally amiable, employed to paint delicate designs on glass. The only thing in common between them was their misfortune in having been with the murdered woman shortly before her death. But how, even in this regard, did their records compare ? According to his own confession, the ship's cook had spent the three nights before the last one with the dead woman, on each night giving her a " present " out of his hard-earned savings, giving her less and less each night, till they were nearly exhausted. She must have been very attractive to him. Further, he had been waiting for her at the " Rising Sun " late on the night of the murder. True, he could establish an alibi by a friend and his landlady, but so could Wood by his father and stepbrother. The only circumstance in which Wood's record compared unfavourably with the ship's cook's, except for the evidence of the ship's cook himself, was that Wood had been seen last with her—at the

" Eagle," by his friend Lambert. It was not that Orr saw the
ship's cook as the real murderer, but, the more the cook's
predicament was probed, the stronger would seem to be his
motive to be seeking out and blaming someone else. He had seen
Wood with her, and the suspicions of his simple and frightened
mind naturally fell on this strange little man with the deep-set
eyes. But how did the woman May know about the burnt letter,
if she had not seen Phyllis on the Wednesday, as seemed almost
certain ? This was the woman who, unless her evidence had
been disbelieved at once, would have brought the crime home
to Wood. If the ship's cook had told May about the burnt
letter, this would account, of course, for her knowledge of it.
If he told her, why did he do so, and for what purpose did he
discuss the matter with her ? Might he not have known her,
and gone to her for information about Wood and told her his
suspicions about him ? Might he not have asked her to help him
establish *his* innocence, just as Wood had with Ruby Young ?
May's evidence was obviously tainted and a tissue of lies ; why
should she attack Wood, identify him as " Scotch Bob," and
tell in great detail a story, manifestly false, of how she had seen
Phyllis with him late on the night of the murder ? There was
absolutely no evidence of the ship's cook's acquaintance with
May, but Orr felt sure they knew each other, and had talked the
matter over thoroughly together. It was from a description
which they had given to the police that they started their
investigations. If the ship's cook's evidence could be assailed,
Wood would be much nearer to safety. As soon as the idea struck
him, he went and put it to Marshall. The latter behaved in a
most characteristic way. No man could be more positive at
the very outset than Marshall Hall. No man would swing round
more completely from a former view. This certainty and positiveness impressed clients very deeply. " There's only one way to
run this case," he would say at the consultation, but in all
probability he would not approach that line at the trial. He was
a man very easily influenced, and I wonder how much greater
the anxiety of his clients would have been if they knew the
volatile changeability that lay behind the great man's positive
manner. When Orr told him his theory as to May's knowledge
of the burnt letter, at first he simply did not see the point of it.

He ridiculed the whole idea. " Put it out of your mind, my dear
Orr ; that fellow's a most dangerous witness ; far best to leave
him alone." But, before Orr had left the room, he knew Marshall
had seen the point and appreciated it, and knew what would
happen. Marshall sent for Newton. " I've got it," he said,
with great certainty. " The ship's cook and May got together,
and he got her to try and protect him. Just like Wood and Ruby
Young—it's clear as day, my dear Newton." But Newton
thought nothing of this theory, and, with his usual deference
and extreme politeness, he waved it aside ; at all events, Marshall
had been won back to his original view when he saw Orr again
after his consultation with Newton. But the young " devil "
was very persistent, and knew that he usually got his own way
with Marshall in the end. He had a very definite idea as to how
Wood was to be saved. The ship's cook was to be closely cross-
examined as to his acquaintance with May, and Wood was to be
called in his own defence. As heretofore no prisoner called in
his own defence at the Old Bailey on a capital charge had escaped
the verdict of " guilty," Marshall shunned the responsibility of
calling him. Finally, he went to see Wood, in order to decide
this very matter, at Brixton Prison, and came back greatly
upset and excited.

" I can't call him," he said ; " I can't call him."

" Why not ? " said Orr. " Remember what you've always
said about Bennett."

" He's raving mad," said Marshall. " Wood's raving mad."

" Why do you say that ? " asked Orr.

" Oh, from his whole demeanour."

" Mad or sane, innocent or guilty," said Orr, " he'll swing if
you don't call him."

Evidently, the impression made on Marshall was that Wood
was not himself ; indeed, it would not be surprising if his dreadful
situation had temporarily affected this young man's balance,
were it not for his amazing calmness at the trial. He described
afterwards how he was not allowed to shave with an ordinary
razor, but was compelled to use a safety razor, which the warder
told him had last been used by Rayner, the youth who had
murdered the merchant prince, William Whiteley. As an artist,
he had, of course, resources within himself not available to most

persons awaiting trial. He passed his time in making sketches, some such as the two I have described, relating to his own tragedy, others of a humorous and quite irrelevant kind. They show a flippancy and an objective manner of looking upon himself which can hardly be normal. His trial took place in the height of the diabolo craze, and he made a sketch of a " Lady Diabolo of Monte Carlo " spinning one man after another on her string, tossing them up on her string and breaking them. In another he depicts an artist in prison painting a living woman with a stuffed dummy as a model. On the other hand, he made a sketch of his meeting with Phyllis at the " Rising Sun " ; of himself going unconcernedly to work under the rays of the rising sun ; and of the rising sun shining down and withering a little backyard plant, which Marshall, to whom he gave this and other sketches, said was meant to represent Wood himself. His sketch of the identification parade is an exaggeration, but seems to me to bear a touch of genius.

Until the very day before the trial, Marshall's mind remained uncertain as to which course he should take, and to the last minute Wellesley Orr gave him no peace till he had achieved his object. The latter obtained special leave, though not briefed in the case, to attend the final consultation. Marshall had expressed a final opinion that Wood should not be called, and Wellesley Orr, a very short man, rose to his feet in his excitement. " Marshall Hall," he said, using the formality which barristers show to each other before solicitors, " unless you call him, Wood will hang as high as Haman." Marshall was struck by the ring of conviction in his voice. Orr looked at him and knew that, though nothing would have made him say so for the present, he had changed his mind. Arthur Newton had clearly not guessed his changed decision, for he wrote to Marshall this letter on the eve of the trial.

" 23 Great Marlborough Street,
December 11*th*, 1907.

" DEAR MR. MARSHALL HALL,—I spent an enormous time with Wood.

" We cannot call him.

" You were perfectly right in every way.

" You must forgive me for not coming to-night, but I have a most important piece of information which I think may turn the whole course of events. I shall be at the Old Bailey to-morrow at about ten minutes past ten.

" In great haste, yours very sincerely,

" ARTHUR NEWTON."

The important piece of information was the advent of a new and very useful witness, and had nothing to do with the calling of Wood. Just before the case began on the next day, Marshall Hall whispered to Orr, " I thought you'd like to know. I'm going to call Wood, and I'm going to cross-examine the ship's cook on your lines."

The case opened on December 12th, at the newly built Palace of Justice which had arisen on the site of the Old Bailey. Marshall had clamoured for the demolition of the old building, and this was his first murder trial in the new court. He came into court chatting with Sir Charles Mathews, leading counsel for the Crown ; perhaps they were recalling the dramatic triumph of Marshall against Mathews in the Hermann trial, thirteen years before. They had both learned much since then, and this case was indeed to be a battle of giants. This was much more complex than the Hermann case, and the life which Marshall was employed to save was far more worth salvation ; the life, not of of a poor, seemingly worthless harlot, but that of a man of talent and of exceptionally gentle and lovable character.

Sir Charles opened the case quietly, stressing especially the lies told by the prisoner, the letter torn up and burnt in the presence of the ship's cook, the ransacking of the postcard album, the subsequent discovery of the post-card in the drawer and of the charred fragments, and finally the peculiar walk of the prisoner noticed by the carman and corroborated by Ruby Young. Marshall hardly cross-examined the doctor at all, and accepted Bertram Shaw's alibi without requiring it to be proved, and the only important witness called on the first day was the ship's cook. He came into the box, of course, quite unconscious of the line which the cross-examiner would take. He swore that Phyllis had shown him both the " rising sun " post-card and the letter, which had arrived on the Wednesday morning : he

CAMDEN TOWN CASE
A study—drawn by Robert Wood in prison
[*By courtesy of the " Sunday Dispatch* "

further swore that the fragments of writing in Wood's hand which, preserved between slides of glass, were handed up to him, formed part of the letter he had read.

Now, as Mr. Justice McCardie has told me, Marshall, with his towering figure and piercing eyes, together with his general reputation for being a hard, ruthless, and relentless man, had a power of almost petrifying a witness. He now turned on the ship's cook all the electric force of his personality. An eye-witness has told me that the witness looked frightened before he spoke a word.

" Tell me," Marshall said, " do you know a woman called May ? "

The witness, taken completely by surprise, first denied it, but then in a most hesitating manner admitted that he knew her by sight. The connection between this man and May, which Orr's cleverness had seen, was already established.

" Have you ever spoken to her ? "—" Yes."

At this moment the witness began to speak in a low voice and to hang his head. " Look up, man," thundered Marshall ; " look up and speak up—you are in a court of justice. When did you first speak to her ? "

" I think it was at the funeral," said the man, dropping his voice again.

" Have you seen her since ? "

The witness dropped his voice again even lower, and only those who were straining their ears to hear the man's words could catch them. " No," he muttered, " she accused me of something, and I haven't seen her again."

The admission was enough, and Marshall did not press the witness on this question ; he was not seeking to make the witness appear to be the real murderer, but only a man frightened to death because he knew that suspicion would fall on him.

" Did you talk about the case at the funeral ? "—" Yes, it was common talk."

" Did she give you a description of the man whom she said was known as a friend of Dimmock's ? "—" Yes."

" Did that description tally very much with your description of Wood ? "—" It tallied very much."

" So that you could easily have picked him out from May's description of him ? "

Thus the ship's cook's confident identification of Wood had been impeached. May had given him a description which would make it easy to pick out Wood at the identification parade. The witness was clearly terrified of Marshall and showed it.

" You were in a great fright, were you not, when you heard of this murder ? "—" No, I was not," said the man.

" When you heard of it, did you realise, except for the murderer——" Before Marshall finished, the witness broke in : " The next man to him "—indicating the prisoner—" next to the prisoner."

This seemed to show that the witness had regarded the prisoner as the murderer from the start.

" No," shouted Marshall Hall, " next to the murderer, which is a very different thing, if you please.

" You realised your danger—it was a very unpleasant situation ? "—" Yes."

Having established that the witness had been apprehensive, to say the least ; that he was prejudiced against the prisoner ; that he had discussed the case with May ; and that she had given him a description which would have made it easy to identify the prisoner—Marshall passed on to cross-examine on the all-important letter. Wood had said that the scrap produced with his writing on it must be part of a page torn from a little address book on which he had been scribbling to please Phyllis, when they met ; Marshall's keen eye had detected blue lines on the fragments which made the statement plausible. The witness still insisted that the scraps were part of the letter which Phyllis had shown him, but again began to hang his head. Again came the ruthless exhortation from leading counsel. " Look up, man, I tell you—we are in a court of justice—don't hang your head." The witness was severely cross-examined as to the part of the letter which he claimed to have read : he repeated his recollection of this as, " DEAR PHYLLIS,—Will you meet me at the ' Eagle,' 8.30 to-night.—BERT." But, as the letter must have been posted on Tuesday night to be received by the first post on Wednesday morning, it was not really feasible that the expression " to-night " could have been used. Somebody in court laughed at the witness's equivocal answer when this point was put to him. Marshall, his nerves strung up to the uttermost limit, could not bear this. Turning round towards the place from which the laughter had come, he said, " I *implore* you not to laugh—a man's life is at stake."

Next he suggested that the ship's cook knew that Phyllis was living with Bertram Shaw, and that, seeking for safety for himself, he had originally said the letter was signed " BERT " in order to throw suspicion on Shaw. He was drawing to a conclusion.

" I put it to you," he concluded, " that this fragment was never part of a letter which passed through the post. I put it that the story of this long letter is an invention."

After a short re-examination by Sir Charles Mathews, the ship's cook left the box with perspiration pouring down his face. The jury began to talk significantly among themselves. Sir Charles whispered a word or two to Marshall.

" No," said the latter, in the hearing of the whole court, " most certainly I do not accuse him of the murder." The first day of the trial was over.

Wood himself had now completely recovered his self-possession, if he had ever lost it, and had been making numerous sketches of the personalities round him in court. When he was back in prison, he penned this remarkable letter to his brother :

" H.M.P., Brixton,
" *December* 12*th.*

" DEAR CHARLES,—I am just back. So sorry I could not grasp you by the hand to-day. Of course, I have nothing now in my possession but the clothes I stand up in.

" My feelings were strange to-day : such that I cannot describe, though quite peaceful. Whispers of good cheer came from every direction ; and even the orderly that tends my room moved silently and with some reverence this morning.

" Little did I think that one day I should appear on the capital charge, under that beautiful figure of Justice (by Frampton, R.A.) that towers above the Old Bailey. I think you have admired it.

" I have a memory of sitting at the same supper with this great sculptor on more than one occasion.

" I liked Marshall Hall's manner when he spoke to me to-day, and he is apparently a splendid man.

" I am rather cut off now from Mr. Newton, so please call his attention to any point, though I expect they view things differently from us—the legal mind, I mean.

" Pardon, dear Charles, if I have omitted any due thanks or remarks.

" To be tried for one's life is, I find, sufficient for the day, and I am very weary.

" I must ask you to be of good cheer, and to take good care of yourselves.

" I understand there are great odds to face that may end disastrous, but I will carry my head high. For I have done no *grievous* wrong. Good-bye—fondest wishes to you all— good-bye.

" BOB."

The first important witness called on the second day was a fellow lodger of the ship's cook, called to prove an alibi for him on the night of the murder. From this evidence arose one of the most dramatic moments of the trial.

Marshall Hall asked him, " Did he [the ship's cook] tell you he was very anxious to prove where he was on Wednesday night ? "—" No."

" Did you know he was anxious to prove that ? "—" No."

" Did you hear that he slept with Dimmock on the Monday, Tuesday, and Sunday nights ? " continued Marshall, purposely inverting the sequence.—" Yes."

" Did he tell you ? "—" Yes, in the course of a conversation."

" When did he tell you ? "—" I knew on the Wednesday morning that he took her home."

" After knowing you only a few days, a man told you that ? "

" He said he had been with Dimmock."

" That was a curious conversation for a man you had only known three days, to tell you he had passed the *three previous nights* in that way ? "—" He did not say that ; he merely mentioned he had been with her."

" Why, I put the three nights to you specifically."

The witness thought that Marshall had made him admit that

the ship's cook had confessed to sleeping with Phyllis on the three nights previous to the discovery of the murder, which, of course, included Wednesday night; this would make him a later companion of hers than Wood. The witness, when he saw what such an answer would have meant, hastened to go back on his actual answer, that he knew that the ship's cook had slept with Phyllis for three nights.

" I never heard you ask me about three nights," he said.

" Nor did I," said the judge, whose view of the case appeared adverse to the prisoner till the very end.

Marshall then became very excited. " I put the days in the wrong order purposely, to mark the question," he said. " I call for the shorthand note."

" There is no need to get excited," said the judge. " There is no good in putting that [the ship's cook's possible statement] to the witness."

Most people in court, including the jury, had heard Marshall's question as to the three nights, and the shorthand note proved it. The jury again began to talk significantly among themselves.

"Very well," said the judge, "if he misunderstood, I did also."

Then there was a pause. The witness was rattled, and Wellesley Orr longed for Marshall to continue this effective cross-examination at length. But a rare inspiration of restraint came over him ; perhaps it was because the greatest dramatic effect could be achieved only by restraint. His eye had surveyed the jury, and seen how the incident of the shorthand note had impressed them ; for the question was well remembered.

" If," he said slowly to the witness, " you put the truth of your evidence on that statement [i.e. that he had never asked a question about the three nights] I will ask you no further questions. Do you ? "—" Yes, I did not say that," replied the witness, possibly glad at any cost to escape from that ruthless cross-examiner. Marshall then sat down ostentatiously, after saying, " Very well, I will not ask you another question."

The next witness to face his enquiries was the carman. Marshall did not attack this witness's character, as Newton had at the police court. Nevertheless, he dealt with him very skilfully. He now put his meeting with the man of the peculiar gait in St. Paul's Road seven minutes earlier than he had before.

Marshall immediately suggested that he made this change in an attempt to get over the difficulty of the lamp, which had undoubtedly been extinguished by five minutes to five, the time first given. Marshall then proved to him that this week had been an exceptionally bright and sunny week for September : the day before had been the hottest day in the year. There was not a drop of rain recorded in London that morning. How had the carman described the weather ?—" A drizzly, foggy morning." Did he know, when the man with the peculiar gait came out of the house, that the house was number 29 ? No, " he had read it in the papers," and afterwards identified it. This answer, as Marshall afterwards said in his speech, was better than he could possibly have expected. Moreover, the carman admitted that he had not mentioned the " peculiar walk " at all in his first statement to the police ; Marshall Hall at once called for that statement, which was not available. It had been taken by a junior officer, and had been lost. The witness excused his omissions by saying, " When we go to make a statement, we are not so ' fly ' as when we come to be cross-examined. I was not so particular."

" You were not so ' *fly*,' " burst out Marshall Hall. " Do you mean to say that—knowing this man's life might depend on your description—you did not take particular notice of what was read over to you ? Have you no regard for human life ? "

The carman had described the man he had seen as being of stiff build with broad shoulders. Wood was a frail, little man. The witness's answer was that in an overcoat he would appear broader, and that, at all events, Wood was broader than he himself was. " Would you describe a bluebottle as an elephant," rejoined the advocate, " because it is bigger than a fly ? "

The third day provided a sensation by the production of the mysterious " Scotch Bob," who had known the dead woman. Thereafter the prisoner could not be confused with him, and the girl May's story became more incredible than ever, for " Scotch Bob's " late employer proved that he was far away on the night of the murder. Everybody in court had a good look at a tall, pale-faced young Scot, as he stood up in court. Later in the day, Marshall Hall administered a bold rebuke to the judge. A fellow employee of Wood's, named Moss, gave evidence that Wood was a creature gentle and affectionate to a degree altogether out of the ordinary. But here the judge broke in with the question, " Had you any idea of the life you have now heard he was leading—an immoral life ? " The witness said he was unaware of anything abnormal, and Mr. Justice Grantham then said, " You had no idea he was leading the life we have heard he was ? " The witness replied in the negative, but Marshall was already on his feet. He saw that the judge already assumed that Wood had been Phyllis's lover, which was some way to assuming his guilt. Ruby Young had not yet given evidence, and there was as yet no evidence of his immorality. " I do not understand your lordship's question." The judge then, lest there might be some misunderstanding, asked an even more objectionable question : " Had you any idea that he was living with such a woman as that ? " Marshall assumed that the judge meant Phyllis Dimmock, as he probably did. " My lord," he insisted, " there is not one tittle of evidence——"

The judge retorted severely, " I am addressing the witness, and I must ask you not to argue with me."

This was an example of the usefulness of Marshall's quick and reckless courage. A more tactful advocate might have let this incident pass. Here is an instance where he was absolutely right in a quarrel with the Bench. Quite undaunted, he had the last word. " I want to point out," he said, with a piercing glance, first at the judge and then at the jury, " in the interests of justice, that there is not a particle of evidence that the prisoner ever had any improper intercourse with Emily Dimmock."

Later, Marshall objected to the evidence of a barmaid at the " Eagle " as to the last meeting between Wood and Phyllis ; she failed to identify either Wood or his companion Lambert. " I implore your lordship," he said, " to note that this witness has not identified these men." The judge retorted, " You have said that before ; I have not forgotten it."

" I thought your lordship did not *appreciate* it," he said.

The really important business of the third day was the evidence of Ruby Young. The girl, when it came to the story of her last kiss and betrayal of Wood, and his words of farewell to her, burst into sobs, and could not continue her evidence for some minutes. Marshall Hall dealt gently with her ; it was not necessary to be brutal to the poor creature who had been pursued with the maledictions of the crowd, now thoroughly roused on behalf of Wood, and who was to be almost lynched as she drove in a public conveyance well guarded by police. But as to the false alibi he put one question that compels admiration. " Having regard to Doctor Thompson's evidence that the deceased woman was murdered between three and four in the morning, has it ever struck you that this was a perfectly useless alibi for the murderer, but a perfect alibi merely for a meeting with the girl ? " Ruby answered " No."

This question was the very foundation of Marshall's wonderful defence ; once again he turned the most damaging evidence for the prosecution into a corner-stone of the defence. For this false alibi, so understood, might even tell in Wood's favour ; it showed that his one concern was merely to avoid the publicity of being known as an associate of this girl, and not his trial for murder ; or, if he was afraid of being arrested for murder, it showed that he did not even know at what time the girl had been murdered, and was therefore an innocent man.

The only dangerous part of Ruby's evidence was her statement, which caused a great sensation in court, that in his walk Wood " had a peculiarity which no one else could copy." But much of the sting of this was removed when she admitted that she would not have mentioned it at all had not the carman's evidence been ridiculed.

It had been generally expected that Marshall Hall would savagely attack Ruby Young, as Newton had done at the police court ; his gentleness took everyone by surprise, and he always regarded this cross-examination as one of his best achievements.

On the fourth day a number of young women, of more or less disreputable character, were called to prove Wood's previous association with Phyllis Dimmock. Their evidence was very inconsistent, and not difficult to handle in cross-examination. One of them said to Marshall, " You are trying to make me into a bad character."

" God forbid," said Marshall sadly, " that I should *make* you one."

SIR CHARLES MATHEWS

Sketched by Robert Wood at the Police Court

RUBY YOUNG

Sketched from the dock by Robert Wood

Another of them had stared at the prisoner in a noticeable way while giving her evidence.

" What is the origin of your feeling against this man ? "— " I have no feeling."

" Oh, come now, why have you looked at him as you have, while you have been standing here ? " " Good gracious," said the woman, " my eyes are my own to look round with ! "

The last witness called to prove the previous acquaintance was a very remarkable gentleman. His name was John William Crabtree. He described himself as of " no fixed abode," but very lately he had had a very fixed abode as a guest of the King ; he had just completed a sentence for keeping a disorderly house, of which offence he had been convicted more than once. Phyllis had lodged at one of these houses, and he said Wood had called there very many times. He professed to remember, in some detail, a quarrel between them about a silver cigarette-case. Now Marshall had seen this man's statement and knew that there was a great deal which he might say in the prisoner's favour ; but he also knew that this wholly unreliable gaol-bird might wish to curry favour with the police. He wished first to discredit the evidence as to the previous acquaintance, and then, just as the Romans got the truth from slaves by torture, so to frighten him that he would blurt out the first thing that came into his head, which, in the case of this witness, was the best way to elicit the truth : once let Crabtree think over the matter, and he would tell a lie. Marshall had learned from the Hermann trial how to cross-examine such a witness, and his line was almost exactly the same as it had been with the witness in that case.

" What was the first thing you went to prison for ? "— " That has nothing to do with this case."

" You are going to answer my question. Turn round so that the jury can see you. Now, what was it ? "— " Horse-stealing."

" When was that ? "— " Four or five years ago."

" What was the sentence ? "— " Three years' penal servitude."

" For the last twelve or fifteen months have you been in prison on and off ? "— " Yes."

" You seem to treat this as a matter of levity ? "— " Not at all."

" Do you ever tell the truth ? "—" I think so ; I try to."

" Do you ever succeed ? "—" Not always."

" Have you ever tried to lead an honest life ? "—" Yes, I have lived fifty-six years, and I have only been in prison three times."

" Will you swear you ever saw the prisoner in any house you ever kept ? "—" Yes, most implicitly I swear it on my oath."

" What time of the day would he be there ? "—" Always in the evening."

" That incident when you saw him in bed—what time was that ? "—" Early in the morning, between six and seven."

" What was the date ? "—" I can't tell."

Marshall now put to him the questions which he had not dared to put till he had destroyed the effect of his adverse evidence, and frightened him by his fierce enquiries. He read out to Crabtree a description given by him to the police of a man who, in his opinion, might have committed the murder. Crabtree's comment on this was again better than could have been hoped. " Yes," he said, " but that man was ' Scotty,' a motor-driver, not the prisoner."

" Oh," said Marshall, " then they have got hold of the wrong ' Scotch Bob.' "

Crabtree went on to say that several men had a certain terrible grievance against poor Phyllis. Among them, " Scotty " had threatened to cut her throat, as he said that she had ruined him for life, and a certain sailor called " Biddle " had actually threatened her with a razor and taken money from her with menaces. Crabtree said he fully expected to see " Scotty " when he went to the police station ; he had merely identified Wood as a man who had been her lover and written her letters.

Finally, with the calling of " Scotch Bob " himself, who was not Crabtree's " Scotty " and who proved an incontestable alibi, the case for the prosecution closed.

Marshall Hall then rose and submitted confidently that there was no case against Wood to go to a jury, there being no motive, or reliable evidence of identification, or trace of the crime brought home to the prisoner. But, of course, the case went on, and Marshall opened the defence. For the first twenty minutes he did not touch the facts of the case, but used all his eloquence and dramatic power to instil into the jury a sense of their tremendous responsibility. J. B. Melville, K.C., now Solicitor-General, then a very " white wigged " spectator, describes this prelude as a masterpiece of advocacy, the most effective jury-speech he ever heard. " After twenty minutes of this passionate and pulverising rhetoric," he said to me, " the jury were in a state of pulp." Small wonder that one of their number was physically overcome and actually fainted. Marshall began with a reference to the contempt with which the Old Bailey Bar was at one time regarded. " But now," he said, " times have changed, and I am proud to boast myself a member of the Old Bailey Bar, into whose hands are entrusted the lives of their fellow citizens of London. . . . Gentlemen, in the last three days you may have thought that, now and then, I was pressing a witness unfairly, that I urged an unfair advantage, that I asked an unworthy question. If I seemed to exceed the proper limits, gentlemen, I implore you to forgive me ; but, after all, why should not I have ? My whole anxiety was for my client. Gentlemen, his life is at stake. I cannot rob the witnesses for the prosecution of that. They have far less to lose at my hands than he has at yours. Gentlemen, this burden has been lying very heavily on my shoulders. It will pass to yours all too soon." Finally, before turning to the case for the defence, he urged upon them an argument, at once challenging and flattering to the spellbound jurymen : " I must leave nothing to chance. If there be anything that I omit to say, I implore you not to pass it over. If any point occur to you, and I have missed it, give it the same weight as if it *had* been given you by the most unworthy counsel for the defence." He then turned to the defence. Some of it had already been disclosed by Newton at the police court. The defence was, as in the Yarmouth case, an alibi. The prisoner would say that he left the " Eagle " rather after eleven, and went straight home : his father and young brother had heard him come in at about midnight. There was nothing new in this evidence, but Marshall had again an important surprise witness who had only come to his knowledge during the progress of the case. This man, a ticket-collector named Westcott, had left " 26 " St. Paul's Road to go to his work at about 4.55 a.m. on the morning of the murder. He was broad-shouldered, and had a brisk walk. He had been wearing a bowler hat and a long, dark overcoat. He had also seen in the street a man who bore a resemblance to the carman. But the real sting came in the end of the opening speech. Two witnesses, said Marshall, had given statements to the Crown that they had seen the woman in the company of a man, who was *not* the prisoner, as late as 12.30. The prosecution had not thought fit to call them, and he was compelled to do so for the defence, to the disadvantage of the prisoner, for now the Crown would have the right to cross-examine them. " If the Crown condescended to call Crabtree, these two men should have been called. For what do you think, gentlemen, of a charge of murder that can rely upon the evidence of a man like the thing that we saw in the witness box just now ? No word I can invent can express the horror and contempt anyone would feel for a man like that—glorying in his wrongdoing—convicted horse-stealer, brothel-keeper, and liar. The prisoner has, under the stress of temptation, told untruths. He may have been immoral ; but, even had he been twenty times immoral, that is a long way from proving him guilty of one of the most atrocious and skilful murders of modern times."

Spontaneous applause broke out as Marshall Hall sat down, and the fourth day of the trial was over.

A rule of practice has now become established that a prisoner called in his own defence must give evidence before any other witness for the defence. This is not a rule of law, and Marshall did not follow it in this case. His decision to call the prisoner was a very bold step and historically interesting, as up to this time every prisoner called in his own defence on a capital charge at the Old Bailey had gone to the gallows.

The first witness called for the defence was the prisoner's father, a venerable old Scotsman. He said he remembered his son coming, on the night of the murder, into his room at about midnight ; he came to fetch a clock of his own which the witness had borrowed. Robert had commented on the pungent smell in the room : witness had bought some lotion for a skin complaint on the day before, and had spilled some on the Wednesday. That was how he was able to fix the date. Sir Charles Mathews asked him at once when he had gone to purchase some more lotion. The old man said on the following Monday. Why ?

—Because he had not spilled the whole of the first bottle. Why hadn't he said that before at the police court ?—" Because no one asked me," replied the old man truthfully, fighting for his son's life.

Young Charles Wood, a half-brother, corroborated his father's evidence ; and after him was called one Rogers, a jeweller by profession, by recreation a fisherman, and an officer of the Great Northern Brothers' Angling Society. This man lived in the flat below the Woods.

" Although a fisherman," began Marshall Hall, " your stories are not necessarily untrue ? " Rogers then told his story : at about midnight on September 11th he had been preparing bait for the annual outing of his angling society, and he had seen the prisoner come in at about 11.50. He had come forward with this statement from the very first, and had been very angry at not being called at the inquest. The last witness for the alibi was Westcott.

" Are you conscious that you have got a swing in your walk ? " asked Marshall Hall.

" Yes," said this bluff, broad-shouldered young man, " especially in the morning. They say it is a good exercise, and out with your chest." He then put on his bowler hat, turned up the collar of his overcoat, and walked up and down for the benefit of the jury. He was corroborated by another witness, named Barrett, who said that he had called him at 4.15 on that morning, and that he had always noticed a peculiar jerk in Westcott's shoulders as he walked. Wood's employer came forward to say that the prisoner was almost the pet of the works, of excellent ability and exceptionally amiable character. Marshall Hall then tendered the evidence of sixty-five of Wood's fellow employees, to the effect that Wood had no peculiarity in his walk, but Sir Charles accepted the evidence as given. Then the two witnesses, Sharples and Harvey, who were not called by the prosecution, but who at the very first had come forward to say that they had seen Phyllis with a man not the prisoner at 12.30 outside the " Rising Sun," gave their evidence. They said that her companion was a head and shoulders taller than Wood, and " much smarter built."

Then, amid tense excitement, Marshall said, " I call the

prisoner, Robert Wood." All eyes were on him as he walked to the witness box. It must have been a terrible ordeal. Everyone in court was watching for a peculiarity in his walk, and he wisely put his right hand in his coat pocket. As he passed by his father, he gave him a gentle smile, and said, " Well, dad, cheer up."

Marshall had been convinced by Orr that it was essential to call Wood in order to save his life, but the reason of his hesitation and anxiety soon became apparent. He was a very bad witness. He could not cast aside his affectations and his vanity even when fighting for his life. He was a young man who had been almost loved by his intimate friends, but to chance acquaintances he would have been thought, at the best of times, something of a *poseur*. Marshall put his first question with great force and dramatic effect.

" Robert Wood," he asked, " did you kill Emily Dimmock ? "

But the prisoner merely smiled, and remained silent.

Marshall repeated the question, but much of its effect was gone. " You must answer straight," he said.

" I mean it is ridiculous," said the foolish young artist.

Marshall then, much distressed, implored Wood to answer his questions directly, but throughout his evidence the prisoner's inability to obey him caused him much anxiety. When he was asked whether the evidence of Crabtree was true or false, he made an attempt to be dramatic. " May God destroy me," he said, " if I ever knew Crabtree, or if I was ever in his house." When asked if Phyllis's hair had been in curl-papers during their last meeting at the " Eagle "—a comparatively harmless fact for which there was abundant evidence—he said that he would not allow himself to be seen with a girl in public whose hair was like that. On the contrary, she was " very neat and dainty." He had talked to Phyllis because she was bright and merry, and " had an intelligence to appeal to." Wood had known William Morris, and really had a vein of sentimental poetry in his character. Afterwards he wrote of Phyllis, " She impressed me as a crushed rose—that had not lost all its fragrance, and had been thrown aside. She seemed a girl who might have seen better days, who might have made a good wife in other circumstances. It delighted me to sit with and talk to her. She was in

CAMDEN TOWN CASE : LADY DIABOLO OF MONTE CARLO

Sketch drawn by Robert Wood in Brixton Prison while awaiting his trial

[*By courtesy of the " Sunday Dispatch "*

herself an exceedingly attractive girl. She had a sort of rough refinement. I was not in love with her. She appealed in some way to my sense of the artistic." It was almost as if he had been reading " Jenny " by Dante Gabriel Rossetti. He did not say these words to the jury, but he would have if Marshall had let him. He seemed unconscious that he was in any danger at all. The calm self-possession which had allowed him to draw those masterly sketches in prison with a bold firm pen led him into indiscretion and dangerous prevarication in the witness box. He was much concerned to show that he did not " frequent " public houses ; he did not go at all " unless he was accompanied by a friend." As for the " Rising Sun," well, he did not want to hurt the feelings of the proprietor, but the place hardly had a good name. When Marshall questioned him about the writing on the charred pieces of paper, which was undoubtedly his, and which it was vital that he should admit and explain, he said fatuously, " It bears the appearance of a copy." He had to be pressed by Marshall to make the necessary and obvious admission. He disliked the poor, dead girl being referred to as " Dimmock." " I met Dimmock, or rather Phyllis, in Camden Road." The Court was adjourned after his examination in chief, which, according to Marshall Hall, was harder than any cross-examination that he had ever conducted.

On the sixth and last day of the trial, Wood had to face the ordeal of cross-examination by the terrible Sir Charles Mathews, then at the zenith of his career as a criminal advocate. Indeed, the affected, almost feminine little man on trial for his life, who seemed unable to give a straight answer, seemed hardly worthy of his steel. It was in very truth a case of *impar congressus Achilli*. The senior Treasury counsel was every whit as dramatic as the counsel for the defence. As Wood wrote afterwards, he created an atmosphere : " When he described night, one actually saw night : if he described blood, one saw blood." He would lift his shrill, compelling voice to a scream, and drop it to a whisper, his old gown dropping from his sloping shoulders, so that when he raised his arms, as he often did, in some dramatic gesture, he resembled a sinister little black raven with flapping wings ; but beside him sat the massive figure of Marshall Hall, with his aquiline nose, and eagle eyes that were fixed eloquently

on the jury whenever one of his opponent's questions mis-
carried, or seemed to go too far. But, as a whole, as Wood himself admitted, the cross-examination was scrupulously fair.
He was asked about the family ring which he had given to Ruby
Young, and Mathews suggested that it was an engagement ring.
" No," replied Wood, " it was something pleasing to her. She
would add more to it than I would, perhaps." Then came a
change in the prosecutor's voice—" Give us the English of that
answer," he said. Under that same question from Mathews,
Devereux the murderer had faltered a few years before, and
lied himself to the gallows. When Wood was asked where he had
been with Phyllis on the Monday night, he merely answered
that "he could not say." But the real crisis of his cross-examination arrived when Mathews came to the writing on the charred
fragments of paper. Mathews had been able to decipher the
following words and letters, " Will you . . . ar . . . of the
. . . miss . . . Town S . . . ill . . . Wednesday . . . has . . . and
. . . rest . . . excuse . . . good . . . fond . . . Mon . . . from . . . "
Mathews put to Wood a clever reconstruction of these fragments,
which was as follows: " Will you (meet me at the b)ar of the
(Eagle near Camden) Town S(tation on) Wednesday (8.15) . . .
good(-bye) fond(est love) from . . . . " This corresponded
closely to the ship's cook's recollection of the part of the letter
read by him. The word " ill," according to Mathews, referred to
Wood's father's recent illness, and " Mon " was the first syllable
of " Money." Wood had explained these fragments to Marshall
Hall in this way ; Phyllis had on Friday night had all the contents of his pockets in her lap—papers, sketches, post-cards,
letters—and this writing may have been one of these. Indeed,
if his sketches were half as clever and amusing as those made
during his imprisonment, she may well have kept them. Wood
was a man always drawing and scribbling. But, though he
admitted that the words were in his handwriting, he could not
explain them, or give their context. The words were so common
that almost anything could have been written around them.

" No," said Wood, " I can't say what that is. I don't know.
I can make neither head nor tail of it."

Finally, Mathews put to him two searching questions as to
the letter.

" Take these two documents. Does not the ' Rising Sun '
post-card contain an appointment for the Monday night, which
you kept that night ? "—" Yes."

" Does not that letter, which is before you, contain an assignation for the night of Wednesday, September 11th, which you kept
on the 11th ? "—" No, it does not, Sir Charles, you have written
that round it."

The judge intervened at this point : " The jury are judges
of that," he said significantly. He then asked Wood why, if he
had never seen Phyllis before September 6th, he had written
" Phyllis darling " on the post-card. Wood's answer was, " It
was to please, I suppose."

Later, Wood excused his not noticing what Phyllis had been
wearing at the " Eagle " by saying that " her personality was
in my mind, not her dress." Asked about the hat she was wearing,
he answered, " No, I could not describe it ; if I were a girl I might."

He was closely questioned as to whether or no he had been
in Phyllis's house at 29 St. Paul's Road on the night of the
murder. Here Wood gave his evidence splendidly, and fell into
none of the traps prepared for him. But at the end he again fell
into prevarication. Asked very directly as to whether he had
been in Phyllis's rooms on the night of the murder, he replied,
" It is only to you, Sir Charles, that I should answer that question. I should be indignant with the average man. No."

Finally he was questioned about Ruby Young, and whether
he had " given her up " in July. " I have never given up a
friendship with anybody," he said.

His cross-examination had lasted nearly three hours, and
Marshall briefly re-examined. The most damaging part of
Mathew's attack had been with regard to the charred fragments,
and it was in this connection that Marshall addressed a masterly
question. " Assuming that letter to be addressed to Phyllis
Dimmock, which you do not admit, what is the necessity of
indicating the exact locality of the ' Eagle,' which was in her
immediate neighbourhood ? "

Wood's inquisition was over ; he had made a bad witness,
but his very badness as a witness began to tell in his favour.
Could this gentle, talented, and rather silly young man have
murdered Emily Dimmock ? At all events, it would have been

fatal not to have called him. Whatever the uncertainty of his answers, anything was better than the almost certain comment of the judge on the silence of the one man who could have easily cleared himself if he had been innocent. Had Marshall not been persuaded by Orr, it might well have been the Yarmouth case over again.

His debt to Orr was generously acknowledged by Marshall Hall at the very outset of his final speech. It is not often that a devil, not briefed in the case, obtains a compliment of this sort. The beginning of the final speech was in great contrast to that of the opening address. Marshall Hall began by reasoning very quietly with the jury. No motive or premeditation had even been suggested against Wood. Why, he had introduced Dimmock to his friend Lambert within a few hours of her death ! The false alibi, in view of Wood's strange vanity, was really a point in his favour ; his respectability, not his neck, had been his concern. The alibi he had sought to establish only covered the harmless hours of the evening. " Had he been guilty, his memory would have been tortured, not by the evening, but the dawn." Turning to the evidence, he began to speak again with passion. " What is the evidence of murder ? The only iota of evidence against the man is that of the carman. If any one of you, gentlemen, had a poor suffering animal to kill, and whether you killed it or not depended on *his* evidence, would you kill it ? " Then he passed to poor Ruby Young. " I would gladly have said nothing of her. I would have let her go from the witness box—poor, unfortunate, wretched woman, who has no doubt experienced many a moment of mad remorse for her part in this case—but for one thing. The evidence of the carman stood alone in all its glaring improbability till December 4th, when, two months after the arrest of her lover, Ruby Young for the first time said that he had a peculiar gait, similar to that described by the carman. That statement was invented out of revenge for the suggestion that her calling was the calling which in fact it was. So far as she was concerned, it was a gross and vindictive lie. . . . You cannot hang a man on evidence such as that," shouted Marshall Hall, bringing his hand heavily down on the desk below him. " I defy you to do it : I defy you. I do not merely ask for a verdict of ' not guilty '—I demand it."

Then, and with some reason, he turned and savagely attacked the prosecution for not calling Sharples and Harvey. " The action of the prosecution was unpardonable," he said.

Sir Charles was up in an instant, his arms gesticulating, his gown flapping. " I'll not allow that to go, I'll not allow that to go," he shouted.

" I will not retract that the conduct of the prosecution in not putting these witnesses into the box was unpardonable," repeated Marshall Hall calmly.

" I offered these witnesses to my learned friend," went on Sir Charles.

" And so gave the prosecution an advantage," replied his antagonist.

" There was a reason for this course, my lord. I trust an open mind will be kept."

" I apprehend my friend's reason," said Marshall, " but, while it may excuse the course taken, it cannot justify it."

After the judge had told Sir Charles to wait his turn, Marshall continued his speech, absolving his opponent from all personal blame in the matter. He then referred to the mysterious Scotty. Where was this man, and the sailor, Biddle, who had been seen for months knocking Phyllis about, and had threatened her with a razor ? He described Wood going about his work quietly on the day after the murder. How could this delicate, amiable little artist have done this dreadful crime ? Not one trace of blood had been found on his clothes to connect him with it. Could the calm, untroubled prisoner be really the guilty man ? " His unruffled demeanour throughout the trial is based on an unruffled conscience." Then came the conclusion, in which every sentence was an intense athletic effort, and beads of sweat stood out on the face of the big man, as he wrestled with one last unresponsive face on the jury. " I have nothing more to say than to remind you that the responsibility is yours now, and not mine. If you are satisfied beyond all reasonable doubt that the man standing there murdered Emily Dimmock, though it breaks your hearts to do it, find him guilty and send him to the gallows. But, if, under the guidance of a greater than any earthly power, making up your minds for yourselves upon this matter, if you feel you cannot truthfully and conscientiously say you are satisfied that the prosecution have proved that this man is guilty, then, I say, it is your duty, as it must be your pleasure, to say that Robert Wood did not murder Emily Dimmock."

His part had been played magnificently ; but, since he had called evidence, the Crown had the right to the last speech. Sir Charles took advantage of his privilege, and made a most dramatic oration, which, fine as it was, would hardly recommend itself to the present school of Treasury prosecutors, nor was it a speech which should have come as the last word. He first explained why the Crown had not called Sharples and Harvey, and the reason given hardly seems to justify the course taken. In the Crown's opinion, the woman whom these two witnesses had seen with the broad-built man was not Emily Dimmock ; they had seen her outside the " Rising Sun," and it was hardly likely that Emily Dimmock would be so near the " Rising Sun " without going in. On that night Emily Dimmock was not dressed for her calling ; she had been until a late hour at another public house, the " Eagle." The ground was not cleared ; the argument of the defence, that the evidence had been edited, still had force. Sir Charles did not scruple to use bold supposition to make good the chain of evidence. Again and again he said, " It might have been," and " Might it not have been ? " The prisoner, he said, was an unnatural and dreadfully singular man : he had a nerve which literally nothing in the world could shake. His strange *sang froid* throughout the trial was not a proof of innocence. On the contrary, " might it not have been. . . ? " The prisoner was exceedingly cold-blooded. In crimes of this kind, it was not necessary to find a motive. When he had discovered, after a talk with one of his friends, that the " one more unfortunate gone to her death " was Phyllis Dimmock, he showed no sign of surprise or grief. Mr. Marshall Hall had said that there was no blood upon his clothes. " No blood found upon his clothes ? Why ? Gentlemen, when that dreadful murder was committed, might it not have been that he was wearing no clothes ? No blood was found upon his hands ? Why ? The murderer had washed them in the room of death. This was a cold-blooded murder. It has been proved again and again that Robert Wood is a cold-blooded man, and cold-blooded under

the most unnerving pressure. Might it not have been . . . ? "
After this peroration, into which all the pathos and bitterness
of his emotional nature was packed, he concluded by the formal reminder that if there was any doubt, they must acquit the prisoner.

He had spoken for two hours ; the judge then began to sum
up. There was dead silence in court, as every ear was strained
to listen and discover which way the judge was going. They had
not to wait long, and, as it became clearer and clearer that the
judge was making point after point against the prisoner, the
crowd in court, full of his sympathisers, became restless and
uneasy. " It must not be assumed that, because no motive has
been shown on the part of the prisoner, therefore he must be
' not guilty.' . . . There is no doubt the dead woman was
murdered by a man who was leading a double life . . . by a
man whom nobody would believe to be a murderer. . . .
Gentlemen, the whole evidence seems to prove that the prisoner
has been leading a double life. . . . I do not see why the Crown
should have called Sharples and Harvey. . . . There has been
no explanation of the burnt letter, which is very strong indeed
against the prisoner, and would justify the jury in believing
the ship's cook's story. . . . I think there is evidence to show
that the prisoner knew the murdered woman before September
6th. The evidence as to this showed that he was lying at the
beginning, just as he lied at the end. Wood's own story is
extraordinary. . . . There was a poor woman—done to death
—with whom he had been in contact within an hour or two of
the murder. He says he is innocent ; yet he keeps everything
from the police, and from his own brother. . . . " Now the
public had taken poor Wood and his family to its heart. From
three o'clock a crowd had begun to collect in the misty December
afternoon outside the Old Bailey, and by six o'clock it numbered
many thousands, and overflowed out of Newgate Street towards
Ludgate Circus. As Arthur Newton listened to the judge's
heavy indictment, a police officer whispered to him, " If there's
a conviction, I don't know what will happen." Indeed, fifty
mounted police were in reserve outside against an emergency.
In court the feeling was intense, and, as the judge went on, the
people's restlessness changed into open dissatisfaction and
criticism. There were repeated and audible observations of

Rh

" grossly unfair," and so forth, which could not have failed to reach the judge's ears. Marshall Hall himself did not neglect to let scorn and indignation play over his expressive features, and began to " talk to the jury with his eyes." However, there was one man who remained quite unmoved—the prisoner. During the whole trial he had busied himself in sketching every witness and many persons of note in court. He had a rare gallery of celebrities as his sitters. Lily Elsie, who smiled at him, Gertie Millar, Lady Tree, Pinero, Henry Irving, Hall Caine, and many others. A famous mental doctor, watching the prisoner during the judge's indictment of his life, exclaimed, " Good God, I believe he's sketching the judge." A scandalised warder looked up, tapped him on the shoulder, and said, " You mustn't do that," and Wood reluctantly put aside his pencil. He was indeed a man of iron nerve : there is no trace of weakness in these drawings ; all the lines are clean and hard. Doubtless, if the verdict had gone against him, he would have sketched the chaplain giving him a final benediction, and the hangman about to put the white cap over his head.

But, quite suddenly, there came a most dramatic moment. The judge paused and spoke in a new tone : " Although it is my duty to further the ends of justice, so that criminals are brought to justice and are properly convicted, however strongly circumstances may go against him, in my judgment, strong as the suspicion is, I do not think the prosecution have brought the case home against him clearly enough." The listeners were amazed, and a loud cheer burst out from them and continued in spite of the usher's staccato calls for silence. But Marshall Hall was not among the enthusiasts. He had been watching the jury's faces during the speeches and the summing up, and felt sure that his speech had won over the last waverers. With child-like petulance, he turned round to Orr and said, " Bah, he's trying to take the credit away from me." When silence was restored, the judge continued : " Although it is, of course, a matter for you, and for you alone, gentlemen, it is my duty to point out to you that, unless you find that the evidence is so much against him as to warrant a conviction, you must give him the benefit of the doubt. I think, gentlemen, I have spoken plainly to you. You are not bound to act on my view."

MR. JUSTICE GRANTHAM
Sketched during his summing-up by the prisoner, Robert Wood

THE MEETING
AT THE " RISING SUN "

ROBERT WOOD
ON HIS WAY TO WORK
Sketched by Robert Wood in Brixton Gaol
[*By courtesy of the " Sunday Dispatch "*

It is quite certain that Marshall's petulant theory did not explain the judge's sudden change. Was the change planned or spontaneous ? Certainly many of the eye-witnesses thought that the judge, who had seemed hostile to the prisoner throughout the trial, had really intended to sum up against him. Who shall say ? The mind of a judge is at least as difficult to read as those of other men. Judges are but human ; and it may be that, in his very summing up, the judge, looking at the slim, æsthetic youth in the dock, experienced a change of heart. It is no libel on a judge to say that he once, in a matter of life and death, changed his view—even at the eleventh hour. There was undoubtedly an overpowering atmosphere in court in favour of the prisoner, and it may have reached and influenced the judge, sitting there on the bench with so much of the power of life and death. At all events, many of the listeners in court hold the view that the judge changed his mind, suddenly and at almost the last opportunity. This should not be understood as a charge of weakness, but as a tribute to the quality of his mercy. Others say, on good authority, that the judge took a strong view of the prisoner's conduct in his association with immoral women, and of his dreadful behaviour after the poor girl's death, and, while intending all the time to direct the jury as he did, considered it his duty to warn Wood and all other young men of the perils into which such an association and such deceit can bring them.

The judge concluded his dramatic address at 7.45, and retired to his private room as the jury filed out. A great hum of conversation immediately arose, and the general opinion seemed to be that the jury would be out for some hours. But at eight o'clock someone noticed that the usher had returned, and exclaimed excitedly, " They are coming back." Marshall looked up nervously ; he had not expected this sudden unanimity, and remembered the fate of Bennett. But the foreman, in answer to the formal question, said " Not guilty " in a loud voice. A great cheer rose in court, and many of the women were in tears. People rushed forward to embrace Marshall Hall and shake him by the hand. He was tired, exhausted, ill, and very much moved. But Wood himself maintained absolute composure, and, before being discharged, actually completed his unfinished sketch of the judge. He himself described his feelings thus : " After the verdict the reaction cannot properly be conveyed in words. I was not relieved. I felt depressed : I was seized with a sort of fainting feeling at the pit of my stomach, though it did not outwardly affect my composure. I was overwhelmed with sadness. I believe I was the only person who did not rejoice at the result. . . . " He was very grateful to his advocate : " My thanks to Mr. Hall can never be expressed. He was ill ; he should have been out of England, and yet he stayed to help me."

The huge crowd outside heard the cheer in court very faintly, and, when a man ran out and told them the verdict, they took it up themselves. Wood appeared at a window and called for cheers for Marshall Hall. The latter's great figure was too obvious to escape the attentions of the enthusiastic mob, but Wood escaped almost unobserved in a motor with Newton : the latter took him into a famous hotel in the Strand for refreshment, and, as he went in, a newsboy came up to him, shouting, " 'Ere y'are, sir, Camden Town murder—trial and verdict."

But there was one person whom the crowd wished to see more even than Wood and his defender : it was now an ugly crowd, which did not understand the cruel chain of circumstances, combined with an unfortunate young woman's indiscretion and weakness, which had led Ruby Young into the witness box to bring her lover near to the gallows. She had not taken the hundred pounds reward offered for information about the writer of the post-card. But the crowd could not know that. Journalism had found this poor little moth, and justice had broken her on its wheel. " Ruby, Ruby," shouted the angry and menacing mob, " won't you come out to-night ? " Meanwhile, she sat terrified and broken-hearted in a remote little room in that great new building. She kept repeating, " I only told the truth : people don't understand." As to the verdict, she said, " I have thought all along that this would be the result. I have never thought Robert guilty, and my evidence was never intended to indicate that I did." The police did not seem to realise the great danger which threatened her, and Sir Herbert Austin, the clerk of arraigns, performed a graceful act of chivalry. The girl had worn an expensive fur, and he knew that it would be madness for her to wear it when she left the court. He persuaded her to change into the dress of one of the Old Bailey

charwomen. There had been a suggestion that she should take
the charwoman's baby in her arms, but on account of the danger
to it she refused to do this. So, well after eleven o'clock, she
passed out unnoticed among the crowd into night and obscurity
once more.

When the case was over, the newspapers took the view that
the result was a foregone conclusion, but this was far from being
true. It was a great triumph for Marshall Hall and English
justice. But much of the credit must go to Newton, who so
cleverly prepared the ground, and to Wellesley Orr for his
brilliant devilling. The latter was very possibly right : if Marshall
Hall had not put Wood into the witness box—and, indeed, if
Marshall Hall had not defended him—there might have been a
miscarriage of justice ; and Wood himself would have been
responsible for it. But his life, unlike Bennett's, was well worth
saving, and Marshall knew it. Wood's sketches in prison, two of
which Marshall kept among his most treasured possessions,
showed almost a touch of genius. It was clear that, if he could
recover from his terrible ordeal, he was bound to do well.
Years afterwards, Marshall left a provincial Assize court, and
was accosted by a smart, happy-looking little man. " You
don't know me, I see, Sir Edward," he said. " No," said Marshall,
taking his hand, " you must forgive me—I've got a terrible
memory for faces." Then he noticed the man's very deep-set
eyes. " Why," he said, " isn't your name Wood ? " " No,"
replied the other gravely, " it's not, but I'd like you to know I'm
doing very well, and owe it all to you." If this was indeed Wood,
it was a very moving incident, and one which was comparatively
rare in Marshall's experience. The acquitted man shows a
perhaps natural desire to avoid every memory of his trial.
Marshall once defended a financier, and obtained an unexpected
acquittal. Advocate and client met again some time afterwards,
placed next to each other in the stalls of a theatre. As soon as the
client caught sight of Marshall Hall, he excused himself to his
hostess and went out. But, now and then, clients are grateful,
and gratitude can take strange forms. While Marshall Hall
was once buying a railway-ticket, a clever thief ran away with
his precious dressing-bag. This contained many of his treasures,
and a wad of notes. Marshall, always very excitable, nearly

went mad, and immediately advertised the loss. A few days later, the bag, with all its contents, was deposited at his house with an anonymous note to the effect that one good turn deserves another, and that if the thief had recognised Marshall Hall the trouble would never have arisen. Not one note was missing. Thieves, however, do not always turn out to be grateful clients : on another journey he lost a suitcase. The thief was discovered, but too late for restitution. Nevertheless, Marshall interviewed him for the purpose of tracing his possessions, and incidentally upbraided him for his wickedness. " Well, you see, sir," was the disarming explanation, " me and the missus got married on that there bag."

The Wood case restored Marshall Hall to his old position at the Bar. He himself was never sufficiently grateful to the great capital trials which established and re-established his fame. He considered that they impeded his chances of a more general and lucrative practice. But his fee-book, after all, is the surest test. Very soon after this great defence, and the Lawrence case which followed it, he was doing better than before *Chattell* v. *the " Daily Mail."* He never appreciated this fact, and would ruefully tell a story of a rich North-country manufacturer who refused to brief him for his defence in a big financial prosecution, on the ground that, if he briefed Marshall Hall, " everybody would think he was a murderer."

It is worthy of record that after the Camden Town case the *Daily Mail* published an essay by Sir Hall Caine on the trial, in which high praise was given to Marshall Hall. " The defence was conducted with a strenuous and impetuous power which I have rarely seen excelled. Constructing his scheme of evidence with wonderful acuteness, building up his material in really faultless order, and with the cumulative effect of the most skilful dramatist, Mr. Marshall Hall made an almost overpowering appeal to the intellect as well as to the heart of his audience. Impulsive, even passionate, it was at some moments, quivering with emotion almost to breaking point, and liable to the accident of a foul hit sometimes, but never descending to personal attack, and lavish in its generous atonement for a misdirected blow. It was a thrilling and most honourable exhibition of forensic ability, contesting against and (as the sequel shows) breaking and destroying an apparently damning chain of circumstantial evidence." Later, Sir Hall Caine made one point most eloquently, which Marshall would have loved to have made. Throughout the trial, hardly anything seemed to have been thought of the poor broken soul whose life and death were the cause of the whole tragic drama. " Her dead body was there, indeed, with all the horror of its blood upon it, and the crime committed upon her we were always conscious of, but the woman herself seemed never for a moment to be present to our minds. That poor outcast of the streets, who was no vampire, no alluring temptress lying in wait to wreck the lives of men, but only an outcast girl, very poor, perhaps very worthless, though dowered with a little fatal beauty . . . that poor crushed thing, whose existence as the victim of man's lust and the world's grinding poverty had been the prologue to the tremendous drama I had just seen."

.   .   .   .

Early in the New Year, Marshall Hall appeared for Mrs. Robinson in the perjury proceedings which followed the collapse of the prosecution of Mr. Herbert Druce also for perjury. The prosecution of Druce was to be a step in one of the most audacious claims to a great title and fortune ever made. On October 11th, 1907, a small but select band of persons had made their way to Clerkenwell police court to give evidence to prove that Mr. Herbert Druce had committed perjury in swearing, in the Probate Court in 1901, that his father had died in 1864 under the name of Druce when in fact he had died in 1879 under the name and style of George, fifth Duke of Portland. The select little band of witnesses was composed of two old ladies, Mrs. Hamilton and " Miss " Robinson, aged seventy-nine and sixty-nine respectively ; an Irish American named Cardwell ; and a miscellaneous collection of elderly people who had known the fifth Duke of Portland and old Mr. Druce. They were shepherded by an English solicitor, and an Australian lawyer to whom the blameless old maiden lady, " Miss " Robinson, had first told her amazing and romantic story.

For many decades rumour had connected the names of the respectable tradesman of Baker Street and the eccentric nobleman who had built the famous subterranean palace at Welbeck.

It was widely believed that His Grace, who had died in 1879, officially unmarried, and had been succeeded by his cousin the present duke, had really lived as the owner of the Baker Street Bazaar in order to cloak a secret marriage by which he had lawful issue ; it was further believed that, after this lawful wife had died, he had brought his double life to a discreet end by a judicious mock funeral of the old tradesman of Baker Street, whose coffin had been filled with stones. There were romantic tales of a secret tunnel of communication between the duke's mansion in Cavendish Square and the Baker Street Bazaar. How this wonderful tale became current nobody will ever know, but the fact that for many years thousands of people believed it is at least a tribute to the incurable romanticism of the British public. But it is seldom that a scandalous rumour, however widely spread, ever reaches the sober atmosphere of the Court of Probate. Yet in 1901 the widow of one of old Druce's sons, already half demented by her pretensions, brought an action for the revocation of the probate of old Druce's will, and Mr. Herbert Druce, a son of old Druce, but one who would have had nothing to gain by the claim to the dukedom, had sworn that he had seen his father lying dead in 1864. Mrs. Druce conducted her case in the most extraordinary way, and was later put under medical supervision for mental reasons. Her brother-in-law's word was accepted. Meanwhile, another " claimant " had come into the field ; George Hollamby Druce had been a miner in Australia, and now claimed, as old Druce's heir and grandson, to be the rightful sixth Duke of Portland. He was always addressed among his friends as " Your Grace."

This whole pretension depended very largely on the evidence for the mock funeral and the true contents of old Druce's coffin. The whole matter could have been settled by an exhumation, but to this course Mr. Herbert Druce was notoriously opposed. In the previous proceedings he had defeated the demands for exhumation ; his opposition was widely construed by the public as an admission of the story. Indeed, a Druce-Portland Company was formed, and thousands were contributed by the British public, in their credulity, for the promotion of the claim.

The first step had to be the prosecution of Mr. Herbert Druce for perjury ; it was thought that this might goad him into opening his father's coffin. The prosecution's contentions certainly were not lacking in evidence. Cardwell, who said that he had cured the duke of a skin disease, told the story of the mock funeral in detail. The septuagenarian Mrs. Hamilton said that the fifth Duke of Portland was her godfather, that she knew perfectly well of his double life, and had herself, in due course, refused his hand in marriage. This lady's evidence had been " discovered " during the 'nineties by an English newspaper, and it had only become slightly modified with years. Her story was a remarkable one, but it paled beside that of the sexagenarian Miss Robinson ; she, it seemed, had been engaged for the duke, by no less a person than Mr. Charles Dickens, to act as his secretary with regard to the Druce family affairs, after the official " death " of old Druce in 1864. Strangely enough, although his Druce-self had come to an end, she always called him " Mr. Druce." She had lived quite close to Welbeck Abbey and had kept a contemporary diary as a record of her numerous dealings with him. She had brought this diary to England ; but, most unfortunately, just before the case came on, a gentleman had come up behind her in the street, told her there was a spider crawling up her back, and, while she was engaged in freeing herself from this loathsome insect, had stolen the precious diary. In spite of this unfortunate loss, and in spite of the fact that her most treasured " present from the duke " turned out, under Mr. Avory's inspection, to be a worthless piece of glass, many still believed in this remarkable corroboration of a long current rumour. During the progress of the case, Mr. Herbert Druce at length consented to the opening of his father's coffin. When the coffin lid was opened, Mr. Pepper saw lying in its shroud, in a very remarkable state of preservation, the clearly recognisable body of old Mr. Druce of Baker Street.

The prosecution collapsed, and the Druce-Portland Company went into compulsory liquidation. Proceedings for perjury were launched against the three principal witnesses, but Cardwell made good his escape to America. Marshall Hall appeared for Mary Robinson. She pleaded guilty, and Marshall Hall told, in his plea in mitigation of sentence, a story as interesting to a student of human nature as the perjured fiction of the wretched

old woman had been to lovers of romance. Mary Robinson was
a woman of humble origin, who had at one time lived near
Welbeck Abbey, and had no doubt heard stories about the
eccentric duke. She had married a man of her own class, had
emigrated with him to New Zealand, and until the age of sixty-
five had lived a life of hard work and unblemished respectability.
But, unfortunately, she had been gifted with a fatal power of
writing, and she adored the romances of Charles Dickens. By
chance she read one day an advertisement in a newspaper asking for information about the fifth Duke of Portland. She
remembered vague stories connecting him with Mr. Druce, and
answered the advertisement. Pamphlets giving in detail the
whole of the Druce-Portland story were sent to her ; drawing
on these and on her imagination, she wrote the story of her
employment as the duke's confidential secretary in an old blank-
paged journal which she had bought at a sale. Step by step she
was induced by the promoters of the claim to visit England,
and, dazzled by the prospects of great wealth, to giving her
perjured evidence. Perhaps she almost began to believe in her
story herself. Nobody had questioned it, but her associates had
rather encouraged her in wider and wider flights of imagination,
until she came into court to face the cold and pitiless questions
of Mr. Horace Avory. She was sentenced to four years' penal
servitude.

.   .   .   .

Marshall Hall could whip himself into a frenzy of enthusiasm
for any client, however unprepossessing or however impersonal.
In 1908 he was briefed at the last minute by an insurance
company to fill the place of Sir Henry Dickens in a circuit case
at Yarmouth. The company was contesting a claim on a life-
insurance policy on the ground that the deceased's alcoholic
disposition had not been disclosed to them. The local feeling
against the company was very strong, and the jury were all
local men ; indeed, at one point before the defence had opened,
or called a single witness, one juryman announced, " I have
made up my mind against the company," at which there was
loud applause in court. However, Marshall passionately addressed them on behalf of the company, and in the end the jury
gave a verdict upon which judgment was entered for the

defendants. " It is refreshing," said Low K.C., his opponent, in the course of his reply, " in these degenerate days to see someone who can get up so much eloquence and so much enthusiasm over the woes of an insurance company."

During the summer, Marshall Hall himself appeared in the guise of a delinquent under rather surprising circumstances. He was one of the pioneers of motoring, and, in spite of retaining a chauffeur surnamed Innocent, he had already been in trouble with the police. In August 1908, Marshall Hall was sedately driving in the Park behind a trap drawn by a fast-trotting horse, without seeking to overtake it. A police officer stopped the car, but allowed the horse and trap to escape. Marshall thought this preferential treatment grossly unfair, and a bitter altercation followed between the P.C. and the K.C. At the police court the famous cross-examiner, himself under cross-examination, said ruefully, " I did not shake my fist at him, but I *did* use an epithet, and I regret it." The fine was forty shillings and five shillings costs.

. . . .

At the beginning of 1909, Marshall was retained " specially " to fight a case which he himself regarded as the greatest triumph of his forensic career. Most " common " lawyers join a circuit shortly after their call, which entitles them to practise in the ordinary way at the Assize towns of their chosen circuit. Marshall Hall's circuit, the South-Eastern, extends from the Norfolk broads and Cambridgeshire fens to the downs of Sussex. The advent of the motor-car has destroyed much of the good fellowship and character of circuit life on the South-Eastern since his early circuit days, as every town on the circuit can be " operated " from London. But the other circuits still form the most delightful professional clubs in England ; and the barrister who has never gone circuit has missed the best fun in the profession. A barrister accepting a brief on a strange circuit has to demand a special fee of one hundred guineas over his ordinary remuneration. One of the most charming pieces of silver which the mess of the Northern Circuit possess is a present from Marshall Hall given as an acknowledgment of their hospitality to him on one of these occasions, and I believe that nearly all of the other circuits have similar gifts from him.

In 1909 he was briefed for the first time on a strange circuit, the Midland, to defend a prisoner on a charge of murder.

On a bitterly cold snowy night on December 29th, 1908, at about a quarter to ten, a Dr. Galbraith of Wolverhampton was disturbed by the visit of a man obviously distraught and under the influence of drink. " Come at once, doctor," he said : " I have shot a woman." The man was Edward Lawrence, a rich brewer, and a well-known, indeed a too-well-known, character of the town. He had received a good education, become an excellent man of business, and had married a charming woman. But a craving for drink was a failing in his family, had killed his brother, and was fast ruining Edward. His wife had obtained a decree *nisi* on account of a brutal assault upon her, and his adultery with a beautiful barmaid named Ruth Hadley. His wife was, however, devoted to him, and in his own interests had never made her decree absolute. He was a generous, open-handed man, but, when in drink, violent and impossible to deal with. He had recently been convicted and fined for savagely assaulting with his teeth a police-constable, against whom he had a fancied grievance.

As the doctor entered the brewer's house, Lawrence made as if to lock the door, and the former refused to come in without another doctor. The two medical men found a young woman lying stretched on the floor of the dining-room in her outdoor clothes. An almost untasted meal for two persons was laid upon the table. She was the girl for whom he had left his wife and children. There was a bullet wound in her right temple, and a slight wound on her right arm. The case was hopeless, and she died soon after. Lawrence was hysterical, and alcohol seemed to have so unbalanced his mind that his moods alternated between heart-broken anxiety and a brazen pride in what had happened. At one moment he would be saying, " Good God, she's not dead, is she ? For God's sake do everything you can for her," and, the next moment, " I'm glad I did it. She is best dead : she drove me to it. You don't know what a wicked woman she has been."

When the police arrived, one spent cartridge was found in the dining-room, and one bullet had penetrated through the window and lodged in the wall opposite. But in the revolver found upon him there were four undischarged and only one spent cartridge, which seemed to prove that Lawrence had reloaded in an attempt to conceal the fact that he had fired twice. When questioned and charged by the police, Lawrence assumed a bitter, defiant attitude. " Murder," he said, " you say, do you ? That's all right." Up to this point his every word and action seemed to be an admission, indeed a confession, of guilt. Later his attitude changed. " Well," he observed, " there's one thing —I didn't do it. You were not there when it was done. . . . She shot herself." This statement, if anything could have, made matters worse : it seemed a fatuous contradiction of everything he had yet said.

The prisoner reserved his defence at the police court, and on the face of the matter the task of defending him appeared almost hopeless. His bad reputation, his violent character, his statements to the police, and the strong local feeling against him, were all considerations which no Staffordshire jury could easily banish from their minds. On the other hand, some person whom he had befriended printed broad-sheets in verse extolling his generosity and begging for an acquittal for " Poor Old Ted." It is clear from his preliminary note of the trial that Marshall Hall before the trial hoped for a verdict of manslaughter at the best : the proposed defence, if there was any, was kept an absolute secret till the day of the trial, and indeed till later. But Marshall had been seen to enter Wellesley Orr's room with a revolver, and ominous sounds, as of some violent scuffle, were heard by the clerks in the next room. Marshall Hall arrived in Stafford the day before the trial, and the last consultation ended after midnight. The defence was still a mystery.

Mr. Justice Jelf was the judge ; Mr. F. W. Sherwood appeared for the prosecution, and opened the case as " one of murder, wilful murder, and nothing less than murder." He suggested that the case was a simple and overwhelming one, and that, on the evidence, the verdict " guilty of murder " could be the only reasonable decision. The court was, of course, packed with spectators, among whom was Edward Lawrence's wife, who had nobly stood by her husband since his arrest, and who sat in the gallery through every day of the trial.

After the opening the prosecution called their evidence.

Two sisters of the dead woman said that Lawrence had shot at her twice before, and had threatened to murder her. One of them said she had seen him threaten Ruth with a revolver. Marshall Hall put it to them that Ruth was a very violent woman, and drank wickedly ; but the answer to this was that Lawrence had taught her to drink. It also came to light that Ruth had left Lawrence in September, and had been supplanted by another girl : Ruth had only returned after the departure of that other girl just before Christmas. This evidence cut both ways, as the other girl had left him because of his threats and violence. This cross-examination of the sisters, not perhaps so effective as Marshall's usual achievements in this line, was the first suggestion of any defence at all.

The last person to see Ruth before her tragic death was a little fifteen-year-old servant girl. She had seen the beginning of a quarrel between Lawrence and Ruth, in which he had accused her of being drunk, and she, indignantly denying the charge, made as if to throw a cruet at him. The servant girl was then dismissed by Ruth, and Marshall made much of the fact that she heard the key turn in the lock just after she went out, and knew that it was Ruth, not Lawrence, who had locked it. The case for the prosecution ended with the cross-examination of a Dr. Powell. Marshall suggested to him that the revolver had accidentally gone off while Ruth and Lawrence were struggling. But in spite of a dramatic demonstration by Marshall Hall, the doctor would have none of it. He said that her flesh would have been blackened by an explosion at so close a range. Things were now looking very black for Lawrence. The jury seemed decidedly hostile, and the judge did not appear at all impressed by any points made by Marshall Hall.

But with his first sentence to the jury, in opening the defence, the atmosphere began to change. In a short and powerful speech he disclosed the prisoner's defence, and at once obtained the jury's rapt attention. He would, he said, put a score of witnesses into the box, before calling the prisoner himself, to prove that Ruth had threatened the prisoner on many occasions ; that she was a violent woman at all times, but in December 1908 she was maddened by the fact that Lawrence had taken another woman in her place ; that the prisoner had been terrified of her tempers; that just such a scene had happened before in the presence of an independent witness, who had prevented the tragedy on that occasion. Finally, the prisoner himself would go into the box, and swear that he had no thoughts of murder, but that the death of Ruth was the result of a drunken brawl, which terminated in a " fatal accident."

This was a bold line to take : many advocates would have taken the middle course of maintaining that the proper verdict should be " manslaughter," and, indeed, as I have said, this was Marshall's own original line of defence ; probably on some sudden impulse or intuition he was inspired to take the bolder line at the eleventh hour, and he went for a clean acquittal. A score or so of witnesses, sedulously marshalled by the enquiries and industry of Mr. Copeland, the solicitor for the defence, were called to prove that Ruth had threatened to shoot him on many occasions : she had stabbed him with a hat-pin, struck him, and broken on his head the steel handle of an umbrella, and, when he had sat dazed under this wound, she had said in scornful delight, " It has been my privilege to drive him ' potty.' " She had assaulted him with any domestic utensil which was ready to hand. On the other hand, not one of these witnesses could tell of any actual retaliation by the prisoner. She had been heard to say of the very revolver which killed her, " This is the thing I will do him in with. I shall only get eighteen months." She was a fury who had made a hell on earth for the man who had chosen her, and a comparison suggests itself between this wild tigress and poor, gentle Emily Dimmock, who also paid the same price for her immorality.

The judge at first seemed disposed to regard all this evidence as irrelevant to the issue before him, but Marshall ingeniously defended its admissibility on the ground that " it tended to prove the terror that would be in the prisoner's mind on the fatal night, which would make him exaggerate the danger when she faced him with a revolver." Of course, once admitted, the evidence established far more than this in the jury's mind.

On the afternoon of the fourth day of the trial, at about two o'clock, the prisoner went into the box. He was an educated and well-spoken man, but he was suffering from jaundice, and his appearance was ghastly. On going into the box he faced the public gallery for the first time during this trial, and looked up boldly into the eyes of his wife. It was an audacious step for Marshall to put this man into the box : he had been exceedingly difficult to handle in consultation, and his outbursts of temper had put a severe test on Marshall's patience. At one moment, so impossible did Lawrence become, Marshall had actually to threaten to return to London if Lawrence did not behave more properly to his advocate ; needless to say, it was a threat which he would never have carried into effect. Everything depended on Lawrence's evidence. A favourable prologue had been spoken for him, but he alone could explain the drama itself. His two shots, his apparent admissions to the police and the doctors that he had shot her, followed by the statement that she had shot herself, had all to be explained.

He gave his evidence in a cool and collected way. Since adventurous days of his youth in South America, he had always kept an old revolver under his pillow, but had not bought any new ammunition for twenty years. He had become a terrible drinker ; so had Ruth been, even when he first met her, and he had been through hell with her. On the night in question, a few days after Ruth had come back to him, they had both been drinking heavily. She had thrown crockery and fire-irons at him when he accused her of being drunk. She threatened him, and he told her to leave his house for ever. He then went upstairs to his bedroom to fetch his revolver, intending to frighten her. He had fired wide of her to alarm her ; but he must have wounded her slightly on the arm as she lurched sideways. He did not know this at the time. He had then returned and hidden the revolver under the mattress in his bedroom, and come downstairs again. Ruth then rushed upstairs, turned everything upside down in the bedroom, in order to find the revolver. At length she found it. In fact, the bedroom was found to be in great disorder. When they met again in the dining-room, she pointed the revolver at him. He saw the hammer rising, and sprang forward to save his life. He gripped her right wrist, and, as they were struggling, the weapon went off and the girl dropped to the floor. As good fortune had it, there happened to be an expert on fire-arms among the jury as well as on counsel's benches, and it had already been established that there was a defect in this revolver, and that it could be fired without even the pulling of the trigger.

The Court listened in astonished silence. The man was acquitting himself with his own testimony, which was corroborated most convincingly by quite minor details of the evidence already given. The evidence as to the two bullets and the two wounds, as to Ruth's locking of the door, the disarranged bedroom, all fitted into the prisoner's main story like small pieces of a Chinese puzzle. Lawrence demonstrated on his own wrist how the revolver, when the wrist of the holder was gripped by another hand, would automatically point upwards. The judge then ordered him to stand on the bench near the jury, and to demonstrate with his clerk what had happened on the night of December 29th. Lawrence did this three times within a foot of the jury, and each time the experiment was successful. Whilst he was doing this, to those who know the procedure of murder trials, a most sinister and dramatic interruption occurred ; happily the prisoner himself could hardly have appreciated its significance. Another murder trial had just come to a conclusion in the next court. When any prisoner is convicted of murder, the judge's chaplain must rise and say " Amen " when the judge has completed the awful liturgy of the death sentence with the words " May the Lord have mercy on your soul." The judge in the next court had now to assume the black cap, but the chaplain was listening to the Lawrence trial by the side of Mr. Justice Jelf ; and, while Lawrence was performing the demonstration on which his life literally depended, a messenger arrived to ask for the chaplain's presence in the next court : so for a moment the trial was interrupted.

The judge had really been hostile to the prisoner at first, but was won over completely by his demonstration. " It shows," he said thoughtfully, after it had taken place, " that it was possible to be done." It was noteworthy that henceforward he addressed the prisoner as " Mr." Lawrence, and not " Lawrence," as he had done before.

The fifth day was occupied by speeches. Marshall Hall made one of the most dramatic and masterly orations of his life, and for the first time performed the dramatic exhibition which came to be known as " Hall's scales of Justice act." He began by admitting, and almost making capital out of, Lawrence's previous bad character. " We are not trying this man for drink. We are not trying this man for immorality. We are not trying this man for error of judgment or human frailty. We are not trying him because, like a fool, he has left his wife and children for other women. One thing stands out in this case, and that is that his wife, in spite of the provocation, has not deserted him. When this awful trial is over, I hope there will be one verdict which you will see your way to find, a verdict of ' not guilty,' and thereby restore this man to his freedom. I trust he will make use of that freedom, and repay with that freedom the devotion of his wife, and endeavour to devote the rest of his life to making her happy, and to making amends for the misery he has caused her in the past." He drew the portrait of the drunken, jealous woman in broad, eloquent phrases. Always jealous and violent, from the moment Lawrence had turned to other women she had become mad, and when, a few days after her last return, Lawrence ordered her out of the house, she was in a frenzy. " She had taken that revolver down, knowing that her life with Lawrence was finished, and intending to finish Lawrence too. She was desperate, defiant, dangerous." Then, dealing with the final tragedy, Marshall, seeking as he always did to make each juryman put himself into the place of the prisoner, took up the revolver. " When he entered the room," he said, " he saw her pointing the revolver like this." As he spoke, he pointed the revolver straight at the jury. " He saw the hammer rising, as you may see it rising now as I pull the trigger. It was hard to pull, and it might have been that her arm was weakened by the injury of the first shot. It might have been that she was feeling the sting of that injury, and that it aroused all the worst passions in her beyond her control, and that she was then in the act of shooting him. . . ." Finally came the peroration in which he made the comparison of a trial of a man for his life with the weighing of a substance in a pair of scales. But the time-honoured simile became original and compelling with his dramatic treatment. With outstretched arms he illustrated his words by the swaying of his body and the gestures of his hands. " It may appear that the scales of Justice are first weighed on one side in favour of the prisoner, and then on the other against the prisoner. As counsel on either side puts the evidence in these two scales, I can call to my fancy a great statue of Justice holding those two scales with equally honest hands. As the jury watch the scales, they think for a moment that one scale, and then that the other, has fallen, and then again that they are so level that they cannot make up their minds which was lower or higher. Then in the one scale, in the prisoner's scale, unseen by human eye, is placed that over-balancing weight, the weight of the presumption of innocence. When the balance is so struck that you cannot tell which pan is nearest the ground, then it is your duty to remember the invisible weight of that invisible substance—the right of every man to demand the acceptance of his innocence until he is proved guilty. . . . I will leave it in your hands. Try this case upon the evidence, and upon the evidence with the help of God."

Mr. Sherwood in his reply, constantly interrupted as he was by the judge, who was now obviously in favour of an acquittal, threw over his original demand for a verdict of " murder " or nothing, and asked the jury for a verdict of " manslaughter " if they were not satisfied as to murder.

The judge summed up in favour of the prisoner, being obviously impressed by his evidence. He had been more than doubtful as to the wisdom of the Criminal Evidence Act, but in his summing up he boldly stated his conversion. " If this was the only case I had ever tried," he said, " I would be thankful because of this change in the law. Had it been that this man's mouth had been shut, I do not think he could possibly have escaped *at least* a verdict of ' manslaughter.' "

The jury retired and returned after twenty minutes. " We have carefully gone through the evidence with honest sincerity," the foreman said, " and our verdict is one of ' not guilty.' " Addressing the prisoner, Mr. Justice Jelf said, " Before I discharge you, I have to add a few words of advice to those which your brilliant counsel, I have no doubt, has already given you. You have had a most terrible lesson. . . . You have seen that your wife is ready to forgive you. . . . If you will turn over a new page in your life, you may yet have a happy time with your lawful wife and children, and then, perhaps, God will forgive you for the life you have led. . . . I earnestly trust that what I have said to you will bear fruit in your heart and in your life."

It is sad to know that Lawrence learnt very little from his troubles, and paid no heed to the kindly judge's warning. For, only three days afterwards, he was charged with a violent assault on a man in an inn at Wolverhampton. However, his acquittal was received with wild enthusiasm in the town, for Marshall Hall had not merely convinced the judge and jury, but turned the tide of public opinion, which at first had been running strongly against the drunken and immoral brewer. Thus ended, according to Marshall Hall's expressed opinion, his greatest victory in a murder trial.

.   .   .   .

Two such wonderful successes as the Wood and Lawrence cases made Marshall Hall's reputation, like that of his friend Maître Labori, international. But he gained something more substantial than mere fame by his visit to Stafford. While he had been there, he had won the youthful admiration of his junior's young clerk, Archibald Bowker. The young man was fascinated by his personality into something near to hero-worship, and made it his business to assist him and make him comfortable in every possible way. Soon afterwards, Marshall Hall was compelled to look out for a new senior clerk, and, when Bowker applied for the post, he replied with a wire asking him to come to London immediately. The result was that Marshall Hall obtained, besides one of the most efficient clerks in the Temple, an affectionate friend with real personal devotion to him, and a faithful servant who put his interests before everything else.

Mr. Justice Jelf remembered Marshall Hall's conduct of the Lawrence case, not only with admiration, but even with gratitude. He had perhaps been saved from making a grievous mistake. On his retirement from the Bench in the autumn of 1910, he wrote to Marshall, " It will be long before I forget the Stafford trial, and the reconstruction of the crime on the Bench. All good things come to you. . . . I hope you will defend Crippen, but what a task it will be ! "

In fact, Arthur Newton, as soon as he was retained for the

defence of Crippen, at once wished to offer the brief to Marshall Hall. Marshall had taken a great interest in the case, as he was acquainted with, and very much interested in, the new drug called hyoscin with which Mrs. Crippen was alleged to have been poisoned. With his quick intuition, he had formed a definite view as to the circumstances of Mrs. Crippen's death, and he was convinced that there was only one possible defence for Crippen, and that was to admit everything except the intent to murder. He thought from the very first that Crippen was an innocent man, and continued to think so until 1927. He was abroad for the long vacation, and, when he returned, the police court proceedings were already over, and a line of defence had been adopted at the police court, on Crippen's specific instructions, which would have made it quite hopeless for Marshall Hall to put forward the theory of defence which he was convinced was the truth.

The facts of this most celebrated trial are well remembered. Dr. Crippen, an amiable little medical man of middle life, came to live in England in 1900. His wife joined him : she was a handsome, flamboyant person of Polish-American birth, who had high ambitions, but no aptitude, for the stage. In 1905, they went to live at Hilldrop Crescent, in the north of London. Crippen was exceedingly generous to his wife ; her wardrobes were filled with fine clothes, and her jewel-box with expensive gems. Crippen had married her to take her away from a protector, and it is probable that she took lovers even during her married life. At any rate, at Hilldrop Crescent they had separate bed-rooms, and probably the poor little doctor was a much wronged and much tortured man during the last years of his married life, for Cora Crippen was at once a peacock and a slut. To the outside world she appeared in all her finery ; at home she kept no servant, and her husband seems to have performed what little housework was done. Then was repeated what has happened since the beginning of monogamy. The distressed husband took consolation in a romantic affection for another woman. A delicate and ailing girl came into Crippen's employment as a typist. They fell in love, and their hearts became set on each other. In the course of time she became his mistress ; yet she felt her position very bitterly, since Mrs. Crippen was nice to her, and did not know. She was a gentle and good-hearted girl, and won affection wherever she went. On January 31st, 1910, the Crippens gave a little dinner-party, and Mrs. Crippen was never seen alive again.

Dr. Crippen at once gave out that his wife had gone to America, and later that she had died from pneumonia on the voyage. But, on February 2nd, Ethel le Neve, his typist, slept at Hilldrop Crescent, and Crippen began to give her clothes and jewellery which had belonged to his wife. She wore a brooch of Mrs. Crippen's at a ball which she attended with Crippen ; some of Mrs. Crippen's friends noticed it, and began to talk. But Ethel, nevertheless, became her lover's housekeeper, and began to live with him openly at Hilldrop Crescent. In July the police interviewed Crippen, and he at once changed his story. Mrs. Crippen had left him, he now said, for another man, who was unknown to him, and she had begged him to cover up any scandal. He was exhaustively examined, and Inspector Dew carefully went with him over every part of his house, including the cellar. Nothing suspicious was found, and Crippen would probably have escaped altogether if panic had not over-come him. Inspector Dew, before dropping the matter, paid another visit to Crippen's consulting-room in order to ask a few supplementary questions, and was told that he had gone abroad. So had Miss le Neve.

Inspector Dew then made a more thorough investigation of Crippen's house, and, seeing a brick in the cellar which looked looser than the rest, he took up part of the floor and began to dig. He found there, buried in quicklime, some small pieces of flesh wrapped in an old pyjama coat marked " Jones & Co., Holloway." There was no head, no bones, nothing to indicate whether the flesh was of a man or a woman, or even whether it was human or animal. On analysis it was considered that the remains had been there several months, and in the remains was found two-sevenths of a grain of hyoscin ; Crippen had recently bought five grains of that drug. Further, on one piece of skin was found the scar of an abdominal operation which had been performed on Mrs. Crippen. This almost labelled Dew's ghastly discovery as " The Remains of Mrs. Crippen." Indeed, it was really as clear as day from the first that the remains were those of Mrs. Crippen, and that they had been mutilated and buried by her husband. Indeed, in the late stages of the trial, the delivery of the pyjama jacket in which the remains were packed was traced to Crippen's house in Hilldrop Crescent during his tenancy. All this Marshall saw, and knew that any attempt to combat these facts would be disastrous. What, then, was the more hopeful line of defence that Crippen would not adopt after Inspector Dew had raced across the Atlantic in a fast liner and arrested him and his mistress—who was dressed in boy's clothes—just as they were about to disembark and start a new life together in Canada ?

In November 1926, Marshall Hall was ill in bed, and, as he was by himself for the week-end, he asked me to spend the Saturday afternoon with him. Rarely have I spent a more enthralling afternoon. I had just been reading Lord Birkenhead's account of the trial of Ethel le Neve, and also Marshall Hall's appreciation of H. B. Irving, which appears at the commencement of the *Trial of the Wainwrights*. In the first, the author does full justice to Crippen's unselfish devotion to his mistress, and quotes his last " letter to the world " published on the eve of his execution. " In this farewell letter to the world, written as I face eternity, I say that Ethel le Neve has loved me as few women love men, and that her innocence of any crime, save that of yielding to the dictates of the heart, is absolute. . . . I give my testimony to the absolute innocence of Ethel le Neve. She put her trust in me, and what I asked her to do, she did, never doubting. . . . " Finally, Lord Birkenhead gives him a great epitaph, " He was, at least, a brave man, and a true lover." Marshall, in his appreciation, wrote : " Of one thing both Irving and I felt convinced, that if Crippen had cared to throw over the companion who was eventually arrested with him, he might have made good his escape." I was greatly interested in this statement, and asked him what lay behind it. Marshall then told me. What he said is clearly in my recollection, and it is only fair to say that my recollection differs materially from the version of Marshall's theory which appears in Mr. Filson Young's preface to the *Crippen Case*, and which is there turned down as " ingenious " but not warranted by the facts.

Hyoscin was a comparatively new drug, the potency and use of which were not universally known or appreciated among medical men in 1910. Marshall had been told of it by his father in the 'nineties. Crippen said he had been acquainted with it in his student days, and had used it for homeopathic remedies. In many of the early medical dictionaries of the century it is not mentioned ; and, indeed, it was Dr. Crippen himself who made it notorious. To-day it is widely used, and because of its powerful narcotic effects it has brought peace and forgetfulness to thousands of agonised sufferers. The British Pharmaceutical Codex for 1923 says that " it is much used as a hypnotic, especially in mania and cerebral excitement. . . it is used as an anæsthetic in operations," and by its means, " a complete surgical anæsthesia can be obtained." In a modified form it can achieve partial anæsthesia, and " the so-called ' twilight sleep ' has become popular in labour. It is not claimed that it abolishes pain, but rather that it destroys the memory of the events."

Now poor little Dr. Crippen was not a high-class physician ; he had become little more than agent for the sale of patent medicines. He was involved in a wretched but commonplace matrimonial tangle. He loved a young girl, and had lived with her in adultery for at least two years. This girl shared with her lover a pitiful and almost morbid respect for " respectability," as it was understood in Hilldrop Crescent. Meanwhile, he had to go on living with his wife, and, with his passion for Ethel le Neve, the demands made on him by his wife had become revolting. Moreover, in order to gratify the former, he probably had to take this refined and retiring girl to undesirable hotels. The whole position was loathsome to both the lovers. But he had endured it for years, and it is unlikely that this respectable and methodical little man would suddenly become a murderer without an immense stimulus, or at least without careful preparation ; yet Crippen's conduct after the " disappearance " of his wife bore all the marks of panic and improvisation. He behaved like a man telling the first lie that came into his head. His first story would not have borne the most superficial examination, and was bound to lead to detection. What, then, was the explanation ? Crippen wished for his mistress's company at night, undisturbed by the demands or suspicions of his wife.

His cheerfulness at the dinner-party on January 31st may have been accounted for by the fact that he was soon to meet his mistress. Very likely she was going to meet him in his own house. There were no servants, no one would know, if only his wife was out of the way. Crippen thought he knew how to achieve this result by a very clever method. She would be there, and she would not be there. Something of a quack, he knew a little of the marvellous and peculiar qualities of hyoscin, and resolved to administer it to his wife. It would serve two purposes ; it would render her deeply unconscious and forgetful of anything that led up to her unconsciousness ; it would also serve as an anti-aphrodisiac to this exacting woman. Very probably he had frequently used this drug on his wife to serve this double purpose, and, if so, he would have to give her ever increasing doses in order to ensure unconsciousness. " Many years after-wards," said Marshall, " I knew of a young officer who was given an overdose of hyoscin preparatory to an operation ; he slept for forty-eight hours, and his case was almost given up : in the end he unexpectedly recovered. He had not only been absolutely unconscious while under the influence of the drug, but, when he came to, he was unconscious that he had been unconscious."

Marshall Hall's theory was simple. Crippen, in order to spend the night with his paramour, whether at home or elsewhere, drugged his wife with a new and rare drug of which he knew little, and of which he had lately purchased five grains. But a little learning is a dangerous thing. To be on the safe side he gave her a large dose, which turned out to be an overdose ; or perhaps his continual dosing of her necessitated a big dose to ensure unconsciousness. No doubt it will be objected that two-sevenths of a grain was found in her body, whereas a safe dose, according to the text-books, is at most one-hundredth. But the prescriptions of the text-books presume that the drug will be injected hypodermically, which is the normal method, and thus administered it is many times more potent than if taken by the mouth, as Mrs. Crippen must have done ; of this Sir William Willcox has himself assured me. He also informed me that he has known cases where patients have died from the results of overdoses of hyoscin administered by unqualified practitioners, and that a patient constantly taking hyoscin will naturally have to be given bigger and bigger doses, as time goes on, if the purpose of the drug is to be achieved. In the morning he found his wife dead, and in a panic he made away with the remainder of the hyoscin, and with all a surgeon's skill cut up her body, rising above his inexperience with the inspiration of despair. Then, hurriedly wrapping the flesh in an old pyjama jacket of his own, he buried it in quicklime, thinking it would thus be destroyed ; as a matter of fact the quicklime had the reverse effect, and preserved the remains. Then he proceeded to write to a number of his friends a transparent tissue of lies. Crippen admitted that Miss le Neve had slept at Hilldrop Crescent on February 2nd. Might she not have slept there on one or both of the previous nights, and frequently before that, while his wife was drugged with hyoscin and unconscious ?

One witness in the case referred to Crippen at the trial as " the nicest man she ever knew," and no one could be found to say, either before or after his arrest, that he was otherwise than an honest, friendly, thoughtful, patient, unselfish, and unassuming little man. Is not this theory more consistent with the facts, and with experience in general, than the theory of murder ? Taking Lord Birkenhead's words in his defence of Miss le Neve from their context, we must all agree that " no one suddenly becomes base." At the lowest, the theory was so ingenious that it seems a thousand pities that Marshall Hall was not able to put it forward with all the passion of conviction, and with a thorough knowledge of medicine, and of the drug in question, to help him. In many of his cases he had far less than this to work upon.

It was not to be ; for Crippen gave definite instructions as to his defence. He denied any knowledge of the remains found in his cellar ; he had last seen his wife alive and well on February 1st ; she must have left him for another man unknown. From that moment his fate was sealed. Many may criticise Marshall Hall for not accepting the brief even then, bearing in mind his stated convictions on the subject of accepting briefs, especially when it was offered to him by an old client. These were, however, very exceptional circumstances. Marshall was convinced of the truth of his hypothesis, but he knew it would be worthless without the testimony of the prisoner ; the theory was absolutely inconsistent with the prisoner's instructions to his solicitor, and with the line of defence disclosed by that solicitor at the police court. Beyond a point, counsel and solicitor alike must cease to advise, and begin to obey ; and neither Marshall Hall nor Sir Alfred Tobin (who defended Crippen) could have properly imposed on him a defence with which he would have nothing to do. As Marshall Hall said himself, " Can counsel be called upon to take the responsibility of defending a man, of whose innocence he is convinced, if that man ties him down to a line of defence which that counsel knows to be a plea of ' guilty ' ? There were many members of the Bar, as able as myself, who were not handicapped by my convictions on the matter. I *could* not have defended Crippen on those lines."

" But, Marshall," I said, " why wouldn't Crippen let his advisers run your line of defence ? "

" Because he considered," he replied, " that it would have made Miss le Neve his accomplice. If she was in the house with him at the time that Mrs. Crippen lay dying or dead from a drug administered to her by Crippen, it would have been very difficult for her to escape from the charge of complicity with him. If this defence succeeded, Crippen would have been convicted of manslaughter or of administering a noxious poison so as to endanger human life, and Miss le Neve would have been embarrassed in her defence ; and, if the defence were to go wrong and he were convicted of murder, what might not happen to her at her trial ? Crippen loved Miss le Neve so tenderly and whole-heartedly that wished her to escape *all* the legal consequences of his association with her. He had, indeed, brought the tragedy upon her, but to ensure her complete scathelessness he was willing to die for her. He died with a declaration of innocence on his lips ; and, if my theory is right, he was rewarded, for Miss le Neve was very properly acquitted of any privity with the murder of Mrs. Crippen."

Marshall's medical knowledge and his romantic imagination made him an unquestioning believer in this theory, and his enthusiasm and conviction lent strength and power to his words ; and, as he sat up in bed, addressing me, his sole juryman, so passionately, about this seventeen-year-old tragedy, I began to be carried away and to see Dr. Crippen, whose very name has acquired a sinister sound, not as a sordid and cold-blooded murderer, but as a martyr and a hero of romance. I went away wondering what Marshall Hall would have made of it, in 1910, before a jury at the Central Criminal Court. The case would have been his first great poison defence, and I could not help thinking that, whatever Sir William Willcox and Sir Bernard Spilsbury might have said about hyoscin, twelve reasonable men might have preferred to believe Sir Edward Marshall Hall. " At any rate," he said, " I would not have liked to return to my little white bed with the knowledge that my verdict had sent that poor man to his doom."

CHAPTER IX

Return to Fortune

MARSHALL HALL had now more than recovered his old position at the Bar. The times were indeed very favourable to him, for by the end of 1910 there had been promotions to the Bench and to public appointments on a very large scale. The commercial, criminal, and special jury courts all lost leading figures. Over a period of months, Horace Avory, Montague Lush, Eldon Bankes, Thomas Horridge, and Thomas Scrutton became King's Bench judges, while Rufus Isaacs and John Simon became law officers. This left Sir Edward Carson and Duke as the two great commanding figures at the Common Law Bar, and Carson was preoccupied more with the burning question of Ulster than with the Bar. Marshall Hall and F. E. Smith stepped into much of the work which was released wholesale by these promotions, but Marshall must have seen with some sadness so many of his contemporaries, whom he had once outstripped, climbing into positions which he could not now hope to attain. The " front row " was already becoming denuded of men of his age and standing. Fine advocate as he was recognised to be, his stormy past was really a bar to official promotion. However, he was always enthusiastic in his congratulations to his more fortunate colleagues, and never failed to write a letter expressing his pleasure at their appointments. When Horace Avory, whom he had fought so many times from his earliest days, was made a judge, he at once wrote a letter from Normandy, where he was holiday-making.

" MY DEAR HORACE,—You will, no doubt, receive many letters of congratulation, but from no one will those congratulations be more sincere than those I now send you. . . . I am sure that the profession as a whole will be glad to have you on the Bench. I only hope that you won't find the work too hard. For, from all accounts, it is no sinecure now to be a judge of the High Court. I trust, too, that you may have good health, without which any form of honour is such an empty thing to possess. I am battling with varicose veins and villainous weather, but hope to get to Sandwich ere the end of the month. . . . Don't bother to reply to this, I know you will be swamped, but I know also that, if I may judge from the many kindnesses I have received from you in the past, you will be pleased to get a letter of sincere congratulation from

"Yours very sincerely,
"E. MARSHALL HALL."

Mr. Justice Avory replied :

"MY DEAR MARSHALL,—It was a great pleasure to me to receive your letter of congratulation. I appreciate its sincerity and hope you will continue to prosper, and that you will not find me more *trying* on the Bench than you have found me at the Bar.

"Yours sincerely,
"HORACE E. AVORY."

It is difficult to imagine, within the bounds of one learned profession, two men of more different gifts. Respect and admiration for each other's powers had been forced on them by an experience of professional antagonism lasting for a quarter of a century ; further, this respect and admiration had developed, as so often happens between hard fighters constantly in opposition, into a secret affection and sympathy between them, the most vigilant and learned prosecutor and the most brilliant defender of the time. Each approached and carried out his work in the spirit of a high public duty. Yet few guessed the true facts which this correspondence reveals, and public opinion credited them with a personal antipathy for which it was not difficult to find much superficial evidence in the years to come.

In 1910 Marshall recovered his seat in Parliament. Two years previously, Mr. F. E. Smith had persuaded him to take over the Conservative cause in the East Toxteth division of Liverpool, which had been abandoned by Mr. Austin Taylor. The latter had been returned as an unopposed Conservative in 1906, and had soon afterwards crossed the floor of the House. Marshall won the seat by the narrow margin of 285 in

January 1910, but increased his majority to 966 in the December election of the same year. It is worthy of note that his main refrain throughout these two elections was the peril from Germany. He said that war with Germany was inevitable, and he had better means of knowledge than most members of Parliament. " Germany's boast," he said, in one of these Liverpool speeches, " is that, when the moment is ripe, in the opinion of their Government of the day, to advance the interests of their country they will do so regardless of the consequences to those they propose to attack. They will think only of their own ends, and my warning is ' Wake up England ; wake up Lancashire. . . . ' If we do not, we shall be one more victim to be dragged after the chariot of German magnificence."

Although elected to the House of Commons, Marshall Hall took no greater part in its debates than he had done ten years before, in spite of repeated requests from his friends in the constituency to speak " upon some major question." But nothing induced him to work hard in the House of Commons, and by 1913 he had already announced his intention of not offering himself again for re-election.

In November 1910 his leading position in the profession was acknowledged by his election as a Bencher of the Inner Temple. Sir John Simon and Lord Robert Cecil were called to the bench on the same night. Hereafter, " dining at the bench " became one of the greatest pleasures of his life, and his expert services were utilised by his brother Benchers in compiling a catalogue of their silver plate.

Marshall Hall's life after 1908 was an extraordinarily interesting one till his death. He lived from sensation to sensation, and human nature assumed the most extraordinary patterns for his observation. His practice was most varied. He still went on circuit, and on one occasion at Cambridge he defended a young man of great ability who had been charged with winning money at cards from unwary undergraduates by dishonest means, making use of a beautiful girl as a decoy. He was a charming person, a real " gentleman crook " of detective romance, and a man of genuine talent ; his name was Vernon Cecil Ellingham Musgrave. He absconded from his bail, and had to be brought back from France under extradition. Like

Wood, he was a clever artist with a strong sense of humour, and his sketches of the personalities on the voyage and in court are quite brilliant. He really contrived to enjoy his enforced journey and detention. Marshall Hall defended him without success, but the teetotum and dice found in his rooms were so ingenious in their contrivance that Marshall begged them for his museum of criminal curiosities. Indeed, during the speech for the prosecution, Marshall could not resist the temptation of spinning this teetotum again and again. The Lord Chief Justice thought so highly of Musgrave's charm and abilities that he gave him only nine months' imprisonment, and also sent for him for a personal interview after the trial. " Now, young man," he said, " it seems such a pity that you should waste yourself in this way. You have real abilities—why don't you settle down, and make good ? You can, you know."

" How much do you make in your present job ? " said the young man, unabashed.

" The State gives me eight thousand a year," said old Lord Alverstone, with a smile.

" I make twice that already," the prisoner is said to have observed. But the Lord Chief Justice was right. Not regarding the wisdom of the old judge, he eventually, his charms and his reputation maturing, sank from grandiose to quite insignificant frauds, and many years afterwards, after quite a gallant war record, he came before Mr. St. John Raikes, K.C., as chairman of Quarter Sessions—the very man who, as counsel, had prosecuted him to conviction at Cambridge—for a series of cruel and petty thefts. For these he was given five years' penal servitude.

One of the most amazing civil cases of Marshall's life was fought in 1910. He appeared for a London doctor, a physician of wealth and skill, who had been in practice for thirty years. This worthy gentleman became acquainted with a fascinating little lady, who called herself " Madame Cresbron," but whose real name was Pesnel. Her charm is vouched for by the fact that, after being sentenced to prison for five or six terms, she succeeded in marrying the governor of a gaol ! The *juge d'instruction* in Paris said of her, " It is a merit we must recognise in her, that in these last swindles, after an experience of twenty

years, she has attained perfection." This accomplished lady,
when she met the estimable doctor, had two irons in the fire—
marriage brokage and a marvellous invention. She introduced
French gentlemen to Anglo-Saxon heiresses for the purpose of
matrimony. In consideration of her introductions, the gentlemen subsidised, in large sums, her new process for sterilising
milk ! She used the innocent doctor's house in London for the
purposes of her introductions, and two French gentlemen went
thither, with the most honourable intentions in the world, to
meet " Miss Northcliffe " and " Miss Mary Smith," both "huge
heiresses "; they were told by Mme. Cresbron that the doctor
was the girls' guardian. Shortly afterwards the doctor went to
stay with M. and Mme. Cresbron in their luxurious mansion at
Versailles. As he was sitting writing letters one evening, M.
Cresbron shot him from behind, and wounded him slightly in
the head. The excuse given was that the doctor had wickedly
assaulted Mme. Cresbron, and that her " husband " was therefore jealous. The doctor had not assaulted Madame ; Cresbron
may or may not have been jealous, but he certainly was not her
husband. Adding insult to injury, the French police arrested
the doctor for complicity in the lady's frauds. He at once
applied for bail, and wrote a cheque to his bank, the Crédit Lyonnais, in order to obtain funds. Owing to a mistake, they dis-
honoured the cheque, and the unfortunate English doctor was
incarcerated for some time in a French gaol. He now sued the
Crédit Lyonnais for damages, and, after eloquent speeches by
Marshall Hall and Rufus Isaacs, and a pithy summing up by
Mr. Justice Darling, the jury awarded him £200.

.   .   .   .

Very different from the amiable little Dr. Crippen was the
insurance agent, Frederick Henry Seddon. None of the circumstances which explained and extenuated Crippen's conduct
appeared in the latter's case, nor was there any such gentleness
or unselfishness in his character to excite pity or sympathy.

One day, a very young solicitor in north London, aged twenty-
two, whose name had only just appeared on the roll, had a piece
of luck ; a new client called on Mr. T. W. Saint of Islington.
The new client was a superintendent of the London and Manchester Industrial Assurance Company, and lived in the same

street. He had in his hand a summons to attend and give evidence at an inquest. It was all very awkward ; an " old girl " who had been his lodger had suddenly died in his house a month or two ago ; her body had been exhumed, and it appeared that poison had been found in her remains. Would Mr. Saint represent him at the inquest ? Mr. Saint, very young himself, had recently briefed a very young counsel, Mr. Gervais Rentoul, in a country case. Although the fee was only one guinea, Rentoul had taken a great deal of trouble, and Saint rewarded him with the brief for the Seddons at the inquest. During the progress of the inquest, Seddon and his wife were arrested, and Rentoul represented them both throughout the police court proceedings. They were committed to trial for murder, and the case became, not only the great sensation of the time, but deeply interesting as a scientific enquiry. Obviously a leader had to be briefed. " Who shall we have ? " asked Walter Saint. " You can have any leader you like."

" Oh, if that's the case," said his young counsel reverently, " I think we ought to have Marshall Hall."

For Marshall had now reached a unique position at the Bar : as a defender of prisoners on the capital charge, it was now recognised that he was second to none, and his name had acquired a high prestige. In this case, at any rate, no better choice could have been made. For he had a knowledge of scientific medicine unequalled by any member of the Bar ; it was a store of knowledge upon which he had had, as yet, no occasion to draw in a capital case.

So Marshall Hall was briefed in his first great poison defence through the choice of a very " white-wigged " admirer, who, in turn, had won this golden opportunity by doing a young solicitor a favour. It was decided better to leave Marshall Hall, in effect, to lead for the defence for both prisoners, though Mrs. Seddon was nominally defended separately by Rentoul. Marshall Hall had as juniors Mr. R. Dunstan and Mr. Wellesley Orr. On its scientific side, Marshall was enthralled, but after reading the papers he became very unhappy and depressed about the personal aspect of the case. " This is the blackest case I've ever been in," he observed at the first consultation.

This pessimism and lack of faith in his client at the very

outset was almost unique in the history of the great defender. He would have to conduct this case without that passionate personal belief in his man's innocence which had carried him through so many of his trials. But this did not affect his devotion to the great task before him. He returned all other work, and could think of nothing but the Seddon case. In the many anxious consultations, he repeated again and again, " Remember, two people's lives depend upon us." He said to Saint, " If ever you want to see me, come—night or day, I shall be at home to see you." He went into training like an athlete for a race and a student for a fellowship examination, going to bed early and saturating his mind with works on the scientific questions involved in the case.

If Seddon was guilty, the case was certainly an exceedingly black one. For there was no great overmastering passion, no sudden, mad impulse, no long, harrowing tragedy, no bitter provocation to excuse this sordid crime, if crime there had been. Mere greed of gold had driven the man to it. The accused was now forty years old, and had for twenty years served his insurance company with efficiency and credit, rising from the very lowest rung to his present post of trust and responsibility. He was a hard taskmaster, disliked by his subordinates, but his credit stood high with his employers. He had married a North-Country woman, who had borne him five children ; he had been an eloquent lay preacher ; and was quite a light in the Masonic world. Owing to great thrift, he had a little money put away : his income amounted to about £400 a year. Some of his savings had been invested in a house at 63 Tollington Park, in which, not being able to find a tenant, he decided to reside himself, using the basement as his office and the top floor as a separate flat for lodgers. So far, nothing was known against Mr. Seddon, except, perhaps, an excessive devotion to money-making, and much to his credit. In his little world he was no doubt regarded as a pillar of society and a coming man.

In response to his advertisement during July 1910, a middle-aged spinster of forty-eight years, named Eliza Barrow, came to lodge on his top floor ; she brought with her a little boy named Ernest Grant, whom she had practically adopted, and a married couple, a Mr. and Mrs. Hook, who were related to him. Miss

Barrow was devoted to the little boy, and the Hooks were to be allowed to live rent free in her rooms. Very soon a quarrel occurred between Miss Barrow and the Hooks, and Seddon gave them notice on Miss Barrow's behalf.

Miss Barrow was now left alone at the Seddons' with the little boy. She became very depressed and worried : at the best of times she was an extraordinary woman of quarrelsome and offensive habits. She had stayed, immediately before her arrival at the Seddons', with some cousins of her own called Vonderahe, and, when residing there, she had been known to spit in her hostess's face. Her chief characteristics were slovenliness, parsimony, and love of gold. She was a real miser : she loved to keep bank-notes and golden coins in her possession, and hoarded hundreds of pounds in this way. Her chief interest in life was her little inherited fortune of about £3,000 capital value ; but what little natural affection was left in her she gave to little Ernest Grant. Her money was invested in India Stock, and in the lease of a public house. The India Stock had lately depreciated considerably, and the Liberal policy of licensing and taxation threatened her public house. Seddon discovered that these worries were preying upon the old maid's mind, and she soon found him a very plausible and efficient man of business, as indeed he was. Seddon, as an insurance monger, considered that Miss Barrow's life was not a good one to insure ; but, conversely, an excellent one on which to grant an annuity ; and, after she had lived with him for twelve months, he persuaded her to make over her entire fortune to him in return for an annuity of £150 a year or thereabouts. Miss Barrow, as her relatives said, was a " hard nut to crack," and no doubt considered that she had made a good bargain, as she thus obtained about £30 more a year from Seddon than she could have wrung from an insurance company or the Post Office. Seddon paid her the annuity punctually until September 1911, usually in gold, but the poor lady had further financial worries. The Birkbeck Bank trouble caused her acute anxiety ; perhaps she talked the matter over with Seddon. At any rate, in company with Mrs. Seddon, she went to the London and Finsbury Savings Bank, and drew out £216 of her savings in gold, and took it home. After her death, Seddon said that he had raised objections to her storing so much gold in his house, and that Miss Barrow had replied, " I know what to do with it."

On September 1st, Miss Barrow was taken ill, and Dr. Sworn, the Seddons' family physician, found her to be suffering from acute diarrhœa and sickness. As the next few days went by, Miss Barrow became worse, and admittedly certain chemical fly-papers, soaked in water, were used in her sickroom to destroy the flies that buzzed in extraordinary numbers round the bed of the invalid, attracted by the pungent odour of the sickroom. Her selfishness and eccentricity were shown by the fact that she insisted on the little boy, Ernest, sleeping in the same bed with her during her illness. She was a troublesome patient, and refused to take her medicine. A new one was prescribed, which Seddon on one occasion induced her to take. Mrs. Seddon nursed her attentively, and Miss Barrow told the doctor that she would far rather be looked after by the Seddons than go to hospital ; but, though she " dictated " a will to Seddon, which she signed, leaving her personal effects (all she now had to leave) to Ernest Grant and his little sister, with Seddon as executor, the Seddons did not take her illness very seriously ; for, on September 13th, Seddon's sister and his niece came to stay in the house, and he himself went to the Marlborough Theatre. He came back late with a story that he had been cheated of sixpence by the box-office clerk. This was very typical of the man. At about 11.30, the little boy said that " Chickie," by which name he knew Miss Barrow, wanted Mrs. Seddon. The wretched woman had crawled out of bed, and was sitting on the floor in agony. " I am dying," she said. During the night the little boy was sent to a separate room, and Mrs. Seddon sat by the lodger's bed, while Seddon sat on the landing outside, reading a paper, smoking a pipe, and occasionally fetching himself a drink from downstairs. At 6.30, Miss Barrow began to breathe heavily and died. Seddon, as executor, immediately began to search for her money ; but, according to his own account, he found only £4 10s. 0d. in her cash-box, and £5 10s. 0d. hidden in a drawer. In the morning, Seddon advised Dr. Sworn of her death, and, without a visit, the latter gave him a certificate that Miss Barrow had died of epidemic diarrhœa. Seddon paid a visit to the undertaker, and, although in Miss Barrow's papers was a document showing that she had a right to be buried in a family vault at Kensal Green, he arranged for her to be buried for an inclusive fee of £4 in a common grave. Indeed, he accepted a commission of 12*s*. 6*d*. from the undertaker for introducing the business. Meanwhile, Ernest had been packed off to Southend, and no relatives of Miss Barrow's received any notification from Seddon, although the Vonderahes, her first cousins, lived, to Seddon's knowledge, in the near neighbourhood. Seddon afterwards claimed to have written to them, and certainly kept a " carbon " copy of such a letter. The corpse was removed from the house that day ; Mrs. Seddon ordered a wreath of her own design, and kissed the poor dead woman's face. Seddon took round to a jeweller's a watch which Miss Barrow had " presented " to Mrs. Seddon, to have the name of her mother removed from it. Moreover, he attended to his business on the day of Miss Barrow's death, and was seen by two of his subordinate canvassers to be counting out quantities of gold. He took a bag of gold, and said to one of them, as a joke, " Smith, here's your wages." However, the strain of Miss Barrow's death and of overwork had told on him, and, at the end of September, Seddon and his family joined Ernest Grant at Southend for a fortnight's holiday.

Meanwhile, the Vonderahes had begun to talk, and, when they discovered in a personal interview that all their cousin's money had been made over to Seddon in return for an annuity, they drew the most unfavourable conclusions. The body was exhumed, and Sir William Willcox found, on a careful scientific analysis, that the corpse contained two and a half grains of arsenic. An inquest was held, and Seddon was required to give evidence. It was then that he consulted Mr. Saint, and told him that the " old girl " must have drunk some of the water in which the fly-papers had been soaked. " Oh," said Mr. Saint, " you can't buy poisonous things like that, can you, at an ordinary chemist's ? " (In fact, each fly-paper contained enough arsenic at least to kill one person.) " Can't you ? " said Seddon. " You can get them at any chemist's " ; and Mrs. Seddon sent her little daughter, Maggie, round to the shop of a Mr. Price to prove it. When she gave her name, the chemist refused to supply her. Meanwhile, she had been closely watched by the police, who knew that another chemist in the neighbourhood, Mr.

Walter Thorley, had supplied a packet of these papers to a fair-haired girl on August 26th. Thorley was taken to the police station and identified Margaret Seddon as the girl who had made the August purchase. Seddon had been arrested on December 4th, and on his arrest he had made a very curious statement which did not at all help him. " Absurd," he said. " What a terrible charge, wilful murder ! It is the first of our family that have ever been accused of such a crime. Are you going to arrest my wife as well ? Have they found arsenic in the body ? "

The trial came on at the Old Bailey on March 4th, 1912. In accordance with the custom in poison trials at the Old Bailey, the Attorney-General himself came down to lead for the Crown. The holder of that office was now Marshall's old friend Sir Rufus Isaacs. With him were Muir, Rowlatt (soon to be a judge), and Travers Humphreys, surely as strong a combination as has ever appeared at the Old Bailey. The Crown had indeed brought down their heavy guns against the two wretched people in the dock, and in truth they had not miscalculated. Seddon himself was a man of great ability, and all the Attorney-General's powers of penetrating enquiry were needed to break down his facile fencing. After his exhaustive and masterly opening, Marshall whispered to a colleague, " They're all out for a conviction, aren't they ? "

This trial, the longest capital case in which Marshall was ever engaged, lasted for ten days, and was remarkable for two great forensic duels, in which the combatants were well matched. Until the trial was over there were no very dramatic incidents such as characterised the Yarmouth or the Camden Town cases ; it was a hard, dogged fight—question and answer, argument for argument, day after day.

The first great duel was a scientific one. The theory of the prosecution, supported by the expert evidence of Sir William Willcox, was that Miss Barrow had died of " acute " arsenical poisoning, that is, a fatal dose administered within twenty-four hours of death ; and that the only people who had the opportunity of administering such a dose were the Seddons. For this contention evidence of motive was obviously relevant. The defence was twofold ; negative and positive. The negative defence, which had great cogency, was that the prosecution rested entirely on indirect evidence ; the second, that Miss Barrow had died of epidemic diarrhœa, as the doctor had certified, perhaps aggravated by " chronic " arsenical poisoning, or arsenic taken for a long period of time before death. The defence also kept in the background, as a possibility, the alternative theory of suicide.

Now, if Marshall Hall could prove that Miss Barrow died, not of acute, but of chronic arsenical poisoning, Seddon was as good as saved, as it was admitted that such taking of arsenic over a prolonged period might reasonably aggravate the effects of a violent attack of epidemic diarrhœa. The evidence by which the prosecution stood or fell on this point was that of Sir William Willcox, the Home Office analyst. Now, calculation of the total quantity of arsenic found in the body was based upon the results of a scientific experiment, which had never before been brought forward as evidence in a court of law. Whereas in two component parts of the body, viz. the liver and the intestines, it was practicable to *weigh* the arsenic found in the body, it was not practicable to weigh that found in the other more widely distributed parts. In the liver and the intestines, by a process of weighing, ·63, or well over half, of a grain of arsenic was found. Indeed, over a quarter of a fatal dose was found, by a simple process of weighing, in those organs alone. Two grains of arsenic make a fatal dose, and it was therefore necessary to make further researches to bring home the case against the prisoner. Arsenic is a poison which very rapidly spreads throughout the whole body, and it necessarily follows, to any mind conversant with medicine that, if so much arsenic was present in the liver and the intestines, it was present elsewhere. But it was not practicable to ascertain, by weighing, a substance so widely distributed, and Sir William had recourse to Marsh's test, a chemical experiment by which arsenic is extracted from a minute specimen of a part of the body in the form of a gas, and deposited on the surface of a tube, technically called a " mirror." For instance, from a minute part of the stomach a minute proportion of arsenic is found. The minute portion of arsenic is multiplied proportionately to the total weight of the stomach as compared with the minute part of the stomach analysed by

Marsh's test. In this way the total amount of arsenic found in the whole stomach is ascertained. Thus all the main component parts of the body, stomach, bone, muscle, etc., were analysed in this way, and the total arsenic found in the whole body, by weighing in the case of the liver and the intestines, and by Marsh's test as regards the rest, was 2·01 grains. Tiny quantities were found in the skin, the nails, and the hair, but these were not counted. Now 2·01 grains was enough for a fatal dose, but arsenic, being a poison which is very quickly expelled from the system, Dr. Willcox estimated that at least 5 grains of arsenic had been administered to Miss Barrow, within a short time before her death, to leave 2·01 grains therein after death.

This experiment was no doubt sound, and even conservative, in its solution ; but it is one thing for a scientist to prove to his own satisfaction that, for obvious scientific reasons and by an elaborate scientific experiment, 5 grains must have been administered to the dead woman shortly before death, and another thing to convince a sensible British jury as to the truth of this theory, when only ·63 of a grain, or less than a third of a fatal dose, had been found in the body by the only rational and intelligible method, that of weighing. None knew this better than Marshall Hall, and he attacked the whole experiment. He first made Sir William admit that any initial error made in the experiment itself would be multiplied hundreds, or, in the case of some parts of the body, thousands of times in the calculation which followed it. Having established this, he made an excellent point : the muscle, one of the largest component parts of the body, two-fifths of the whole, in Willcox's calculation, contains a greater proportion of water than any of the other parts. But the corpse of Miss Barrow, in the ordinary process of decay, had shrunk from ten stone odd, her weight when alive, to something round about four stone at the time of exhumation. Now water is the first substance in a corpse to evaporate ; therefore the weight of the muscle, being so largely composed of water, would decrease much more quickly than the other parts. But Willcox had used as his basis of calculation that the muscle was two-fifths of the weight of the whole body, and this would only be true for a short time after death, owing to the rapid evaporation of water. The vital question was then put.

" And I am sure it was an oversight—I mean—I may be wrong—but in making this calculation you have made no allowance whatever for the loss of water ? "—" No, I have not."

Marshall had thus established a great deal : he had successfully assailed the scientific experiment in an important particular, and Englishmen always appreciate the spectacle of science confounded on its own ground. Much had already been achieved when he passed to a simpler point, a stronger one and more easily comprehended.

Among the abundant literature which he had been perusing for the purposes of this case was the report of the Royal Commission on Arsenic, convened at the beginning of the century as a result of a widespread epidemic of arsenical poisoning arising from beer-drinking. Now Marshall Hall had in the forefront of his mind every detail of the conclusions of this commission ; Sir William Willcox, on the other hand, had them stored in the back of his memory, but had not read the report for some time. From a wide examination of cases the commission had reported this : that arsenic does not penetrate even into the " proximal " hair (that is, hair nearest the scalp) unless taken by the person affected some weeks before, and does not penetrate to the " distal " hair (the hair away from the roots) unless the person affected has taken arsenic at a considerably distant period—months, perhaps years, ago. For the arsenic remains in the hair as it grows ; and, the hair growing about five or six inches a year, it is possible to compute how long ago the arsenic was taken by the distance it is away from the scalp in the case of a woman with long hair. Now, Sir William Willcox had examined a portion of Miss Barrow's hair of about twelve inches in length. Very innocently, Marshall asked him first about the proximal, then about the distal, ends of the hair.

" In the proximal end of the hair you found one eighthundredth of a milligram ? "—" Yes."

" What did you find in the distal end of the hair ? "—" One three-thousandth—about a quarter as much," replied Sir William, with a smile at being asked about so small a quantity.

But the questions were not innocent : if arsenic was found in the ends of the hair, as Marshall went on to prove slowly, question by question, then Miss Barrow must have taken arsenic weeks ago, months ago, even years ago, before she ever went to live with the Seddons ; and, if this was so, the defence had as good as won, as the jury, with Willcox's admissions in their ears, would certainly prefer the theory of the defence, that the poor lady had died of epidemic diarrhœa, aggravated by chronic arsenical poisoning, rather than the theory of the prosecution that she had died of acute arsenical poisoning, administered by the Seddons. When everything was prepared, Marshall obtained these answers from Dr. Willcox, which were indeed a triumph for his painstaking advocacy.

" Is the finding of the arsenic in the hair corroborative of acute arsenical poisoning, or of chronic arsenic taking ? "— " If arsenic is found in the hair it indicates that probably the arsenic had been taken for some period."

" I am sure you will give me a fair answer. Apart from all other symptoms, or any other questions, if you only find arsenic in the hair, you would take that as being a symptom of a prolonged course of arsenic ? "—" Of a course of arsenic over some period."

" And the minimum period would be something about three months ? "—" I think that."

" In the proximal portion, but . . . you would not expect to find it in the distal ends in three months, would you ? "—" Not in large amounts."

" Not in the amount you have got here . . . ? This minute quantity in the distal end might possibly mean some arsenic might have been taken, perhaps a year or more ago. . . . A year ago or more ? "—" More than a year ago."

Here, I think, Marshall Hall should have sat down. If he had, Seddon might well have gone free, and Marshall, by sheer scholarship and skill in using it, would have achieved a marvellous forensic triumph. " I had not got that part of the report in my mind," Sir William told me. " He very nearly tied me up. I don't think I've ever been so nearly trapped as I was then— it was extraordinarily clever of him." But, unfortunately—or, rather, fortunately for the ends of justice—Marshall went on driving the point home so that the jury could not possibly mistake the importance of the admissions, and all this time his learned and brilliant antagonist was thinking hard. " He is quite right," thought Willcox ; " if the arsenic got into the hair through the system—but I am certain that the woman died of *acute* arsenical poisoning, which would be surprising if she was a confirmed taker of arsenic. Could the arsenic have got into the hair by any other means ? "

Before Marshall had finished giving the famous analyst a lesson in analysis, Willcox had thought of the true explanation. Miss Barrow's long hair had become contaminated by the blood-stained fluid which was dispersed all over the coffin, and in this way had become tainted with arsenic. Before he left the box he made a discreet suggestion that this was the true explanation. Marshall poured scorn on this as an afterthought, as indeed it was. " Did you not wash the hair with all care, before making the experiment ? " he asked.

That was late on the Thursday afternoon. The case now literally hung by a hair. Willcox quietly went home and thought more about the matter. Then he paid a visit to his hospital, and begged a long length of hair from one of his fair patients. This lovely strand of hair was then soaked in the blood-stained fluid from Miss Barrow's coffin, in which the latter's hair had been found matted at her exhumation. The experiment was then entrusted to another medical man, Dr. Webster ; the hair was washed just as Miss Barrow's had been, and it was found to contain arsenic just as Miss Barrow's had done. On the following Tuesday, Sir William was recalled to give evidence as to this experiment. The experiment was a simple one with a successful result, which any juryman could appreciate, and the effect of Marshall's brilliant cross-examination was gone.

The other duel in the trial—and it was a real duel—was that fought between the Attorney-General and the male prisoner. Seddon was an exceedingly vain man, with a great belief in his own abilities. When he heard that the Attorney-General himself, the great Sir Rufus Isaacs, was coming down to prosecute him, far from being alarmed, he was delighted, and from that moment made up his mind that he would cross swords with him. Marshall Hall from the date of his first interview with Seddon had been strongly opposed to calling him as a witness. " If the evidence does not convict this man," he said, " his conceit will." He told Mr. Saint that he must on no account prevent Seddon from going into the witness box, but that he must warn him in the clearest way of the dangers. Just before the case for the prosecution had closed, he himself went over to the dock, and gave Seddon a final warning. But the prisoner was determined. He had heard Rufus Isaacs's masterly opening, and thought that he, Seddon, could easily defeat him. He was, in fact, longing for the fray. So, after Marshall Hall had called two witnesses to prove that Seddon was in the habit of keeping large sums in gold in his house, Seddon went into the box on the afternoon of the fifth day of the trial. For over two hours on that day he was examined by Marshall Hall, and made a clear and admirable witness. Finally, late in the morning, he stated, " I never purchased arsenic in my life, in any shape or form. I never administered arsenic. I never advised, directed, or instructed the administration of arsenic, that I swear."

The Attorney-General rose to cross-examine. The first two questions could not have been more skilful, and dramatic in their effect, spoken as they were in a cool, courteous tone.

" Miss Barrow lived with you from the 26th of July, 1910, till the morning of the 14th of September, 1911 ? "—" Yes."

" Did you like her? "—" Did I like her? " echoed the prisoner.

" Yes, that is the question." Seddon now hesitated, for the only time in the whole of his ordeal, obviously unprepared for this searching question. The question put him in a dilemma : if he said " Yes," he would be patently a hypocrite; the dreadful meanness of his conduct after her death, culminating in the pauper's funeral which he gave her, would tell even more heavily against him than otherwise. If he said " No," he would be strongly prejudiced at the outset. After some hesitation he gave the best answer possible under the circumstances.

" She was not a woman that you could be in love with, but I deeply sympathised with her."

" During the time that she was living with you at your house did you advise her on her financial affairs ? "—" Certainly I advised her."

Then the Attorney-General went through the details of Miss Barrow's little fortune, and made the prisoner admit them.

" She came to you, then, with India Three and a half per cent.
Stock bringing in one pound a week, the leasehold property
bringing in one hundred and twenty pounds a year, and over
two hundred pounds in the Finsbury Savings Bank; that is
right? "—" Yes."

" She remained in your house from that date, 26th of July,
1910, till the 14th of September, 1911, when you examined
all that there was to see of the property that was left? "—
" Yes."

" On the 14th of September, 1911, when she died, was all the
property that was found of hers a sum of ten pounds in gold,
and furniture, jewellery, and other belongings to the value of
sixteen pounds, fourteen shillings, and sixpence? "—"According
to the inventory taken by Mr. Gregory, a reputed auctioneer
and appraiser, it was sixteen pounds odd." The skill and effect
of these questions needs no comment.

For the rest of the sixth day, and for the greater part of the
seventh day, Seddon stood in the box under the patient, relentless, but increasingly intense light of the Attorney-General's
enquiries, all the more deadly because of the unfailing courtesy
of that beautiful voice. At a dinner of his community that celebrated his return from India, I heard an admirable compliment paid
to Lord Reading. Sir Herbert Samuel had compared him to
Rufus Curtius, a great proconsul of the Emperor Tiberius. " I
am glad," said Lord Merrivale in a later speech, " that even in
those days there was a Rufus—courteous." And courteous he
certainly was to the wretched man Seddon, even in his fiercest
questions. He always addressed the prisoner as " Mr. Seddon."

Seddon had a very quick and agile mind: at first his clever
parries and retorts were very effective. He had an explanation
and a reason for everything. But gradually his very cleverness
and his inhuman coolness began to disgust the jury. His performance in the witness box makes a strange contrast to that of
Robert Wood. Wood, innocent, made a bad, futile witness, and
did not seem to understand the points made against him.
Seddon, guilty, made an excellent witness, and missed nothing.
Yet Wood, by his very incompetence in the box, made an impression of innocence on the jury: Seddon, with all his surprising competence, by his skilful quips and retorts, gave all his

Important. P.S. Family affairs. If the Prosecution have investigated & learnt of all family quarrels & disagreements between myself & wife they may decline to use such information as it would undoubtedly be very prejudicial to them in this case, how could they reconcile this statement that my wife would administer my influence over her in the first place. So relations to my wife & always visitors on her own way & fright against another they know she would not murder my aunt only they know she would not (or any poison her,) Shews me if she knew I was guilty of the crime. I am not under my influence unless she had a wife to do so & was to keep this poison, yet what pain can the Prosecution shew she had motive to secretly poison my wife (since the death of the deceased) to my wife? No! She had no motive nothing more than she had previously, therefore there is no motive against her, & further I would not instruct myself on the crime of my wife on such a serious charge as I have always considered her incapable of such any knowledge against me for when guilty. She would surely admit me I say all manner of things against me to quite sympathy for herself in her hysterical temper, there her family keep so prejudiced against me. Therefore there can be any compact between us in this case.

What evidence had the Coroner Jury that "Annie" had been feloniously administered? There has been no such evidence.

AUTOGRAPH NOTE

from Seddon from the dock to his Counsel—during the course of the trial

hearers a secret conviction of his guilt. Only towards the end did he break out and lose his composure. When he was asked as to the counting of the gold on the day of Miss Barrow's death, he showed his first sign of anger.

" The prosecution are suggesting that I am dealing with the deceased woman's gold. That I should bring it down from the top of the house to the bottom, into the office in the presence of my assistants, and count it up—is it feasible ? . . . I am not a degenerate. That would make it out that I was a greedy, inhuman monster. . . . The suggestion is scandalous."

Seddon did himself more good by this angry outburst than by all his cool cleverness, but he ruined its effect by adding, with a sarcastic smile, " I would have all day to count the money."

He again became very indignant when Mr. Attorney came to the statement made by him on his arrest, when he was alleged to have said, " Are you going to arrest my wife too ? " He said the explanation of this was that the officer had first said, " You will see your wife at the station." " That," he said, " I swear before God, is the words that took place, and I have been waiting the opportunity to get into this box for to relate the true words that were spoken on this occasion."

" All the statements," commented the Attorney-General quietly, " that you are making are statements before God."

Little by little, Sir Rufus gained ground, and for all his cleverness the soul of Seddon was laid bare before the Court, if soul it could be called ; for its god was gold, and his mean, calculating character, which obviously cared for nothing but Seddon and his worldly possessions, aroused the contempt and loathing of almost everybody in court. Here was a man who would do anything for gain. " Never," said an onlooker, " have I seen a soul stripped so naked as that."

Mrs. Seddon went into the box and was faced by the same ordeal. It was she who had taken Miss Barrow's bank-notes to be cashed, and had endorsed them with a false name and address. She explained lamely that she had never cashed notes before, and that she did not like to give her own name.

" Did you think it quite an ordinary thing to write your name at the back, or rather to write a false name at the back, when you were asked for your name ? "—" No, it never struck me. . . . I never thought there was any harm in it whatever."

She was a harassed woman who had once been pretty : now she was aged beyond her thirty-four years by being Seddon's drudge for so long. She was obviously deeply moved and broken by the tragedy of her position. Even in her examination she broke down when she was asked about Miss Barrow's death scene. She was, nevertheless, able to describe it in detail till she reached the stage where her husband had " lifted up her eyelid and said——" At this point she began to sob helplessly. " I cannot say it. . . . I don't like to say it."

" Never mind," said her young counsel, " say it low."

" He said," she whispered, " ' Good God, she's dead.' "

She was one of those people who have a nervous habit of smiling. She was asked about the last dreadful night, when Miss Barrow had called out, " I'm dying," and she had taken no steps to fetch a doctor.

" Did you tell your husband about it when he came in ? "— " Yes, I did," answered Mrs. Seddon, and with tragic inappropriateness she gave one of her nervous smiles.

" Did you smile at it ? " asked the Attorney-General sternly.— " Well, I have a usual way of smiling at almost everything, I think. I cannot help it. It is my way. No matter how serious anything was, I think I would smile. I cannot help it."

When she crept back to the dock, poor, miserable, forlorn woman, she had created an impression on the jury—which foreshadowed an acquittal—as a woman who had been used and broken by the cruel, cold, mean man her husband, and who counted for nothing in his life but as a tool and a household drudge. Quite unobtrusively the truth, for all her loyalty throughout the trial, slipped out. " He never used to take any notice when I said anything to him ; he always had other things to think of. . . . I did not tell my husband everything I done : he never told me everything."

When Sir William Willcox had been recalled towards the end of the eighth day and gave the result of his experiment, the atmosphere in court had turned strongly against Seddon. The one great scientific attack on the evidence against him had been defeated. There was only one link in the chain of circumstances which was still open to a real doubt, and it was a very material one. Mr. Filson Young inclines to the view that the Crown did not, at any rate without Seddon's own evidence, make out its case against him. But it is difficult to see how, save for one weak link in the chain of circumstances alleged, short of producing a witness who had actually seen him administer the poison, they could have proved more. There was overwhelming evidence of motive, overwhelming evidence of opportunity; further, there was overwhelming evidence as to the prisoner's furtive attempts, after Miss Barrow's death, to prevent suspicion falling upon himself; furthermore, the dead woman was proved to have died of acute arsenical poisoning, and enough arsenic to poison several people had admittedly been purchased by the Seddons. The weak link in the chain was one of identification. Thorley, the chemist who ultimately had identified Maggie Seddon as the girl who had bought a packet of arsenic fly-papers on August 26th, did not come till late upon the scene. Maggie Seddon was a friend of his daughter's, and had called several times to see her at the side door of the shop. He had seen her on one of these private visits, but did not know her name, and it was only after he had seen Maggie Seddon's photograph in the newspapers in connection with the case that he was asked to come down to the police station to identify, among twenty women and girls, the girl who had bought the arsenic papers from him on August 26th. He at once identified Maggie Seddon, but she and another among the twenty were the only girls with their hair down. Marshall Hall was confident throughout that Thorley was an honest but a mistaken witness, and this weakness in the identification of Maggie was a real point for the defence. The matter was made worse by the fact that the police had cross-examined poor little Maggie Seddon before she gave evidence in any court, and had asked her difficult questions which she had answered inaccurately. She was asked, when the police knew perfectly well that she had done so on December 6th, whether she went to a chemist's " to purchase fly-papers." She answered " No," but her explanation for this was that she misunderstood the question, and thought that the police were asking whether she had ever gone and actually purchased fly-papers. At all events, the girl's slip was used to discredit her evidence at the trial by the Attorney-General, and Marshall Hall was able to comment on the un-English and inquisitorial method by which the police had approached the daughter of the prisoner at the very outset, not in the interests of truth, but in order to discredit whatever she might say on behalf of her father.

Eight days of this trial had punished Marshall cruelly : he had felt the responsibility of *two* human lives on his shoulders, one of whom, the woman, he was sure was innocent ; for this paramount reason he kept an iron grip on his self-control, and, knowing his own weakness, studiously avoided any kind of friction with the Bench. The Chattell case had made him, in the end, a much finer advocate. Undoubtedly his was the commanding personality in that great court, even with the Attorney-General there against him. In no way did Marshall Hall show an inferiority, throughout this memorable trial, to the leader of the Bar. Those who consider that Marshall Hall was a superficial man, who won his fame and victories by an overbearing, masterful personality and flamboyant rhetoric, would do well to study his cross-examination of Sir William Willcox, which was a profound, scholarly, and patient effort, and an intellectual achievement of which any man could be proud. Indeed, it showed an academic knowledge which could only have been derived from days and nights of careful research, and which, at one point at any rate, gave him the advantage over a man whose life's business it was to pursue this special and intricate branch of science.

When Marshall Hall rose to address the jury on the ninth day he looked tired and haggard, and, as a witness has told me, years older than at the beginning of the trial. The strain had been so great that he expressed the hope that this would be the last capital case of his career. " Gentlemen," he said at the commencement, " nobody can attempt to deny that this is one of the most interesting cases that probably has ever been tried in this building or in the building of which it is the successor." At great length, and with exhaustive detail, he repeated his arguments as to the scientific evidence, and referred with contempt to Sir William Willcox's " further experiments," made simply because his primary evidence was " self-destructive."

Will it be made clear to the Jury that all these notes were cashed during the lifetime of the deceased & extended over a period of 11 months thereby proving the deceased's knowledge.

Yesterday was the first time that Robt Hook stated that the £420 had reduced to £380 He contended at Police Court it was £420.

There was only 2 weeks annuity due at time of death & I had paid her £10 on Sept 2nd in advance

FURTHER NOTES FROM SEDDON TO COUNSEL

He went carefully into Miss Barrow's financial resources, Seddon's agreement to give her an annuity, and proved that Seddon only benefited by her death to the extent of £1 8s. 0d. a week. " People," he said, " do not commit murders for one pound ten shillings a week." He maintained that, if the prisoners were guilty, they had shown a refinement of cruelty that was incredible. He asked the jury to think, if the Seddons were guilty, of their cold-blooded patience in sitting near her to watch her die, tortured by an agonising poison, even administering palliatives to prolong her agony in order to simulate a natural death. One would search the annals of Italian poisoners in vain to find a parallel. During this passage, Mrs. Seddon broke down completely, put her face in her hands, and sobbed hysterically. Marshall put forward finally as the theory of the defence " that in some way or other some portion of the arsenic, not sufficient to cause her death, but sufficient in the state in which she was to aggravate the symptoms from which she was suffering—some portion, by some means or other, got into this unfortunate woman's stomach, and so into her body."

Then came his peroration ; once more he repeated, almost word for word and gesture for gesture, the scales of Justice simile, which had been so effective in the Lawrence trial ; but more effective still was his last argument of all, a reference to the scientific evidence upon which the Crown sought to hang these two people.

" Gentlemen," he said, " the great scientists who have been here have told us much of the marvels of science and of the deductions that can be made from science. But there is one thing all scientists have never been able to find, never yet been able to discover, with all their research, and with all their study, and this is, how to replace the little vital spark we call life. Upon your verdict here depends, so far as I am concerned, the life of this man. If your verdict is against him, that vital spark will be extinguished, and no science known to the world can ever replace it."

Marshall Hall had pleaded for a little over four hours. In that space of time he had spoken with his usual rapidity : altogether, something above thirty-seven thousand words, thus averaging nine thousand two hundred and fifty words an hour. The Attorney-General, who followed with the final speech, spoke for about the same time, and spoke nearly twenty-nine thousand words. Thus Marshall Hall packed into each hour nearly two thousand words more than his antagonist. When he sat down, Richard Muir scribbled a note and sent it to him : " MY DEAR MARSHALL,—A truly great speech—of many good things I have heard you do, quite the best. Yours always, R. D. MUIR."

The Attorney-General's speech was masterly ; speaking in an even, courteous voice, he missed no single point against the prisoners. Marshall had said, " People do not commit murders for one pound ten shillings a week." Rufus Isaacs showed that this was precisely what this man Seddon might do, and every circumstance seemed to prove that he did. To show how much thought and care had been spent on this speech, one point of detail serves. Little Ernest Grant went to the same school as the Vonderahes' little boys. Seddon said he sent a letter to the Vonderahes to announce Miss Barrow's death ; the Crown's contention was that Seddon never sent such a letter, and that he did everything to keep the news of Miss Barrow's death from them. Rufus Isaacs then brought forward the seemingly insignificant fact that the Seddons had not let Ernest Grant go to school on the morning of Miss Barrow's death, but had sent him down to Southend. Had he gone to school, he might have met the little Vonderahes and told them something.

Rufus Isaacs continued hour after hour, piling up his terrible indictment against both prisoners. The speech was really almost as deadly against Mrs. Seddon as her husband. At the very end, Mr. Attorney gave a slight hint that there was a distinction between the two cases. " Supposing you come to the conclusion that you have no reasonable doubt with regard to the male prisoner, but that you have some doubt—you are not quite satisfied beyond all reasonable doubt—that the woman is guilty, then it would be your duty to acquit her."

After this last speech, came Mr. Justice Bucknill's summing up. After the ten days' trial it was expected that he would sum up for the best part of a day ; actually he spoke something above two hours. Many were disappointed that he did not give the jury the benefit of a more exhaustive analysis of the evidence.

Important. Mrs Seddon knows that it was my intention to take the "Will" to Mr Keeble (Solicitor) & have a proper one drafted from it, the one I made being only temporary to satisfy Miss Barrow for the time being. We did not expect her death so soon.

My Wife also knows that I took all monies out of my office Safe to Bedroom Safe every Thursday night for Safety, as men paying in the Company's money it would become known I had the week's collections on hand, & banked on Fridays, So Thursday nights would be the most likely night for a Burglary - as we once experienced 9 Years ago in Victoria Rd Holloway. That happened on an office night - So I took special precautions, afterwards, to leave no large amount of cash in office over Thursday night. ·X· I had no Safe then when Burglary was committed.

Mrs Seddon also knows that Funeral Arrangements made by me were only temporary & I expected Relatives to answer my letter & arrange to their Satisfaction. They did not turn up so arrangements were not altered as Mr Nodes had promised a thoroughly decent turnout, & we expected such as he knew us so well, So I was guided by Mr Nodes, it was quite a respectable funeral. My Wife heard deceased say the family Vault was full when her brother was buried, & the Vault was not in her name.

N.B. If I had not money enough on hand (viz £200) to pay off the Mortgage on my house I would have paid it off when I sold the £1600 India Stock, or held that amount.

A FURTHER NOTE
from Seddon to Counsel

As to the scientific controversy, he said, " I should not be surprised if you said that you are satisfied beyond reasonable doubt that this lady died of acute arsenical poisoning as distinct from chronic. . . . " He gave a clear hint to the jury to acquit the woman, but his directions as regards Seddon excited much comment at the time. After referring to his mean character and to the fact that he did not send for a doctor when the woman was in such agony, he said, " Do not be too much prejudiced." These words implied that there must be some prejudice, and of course prejudice in general is wrong. But Marshall Hall had himself denounced Seddon's meanness in the strongest language, and the judge's language was moderate and sensible ; he could have used these circumstances in a far more deadly fashion against the prisoner, had he so chosen, and remained strictly within the proper limits.

The jury retired at 3.58, and returned into court exactly an hour later. They found Seddon guilty. His face flushed, but otherwise he maintained his composure. Immediately afterwards they pronounced his wife not guilty. Seddon went across, embraced her, and kissed her on the lips. So silent was the court that every one present must have heard the sound of that tragic gesture of farewell. Immediately afterwards she was taken away to be discharged. Much of the prejudice that had gathered round the prisoner was dissipated by this one incident. Many were moved to tears by it. Then the formal question was asked, by the officer of the court, to which very seldom is an answer given by the prisoner, at any rate in capital cases, where no words of his can affect his sentence. " Frederick Henry Seddon, you stand convicted of wilful murder. Have you anything to say for yourself why the Court should not give you judgment of death according to law ? "

Then a surprising thing happened. " I have, sir," replied the prisoner. He cleared his throat, took out some notes, and made a calm and admirable little speech in his own defence. He declared his innocence of the murder and denied any knowledge of it. Finally, knowing the judge to be a zealous Freemason, he made it clear to the judge that they belonged to the same brotherhood, whose members bind themselves solemnly to help each other through life, and especially in extremity. " I declare,"

he concluded, " before the Great Architect of the Universe, I
am not guilty, my lord."

This appeal utterly unnerved the judge. His clerk arranged
the black square of cloth upon his head, which seemed to overshadow and darken his whole face. The chaplain was summoned,
and the usher called out, " Oyez ! Oyez ! Oyez ! My lords the
King's justices do strictly charge and command all persons
to keep silence while sentence of death is passing upon the
prisoner at the bar, upon pain of imprisonment. God save the
King ! "

But no words came from the judge : in a silence that could
be felt there were only two sounds to be heard—the ticking of
the court clock and the loud sobs of the judge about to speak the
words of condemnation. It seemed a long time before he could
pull himself together, yet it could not have been more than a
minute in all. Then, in a voice broken with emotion, the judge
admonished the prisoner for his barbarous crime. " It is not for
me to harrow your feelings," he said.

" It does not affect me," said the prisoner ; " I have a clear
conscience."

" Try to make peace with your Maker," the judge continued.

" I am at peace," said the prisoner.

" You and I know we both belong to the same brotherhood,
and it is all the more painful to me to have to say what I am
saying. But our brotherhood does not encourage crime ; on the
contrary, it condemns it. I pray you again to make your peace
with the Great Architect of the Universe. Mercy—pray for it,
ask for it. . . . And now I have to pass sentence. The sentence
of the Court is that you be taken from hence to a lawful prison,
and from thence to a place of execution, and that you be there
hanged by the neck until you are dead ; and that your body be
buried within the precincts of the prison in which you shall
have been confined after your conviction ; and may the Lord
have mercy on your soul."

The great battle had been both won and lost ; it needed the
most athletic advocacy to conduct the defence of both prisoners
without prejudicing either of them, and for this reason, perhaps,
Marshall Hall's oration for the Seddons was the most artistic

MR. JUSTICE BUCKNILL
sentences Seddon to death

THE CHAPLAIN

(The only photograph of a death sentence)

of all his speeches. The Attorney-General sent him a glowing tribute. He wrote on March 15th :

"My Dear Marshall,—Quite frankly, and sincerely, not as A.-G., but an old friend, do let me say how much I admired your defence and whole conduct of the Seddons' case. Your five minutes' outburst for Mrs. Seddon made a most powerful impression ; and, in my view, did much—if not the most— for her acquittal. His case was a terribly difficult one—the chain was as complete as circumstantial evidence can make it—and you had a very hard task, when it was so plain to all that the man had such a covetous nature, and was such a shrewd, cunning fellow. But I didn't mean to discuss the case. I wanted to say again what I had said in your absence, in my speech, that it was a really magnificent forensic effort, and the whole defence was conducted by you in accordance with the highest traditions of our profession. I know you won't think it impertinent for me to write this to you. It is meant, and will be understood by you, as the expression of an opponent, who loves to see work well and nobly done— and of a friend who has always received such generous (over-generous, I think) recognition from you.

"I am so glad I went away before the verdict was given. I hope your wife is better. Please remember me to her.

"Yours ever,

"Rufus D. Isaacs."

For his own part, Marshall Hall had expected the verdict to be as it was. He regarded the appeal as hopeless, but for two days he argued for Seddon in the Court of Criminal Appeal. Although this court had been founded in 1908, this was the first appeal of importance which Marshall Hall had argued. He hated appearing in any court of appeal, but he argued this case splendidly, the chief argument being that there was not sufficient evidence to go to a jury. He was unsuccessful, but one observation in the course of the argument by Mr. Justice Darling is interesting as showing how far the interpretation of the Criminal Evidence Act had changed in the course of years. "No one," said the learned judge, "who is well acquainted with criminal administration is ignorant of the fact that, to-day, prisoners are practically bound to go into the box, and that in the great majority of cases they say what is not true."

If this judicial dictum was well founded, Marshall Hall himself was largely responsible for the change in the practice. At the beginning of the century, counsel were very cautious in advising their clients whether to make use of the " privilege " conferred by the Act. But his great triumphs in the Wood and the Lawrence cases, in which he had put the prisoners in the witness box, had made a great effect. In the latter case the judge had expressly said that the prisoner would probably have been found guilty if he had not given evidence. From this time many more prisoners went into the box, and to-day it is a bolder thing to keep a prisoner out of the box than to put him into it.

After Seddon's appeal had failed, the public conscience began to grow uneasy : it was widely known that Seddon had been convicted on scientific evidence, and, with the usual British distrust and dislike of science, over 300,000 people signed the petition for his reprieve. But the Home Secretary did not reprieve him, and Seddon was executed on April 18th, 1912. When he knew all was over, he seemed quite unmoved. " This is nothing to me," he said, in his last interview with his solicitor, and went on to discuss the sale of his property. He could not be made to talk of anything else. When he heard how little his goods had fetched at the auction, he said, " That's finished it," and he was really upset when he heard that his motor-car, of which he had been inordinately proud, had gone for a smaller price than he had paid for it. He would not talk of his wife or family, or their prospects. Perhaps this was from indifference, or perhaps from some more human reason he found himself unable to do so. Who shall say ? " There is no question of my confessing," he said. " If you hear it, do not believe it." He wrote to the same effect to his wife and family, expressing his absolute innocence and his trust in Jesus Christ. So he died, an obstinate, conceited, hypocritical, cold-blooded, avaricious man. In him all the common virtues of the Anglo-Saxon were distorted into vices : he had but one real virtue, and this was courage ; yet, if he had not had that one great temptation, the arrival of a helpless, well-to-do old maid to lodge in his house, he might to-day be a pillar of

THE POISONER SEDDON

Islington municipal life, a director of an insurance company, hated as a hard taskmaster by his subordinates, but high in the favours of his board. His best epitaph, and one of which he would have been proud, was one given to him by Marshall Hall: " The ablest man I ever defended on the capital charge."

After his death a new sensation brought back his tragedy to the public mind. A few months afterwards his wife married again, and suffered much persecution. Two articles appeared over her signature in the *Weekly Dispatch* in which she admitted that she had seen Seddon give Miss Barrow arsenic, and that he had threatened to kill her, his wife, with a revolver if she gave him away. She had stood by him at the trial for the sake of her children. She described in some detail her miserable life with Seddon, and begged the public not to regard her as a murderess. Much public outcry arose at this " confession," which of course, if true, would have exposed her to a prosecution for perjury. Soon afterwards, by the instrumentality of *John Bull*, she was asked to sign a recantation of her confession : she did so. She said that it was false, and that her evidence at the trial was the whole truth. She was obviously a woman easily influenced. Later, she went out, with her husband, to Australia to try and make a new life for herself. Incidentally, she was only able to do this through the generosity of the young solicitor who had defended her. Only one comment needs to be made as to her " confession " in the *Weekly Dispatch*. Seddon *had* a revolver. One of his legal advisers went to view his house before his arrest : there was a picture in the worst of taste hanging on his dining-room wall, depicting a husband shooting his wife's lover. " There," said Seddon gratuitously, calling attention to the print, and throwing down a revolver on the table, " that's the sort of man I am—only I would have shot them both."

.   .   .   .

In 1913, Marshall Hall appeared in two very amusing libel actions before Mr. Justice Darling. The first action, *White* v. *Barnes*, was a political libel action, brought by a Derbyshire J.P. and county councillor, claiming damages for libel and slander published by a newspaper reporter of opposite political tendencies. He was alleged to have said that the plaintiff was a " pub-crawler," and had been " frog-marched " from a public

house. Marshall Hall appeared for the defendant, who " justified " the libel. A number of amusing incidents took place ;
perhaps the best was the reference to a conversation in a public
house, between a Conservative local light and the plaintiff, as
to Tariff Reform. " If a ten per cent. tariff were put on," said
the staunch Conservative, " it would pay half the nation's
taxes."

" Then why not put on a tariff of twenty per cen.. and save
all taxation," said the plaintiff.

" That won't do," said the Conservative. " That's like the
advertisement about stoves : ' Buy Smith's stoves and save half
your fuel.' If your argument is good, why not buy two stoves and
save all your fuel."

Marshall Hall was able to call the cab-driver who had actually
taken the plaintiff round the public houses on the day after the
county council elections which the plaintiff had been celebrating. Over a considerable distance they only missed one public
house, and that was only because the sagacious horse, the best
" pub-crawler " of them all, did not know it ; but, from constant
practice, he knew all the others. The evidence as to the horse,
clinched the matter, and the jury found a verdict for the defendant.

In July 1913 he appeared for the *Winning Post* in the celebrated libel action brought against that newspaper by Mr.
Richard Wootton, the well-known trainer, which occupied eight
whole days of the business lives of Mr. Justice Darling and a
special jury. Mr. Robert Sievier, the editor, had published a
series of articles, in substance accusing the plaintiff of ordering
his jockeys and apprentices " to pull their horses " when they
were not backed by the plaintiff, and, together with other
trainers, of pre-arranging the results of races by unfair means.
Mr. F. E. Smith, K.C., Mr. Eldon Bankes, K.C., and Mr.
McCardie—as they then were—appeared for the plaintiff.
Representatives of the entire racing hierarchy were called by
one side or the other, from Lord Derby, Lord Lonsdale, Edward
Hulton, Francis Lambton, and George Lambton, down to
jockeys and stable-boys : as Robert Sievier, who conducted his
own defence, said, the Turf " extended from King to card-
seller." Wootton's sons had got into trouble for unfair riding,

and their cases had been previously tried by the stewards—that of one of them, Frank, when he was only thirteen. " Why," said the judge, " if he had not been a jockey, he would have been tried in the children's court." But Richard Wootton made a distinction between being in trouble for trying to win and being in trouble for trying to lose. Lord Derby agreed that the latter was the more heinous offence, but he said that he thought all the articles in the *Winning Post* were " reasonably sensible," both the sporting ones and the others, " for he read them all." Lord Lonsdale explained that he wished to get away to the meeting at Sandown, where he was a steward. " I understood," said Lord Darling, " that, as everybody was engaged here, there was to be no meeting to-day." At another opportunity, Lord Darling made what Marshall Hall said was the best joke he ever heard in a law court. A little jockey of seventeen, who had run off after a race without weighing-in, after being cross-examined severely as to this delinquency, almost ran out of the witness box. But Mr. F. E. Smith had risen to re-examine. " Wait a minute," said the learned judge, his Voltairean features illuminated by an expression indescribably mischievous ; " Mr. Smith has not weighed in yet."

" You have not forgotten to weigh in again ? " asked counsel. " No," said the jockey ; whereupon the judge said, " He nearly forgot again just now."

The judge, a keen rider himself, took a great interest in the case, and did not lose his chances of contributing to the discussion. He obviously disapproved of the modern fashion of riding with very short stirrups. Marshall Hall was commenting on the fact that a certain jockey only got £15 out of riding " over the sticks." " They will cross the other Styx," observed the judge, " if they continue to ride with short leathers."

At one point in the case a jockey said he always took orders from Mr. Wootton before a race ; and when, towards the close of the case, Marshall began to read from a mass of documents, " Finish that up," said the plaintiff. Marshall Hall turned on him. " *I* don't take riding-orders from you, Mr. Wootton," he said.

One of the most amusing witnesses was a rider called for the defence, who, as Marshall said, was the most candid witness of them all.

" Have you been drunk often during the last three weeks ? " asked Mr. Smith.—" Yes, pretty often."

" Have you hardly gone to bed sober in the last three or four years ? "—" Very rarely."

" There is a maxim," said Mr. Justice Darling, " that drunken people tell the truth."

" But that," retorted Mr. Smith, " is when they are drunk. Are you sober now ? " " Yes," replied the poor man, now robbed even of his one virtue as a witness—intoxication !

Mr. Sievier, in the course of this long case, became quite a good advocate, and received several compliments from the Bench. All through the case he had a refrain, and this was, " Money talks " ; and, whenever he said this, he produced a farthing and held it up to the jury as a suggestion. Both the plaintiff and the defendant had their *claques*, who loudly applauded each point made by their respective factions. In the end the jury found that the words complained of were not true, or fair or honest comment, but that they were published without malice. Finally they adopted Mr. Sievier's tactful suggestion as to the damages. The costs, however, amounted to many thousands of pounds.

Just about this time, as one of the most fashionable leaders of the day, Marshall made his last appearances in the county courts. On each occasion his advent into that humbler atmosphere achieved notoriety. Sir William Bull, M.P., briefed him with a junior in the Westminster County Court to defend a small claim which involved a big principle. The advent of the great man so alarmed the plaintiff that his counsel was instructed to apply for an adjournment. This so annoyed Marshall Hall, who had come down at great personal inconvenience, that he suggested that he should retire and leave the two juniors to fight the case out together. Whereupon his own junior rose in alarm : " I had to see my doctor yesterday—I am not feeling at all well." Eventually it was agreed that the case should be fought out in the High Court.

Two years later, being known to be an enthusiastic dog-fancier, he was briefed to appear for a St. Bernard dog, in a county court action brought against him by a tiny White Jap for assault. The latter was represented by his mistress in person. She was a clever young American lady, who certainly gave a good performance against her formidable opponent. The White Jap, she said, had not done anything to annoy the St. Bernard, who leapt at him and took him in his mouth. The poor little fellow had suffered such pain and shock that he was now useless for breeding purposes !

" I can relieve Mrs. Turnbull," observed Marshall, " of one difficulty. We are not contending that the St. Bernard did this in self-defence."

However, Mrs. Turnbull had heroically saved her little pet by breaking a parasol on the big dog's back, and by twisting his tail very violently. " Your honour," interrupted Marshall, " the St. Bernard alleges no counterclaim."

On one point the plaintiff himself was produced and placed on counsels' table, and Marshall could not resist caressing him, and received an answering wag of the tail. His advocate was most ingenious in her advocacy, but unfortunately the St. Bernard had a good defence in law. Unless it could be proved that his master knew of his vicious tendencies he could not be mulcted in pecuniary damages. There was therefore judgment for the defendant. Marshall Hall was much impressed by the advocacy of this " modern Portia," whom he had plaintively and repeatedly requested to " leave him alone." In the course of the trial she had tried to inform the judge of the vicious characteristics of St. Bernards in general.

" That is not evidence," objected Marshall Hall.

" What do you know about dogs ? " said the scornful Portia.

" I know something about ladies," was the K.C.'s dry retort.

. . . .

In spite of his intention after the Seddon case never to appear again in a murder trial, during the years immediately preceding the war he defended two prisoners on the capital charge, and both defences were interesting. In June 1912 he appeared for a young man, aged twenty-three, educated at an English Public School and a foreign university, who had killed his sweetheart in a Marylebone flat. He had taken her from a life of promiscuous immorality, and they had lived happily together for some time. One morning they quarrelled : the girl said she was going to leave him, and she prepared to go ; he tried to prevent her ;

while doing so, he caught her by the neck, whereupon she instantly gave two screams and fell back dead. She was in a medical condition called *status lymphaticus*; the thymus gland in her throat, which usually disappears altogether in adult life, had become enlarged, with the usual result of great weakness of heart. Any shock, however slight, to a subject of this complaint may result in death. On these facts, Marshall Hall persuaded Muir, for the prosecution, to accept a plea of " manslaughter " from the prisoner, and so moving was his plea in mitigation that Mr. Justice Bankes gave a sentence of only nine months. " It would require," he said, " the pen of a Zola or the pencil of a Hogarth to depict the prisoner's abject horror at finding she was dead." This was the first occasion on which *status lymphaticus* in the deceased was raised as a legal defence.

Years afterwards, indeed a few weeks before his death, Marshall Hall received a very sad letter from this unfortunate young man, revealing as it does the cruel disadvantages under which a man in his position suffers when he tries to resume his place in the world, whatever the extenuating circumstances of his case may be. This man, after his release, went out to America and " made good " for a time under an assumed name. Then came the war ; he enlisted in the American Expeditionary Force, and earned a commission on the field. After the war he " decided to give England a chance " again, and married a young wife. After a while his true identity was discovered by his wife's family, and in January 1927 he found himself again utterly alone in the world.

.   .   .   .

The next capital defence which Marshall Hall undertook was that of Jeannie Baxter. The circumstances were strikingly similar, up to the very last act of the tragedy, to the case of Edward Lawrence ; but on this occasion it was the man who paid the price with his life and the woman who stood her trial for murder. A young pioneer of the air, magnificently built, named Julian Hall, and an extraordinarily beautiful girl met in a night club, and became violently attracted to each other, with the result that the girl left a far richer man than Julian Hall to live with the latter, and the airman threw over another young woman for whom he had cared before. But, in spite of his wealth and wonderful physique, Julian Hall was in a bad way when he met Jeannie Baxter. Like most airmen, he was absolutely without fear of death; he would frequently talk of death, and indeed he was, like Lawrence, drinking himself into his grave before ever he knew Jeannie. When he and Jeannie's former lover met, he said, " Do you love this girl ? . . . So do I, I am going to have her, and if you do not agree, come into the sitting-room." He then challenged his rival to a duel by shooting, but the challenge was naturally declined by his more sensible rival. When his own former sweetheart came to upbraid him, Jeannie said he must choose between them, and Julian turned to Jeannie and said, " I choose you." Jeannie had lost a great deal by going to him, and she grew to love him passionately. " I loved him better than anybody in the world," she said at the trial. But there were violent quarrels. Hall would fire his revolver, and, being a man of gigantic strength, once broke with his own hands a strong oak table. There would be reconciliations, for Jeannie loved the big, strong man, and was even proud of his bouts of violence : it was eventually arranged that they should marry. Hall made a will in her favour, and Jeannie even got as far as choosing a wedding-dress. But Hall was of most unreliable character, and it seemed that he had a man friend and constant companion who opposed the marriage. At all events he began to go back on his promise. According to her own maid, Jeannie had said, " Do you think, Theresa, that anybody should be punished very much if they shot Mr. Hall dead, after he has spoilt everything between me and my friend? " To Julian Hall's man friend, according to the latter's evidence, she had said, " Either Julian must get me back my friend, or he must marry me, or I will kill him."

Julian Hall lived in a flat in Denman Street, and was very ill one night from the effects of drink, and, obeying a summons from the friend, she came in the very early morning to see her lover. He was in bed, and kissed her good morning. They began to discuss the question of marriage, and Julian said that his friend was very much against it. However, a little later he sent for two servants, told them he was going to be married, and they were asked to sign a document, which purported to leave Jeannie's interest in his fortune, under a previous will, to her baby daughter. But afterwards, according to Jeannie Baxter herself, he said, " It's no good—I can't keep my promise—it's better to finish it. This drink is killing me." Then a fusillade, six shots in all, was heard, and Jeannie ran out, the tears pouring down her cheeks, and sobbed out, " I have shot him—four times—he dared me to do it. Oh, why did I do it, when we had arranged everything so nicely for to-night."

Julian Hall had two wounds, and died soon afterwards ; he tried to speak, but he could not do so, and Jeannie Baxter was committed for trial at the Old Bailey. She had a difficult case to answer ; her desire to marry him, and her maid's evidence as to her threats, were strong evidence both of motive and intention, and her own admission that she had shot him four times seemed at first to make the case conclusive. But Jeannie Baxter felt sure of her acquittal. Marshall Hall, and his junior, Mr. Jack Valetta, had to interview the prisoner in a special room in the gaol. She seemed amazingly confident, and made a strange and incongruous figure, with her fashionable dress, her beautiful, almost childish face and red-gold hair. When the interview was over, Marshall Hall looked out of the window and said, " My God, Valetta, look at that ! " Their client, about to be tried for her life, was executing a little *pas seul* as she crossed the snow-covered prison yard on the way back to her cell. It was not a sight to be forgotten. She was dancing back to prison.

Mr. Cecil Whiteley, only lately appointed a prosecuting counsel to the Treasury, led for the prosecution ; he was very nervous at the prospect of his first capital case in that capacity, and felt the task of prosecuting and cross-examining the beautiful girl in the dock an odious one, as any man would have done. He opened the case with admirable fairness, and Marshall, always generous to a young opponent, scribbled a note to him and sent it along, " Admirable, my dear Cecil, just what an opening ought to be."

Marshall Hall cross-examined the dead man's friend and the accused's maid with great effect, but the most useful witness to him was Julian's former sweetheart, who, forgetting all jealousy, generously came forward to say that Julian and Jeannie were obviously very much in love with each other, that he had been very violent and struck her with a revolver, and that she, the witness, bore no ill-will to Jeannie whatsoever.

As in the Lawrence case, only two people knew what had happened to bring about the tragedy, and the only person alive to know was the prisoner. All, then, depended on her evidence. She came forward and gave her evidence with calmness and great assurance. The defence was that Hall was besotted with drink, and was teasing her, as he often had, about suicide. " You seem to think death an awful thing," he had said, " but we all have to die some time." " Yes," Jeannie had replied, " but we are not all like you." Then Hall began playing with the revolver, and, pointing it towards his breast, dared her to pull the trigger. She refused to do so, but, terrified, sprang forward to take it out of his hand, and in the struggle the revolver had wounded him twice, while his thumb was still round the trigger. Jeannie then fired four more shots into the air to empty the revolver, and ran to get assistance. The dead man had on many occasions been violent to her when in drink.

" Did that make you hate him ? " asked counsel.

" No," she sobbed, " it made me love him all the more."

Much turned on the meaning of the words spoken. When Hall said " finish it," did he mean the end of their love, or the end of his life ? What exactly happened no one will ever know. Marshall's speech was a magnificent effort ; he was always at his best when his case had a strong romantic interest. After a summing-up by Mr. Justice Rowlatt in favour of a verdict of " manslaughter," the jury found her guilty of that offence, and strongly recommended her to mercy. She was sentenced to three years' penal servitude, from which sentence she appealed in vain to the Court of Criminal Appeal. Her tragedy gave rise to a leading case in the civil courts. She was a beneficiary under Julian Hall's will, and the Court of Criminal Appeal decided that no person who feloniously causes the death of a testator can benefit under that testator's will. It had been already established, in regard to the estate of Mrs. Crippen, that there can be no claim to a murdered person's estate by the murderer or through him, but this principle had not been established as to manslaughter until the case of Jeannie Baxter.

In some ways this case of Julian Hall and Jeannie Baxter
WH

was as sad as any case in the experience of Marshall Hall. Julian Hall had the makings of a splendid man : everyone spoke of his indomitable courage and his gentle character when un- affected by drink, and his strength was a thing to marvel at. He was one of those fearless adventurers who were just then conquering the air, and on one of his very first flights in those early machines he had hoodwinked his instructor and taken the air by himself. Had he lived for another year, his opportunity would have come, and he might have been one of the great heroes of the war. " The most distressing feature is the loss of the man's life," said Marshall Hall, in his final speech. " He was a man of magnificent physique. He took to a branch of national defence which hereafter will be of immense value to the country. He was a man who might have used his life to great advantage, and if he was reckless of it he might have sacrificed it in the magnificent service of his country. Yet he allowed himself to be brought down by drink and passion to a level lower than some animals." Indeed, the race is not always for the swift, nor the battle to the strong.

Chapter X

Wartime

THE war did not come as a surprise to Edward Marshall Hall. He had foreseen it for years, having a better knowledge than most men concerning the temper and strength of the German War Party. He was in the middle fifties, and physically quite unfit for any form of active service. Therefore, he had to remain at home, and, in the words of our first national war slogan, to carry on his " business as usual." He was personally in the painful and embarrassing position in which all Englishmen with German wives found themselves. To Marshall Hall, the most patriotic, sensitive, and affectionate of men, the position was distressing in the extreme. He tended to see less of his friends, and absorb himself even more than ever in his professional duties.

Many barristers of military age, as in every other profession, joined the colours, and those who, from necessity or other circumstances, stayed in the Temple, were naturally the gainers. Marshall Hall profited among the rest, and obtained many of the returned briefs of those of His Majesty's counsel who were serving His Majesty in the field. But here, too, his generosity and patriotism were conspicuous. Lord Birkenhead has informed me that Marshall Hall, and one other, were the only leaders who forwarded him half of the fees of the briefs, returned by him on account of his military service, and delivered to them.

His war-time practice is interesting, as showing the spirit and circumstances of war as reflected in the national courts of law. New crimes were created and committed ; queer litigation was brought to light by strained and sensitive nerves. Men required the services of counsel for purposes unknown in times of peace.

It will probably be thought that in those terrible first twelve months, when the British Empire and the French Republic were fighting with their backs to the wall and squandering, for their actual existence, hundreds of thousands of lives and untold treasure, the paramount interest of war would have diverted or extinguished the limelight which usually plays so fiercely on our courts of justice. Yet this was not so. Perhaps the popular mind turned with relief to some other subject than the war, but the fact remains, that the public interest in the trial of George Joseph Smith, in the advocates who prosecuted and defended him, in the judge and jury who tried him, was no whit less than that displayed in any of Marshall Hall's trials. Yet, though this was perhaps the most extraordinary case in its circumstances, it was, in its conduct, the dullest of all. Throughout the trial the atmosphere of the court was not, " is this man innocent or guilty ? " but " is there sufficient evidence in law to convict this undoubtedly guilty man ? " Yet the case, the most overwhelming, as regards the facts, ever brought against one of Marshall Hall's prisoners, was the weakest in law. Further, the case has, for other reasons, an important place in the life of Marshall Hall, bearing, as it does, on the whole question of defence funds raised on behalf of poor prisoners, and on the relationship of defending counsel, before and after conviction, to prisoners whom they personally believe to have been responsible for the crime charged to their account. The writer will attempt to tell this difficult story, so as to make clear the only really important issue in the case for a lawyer, the admissibility of certain evidence ; upon this point alone was the issue of the trial ever in doubt ; but he will not attempt to deal in detail with the medico-legal questions, already so ably covered by Mr. Eric Watson in his edition of the trial.

In May 1912 a man named Henry Williams, by trade a dealer in antiques, took a house on a yearly tenancy for himself and his wife, whose maiden name had been Bessie Mundy, at 80 High Street, Herne Bay. In an interview with a Miss Rapley, the house-agent's secretary, he confidingly informed her that his wife had all the money, and that he had none. They lived there without servants, and the house was an inconvenient one, in some ways, for a lady of " Mrs. Williams's " position in life ; she was a bank manager's daughter, and had inherited a little fortune of £2,500, carefully invested in trustee securities for her. The house had no bath ; however, this defect was soon made good, for Mr. Williams bought one from an ironmonger's on July 9th, and had it installed in their little home. Two days later, the fond husband took his young bride to a Dr. French, saying that she had had some sort of a fit. The doctor could not gather from either husband or wife any definite evidence of the symptoms of her seizure, but, by leading questions—Dr. French had been a solicitor, and was skilful in putting them—he concluded that she had been suffering from an epileptic fit. He was called in a night or two later, and found Mrs. Williams in a slightly feverish state ; that same night, Mrs. Williams wrote to her uncle to say that she had had two bad fits, and that " her husband had been extremely kind. . . . " The letter concluded, " I have made out my will, and have left all I have to my husband. That is only natural, as I love my husband." The next news Dr. French heard about Mrs. Williams was a message from her husband on Saturday morning, July 13th, that she had died in her bath. He went round and found that this was indeed true. There was no sign of violence upon her. Mr. Williams wrote to his wife's relatives, " Words cannot describe the great shock I suffered in the loss of my wife." But they were not given an opportunity of attending the inquest, which was held on the following Monday morning. However, the coroner, Mr. Mowll, in his own words, exercised " more than ordinary perspicacity," and " thoroughly and carefully thrashed out " the case, with the result that the jury found that the bride had died from misadventure. There was plenty of evidence, the coroner said, that the husband had been devoted to his wife. " He did not see any evidence on which to censure the husband at all." Rather, " it was a terrible blight upon him."

Now, had the coroner waited for the relatives to be present at the inquest, as they had requested to be, he might have given his " perspicacity " a better chance. For the matrimonial history of this couple had been very curious, almost unique. In 1910, Henry Williams had met Miss Mundy at Clifton, in a boarding-house, where that lonely spinster of thirty-three was then residing. She opened her heart to him, and he found it worth winning. No doubt, with a full knowledge of her financial position, he married her at Weymouth on August 20th. On his wedding day, he wrote for a copy of the late Mr. Mundy's will, and discovered that his wife had executed a voluntary settlement of her property to trustees, and that she received her income monthly. However, the trustees had accumulated a sum of £138 from the income. The payment of this sum, in

gold, he obtained through a solicitor in September. As soon as
he received it, he abandoned his wife, leaving her almost without clothes and without a penny in the world. He excused his
betrayal of her by a letter, which was a disgraceful piece of
blackmail. He said that, through living with her, his health
had become terribly impaired, and a long cure was necessary
before he could return. The deserted wife was, at first, broken-
hearted, but soon began to regard her husband's departure as a
blessing in disguise. She was well out of it, and, very probably,
the poor woman thought she was done for ever, not only with
Henry Williams, but with all men.

It was not to be ; Mrs. Williams went to live at Weston-super-
Mare with a worthy woman named Mrs. Tuckett. On March
14th, 1912, she went out to buy some flowers, and, while on the
esplanade, she began looking dreamily out to sea. Looking
sideways, she saw, a few feet away, the familiar features of her
errant husband. If this was a coincidence, it was surely the
most cruel that ever happened. Then the most amazing thing
occurred. Instead of running away from this monster who had
betrayed her, or going to fetch a policeman, she again fell completely under his charm. For this woman, at least, Henry
Williams must have had a most abnormal attraction. She left
her kind landlady's house, to spend the night with him, without
even taking a nightdress with her. Her relatives were advised
of the reconciliation, and deeply shocked by it.

The following month, the reunited couple moved to Herne
Bay, and there he went to consult a solicitor. His wife had made
a voluntary settlement ; she now wished him to have the
unfettered benefit of her capital. Was there any means of avoid-
ing the settlement ? or, if not, if husband and wife made mutual
wills, leaving everything to each other, did that make each will
irrevocable ? Now these were searching and difficult questions,
and Mr. Annesley, the local solicitor, very properly thought
them worthy of counsel's opinion. Mr. G. F. Spear, of Paper
Buildings, was consulted, and he advised, most emphatically,
that it was impossible to avoid the settlement, that if, after the
mutual wills were made, Mrs. Williams made another will,
disposing of her property elsewhere, Mr. Williams would not
have a right to claim against the estate. Further, the trustees

could always make the effect of the mutual wills nugatory by purchasing an annuity for Mrs. Williams. He further suggested that Mrs. Williams should be told clearly that the proposed arrangement was not to her interest. A very proper opinion ; and, of course, learned counsel, as he wrote out his erudite conclusions, had no suspicion that he might be composing his poor client's death warrant. Even behind the formal " instructions to counsel " this astute denizen of Paper Buildings had obviously formed an unfavourable view of Mr. Henry Williams. But, of course, learned counsel who write opinions on probate law do not think of their clients' husbands as potential murderers. Mr. Williams, however, was quite furious with the opinion, and took it home to peruse. Mr. Spear's advice made it abundantly clear that he could not be sure, by any means, of securing his wife's capital. Those trustees would be sure to purchase an annuity. Only if his wife were to die in the immediate future, very soon after she had made a will in his favour, could he possibly be sure of that £2,500. Mr. Spear had not said that, of course, but he had cleared all other avenues. It was a chance in a million, yet, strange to say, it happened. Some days after the funeral, Mr. Williams went round to see Miss Rapley, of the house-agent's office, to tell her of his wife's death and his imminent departure from Herne Bay. He broke down badly in her presence, and began to cry. Then he looked up and said more brightly, " Was it not a jolly good job I got her to make a will ? " Miss Rapley, a very intelligent lady, rightly thought this remark extraordinary, and said so. Mr. Williams explained that he also had made a will in his wife's favour. Then Miss Rapley looked him very straight in the face. " I thought you told me, when you came here first, that you had not anything," she said. She did not give this evidence at the inquest, for the good reason that the inquest had taken place some days before this strange visit of Mr. Williams. Nor, of course, could it have been guessed by the coroner or his jury, that Mr. Williams, who was " so fond of his wife," and had profited so richly from her will, would give her, as Seddon gave to Miss Barrow, a pauper's funeral in a common grave.

The trustees of the poor dead woman entered a caveat when Williams sought to prove the will, but, though they were suspicious, the verdict of the coroner's jury stood as a barrier to any effective opposition, and, in September 1912, the widower was able to possess himself of his wife's fortune. He first invested the proceeds in house property ; then he sold out at a considerable loss, and, finally, with £1,300 he bought an annuity of £76 a year. Clearly the fellow had an expectation of a long life.

For nearly three years, Mrs. Williams's inconspicuous grave rested unnoticed and undisturbed, and, for the same time, Mr. Williams went as he pleased. But on February 1st, 1915, in consequence of information which had reached Scotland Yard, a certain John Lloyd was arrested in North London. He was charged with the murder of Bessie Mundy. His name was known to the police to be neither John Lloyd, nor Henry Williams, but George Joseph Smith.

Marshall Hall was briefed, with Montague Shearman and Grattan Bushe, to appear for this man at the Old Bailey. His case excited the widest public interest. Smith, however, his capital gone in the purchase of annuities, was almost without resources. The police had taken from him all the money in his possession when arrested. It was not fairly to be expected that a great leading counsel, like Marshall Hall, with a practice worth many thousands a year, could appear for the prisoner for a paltry fee. Except in cases of personal friendship or special charity, the clerks of counsel are justified in asking a fee to which their position at the Bar entitles them : indeed, it would be unprofessional to do otherwise.

Now, so great was the publicity value of George Joseph Smith, that certain newspapers approached his solicitor, Mr. W. P. Davies. If the Press provided funds for his defence, which would enable him to employ the ablest counsel at the Bar, would Smith, after the trial, assign the copyright of anything he might write to these newspapers ? Mr. Davies considered such an arrangement would be very greatly to his client's advantage, and drew up a deed, embodying the terms of the proposed contract. He took an opinion of counsel, not to be briefed at the trial, as to the legality of the agreement. Relying on the completion of this transaction, and anticipating that he would have considerable funds at his disposal, he went to Temple Gardens and briefed Marshall Hall for the defence. Even in these circumstances, Marshall accepted the brief with great reluctance. Mr. Montague Shearman, the son of the judge, and Mr. Grattan Bushe, were instructed as juniors. But Smith was in prison, and it was necessary to obtain the sanction of the Home Office for his signature to the deed. The Home Secretary of the time was one of the most distinguished of living lawyers, Sir John Simon, lately Attorney-General ; on June 19th, three days before the trial, the Home Office, on the instructions of the Secretary of State, vetoed the arrangement as contrary to public policy. Both Mr. Davies's and Marshall Hall's letters to Sir John make the view of the Home Office clear. The proposed method of raising funds was very unfortunate ; the Poor Persons' Defence Act had been expressly provided to meet this contingency. It was an obligation of honour for counsel, who had once undertaken a defence, to persist in it. Further, the Secretary of State seems to have expressed the view, that no member of the Bar would ever, willingly, allow his fees to be paid out of such a fund.

Now this view, expressed by a colleague, wounded Marshall Hall. He considered it wrong ; and, since it concerns a matter which is still of great public interest and importance, and about which Marshall Hall felt very deeply, both in its personal and public aspects, it seems only just to quote his eloquent letter to the Secretary of State at length. From the public point of view, it is, of course, deplorable that it should be necessary to exploit the publicity value of the life of a man like Smith, in order to procure sufficient funds for his defence, and those who choose to do so are entitled to criticise the Press which makes the bargain. But, from the point of view of the prisoner and his advisers, it is, at least, better to make such a bargain than to leave the prisoner practically undefended, when confronted with all the resources of the Public Prosecutor, or even to draw for his defence on funds of his own, which may well be the fruits of his crime. The utmost that the Poor Prisoners' Defence Act allows to counsel is the sum of £3 5s. 6d. It is interesting to speculate on the manner in which Sir John's own clerk would have commented on this sum, as a remuneration for his master's superb services during a nine days' trial. The whole incident is a bitter commentary on the present machinery for the defence of poor prisoners, and a strong argument for the institution of the office of a Public Defender.

3 Temple Gardens.

" MY DEAR JOHN,—I am writing to you direct, as Ernle Blackwell tells me that the letter from the Home Office to Mr. Davies, the solicitor, *in re R.* v *Smith* (Murder), although signed by him, was, in fact, your letter. As you have been so recently Attorney-General and, therefore, custodian of the Bar's honour, I attach much importance to some remarks you make, and regret to say that I am quite unable to understand or accept them. As I understand the facts, they are as follows :

" Some time ago, Mr. Davies, a solicitor, gave my clerk a retainer for me on behalf of the man Smith, accused of murder. My clerk informed him that the brief would not be accepted unless a very substantial fee was paid with it. This condition was acceded to. Later, the solicitor informed my clerk that the fee required would be forthcoming, as he had made arrangements, on behalf of the accused man, whereby certain people were prepared to provide the funds necessary for his defence.

" The brief was not then delivered, but, on the faith of the statement, I consented to have a consultation, and actually to see the accused, which I did. The brief was delivered on Thursday, June 18th (the trial being definitely fixed for June 22nd), and the solicitor then informed my clerk that, as the arrangement for obtaining the money involved the signing of a document by the accused, and the prison authorities had referred the matter to your department, owing to the fact that no reply had been received from you, the fee would not be paid, as arranged, with the brief. My clerk was informed that there would be no delay, and, on this assurance, I consented to take the brief, and devoted the whole of Friday, Saturday, and Monday to getting it up. On Monday afternoon, I was personally shown your letter and informed of the further facts.

" I understand that the proposal, which you so strongly vetoed, was that the accused should assign to certain named assignees the copyright of anything he might write for publication, the consideration being the provision of a certain sum of money to be used by the solicitor for the purposes of his defence. I understand further, that this assignment (which your department have and which I have never seen) was, in fact, prepared by counsel (having no connection with counsel for the defence), who had advised that there was no objection to the execution of such a document by the accused.

" In spite of your expressed opinion, I regret to say that I cannot see your objection. ' A ' charged with murder, and protesting his innocence (and moreover by our law *presumed* to be innocent), has arrayed against him all the resources of the Treasury and the Public Prosecutor, who propose to call some 120 witnesses against him on his trial, which will probably last fourteen days. ' A ' has been deprived of all funds in his possession by the action of the police, and he is anxious to be defended. He is told that the particular counsel, whose services he desires to secure, insists on payment of a fee which he cannot provide. An offer is made to ' A ' to provide sufficient money for this purpose (note please, nothing for the accused himself) if he will write the history of his life and assign the copyright to the person finding the money. ' A ' agrees, but the Home Office authorities decline to allow him to sign the document, and go on to say that the late Attorney-General is of opinion that no counsel at the Bar would accept fees coming from such a source.

" For the life of me I cannot follow this, but, as you are such a great friend of mine, I feel very strongly the opinion you have formed, and I tell you quite frankly, I was quite prepared to accept fees so provided, and cannot see the objection to my so doing.

" If ' A ' had been on bail, he could have executed the assignment at his free volition, and the fact that he is detained in custody cannot affect the proposition.

" ' A ' is entitled to be defended by counsel, and counsel are entitled to be paid reasonable fees. In fact, they are not entitled to refuse any brief, if it is for a court in which they practise, and the fee paid is reasonably adequate. This was the opinion given to me by Lord Alverstone and Lord Loreburn, when I consulted them, many years ago, as to refusing a brief which I much wished to refuse at the C.C.C.

" Now ' A ' is entitled to procure funds for this purpose by any legitimate means, and he can, for this purpose, sell anything that belongs to him which is marketable, e.g. he could execute the necessary conveyance to enable him to sell house property in his possession. Surely he can sell the product of his brain and pen in the same way.

" Further, from the counsel's point of view, your experience, fortunately, has not been so long or so sordid as mine, of this class of case. What has sometimes made me feel very unhappy is to know that fees that have been paid to me for the defence, once the accused has been convicted, have obviously been ear-marked as the proceeds, more or less direct, of the crime itself. But the only protection open to a man like myself (who quite against his will has attained a widespread reputation as a defender of prisoners), against being briefed in any important case of the kind that may arise, is to insist that substantial fees should be paid before the brief is delivered. If the solicitor at the last moment is prevented from finding these fees, you say that counsel, in spite of this arrangement, is in honour bound to conduct the case. Although I deny your premisses, I accept your conclusion, and, in spite of every inclination, have consented to represent the accused, and my friend Montague Shearman has adopted the same attitude. Of course, I was not bound to do it, and from every point of view, pecuniary, physical, and professional, I cannot help suffering from being concerned in such a case.

" It is too late to alter this now, but I do most strenuously protest that the proposed arrangement (which was being carried out openly in every way, as your letter admits) was in no way against public morality or public interest, and one within the rights of any accused person—of course, there might be conditions attached, which would make such an assignment highly undesirable, or even against public policy, but no such conditions existed in this case."

This letter produced only a courteous acknowledgment from the Home Secretary, and the release by the police authorities of the money found in the prisoner's possession on his arrest, which it would be difficult to describe as otherwise than " earmarked " in the sense mentioned above.

So, after all, Marshall Hall appeared to defend George Joseph Smith at the Old Bailey on the 22nd June, 1915. The fee was not what was promised, and was inadequate in the extreme to the great position and prestige which were now his ; indeed, in the appeal that followed, his fee, the very modest one of seventeen guineas, was paid, as to ten guineas by the Director of Public Prosecutions, and as to seven guineas by the Kent County Council. The prisoner's funds had been totally exhausted. Many will say that he could hardly have refused to give his services under the circumstances, but it is conceivable that other great advocates might have felt that, as a protest, and for the sake of the protection of the Bar in the future, retirement from the case was the higher duty. Such a course was never possible for Marshall Hall's sympathetic and generous nature, and full credit must be given to the great advocate, who, during ten whole days' for a few guineas a day, lavished the full force of his superb advocacy in a hopeless cause.

Archibald Bodkin, Travers Humphreys, and Cecil Whiteley appeared for the Crown. The whole of the first day was occupied in the opening of the case by Bodkin. The prisoner was charged with the wilful murder of Bessie Mundy on the 13th July, 1912, and nothing else was referred to in the indictment presented to the jury. However, Mr. Bodkin was able to adduce a very remarkable introduction to the case. In 1898, Smith, the son of an insurance agent, under the assumed name of George Love, had married Caroline Beatrice Thornhill, who had separated from him in 1903. She was still alive. In 1908 he met a young woman named Edith Pegler in Bristol, and married her under his own name ; till the date of his arrest he had lived with her from time to time, leaving her for long periods, but always returning to her in the end. Then counsel opened the story of Miss Mundy's death, concluding with the words, " This case . . . is of a very grave character, and one to which you will give the most earnest attention in the interests, not only of the prisoner, but also of the public."

There was a dramatic pause, and Mr. Justice Scrutton, the

great commercial lawyer, who was presiding at the Old Bailey, requested the jury to retire while counsel argued as to the admissibility of certain evidence. It was generally known that an important question of law was to be argued, and that *R. v. Smith* might become a " leading case," as well as the most extraordinary trial of recent times.

Now it is a fundamental principle of British criminal juris-prudence that, when a prisoner is charged with an offence, he shall not be embarrassed in his defence either by the allegation of other offences, whether he has been convicted of them or no, or by an attack on his character or reputation, however bad it may be. The law, in its mercy and wisdom, seeks to isolate and, as it were, to disinfect the one charge of everything except its own immediate set of facts, so that the accused shall not be imperilled by prejudice. There are certain exceptions to this rule ; where the defence attacks the character of the witnesses for the prosecution, or puts the prisoner's character in issue by adducing evidence of his good character, such evidence becomes admissible. There is also a further ground on which evidence of other similar acts by the prisoner may be admitted. Where the prisoner, charged with a crime, puts forward a defence of accident or mistake, or ignorance, the evidence of other facts may be adduced to rebut such defences, or to prove a course of conduct which makes accident, mistake, or ignorance, on an isolated occasion, unlikely. A schoolmaster may beat a child to death once, and be innocent of cruelty ; the child's physique may be abnormal and peculiarly sensitive, or the master may plead accident and ignorance. But if three children die under his cane, the man's nature will naturally be thought cruel and violent, and he will be rightly convicted of manslaughter. The exception has a sound basis in logic : it is based on the principle of induc-tion, which is as vital to inference as deduction. Such evidence is technically called evidence of " system."

Now how much had Mr. Archibald Bodkin proved up to this moment ? He was asking the Old Bailey jury to reverse the decision of the coroner's jury, probably as sensible as themselves, and that three years after the woman's death. The second jury had before them evidence of motive in regard to the will, and they had the strange history of the marriage. Further, they had the extraordinary interview of the prisoner with Miss Rapley. They had the bath, which was a very small one, and a difficult one in which to be drowned accidentally. All these things the coroner's jury had before them, but they had heard no evidence of any act by the prisoner or of his presence in the bathroom. Could the jury convict of murder with such gaps in the evidence? If this were all, could the judge even leave the question to the jury? Mr. Cecil Whiteley, one of the prosecuting counsel, frankly said, at a meeting of the Medico-Legal Society, " It might have been very difficult for a jury to have convicted. The prosecution, not proving any act at all of the prisoner, it would have been very difficult indeed to have satisfied the jury beyond reasonable doubt that he was responsible for the death ; if we had gone on it would have been hopeless for the prosecution, and there can be no doubt that he would have been acquitted."

But this was not all ; it was well known to Marshall Hall that, in the mountain of documents piled up in front of his adversary, there was evidence that the prisoner had married two other women ; that the two had died in their baths ; that he had been the sole beneficiary under their wills. He knew that, if once this evidence was admitted, Smith was as good as hung. The jury would as certainly infer murder as if he had drowned his brides under their very eyes. Here then was the prisoner's life dependent on a legal argument, and, as Marshall so frankly admitted, he was not skilled at arguing points of law : but here he had a fine point to argue, and, putting heart and soul into it, he argued it finely, both at the Old Bailey and afterwards in the Court of Criminal Appeal. The whole principle of the presumption of innocence, he said, was at stake. Evidence of " system " was only admissible where a defence, denying intent or the like, was to be set up. Here no defence was necessary. There was no *prima facie* case to answer at all. He cited all the relevant authorities, and said that no previous decision had allowed evidence of system to be set up when there was, as yet, not sufficient evidence to go to the jury to displace the primary presumption of innocence. In Palmer's case, although it was known that other patients had died under his treatment, no evidence of this was tendered by the prosecution. The utter depravity of Smith naturally tends to blur the force of the argument, and to degrade it into a mere technicality. But it was more than this ; if Marshall Hall was right, it was of importance that his contention should prevail. According to his view, the great principle that a man is innocent until he is proved guilty was at stake, together with the only less important principle that a man shall not be embarrassed in his trial for one offence by the allegation of others. It is better that one guilty wretch should escape, utterly worthless and a danger to society though he may be, than that the necessity for his conviction should impair the common law.

The judge, however, admitted the evidence, warning the jury that they must not use it to infer that the prisoner was a man of bad character and infamous acts, likely to have committed the murder, but to help them to decide whether the death of Miss Mundy was accidental or designed by the prisoner. From this moment, though the case dragged on for nine days, the prisoner's fate was sealed, and, gallantly as he fought, Marshall Hall was never for a moment able to put the issue in doubt.

Mr. Bodkin then proceeded to open the facts of the second murder. In the autumn of 1913, Smith left Miss Pegler, as he said, " for a run round " in the antique furniture trade, which she always understood was his business. He always explained the profits which arose from his marriages by saying that he had done very well out of the sale of a work of art : on one occasion it was a Turner ; on another, a Chinese image. While he was " running round " he visited a Nonconformist chapel at Southsea, where he went, as Mr. Bodkin said, not to pray, but to " prey," on young women of simple faith. His fascinating and predatory gaze fell upon a buxom young nurse named Alice Burnham. She felt his gaze fixed on her all through the service, and he spoke to her outside. She soon fell a victim to the charms of " George Joseph Smith, Esq., a gentleman of independent means," and wrote an unaffected letter to her married sister telling her of her happiness. They had " met at the chapel I attend. George was brought up Wesleyan. . . . I am so happy, Rose dear. My heart and soul thank God continually for joining me to the love of so good a man—a perfect gentleman, very homely. You cannot fail to like him, so genuine, kind. . . . I am the most fortunate and happiest girl in the world." On November 4th, they were married. Mr. Burnham, her father, had been keeping a sum of £104 for his daughter. For this Smith made a formal demand, and, when his father-in-law dared to ask questions about him, he wrote the following astonishing letter.

" Sir,—In answer to your application regarding my parentage, my mother was a Bus-horse, my father a cab-driver, my sister a roughrider over the Arctic Regions. My brothers were all gallant sailors on a steam-roller. This is the only information I can give to those who are not entitled to ask such questions contained in the letter I received on the 24th inst.
" Your despised son-in-law,
" G. SMITH."

In the end, he obtained through a solicitor payment of his wife's £104. Smith had now learned by experience not to ignore opportunities ; if this spouse should also die, he did not wish to be left uncompensated. There had been no need to insure Miss Mundy's life, as she was so well off. But he saw to it that the new " Mrs. Smith's " life was insured for £500, and on December 8th she went alone to a solicitor and made a will leaving everything to the prisoner. The couple then went on a visit to Blackpool. They rejected the first lodgings they visited, because there was no bath, but at Mrs. Crossley's, in Regent Road, they found all they wanted. Then almost in the minutest detail the fate of " Mrs. Williams " dogged " Mrs. Smith." Headaches came, and there were visits to a doctor ; this bride wrote home just as her predecessor had done. " My husband," she said, " does all he can for me ; in fact, dear, I have the best husband in the world." In the, evening the bride took a walk in the gay, Christmas-lit streets of Blackpool—the last walk she was ever to take on earth. At 8 p.m. on the Friday night, December 12th, she took a bath. While she was taking it, the landlady below saw water coming through the ceiling. A little later the bridegroom knocked at the door ; he had been out to buy some eggs for his wife's supper (he had gone out to buy fish when Miss Mundy died). He then went upstairs, and his wife was found dead in her bath ; no bruises were found on her body. If he had been hysterical and

X H

unnerved by the death of his other bride, he had now become
hardened by misfortune. He struck Mrs. Crossley as shockingly
callous. He wanted to sleep in the room where the dead woman
lay ; he ordered her a deal coffin and a pauper's funeral ; and,
when the Crossleys protested, he said, " When they are dead,
they are done with." On the other hand, he wrote to Mrs.
Burnham that " he had suffered the greatest and most cruel
shock that ever a man could have suffered." The inquest was
held on the Monday morning following, before the Burnhams
could possibly arrive. The coroner, having a train to catch, was
in a hurry, and Smith's tears now flowed freely. The coroner's
jury might say that " the deceased suffered from heart disease . . .
the cause of death was accidental," but Mrs. Crossley was not
deceived ; she wrote on the back of a card on which Smith had
left his address, " Wife died in bath ; we shall see him again " ;
and, as he departed down the street, she called after him,
" Crippen ! " She was underestimating him ; he deserved a worse
name.

It was now nearly Christmas-time, and Smith naturally
returned to the bosom of his family for the festive season ; that
is, he went back to the other and well-beloved " Mrs. Smith " of
Bristol (Miss Pegler). He spent Christmas with her mother.
There was a party, and the versatile antique dealer, having, as
he said, just returned from a profitable journey in Spain, was
most agreeable, and kept everyone laughing by his musical and
story-telling talents. For he was a good musician, and " could
play anything by ear." In January he received the £500 insurance
money on Alice Burnham's life, which he prudently handed over
to the insurance company in order to increase his annuity by
about £30 a year.

Bodkin, in what is generally thought the most brilliant speech
of his career, had opened these two terrible stories in strict
chronological order, dealing with the meeting with the women,
then with their financial resources and their marriages, then
with Smith's obtaining of their money, followed by the visits to
the lawyers and the doctors, the letters home, the deaths, the
discovery of the bodies in the baths, and the realisation by
Smith of the assets, and finally his disappearance. When he
came to the third story, he went straight to the discovery of the

body in the bath, and then worked backwards, showing that in every aspect of the case it was similar to the first two, so that the jury could see that every detail, opportunity, access, motive, were the same in each case. Nothing could have been more effective or dramatic.

At a lodging-house in Bismarck Road, Highgate, London, N., on December 18th, 1914, a distracted husband named John Lloyd found his bride of one day dead in her bath. He ran at once to fetch first a policeman, and then a doctor. The police officer, knowing something of these things, tried to restore her to life by a system which had been invented by old Dr. Marshall Hall. But it was all in vain. The tragedy had happened this time while the bridegroom had been out buying tomatoes. It was a Friday night, and a bath, having been specially asked for, had been prepared for the bride. A few minutes later the sound of splashing was heard from the bathroom, and the noise of the slapping of wet hands on flesh ; then there was a sigh. Soon afterwards the landlady heard the mournful strains of the stately hymn, " Nearer, my God, to Thee," which someone was playing on the organ in the Lloyds' sitting-room. Soon afterwards the door slammed, and a little later Mr. Lloyd knocked at the door. He had forgotten that she had given him a key. " I have bought some tomatoes for Mrs. Lloyd's supper," he said.

A third coroner's jury exonerated the husband, who showed great emotion. " We were only married Thursday," he said. This was the eldest of Smith's three brides, and she lived the shortest time of all after her marriage ; she was the most well born of all his brides, being a clergyman's daughter who had spent her adult life as companion to elderly ladies. But she was the poorest of them all. She possessed only £19 in cash, which her husband easily induced her to draw from her savings bank account on the day before her death. However, shortly before her marriage she had effected an insurance on her life, and on the day of her death she visited a solicitor and made a will leaving everything to her husband. Her quiet life with her old lady friends had been disturbed by an unfortunate love-affair with a man who turned out to be married ; this may have made the way easier for Mr. John Lloyd, land agent, when, a year later, he laid siege to the poor woman's affections. On the day of her marriage she wrote to her family, " No doubt you will be surprised to know that I was married to-day to a gentleman named John Lloyd. He is a thorough Christian man whom I have known since June. I met him at Bath. . . . Our tastes and temperaments were exactly in harmony. . . . It is only natural I should do anything to secure the one I love, and I have every proof of his love for me. He has been *honourable* and kept his *word* to me in everything." Poor, simple, deluded companion to old ladies. From the bells of a cathedral close to the arms of George Joseph Smith!

Perhaps Smith was anxious to get back to Bristol to spend another merry Christmas with Miss Pegler ; or perhaps he was growing in confidence ; at any rate, the programme, which otherwise so exactly followed precedent, had two peculiarities. The drama had been greatly accelerated, and the scene was this time laid in London. " The Bride of one Night," dying on Friday night in London, was sure to attract the attention of the national Sunday Press. In the *News of the World* it was made quite a feature. " Bride's Tragic Fate on Day after Wedding. . . . Particularly sad circumstances under which a bride of a day met her death were investigated at an Islington inquest on Margaret Elizabeth Lloyd, thirty-eight, wife of a land agent of Holloway." The previous inquests had been only reported in local papers ; and now, all unknown to him, the meshes were closing round Smith. The *News of the World* has several million readers ; among them was a Mrs. Heiss, who let lodgings at 16 Orchard Road, Highgate. A Mr. Lloyd had applied for lodgings, and had particularly asked for a bath. He was shown the bath, and saw it was very small, and he had said, " I daresay it is large enough for someone to lie in." He engaged the lodgings, but, owing to the fact that he was unable to provide a reference, she had ultimately refused to fulfil the engagement. Mr. Lloyd had been so offensive that she had had to call in a police-inspector, who turned him away.

Among other newspaper readers were Mr. Charles Burnham and Mr. Crossley, of Blackpool. They each read the story of " Mrs. Lloyd," in different corners of England, and said to themselves, " That is Smith." Communications reached New Scotland Yard. When Smith returned from his Christmas with the Peglers of Bristol in order to attend the adjourned inquest, and to consult a solicitor at Shepherd's Bush concerning the probate of " Mrs. John Lloyd's " will, he was already under police observation. On February 1st, 1915, he was arrested when about to deal with this important business.

Finally, Bodkin brought his gruesome narrative to a close. " In each case," he said, " you get the simulated marriage. In each case all the ready money the woman had is realised. In each case the woman made a will in the prisoner's favour. In each case the property could only be got at through the woman's death. In each case there were, we submit, unnecessary visits to a doctor. In each case letters were written the night before death in which the prisoner's kindness as a husband is extolled. In each case there were enquiries about a bathroom. In each case the prisoner is the first to discover the death. In each case the prisoner is the person in immediate association with each woman before her death. In each case the bathroom doors are either unfastenable or unfastened. In each case he pretends to do something which shall take him away from the scene where the particular tragedy has been enacted. In each case there is the immediate disappearance of the prisoner." Mr. Bodkin might have added that in each case the bride died either on a Friday night or a Saturday morning, so that an inquest could be held over the week-end, before her relatives could arrive.

For six days witnesses were called to narrate the miserable tragedies of these three confiding and simple ladies. Theirs were humble lives, which would normally have been spent in quiet, uneventful surroundings. That seemed to make their tragedies the more poignant. For these women asked so little of life ; until Smith came along they did not even claim love. Some strange fascination in him called them from their quiet homes and employment. They learnt what love was ; they became adventurous and passionate, and paid for it with their lives. The witnesses' stories were made more graphic by the production of the three very baths in which the poor women had died, and many of them, from great emotional stress, found it difficult to give their evidence. The near and dear ones of each of them had to go into the box to say what they knew, as well as the poor, respectable landladies, none of whom " ever expected such a thing to happen in my house."

The only bride of Smith to give evidence at the trial was Miss Pegler, the one bride whom Smith loved enough neither to desert, to rob, nor to kill. But once, nevertheless, he had warned her of the danger of baths to women. Shortly before he married Miss Lofty he said to Miss Pegler, while he was living with her, " I should advise you to be careful of these things, as it is known that women often lose their lives through weak hearts and fainting in a bath." This is very curious. However, Miss Pegler could say that Smith, on the whole, had been kind to her.

At the police court, where a multitude of women came to look at him, he had broken out into violent abuse of the witnesses, and especially of Mr. Bodkin. When Marshall Hall and Shearman went to see him at Brixton, they were shown into a room where he was sitting, and his eyes were quite terrible. " He had," said the latter, " a horrible way of looking at one. It gave me a most unpleasant feeling, and we certainly formed the opinion that he had a curious way of influencing people." So repelled was Marshall Hall by his looks that he broke off the consultation, convinced that the man was trying to hypnotise him.

At the trial Smith was quieter than at the police court ; he was obviously distressed when Miss Pegler was giving her evidence. Otherwise, except for feverishly writing notes to his counsel, he remained comparatively calm until the police evidence was called. Then his undisciplined nature burst forth. When Inspector Neill went into the box he lost all control. " He is a scoundrel. . . . He ought to be in this dock. He will be one day," he shouted.

" Sit down," said the judge. " You are doing yourself no good."

When another police officer followed Neill, the prisoner shouted, " He is another scoundrel. He has been doing nothing but bribery for the last five years."

Mr. Shearman was quite unable to pacify him ; he rushed to the front of the dock, banged his fist on the front ledge, and shouted, his face white with wrath, " I don't care tuppence what you say, you can't sentence me to death. I have done no murder."

Conclusive as the circumstances seemed to be, the prosecution had yet to prove how the women died, and how the prisoner had a hand in the business. Inspector Neill induced one of his fair

GEORGE JOSEPH SMITH'S DECISION

not to give evidence, recorded in writing according to Marshall Hall's practice

friends, a strong swimmer, to put on a bathing costume and subject herself to experiment. The inspector pulled up her legs from the foot of the bath so that her head fell under water. She immediately lost consciousness, and they had real difficulty in bringing her round. For, as Sir William Willcox and Sir Bernard Spilsbury said in their evidence, water suddenly and unexpectedly pouring into the mouth and nostrils might produce death from shock before the victim was actually suffocated by drowning. This was the first method suggested by the prosecution as to the way in which Smith killed his victims. It certainly seems surprising, however, that the women were not able to resist by lifting themselves above the water with their arms. Only in the case of Miss Lofty was there any evidence at all of a struggle.

When the turn for the defence came, there was great expectancy, though everything had seemed to go one way. Had Marshall Hall some unexpected surprise to spring upon the prosecution, as he had in the Bennett and the Lawrence trials? He had cross-examined every witness with all his usual vigour and dexterity, yet only one line of defence was disclosed—that the prosecution had not brought home to the prisoner any act which could have caused death to any one of the three women; and this was not enough, or nearly enough, to answer Mr. Bodkin's terrible indictment. Was there anything further? At the end of the seventh day, when the case for the prosecution closed, he rose and said, " I do not call any evidence."

This gave him the last word; for, except where the Crown appears by one of the law officers, who have always a prerogative to the last word, where no evidence is called the prisoner's counsel addresses the Court last. After Mr. Bodkin's speech, Marshall Hall rose to defend Smith. It was a fine speech, and very impressive; but the impression it made was rather this: that with such scanty material, and against such tremendous odds, so much could still be said for the prisoner. For Marshall Hall was never a man to throw his hand in. He began his speech quietly and slowly : " At a moment like the present, when the flower of our youth are laying down their lives for their country, does it not strike you as a great tribute to the national character of level-headedness that, with all the panoply of pomp and law,

we have been assembled day after day to enquire into the facts
of this sordid case, and to decide whether or not one man should
go to an ignominious death or not ? It is a great tribute to our
national system of jurisprudence."

His arguments for the defence were, first, that no act of
violence was proven, and that it would be impossible for Smith
to have committed this crime without leaving marks of violence
and evidence of a struggle. " If you tried to drown a kitten
it would scratch you, and do you think a woman would not
scratch ? " He prayed in aid the mutual affection between Miss
Pegler and the prisoner, and said that to have perpetrated
these crimes was outside the orbit of sane humanity. " Let me,"
he concluded, " with all the solemnity I can, and with all the
power of conviction I can put into words, say to you : be fair
to yourselves, be fair to the prisoner, be just to justice itself
before you decide the fate of this man by saying that this
terrible accusation against him has been proved."

When Marshall Hall sat down, the prisoner gave a deep sigh.
The learned judge paid Marshall Hall's speech the compliment
of summing up for nearly a day ; it was remarkable for one
thing : the judge put to the jury hypotheses as to the method in
which the women might have died not advanced by the prosecution. " Include in your consideration this possibility," he said
" . . . of this having happened. Wife to husband : ' I am going to
have a bath'; husband to wife : 'All right, I will go and turn on
the water for you.' Husband goes to the bathroom and turns on the
water and waits ; the wife comes in her dressing-gown or night-
gown. The newly married husband stays in the room, strips her,
or she strips herself. ' I'll put you in the bath, my dear ' ; picks
her up . . . lowers her into the bath, but holds the knees up." As
he said this, the learned judge rose from the bench, and in dumb
show demonstrated how it was possible to lift the woman up and
put her in the bath, forcing her head down with one hand while
holding her knees up with the other. This theory did away with
the difficulty of the prisoner coming into an unlocked bathroom
and assaulting his wife in a deadly way without surprising or
frightening her into a struggle. Speaking of this judicial demonstration, Mr. Cecil Whiteley said, " It was so vivid that I think
it contributed largely towards the conviction of the prisoner."

Marshall Hall at once protested, and submitted that it was not open to the jury to consider any other theory than that put forward by the prosecution.

" I will give you another cause for complaint," retorted the judge, " if you wish it. If, on looking at the baths, another theory occurs to the jury better than those already suggested, in my view they are quite entitled to consider it."

Indeed, in the course of his summing up he also suggested that the prisoner might have administered a drug to the women. " There is no evidence of drugging," he said, " but you must consider it as a possibility." These alternative theories of the judge made one of the grounds of appeal, and the Lord Chief Justice, while holding that the real question was whether the prisoner had caused the deaths or not, said that it would have been better if the learned judge had not put forward his own speculations as to the exact method used by the prisoner.

Mr. Justice Scrutton, with great effect, compared the knocking at the door by Smith shortly after Miss Lofty had died to the knocking at the gate just after the murder of Duncan in *Macbeth*—" the most dramatic moment in English poetry."

During the summing-up the prisoner interrupted again and again. " You may as well hang me at once, the way you are going on." " Get on, hang me at once and done with it." " You can go on for ever ; you cannot make me into a murderer ; I have done no murder." " It is a disgrace to a Christian country, this is. I am not a murderer, though I may be a bit peculiar."

At 2.48 on the ninth day of the trial the jury retired. At 3.10 they returned. Then an official rapped three loud knocks on the door through which the judge was to enter, in order to warn the Court of his arrival. This formal incident produced, perhaps, the most dramatic moment in the whole trial, the judge's reference to the knocking at the gate in *Macbeth* being fresh in the memory of those in court.

The verdict was " guilty."

This time there was no emotion in the stern voice of the judge as he pronounced sentence. " Judges," he said, " sometimes use this occasion to warn the public against the repetition of such crimes ; they sometimes use such occasions to exhort the prisoner to repentance. I propose to take neither of those courses.

I do not believe there is another man in England who needs to be warned against the commission of such a crime, and I think that exhortation to repentance would be wasted on you."

The sentence had a stunning effect upon the prisoner; his face, save for a patch of red on each cheekbone, went livid. He all but collapsed, but, when he was called on by the clerk of the court, he managed to say, " I can only say I am not guilty." A moment later, be it said to his credit, he pulled himself together sufficiently to speak a word of gratitude to his counsel. " I thank you, Mr. Marshall Hall," he said, " for what you have done for me. I have great confidence—*great* confidence—in you. I shall bear up."

Thus ended the trial of this amazing man. His appeal was heard on July 29th. Rufus Isaacs, now Lord Reading, as Chief Justice of England, presided. He paid a high tribute to the argument of his old friend. It was a substantial argument. The main point had been argued before Mr. Justice Scrutton. The Court decided on the facts that, there being a *prima facie* case against the prisoner as regards Miss Mundy, the evidence as to the other deaths was admissible. This was a decision on the facts, not on the law : whether evidence as to system is admissible where there is not sufficient evidence on one charge to amount to a *prima facie* case, is still a matter of doubt.

Mr. Justice Scrutton in discharging the jury said that the prisoner had married two other women and robbed them. The facts disclosed by the trial, even thus reinforced, give but a scanty idea of Smith's record. He was an habitual criminal, and for twenty years lived a life of lesser crime before he took to murder. Born in 1872, and of respectable parentage, his precocious wickedness had broken his mother's heart : she prophesied that " he would die in his boots." He was sent to a reformatory as a lad, and there bewildered his teachers. " I would give anything to see what you are like in twenty years," said one of them. He showed a great love of poetry, especially of Shakespeare, and could play the piano and draw quite well. In 1891 he received his first term of imprisonment for stealing tricycles " hired " by him. From 1891–3, according to his own story, he served in the Northamptonshire Regiment, became a a gymnasium-instructor and also acted as a sort of barrack-room lawyer, advising his comrades exactly what punishment could be meted out to them. In 1896 he served a year's imprisonment for larceny. This was unfortunate ; but, nevertheless, he had now discovered his true vocation. He began to move among an under-world of attractive women. He discovered that he had a considerable power over them. Posing as a " music-hall song writer," he lived at Chelsea and gave enthusiastic " references " to good-looking servant girls, who shortly after engagement would steal what they could and bring the plunder faithfully to Smith. When he came out of prison, he went to Leicester, where he opened a little bakery shop ; he employed a pretty girl named " Beatie " Thornhill as his assistant. He made passionate love to her, and married her in 1898, under the name of " George Love." He moved to London, returning to his old games, and made his poor young wife steal for him. As early as 1899, he took to bigamy and " married " at a register office in London a respectable boarding-house keeper, from whom he extorted sums of money. This woman was taken to identify him, in her own interests, when he was pacing up and down the exercise ground at Pentonville under sentence of death. Meanwhile, Mrs. Love had to pay the price with a conviction for larceny, but her husband escaped. After she had returned to her parents, George Love wrote his wife passionate love-letters and poems, begging her to return to him. " It seems to me that you were born for me. . . . Remember, love is full of folly and is frantic. . . . Why did the very eyes of you make me so foolish, and make me a mad, loving fool ? Heaven bless you. . . . They say sleep is the balm of each day's care, but, when I try to go to sleep, I cannot, because of you."

However, Beatie Thornhill was more sensible than any of her successors. In 1900 she was in London, and saw her husband looking into a shop. This strange chance meeting is as curious as his later reunion with Miss Mundy. Unlike the latter, Beatie acted promptly, and had him arrested by the nearest policeman ; he was sentenced to two years. The husband swore to murder her when he came out. Beatie's retort was " Treacle is sweet, but revenge is sweeter." When he came out in 1903, he went in search of his wife at Leicester, but only received a sound thrashing from her loyal brothers. His wife fled to Canada, and found safety and prosperity.

Obscurity then falls over the man : the police lost touch with him. Early in the same month in which he married Miss Pegler, he was able to defraud a widow under a promise of marriage. He took her to the White City Exhibition, left her on a trivial pretext, and altogether made himself the richer by £80 or £90. He did not marry this lady. He regarded women purely as commercial propositions, and did not marry them if it was not necessary. In June 1909, when he was actually living with Miss Pegler, he met a Miss Faulkner. He was now " George Rose." Miss Pegler never discovered the intrigue. In October 1909 he was married to Miss Faulkner at Southampton by special licence ; for she was worth about £300, every penny of which he got into his possession. Remembering how successful his method had been with the Brighton widow, he took " Mrs. Rose " to the National Gallery on a free day, left her on the same excuse, rushed home, and went off with all the poor woman's possessions, including her clothing. She never saw him again until after his arrest. The poor woman was, after all, very fortunate. She was the last but one of all Bluebeard's known victims to escape with her life. His next wife was Bessie Mundy.

The evidence at the trial accounts for some of Smith's activities during the succeeding years; but there was still one other poor girl, Alice Reavil, who lost all her worldly possessions through her " marriage " to him. In September 1914 he won the heart of a poor servant girl who had saved about £78. He met her in some public gardens at Bournemouth. He complimented the ingenuous maiden on her pretty figure, and on the third or fourth day she accepted the proposal of " Charles Oliver James," an artist from Canada, for her hand. Besides her savings, she owned some furniture and a piano, which she sold for £14 and gave to her lover, whom she married soon afterwards on September 17th. He took her to London, and, since she had now withdrawn all her savings from the Post Office and handed them over to Smith, there was no need to trouble her further ; for Smith did not take pleasure in murder for murder's sake. He took her for a penny tram-ride, then for a walk in some public gardens, and then left her " for a minute." But he made

GEORGE JOSEPH SMITH
dressed as a bridegroom

his escape for good, taking with him all her possessions. He afterwards gave the poor girl's trousseau to Miss Pegler, saying he had been doing a deal in second-hand clothes.

The record of George Joseph Smith with regard to women is now complete, that is, so far as it is known. Except for Beatrice Thornhill and Edith Pegler, for both of whom he obviously felt affection, he regarded women and their lives merely as commercial propositions. He wanted their money, or, if they had no worldly possessions, the money that their insured lives would yield. Was he not the son of an insurance agent? He did not marry them unless he had to, he did not kill them unless he had to, he did not even make love to them unless he had to. He was no sadist, but a purely commercial murderer. There was a curious incident of his acquaintanceship with a nursery governess whom he asked to tea with himself and Miss Pegler, and whose life he wished to insure. The premium was actually paid, but in the end the policy was cancelled. This transaction, if completed, would have been unalloyed by any show of sentiment.

He must have been a person of very singular personality; in all his history no man friend or associate appears at all; he was a professional and a literal lady-killer. It was the only business which he ever made profitable. He tinkered at many honest trades, from bakery to dealing in works of art and literature, and never made a success of them. But, from the moment when he discovered that he could persuade pretty girls to steal for him, until the evening when he wrestled with Miss Lofty in the bathroom of their North London lodgings, his relations with women were always profitable. He made a trade of love-at-first-sight, and he knew his powers. His success is all the more extraordinary in view of his extreme parsimony, a quality known to be intolerable to women. Was it that he had merely made a careful study of the art of fascinating women by his virile personality, or had he some strange uncanny power of an abnormal character? H. B. Irving at the trial overheard two attractive and gay ladies whispering about his charms as a man. Marshall Hall's own view appears in his letter to the Bishop of Croydon.

Surely Smith was the most extraordinary of all modern criminals. In Seddon, Marshall Hall considered that he had

plumbed the depths of human wickedness ; but Smith's case is
so much more shocking than that of the poisoner, that Marshall
Hall might well have been expected to change his mind. Yet
this was not so. He continued to think that Seddon was as
wicked as a *sane* man can be. Indeed, considering the whole
personality and life of Smith, the reader finds himself in an
atmosphere of nightmare, of unreality, of madness, of ghastly
and inexplicable contradictions. The man who could read
Shakespeare in a quiet garden to a woman whom he genuinely
loved, soon after he had brutally killed another ; who could
himself play his bride's dirge, " Nearer, my God, to Thee,"
immediately after he had murdered her, is a person outside
ordinary humanity. But it should, perhaps, be stated that, in
the present state of the law under the rules of the Macnaughton
case, it would have been hopeless in this case to have put
forward a plea of insanity.

To condemn Smith, as the contemporary Press did, merely as
an unspeakable hypocrite and a human monster, without a
single redeeming feature, is the easiest course. Yet, perhaps,
after all, there was something more interesting and more dreadful
in him than this. Both Marshall Hall and the clergyman, who
came into even more intimate touch with him than his advocate,
formed this view. The chaplain of the prison found him intelligent
and very well read, and the most interesting of all the fifty men
under sentence of death to whom he had administered. Smith
protested his innocence to the last, but this, in view of the
Bishop of Croydon's letter below, cannot merely be explained,
as Mr. George R. Sims sought to explain it, by the fact that his
statements, to his knowledge, would be reported to the authorities and add to the possibility of a reprieve. His one interest in
life during his last days seemed to be for Miss Pegler. He wrote,
on the eve of his execution :

" DEAR LOVE,—Your pure heart and conscience free from
stain helps me to believe that, whilst memory holds a seat
within your sacred brow you will remember me. You are the
last person in the world to whom I shall write, inasmuch as
this is my last letter. I could write volumes of pathos
prompted by the cruel position wherein I am now placed.

But I have too much respect and love for your feelings to do so. I have not asked for a reprieve, nor made a petition, and do not intend doing so. Since we have failed to obtain justice from the earthly judges, I prefer death rather than imprisonment. So an innocent man goes to his untimely end, a victim of cruel fate. God alone is my Judge and the King of kings. It was He who gave me life, who ordained our coming together. My property I give to you. Don't be alone on the last day, when I shall have left this weary ark behind, where perjury, malice, spite, vindictiveness, prejudice, and all other earthly ills will have done its best, and can harm me no more. My time is occupied in solemn and deep meditation. I am preparing my soul for Him to receive. I return to the teaching which I received from my mother. . . . I have gone to God with all my sins with true repentance, and asked His forgiveness and mercy on my soul. I truly believe and feel that my faithful and sincere prayers have been answered. . . . I shall have an extraordinary peace, perfect peace. May an old age, serene and bright, and as lovely as a Lapland night, lead thee to thy grave. Now, my true love, good-bye until we meet again.

" Yours, with immortal love,

" GEORGE."

It is very easy to say with Mr. Sims that this is a " farrago of hypocritical cant." But was this so ? The prison chaplain thought otherwise ; he has written that Smith, coming into prison as a professed atheist, became, before he left it, a sincere convert and penitent. In the interval between his sentence and his execution his hair turned almost white. Hypocrisy could not achieve this : fear might, and so might an agony of remorse and despair. He professed his innocence to the last, both to the chaplain and to the Bishop of Croydon. His death was not cowardly, as was much written at the time, but courageous. He died after partaking of the Holy Sacrament. His last words to the chaplain were, " I beg of you to believe me when I say I am innocent. No one else does, except my wife. I don't care now ; I shall soon be in the presence of God, and I declare before Him I am innocent." As the noose was around his neck and the trap-door fell, he again said, " I am innocent." His body fell into the pit, and George Joseph Smith died, as his three brides had done, by suffocation.

In view of the fact that the prison chaplain has already published the above facts, I feel justified, if for no other reason, in printing the following very interesting correspondence that passed after the execution of Smith between Marshall Hall and the Bishop of Croydon. The latter was most unhappy at the time that the Home Office would not sanction his publication of certain information, and, now that it is already made known, there seems to be no good reason for refraining from publishing these letters.

" *August* 17*th.*

" My Lord,—Your letter *re* G. Smith has interested me very much. I am afraid you had not all the material upon which to base a satisfactory opinion as to his guilt or innocence. On his own admission, the man was abnormal ; and the admitted and undisputed evidence against him, especially two letters in his own handwriting, only one of which has ever been made public, proved conclusively that he was a thief, a liar, and utterly devoid of any sense of decency in his treatment of women. It was because I knew of the overwhelming prejudice against him, and the history behind the case, that I, most reluctantly, acceded to his request that I should defend him, and this I did at great pecuniary and physical sacrifice. But the man was so unlike any other of his type that, after thirty-two years' experience, I felt interested ; and, up to a point, I hoped to save him from the extreme penalty of the law. The moment, however, that the judge, and the Court of Criminal Appeal, decided that the evidence of all three deaths was admissable against him, I knew that the case was hopeless, as no jury, and very few men, will ever accept a theory of triple coincidence to explain what otherwise has a criminal aspect attaching to it. The motive in all three cases was so strong and the series of similarities in all three cases overwhelming. Personally, I have seen some most extraordinary coincidences happen in every-day life—for instance, I have seen the same number turn up five times consecutively on a roulette table. Some years ago at Bournemouth, P. H. Morton (an old Cambridge colleague of mine), playing golf with me on the

public course, holed out the first hole *twice* the same day in one stroke. The odds against both these events are incalculable. Only a few days ago Lord Carnarvon tells me that he and two friends were playing cards at the club and they had to cut for deal ; all three cut a *three*. They cut again ; all three cut a *seven*. They cut a third time ; all three cut an *ace*. My mathematics are rusty, but I believe the odds $(52 \times 51 \times 50)3$ to 1 would represent them. Therefore I have not eliminated the coincidence theory, more especially as in the Highgate case —Lofty—I am extraordinarily sceptical of the cause of death. But alas, allowing for all this, I have most reluctantly come to the conclusion that Smith was responsible for the deaths of all three women, directly or indirectly. That he did not drown them in any of the ways suggested by the evidence, or the *ex parte* suggestions of the judge, I am convinced ; but I am equally convinced that it was brought about by hypnotic suggestion. I had a long interview with Smith, under very favourable circumstances, and I was convinced that he was a hypnotist. Once accept this theory, and the whole thing, including the unbolted doors, is to my mind satisfactorily explained, and it also accounts for his very firm assertion of innocence of murder, he having satisfied his conscience that the act was induced by his will, and became to all intents a voluntary act on the part of the woman. Obviously it is very difficult to write fully upon this subject ; but, if it interests you, perhaps we might meet some day and talk it over. It interests me from all points of view, and I am one of those who think that no man is too bad to try to save. I wrote Smith a letter, in reply to one he sent me protesting his innocence, and I implored him to take the chaplain or someone into his confidence before the end came. I also told him that I was convinced, as well as I could be convinced of anything, that he was responsible for the deaths of all three women, and I further told him that to my mind the means he employed was some form of hypnotic suggestion. This letter was, of course, private, and marked ' not for publication.' He did not answer it, and no doubt, after hearing my four hours' speech on his behalf, he felt it difficult to realise that I believed him guilty. He could not distinguish between the advocate who tries to insist that the onus of legal
YH

proof has not been discharged by the Crown, and the human individual who, outside his professional duties, finds it impossible, knowing all the facts, to accept the theory of coincidence. I am indeed glad, my lord, that you saw him, and did all, I am sure, you could do for a man in his position. The value of human life has, alas, been gravely reduced by the lamentable slaughter that is going on of our bravest and best at this moment. But it is a great tribute to our judicial system that, at a time like this, this man was tried with all the care and precision as if we had been in the midst of peace.

" I judge no man : I know my own life too well to dare to judge others ; but in my heart I feel that it was better for this man to die, even if he were technically innocent, though morally guilty. He apparently died bravely, though with his morbid and abnormal nervous system he must inevitably have suffered acutely, and, though you and I probably look on a future state from a different point of view, I am convinced that he has passed from one plane of existence direct to another, where he will have the chance to prepare for that ever-upward movement that our immortal beings must eventually attain to. Please forgive this long letter. Large sums of money have been offered me to write for publication practically what I am now writing you, but my personal and professional environment make it impossible.

" I have no copy, and I have written as I feel, but I should esteem it a great favour if, after you have read it, you would return it to me, so that I may keep it with other documents concerning this most extraordinary case. As to the letter written to you by Smith, if the authorities see no objection to its publication, I see none.

" I am, my lord, yours very sincerely,
                            "E. MARSHALL HALL."

                            " 18 Collingham Place, S.W.,
                                " *August* 18*th*, 1915.
" MY DEAR SIR,—I am most grateful to you for the long and most interesting letter you have sent me. In compliance with your request, I return it to you.

" I venture to trouble you with a more detailed statement

of my experience in relation to the unhappy man Smith than I gave you in my last.

" When the chaplain of Maidstone Prison wrote and asked me to go there in order to confirm Smith, I found that he was deeply impressed with a conviction of the man's innocence. He told me that whereas Smith, when he first saw him, was hard, impenitent, and a professed unbeliever in a future state, he had become a completely changed man. He was softened, penitent, and a convinced believer in the Christian faith.

" My own experience with him was precisely the same. He told me—not under the seal of confession—that for twenty years he had been a most wicked and abandoned man ; that he had been steeped in every villainy, but never of murder. He knew that there was no chance of a reprieve, nor did he desire it. He deserved his fate. But again he asserted, with the tears coursing down his cheeks, that he had not had anything to do with the murder of these three women. He left a statement to this effect in his cell ; and the last words he spoke, just as he was about to be executed, were ' I am innocent.' I cannot, with a long experience of penitents, believe that he was not sincere in his declaration. He knew perfectly well that he had nothing to gain by deceit then. He declared he was beyond all consideration of what the world might think, and that he desired to make himself right with God above all things ; but, without a complaint as to the injustice of his sentence, he always came back to this : ' I am innocent of murder.'

" As you truly point out, the circumstantial evidence was overwhelmingly against him. I can only conclude that if he was indeed guilty—even of having hypnotised his victims to their deaths—he must have been mad, for I am absolutely convinced that he believed himself innocent of this crime.

" I am in a distressingly difficult position. In his last letter, received by me after his death, he charges me to make his declaration of innocence known. The Home Secretary refuses his sanction to my doing so. I am seeking the advice of the Archbishop of Canterbury as to what my action under the circumstances ought to be. . . .

" Believe me, very truly yours,

" H. H. CROYDON."

Thus we see that the only defence that even Marshall Hall could find for Smith was that of insanity. His views on the law and insanity will be discussed with regard to a later case. Whether Smith killed his victims by virtue of some hypnotic power, or whether it was merely that his strong attraction as a man delivered them helpless into his hands, he was equally guilty of murder. The only thing which can be said, if Marshall Hall's theory was correct, is that it might be a great temptation to a man of an insanely covetous nature and unhinged mentality to make use of such a power, if he consciously possessed it. But, on the whole, expert medical opinion, as Dr. Kingsbury had said in the case of *Kingsbury* v. *Turner*, mentioned above, is against the proposition that a subject can be induced by hypnotism to perform any act, such as suicide, which is repugnant to his or her nature.

. . . .

The prestige of the German Secret Service was very high in England during the war ; it was credited with the most marvellous organisation, and with a ubiquitous personnel of superb efficiency. This prestige caused many quite innocent persons of foreign nationality or extraction to be suspected of espionage. Marshall Hall was in several cases of this nature, of varying importance. The first case of this sort in which he was concerned was the defence of a young Swedish artist named Rolf Jonsson, who was prosecuted before court martial under the Defence of the Realm Regulations. The charge was that " he had signalled to the enemy." He had a house by the sea at Newlyn, in the West Country, and much local gossip credited him with signalling to German ships from his windows overlooking the sea. A naval lieutenant was sent out in a patrol trawler, and proceeded to signal by red and white flashes. According to his account, he received answering flashes from Jonsson's house. Marshall Hall had very little difficulty in securing a finding of " not guilty." He elicited the fact that at the time that the lieutenant saw the flashes coming, as he thought, from the defendant's house, the police, carefully watching the house from the shore, had seen nothing. He suggested that the signals which the lieutenant had seen were possibly produced by the same malicious persons who had been responsible for reporting to the authorities their suspicions of Mr. Jonsson.

Even more ill founded was a prosecution which gave rise to a libel action in which Marshall Hall appeared for the defendant newspaper, *John Bull*. During the night of October 13th, 1915, a Zeppelin flew over London, and an Englishman named Usher went on to the roof of his hotel, the Holborn Viaduct, with the manager, a Swiss, to enjoy a view of the raid. Unfortunately, with the indifference to danger of a true Briton, he lighted a cigarette. This was at once perceived by the vigilant police sleuths beneath, who promptly haled Mr. Usher and the manager to the police station, where they were charged with " vagrancy and signalling to the enemy," and handed over to the military authorities. When the case came on the next day, the stump and ash of the cigarette were gravely produced to the magistrate as exhibits, and the case was dismissed amid laughter. Shortly afterwards a paragraph appeared in *John Bull* which was understood to refer to this incident, and the Holborn Viaduct Hotel brought an action for libel. The case was settled, but, with Mr. Gordon Hewart for the plaintiff, Marshall for the defendant and Mr. Justice Darling on the bench, there was a good laugh all round.

Marshall was successful in obtaining a verdict for Captain Weiner, an American millionaire of Austrian extraction, who had fought for Great Britain in South Africa. An article in the *Evening News* gave a description of Ewell Castle, of which the plaintiff was the owner, containing an obvious innuendo. The garden, with its foundation of " layers of concrete " which could be used " for emplacements of heavy guns directed against London," an " observatory " tower with a significant view of the surrounding country, and a very powerful telescope, were all mentioned. A doctor was called, and testified that the captain had " no German proclivities." " Did you examine him professionally about it ? " asked Mr. Justice Darling. This case is interesting for this reason. The defendants were, as Marshall Hall remarked, " the most powerful association this country possesses at the present time " ; it was the Harmsworth Press, the same defendants as in the Chattell case. On this occasion their advisers did make enquiries, and attempted to call evidence in mitigation of damages in order to attack the plaintiff's character in a way which certainly had no connection with his alleged German proclivities. The judge refused to admit this evidence. " I do not consider," he said, " that a man who brings an action with regard to one matter should be cross-examined up hill and down dale about every kind of private wrong." The jury gave a verdict of £50 to the plaintiff. He had, in fact, laid a heavy concrete bottom in his grounds for the purpose of constructing a lake. The purpose of the telescope was, in fact, rather sporting than military. Captain Weiner had boasted that with its aid " he could see a man wink on the Grand Stand at Epsom."

More serious than any of those was a case which arose out of a conversation among season-ticket holders in a first-class compartment on the Midland Railway. A wealthy wine merchant of British nationality but German origin named Hans Pauer was travelling in August 1917, as was his wont, between Trentham and Stoke. Conversation naturally turned to the war, and the recent sinking of the hospital transport the *Warilda* by the Germans was indignantly discussed. Somebody said that British naval policy would never allow such a thing, and that Great Britain had faithfully adhered to her obligations under the Hague Conventions. To this Mr. Pauer replied that a week or two ago he had heard a British officer say that to his utter astonishment he had himself seen 2,000 men in khaki pour out of a hospital ship at Alexandria. " That," said another occupant of the compartment, " is a bloody lie." One of his fellow-passengers reported the matter to the police, and Pauer was prosecuted under the Defence of the Realm Regulations for " spreading by word of mouth a certain false report." Obviously the prosecution was justified, but the wide publicity given was perhaps, in the circumstances, unfortunate. The stipendiary punished the prisoner with a fine of £100 and six months' imprisonment. Marshall Hall represented Pauer on the appeal heard before the recorder at Quarter Sessions against the sentence, and, as a result, the offender's term was reduced to one month. Major-General Sir William Donovan, Director of Medical Service for the Mediterranean, was called to say that the prisoner's statement was utterly false, and Marshall Hall had an exceedingly difficult task before him. Some of his old violence returned to him in this case. When his opponent, Mr. Graham Milward, after objecting to one of Marshall's questions, rose to cross-examine, the latter said savagely, " This is not a reading from *Pickwick Papers*," and then began talking loudly to his junior. Mr. Milward paused, and gazed angrily at Marshall Hall. When Marshall realised he was being stared at, he repeated, " I said that this is not a reading from *Pickwick Papers*." Later, in his final speech, he was making an appeal *ad misericordiam* for his client, and was saying that he had been ruined by the scandal of this case, having been compelled to sell his business. Strictly, in order to use this plea he should have called evidence as to these facts, and Mr. Milward said so. Marshall Hall offered to do so.

" Well," said Milward, " if you do, do you know I shall have the last word ? "

Now the old lion was thoroughly roused. " Do you think I am afraid of your last word ? " he retorted. " I don't care if you talk from now till Doomsday. I'm not afraid of that. I know I shall not be here to listen to it. You can make as many speeches as you think fit."

Much more important was the trial of Sir Joseph Jonas and his London agent, Charles Alfred Vernon (christened Karl August Hahn), at the Old Bailey, under the Official Secrets Act, which had been passed in 1911. Sir Joseph Jonas had left his native Duchy of Hesse, on account of the conscription laws, shortly after its annexation by Prussia, and came to live in England. He became a manufacturer of steel in Sheffield, and acquired an enormous business. Municipal honours had poured on him before he received his knighthood, and in 1918, when he was prosecuted, his son was fighting for Great Britain. But it appeared that in 1913 Vickers were contemplating the manufacture of rifles on a large scale for the British Government, which was a new departure. One of Sir Joseph Jonas's biggest customers was a manufacturer of small-arms for the German government ; this man made it his business to find out, through Jonas, this and other interesting information concerning the British aircraft estimates, and a new process of steering His Majesty's ships. Jonas himself obtained this information from Vernon, who, in turn, gathered it from a German named Zieschang, a Teutonic foreman, employed in Vickers' works. In one of his letters to Vernon he wrote, " Please get positive news of Vickers' doings in small arms. I am pressed for the news."

It was not till the last year of the war that Sir Joseph was prosecuted for these transactions. The Attorney General himself, Sir F. E. Smith, and Sir Richard Muir prosecuted ; Tindal-Atkinson, K.C., and Travers Humphreys defended Jonas, while Sir Edward Marshall Hall, as he now was, and Huntly Jenkins defended Vernon. The defence was, that the information was obtained and handed on for purely business reasons, and in order to oblige a most important customer. However, there had been an ugly rumour that Sir Joseph had made a bet in 1914 that " we shall be in Paris in three weeks." The truth, however, was that he had, in the privacy of his club, refused, for obvious reasons, to make a bet on this subject at all, for fear of the comment that might arise.

The information was calculated, in view of the outbreak of war, to have done the country's interests great harm ; the prosecution took place in 1918, when the temper of our country had been sorely tried by four cruel years of war, and it is a tribute to our jury system that they acquitted the two prisoners of " felony," that is, of disclosing the information with intent to injure the interests of the State, but they found them guilty of the misdemeanour of communicating information which they had " unlawfully obtained." Sir Joseph was fined £2,000, and Vernon £1,000, and they were ordered to pay the costs of the prosecution.

Marshall Hall also appeared for Eric Brotherton, in the prosecution arising out of the Humber Graving Dock Company at Immingham. The case lasted for over a fortnight, before Mr. Justice Atkin, at the Old Bailey. The Humber Graving Dock Company had a contract from the Government to repair His Majesty's ships. It was, of course, understood that the Admiralty work must come before that of any other customer. Mr. Brotherton, the manager of the company, then hit on a very happy idea. Since he did so much for His Majesty, why should not His Majesty do something for him? If he wanted work to be done in his house or garden, if his plant or the company's buildings needed enlargement or repair, why should not the work be

charged to one of His Majesty's ships? The workmen employed
on any such work, or on the repair of privately owned vessels,
were always instructed to charge their work and material to the
account of one of His Majesty's ships. In this way, the company
was sure of being paid at least once. One workman foolishly
charged his work to a fictitious ship, " H.M.S. *Greenhill*."
Eventually, an honest employee's refusal to be a party to these
frauds, led to the prosecution of Brotherton and his colleague
Walker, for " conspiring together to defraud the King of money
by false representations."

The defence put forward by Marshall Hall was that Brotherton
had done all this in the public interest, and this contention was
not so absurd as it sounds at first. The company, under Brotherton's guidance, had admittedly done good, even brilliant, work
for the Admiralty ; in order to do this work with efficiency it was
necessary to have a large and fully-trained staff of skilled
workmen at beck and call, night and day. This would be impossible unless the men were given regular employment, and,
in the ordinary course, there would be times when there would be
nothing for them to do, and when the company could not afford
to pay them for nothing. But the defence, really, only amounted
to a plea in mitigation. Brotherton was tried on several indict-
ments, and, altogether, he spent twenty-eight days in the dock
at the Old Bailey before being sentenced to imprisonment for a
year and eight months in the second division. The preliminary
investigations in the police court had lasted thirty-four days.
It was estimated that the Government had been defrauded of
at least £25,000, and probably of double that amount, not to
mention the fees of Treasury counsel engaged in the case over
a period of at least two months. All things considered, Brotherton escaped with a light sentence, considering the magnitude
of his frauds, and this was largely due to Marshall's skilful and
eloquent handling of the case. He certainly brought out the
facts, that Brotherton had done fine service and that the frauds
would long ago have been discovered if the Admiralty had been
sufficiently vigilant.

Marshall Hall's fees in this case ran into four figures. He
was instructed by Mr. Freke Palmer, who had briefed him from
the very earliest days. In a very early case at the Marylebone

County Court, Palmer had marked him down as a " winner," by his instant detection of a certain document as a forgery. This was the document on which the plaintiff relied for success, and, although Marshall did not see the original till it was handed to him during the progress of the case, he at once denounced it as a forgery ; and he proved to be right. That year, the year 1888, Mr. Freke Palmer paid Marshall Hall just over £7 ; in 1918 his cheques amounted to over £1,700.

In July 1918, Marshall Hall appeared for a girl whose case, owing to the war and other circumstances, was, as he said in his speech, the " saddest story I have heard in all my thirty-five years' experience at the Bar." She was appealing against a sentence of four months hard labour, and a recommendation for expulsion from England. She had been found guilty of going to Folkestone, a " prohibited " area under the Defence of the Realm Regulations, she being an alien enemy. The girl's father was a naturalised British subject ; but her mother went to Germany to visit her dying father, and, while she was at Leipzig, a daughter was prematurely born to her. The baby was at once brought back to England, and she never learned to speak any other but the English language. When she was aged sixteen, she was left alone with her father, who was sent to five years' penal servitude for drugging and assaulting her. When he came out of prison, he persecuted her until her life became a burden and a terror to her ; in her despair she married a German admirer, who treated her almost as badly as her father had done, and was eventually also sent to prison. She then tried to earn her living as a ladies' hairdresser, and in 1916 she met a British officer, who fell in love with her and wished to marry her if she could obtain her freedom. Her husband refused to divorce her ; then came the final blow. On one of her visits to the British officer, she was arrested under the war regulations, and sentenced to imprisonment and separation for ever from her lover. But the lover had the wisdom and generosity to brief Marshall Hall for the appeal. All his sense of pity was aroused for the poor girl, who, he said, was only an alien by accident. " If you uphold this sentence," he said boldly, " it will be a disgrace to humanity." Of course, he also said, as he had often said before, that neither the pencil of Hogarth nor the pen of Zola had ever depicted a more dramatic or terrible story ; he might have added, that the story was sadder than anything written, just in that manner, by John Galsworthy. But the story ended happily ; the Bench, softened by the eloquence of counsel, reduced the sentence to a fine of ten pounds. The reunited lovers left the court together, and so the curtain falls on their romance. This would hardly have happened in a play by John Galsworthy.

On the whole, from these cases, it will be seen that the courts and juries in England were very fair to the foreigner of Teutonic origin, residing in England during the war, in spite of the bitter hatred of Germany which was then prevalent. Marshall Hall abated none of his passionate enthusiasm because he was appearing for an alien enemy. This conduct was in the true tradition of the English Bar, but it is, perhaps, worthy of record that, during this very difficult time, and in the face of overwhelming prejudice, bold advocates were not lacking in England to plead the cause of " alien enemies," on equal terms with native citizens of Great Britain.

Of course, juries were sometimes prejudiced. An action for defamation was brought by a man whose father was a Russian Jew and whose mother was a Russian Pole, and who had himself been born in German Poland, against a boon companion who had called him a " German spy " in a public house. The defendant was an obvious Englishman of the true bull-dog breed, and Marshall Hall was quite unable to prevent the jury from finding in his favour. On the other hand, when the plaintiff was the wife of an officer and a gentleman, juries would be anxious to find for her. This was so in the case of *Wallis* v. *The "London Mail,"* of lamented memory. A very attractive young lady had been persuaded by the blandishments of a photographer into allowing herself to have her portrait done " for nothing." She was given a few copies, but, unbeknown to herself, she had assigned the copyright to the photographer, who sold it to the *London Mail*. The editor of the periodical used it on the front page, under the title of "The Whitsun Girl." Soon afterwards, the young lady's husband, a lieutenant somewhere in France, picked up the *London Mail*, recognised his wife's portrait at once, and was furious. Mr. Hawke, K.C., now Mr. Justice Hawke, opened the case in black colours. The title " The Whitsun Girl " had a sinister meaning :

it suggested that his client was not of staid character, and, perhaps, worse things : it might mean that she was a girl whom any man could pick up on his Whitsun holidays. Counsel gravely turned over the pages of the paper. " Why," he said, " in the same number there is a picture of a woman entirely naked, sitting in a glass of champagne."

" No," interrupted Marshall Hall, for the defendants, " you are wrong ; she is not sitting, she is kneeling : a very different matter."

" As you please, Sir Edward," retorted Mr. Hawke, " I do not think, however, that it is supposed to be a devotional picture."

The jury were already impressed, and when counsel showed them another picture in the same number, in which "The Stalky Girl " was obviously trying to attract the attention of a passing gentleman, they were shocked. Finally, when the husband went into the box, and said he had been wounded at Vimy, they made up their minds, and awarded the plaintiff £110 damages. In times of peace, the case might have been laughed out of court, merely serving as a warning to pretty girls not to yield to the flatteries of generous photographers.

By one murder trial during the war the public mind was profoundly moved ; in this case, the aggressor was not a man of bad character, but a gentleman and a soldier, who had joined the colours in 1914, and had fought all through the war. His victim was a Russian, who was connected with the White Slave traffic, and was probably a German spy. He used a bogus title, which was not, however, unappropriate to him. His real name was Anton Baumberg, but his card bore the inscription, under a coronet, " Count Anthony de Borch." This man, a person, as one of the police witnesses said, " of whom nothing good could be said," took the advantage of the absence from home of Lieuten-ant Douglas Malcolm, to make love to his wife. Her husband adored her, but was jealous of the attentions paid to her by her foreign lover. He, however, believed passionately in her innocence, and saw himself as his wife's only protector. He returned on leave from France in July 1917, traced Baumberg and his wife to a cottage in the country, where he thrashed the Russian almost into insensibility. He wrote two letters, challenging Baumberg

THE KILLING OF DE BORCH

to a duel, which were not answered. In August his wife wrote
that she could not give up her lover, and asked him for a divorce.
Again Lieutenant Malcolm returned home on leave, and wrote
a passionate letter to " his dear, his very own darling Dorothy,"
saying that he was going to thrash De Borch " until he is un-
recognisable. I may shoot him if he has got a gun." To the Count
he had written, " I will thrash you until I have maimed you for
life. This I swear before God, in whom I believe, and who is my
witness." Early on the same morning on which he had written
a passionate love-letter to his wife, and made a will, leaving
everything to her mother in case of his death, he gained admission
to the Russian's flat, under the name of " Inspector Quinn of
Scotland Yard." Soon afterwards there were loud noises, followed
by the report of four shots. Malcolm at once gave himself up to
the police, and Baumberg was found dead on his bed. A drawer
near by, which contained a revolver in its case was found nine
inches open. Baumberg had said to Mrs. Malcolm that he was
keeping it for his protection against Malcolm. When he was
charged, Malcolm said, " I did it for my honour," and later,
" You can imagine how I felt when I saw the cad who has been
trying to get my wife to go away with him, and *me* in France,
helpless to defend her honour! Can you wonder at what I did on
the spur of the moment, when I saw the cur before me who was
luring my wife to dishonour."

Whether De Borch was reaching out for his revolver, and
Malcolm shot him in self-defence, or whether Malcolm was provoked by Baumberg into ungovernable rage to kill him, the public
sentiment was the same ; it was generally thought that Malcolm
was justified in what he did . . . " and me in France, helpless
to defend her honour." But according to the law of England,
only provocation by an assault or by a threat of an immediate
assault, or, possibly, an admission by a wife of adultery, can
even reduce a wilful assault by one man on another, which
results in the latter's death, from murder to manslaughter.
Here the last alternative was ruled out, because Malcolm believed
implicitly in his wife's innocence till the last. So, unless the jury
were convinced that the " Count " was slain by Malcolm in
self-defence, there was no defence in law to the charge of
murder.

Marshall Hall was intensely interested in the case, and was very much disappointed when the leading brief for the defence was given to Sir John Simon. Marshall was, however, briefed to watch the case " on behalf of a party interested," but this, of course, gave him no right to intervene. It is of interest to compare the technique of the two great advocates in this connection. Had Sir Edward defended, the prisoner would have gone into the box ; there would have been a thrilling reconstruction of the scene between the two men, culminating in the death of the German spy, who was attempting to seduce the British officer's wife, at the latter's hands. Marshall would have pointed the revolver at the jury, and the ring of steel and the click of its trigger would have been heard in court. He would have reproduced, in dumb show, De Borch's stealthy gesture in attempting to reach his revolver. Sir John Simon, in his one great murder defence, pursued quite different tactics, yet his conduct of the case, as a piece of advocacy, could hardly have been surpassed. Malcolm, in his righteous hatred of De Borch, would have made a most dangerous witness ; under the cross-examination of Muir, he might have lost his head or his temper. So Sir John Simon decided not to call him, and to rely on his own powers of advocacy. In the Camden Town trial, Marshall Hall had been very bold in calling the prisoner : ten years later, so much had the practice changed, Sir John took an equally bold and unconventional course in not calling his client. His speech was as near perfect in style and construction as oratory can be ; it commands admiration as a sustained and flawless work of art. Muir had rightly said, that so great a lawyer as Sir John would not ask the jury to break their oaths, by making an appeal to the unwritten law. He was quite right. " I do not appeal to it," said Sir John, " I do not require to do so. It would be contrary to my duty to do so, and contrary to your duty to listen to me if I attempted it.   This is a court of justice, and you are sworn to do justice, and it is justice, and justice according to law, which I stand here to ask you to mete out to the defendant. . . . Nobody will ever hear me . . . defend in a court of justice a review of the law of murder which will make light of the taking of human life. But, for my part, if such a situation were to arise, and it became necessary to discuss and decide it, I should not be prepared to subscribe to the doctrine that, in a case where no other conceivable course can possibly save your wife—not, indeed, from unfaithfulness, but from destruction of body or soul at the hands, not of an admirer, but of a blackguard—that the duty of protecting the woman is thereupon dissolved, and, in the face of such a situation, there is no other course within the common law of this country but that a husband should then retire, and leave his wife to her fate. But that is not the defence here."

Speaking very quietly, very slowly, with long pauses between the words, he told the sad story : how in 1914, Douglas Malcolm, whose sole duty had been that of protecting his beloved wife, undertook greater obligations. Then he spoke of " this black, evil, ugly shadow " which fell across their lives ; then of the thrashing, and of Baumberg's purchase of a revolver, of his baneful influence on the young wife, of the young husband's frenzy and despair. " He went to the room to punish and not to kill, and, in the struggle which took place, it was a choice between De Borch's life and his. . . . Lieutenant Malcolm is here before you in the clothes of a civilian. It is for you to say whether he shall pass from this place to the condemned cell, or whether you, in the words of the jurymen's oath which you have sworn, shall make " true deliverance between our Sovereign Lord the King and the prisoner at the Bar, and will return him to the service of His Majesty, to put on again the uniform which he has done nothing to disgrace and so much to justify."

The jury, after a very short absence, found the prisoner " not guilty of murder or manslaughter." " Thank God," said a woman in a clear voice in the back of the court, and her voice expressed the feeling of the multitude. In the House of Advocacy there are many mansions, and the contrast between the methods of Sir John Simon and of Marshall Hall is vivid indeed. Sir John Simon spoke in an objective way, as if he was but an interested observer and altogether aloof and apart from the tragedy, just as Thucydides wrote the story of the ruin of his native city ; and his conclusions were all the more effective because of this restraint and detachment. Marshall achieved his effects like Thomas Carlyle, by the extreme subjective method, by identifying himself with the central figure of his case, speaking as if the prisoner's thoughts, actions, and impulses were his own. He pleaded not as a historian, but as an actor or a Homeric rhapsodist. He went straight for the hearts of his hearers. Perhaps in only one of Marshall's trials was the prejudice in favour of the prisoner so strong, the case of Madame Fahmy, and the reader will see how differently this trial was conducted. Yet Marshall Hall was the first to rightly appraise his colleague's achievement. He told me that it was by far the finest speech that he ever heard at the Old Bailey.

The Conscription Act, passed in 1916, brought Marshall Hall one class of work, not a very attractive one, for which his knowledge of medicine rendered him peculiarly suitable. He was much briefed by applicants for " exemption," and, for this purpose, he made an exception to his hitherto unbroken practice. He had always held that it is the duty of an advocate to accept instructions from his client, whoever he may be, and to make the very best of them. In exemption cases, however, he would insist on a preliminary consultation, and, if he was satisfied that there was neither substance nor honesty in the application, he would not undertake the case. In one case his medical intuition was justified in a remarkable way. A Jew, with a good business in the City, wished to obtain exemption on the ground that he was a consumptive. His own doctor certified him as tubercular, but the military authorities certified him fit. Marshall Hall felt convinced the man was a consumptive, and advised him to consult, privately, the consultant of the very hospital which had certified him fit on behalf of the military authorities. This distinguished gentleman found he was tubercular. Nevertheless, Sir Donald Maclean's tribunal did not grant him exemption. Finally the man was called up, and the medical officer who examined him on joining up, found him unfit for service on account of tuberculosis.

On all these cases the hall-mark of the European war is stamped, but, in other directions, " business as usual " went on in the Law Courts, and, from day to day, questions of tort and contract were decided as usual in the great building in the Strand. In one of the most interesting of Marshall Hall's civil cases during the war, another similar difference of opinion arose among medical men, as to whether a person was or was not

affected by tuberculosis. The case was that of *Jefferson* v. *Paskell*,
an action for a breach of promise of marriage, brought by a young
girl against a Birmingham manufacturer, aged forty. There was
one very exceptional aspect to this case, in that the defendant,
in the witness-box, expressed himself as being still devoted to
the plaintiff ; in fact, he said, that even now he would marry
her but for one circumstance ; he was convinced that she was
suffering from tuberculosis, and was absolutely unfit for
marriage. This raised a very interesting question both of fact
and of law, and one of the first importance to engaged couples.
In March 1913, after the contract for marriage, the plaintiff
was taken ill. A specialist, Dr. Stanley, of Birmingham, certified
her whole condition as tuberculous. She went to a sanatorium,
where her sister, who subsequently died of consumption, was a
patient. The defendant made up his mind not to marry the plaintiff. In August she was examined by a Dr. Fligg, who certified
her as entirely free from tubercular disease. The physician of the
sanatorium gave evidence that there would be no risk whatever
to the defendant's health if he married the plaintiff. On the
other hand, Dr. Stanley swore than the plaintiff was tuberculous,
and that the defendant was quite justified in breaking off his
engagement. Sir William Osler's view, that ninety per cent. of
the population suffer from tuberculosis, was put to this
witness by Marshall Hall, in the course of cross-examination.
The questions of law for the judge were whether, if either the
plaintiff was in fact tuberculous, or if the defendant was reasonably convinced of this, he was justified in breaking off his engagement. Mr. Justice Bray held that the defendant's belief was
no defence, and directed the jury that it was for the defendant
to prove the plaintiff's unfitness, not for the plaintiff to prove her
fitness. The jury found in favour of the plaintiff on all points,
and gave her £500 damages. The case went to the Court of
Appeal. When Marshall really believed in a point of view, he
could argue it very well, and he won the appeal. *Jefferson* v.
Paskell is really a leading and very interesting authority on
the law of breach of promise ; these cases always provide good
reading in the contemporary Press, but they very seldom
possess any but a transient interest of melancholy comedy.
But here a fundamental question was raised, which was, I think,
ZH

omitted by Lord Birkenhead in a recent essay on " Breach of Promise." Does the unfitness of either party entitle either or both of them to break off the engagement ? The Court of Appeal seem to have agreed with a view expressed by Lord Campbell in an old case, that a party cannot escape scathless from a promise of marriage by pleading his own unfitness, if the other party still desires the union. In what circumstances can a party escape, because of unfitness in the other party ? The Lord Justices agreed with the judges below, that the defendant's belief makes no difference. The only question is : is the plaintiff, in fact, ready and willing, within a reasonable time, to perform the contract ? If he or she is physically quite unfit for marriage, he or she is not " ready." Therefore, the plaintiff must provide some *prima facie* evidence, such as an appearance in the witness-box in apparently good health. It is then the defendant's duty to disprove that he or she is ready for marriage by medical evidence. This the court held the defendant had not proved ; the verdict of the jury therefore stood.

Another *cause célèbre,* fought in March 1917, deserves mention, for several reasons. It was an action brought for damages for " maintainance." " Maintainance " is the giving of assistance or encouragement to a party in an action, by a person who is not interested in the case, and is not actuated by any motives recognised by law as justifying interference ; one of the motives recognised by law is charity. This form of action is extremely rare, and the facts of this case were extraordinary. At the end of the last century a young couple married for love. The man was possessed of considerable private means, was called to the Bar, and acquired a good practice on the Chancery side. His wife made a close friendship with a neighbour in the country, a married man, who constantly gave her personal advice. The husband, although fond of his wife, formed a romantic attachment for another married woman, and for years these four people went about together, and all of them saw a great deal of each other, although the relations between them were innocent. But, owing to several incidents, the wife became suspicious as to her husband's relations with his married woman friend, and, eventually, she instituted divorce proceedings. Her friend and admirer, the married man, paid £200 to her solicitors against her costs, and, in the proceedings that followed, rendered further financial assistance ; he also went to a doctor and pressed him to give evidence at the trial, that the barrister had shown cruelty to his wife (at that time a wife could not obtain a divorce on the ground of adultery alone). The doctor refused to do so. Up to this time the barrister maintained that his relations with his married woman friend were entirely innocent ; they were, however, faced by much circumstantial evidence, and, at all events, if the suit were defended, there would be fearful publicity and scandal. In order to avoid this, he and she decided to do the very thing of which they were accused, and of which they were as yet innocent. They ran away together, and provided, conclusively, the evidence of adultery which the wife required for her divorce suit. The divorce then passed, comparatively unobserved, as an undefended petition. The barrister now sued his former wife's man friend in effect for vindictively promoting the litigation.

In this case, Marshall Hall, for ten days, leading Lewis Thomas K.C., Douglas Hogg, and Grattan Bushe, contended against Sir John Simon, K.C., Disturnal K.C., and Eustace Hills, before the Lord Chief Justice and a special jury.

Great feeling was shown by the witnesses on both sides. When the doctor, who had been approached to give evidence, was in the box, a matchbox in his coat pocket caught alight, and flames and smoke surrounded the witness-box.

" I do not wonder at this," said Lord Reading, " after the heat engendered in this case."

" I thought it was spontaneous combustion, my Lord," said Marshall Hall.

An old solicitor of seventy-four, who had briefed Marshall almost since his call, had been a great friend of the plaintiff's family, and had, in fact, advised him and his lady friend to run away together, and provide the evidence rather than incur the terrible scandal that would inevitably ensue by defending the petition. While the poor old gentleman, who had acted for the best, was in the box, he broke down and sobbed, and had to be assisted from the court, and Sir John Simon chivalrously did not cross-examine.

Marshall's cross-examination of the defendant was a feature of the case. The latter's last answer was, " I have never worked harder at anything in my life than to have these two people reconciled."

" Yes," retorted Marshall Hall, " and the way you did it was to have them watched."

The end was a victory for Marshall Hall and his client. The jury decided that the defendant had paid the £200 before he had any interest in the case, and added, that they were unanimously agreed that he was guilty of unjustifiable intermeddling. After legal argument, judgment was given for the plaintiff, with costs.

Marshall Hall had, on this occasion, as well he might have, a grateful client. " You cannot fail," he wrote, " to realise how impossible it must be for me to express adequately the feelings of gratitude which I entertain for all the kindness and devotion to my interests which you have shown. Never did client have counsel's genius and skill more unreservedly placed at his disposal."

Marshall, at the age of fifty-nine, was a very different advocate from the fiery defender of Bennett ; his indomitable courage, overflowing spirits, and generosity had made him exceedingly popular with bench and Bar, and his name had immense prestige with the public. Scenes with judges, once almost a part of the daily routine of his advocacy, were few and far between. Yet they sometimes occurred. When he appeared before Mr. Justice Ridley, the sparks were always apt to fly. In 1916, he appeared on behalf of a gallant artillery captain, who, with his wife and some brother officers, had been making the most of their leave at a country hotel. There was old brandy, and some noise, followed by an altercation with the proprietress, in which bitter words were used on both sides. The good hostess brought an action for slander and recovered damages. Marshall Hall appeared for the defendant. During the evidence, it appeared that a lady of the party had sung a song called, " He calls me his own Grace Darling," in which the lines occurred, " Why, I like you for your whiskers, dear ; they tickles me and makes me laugh." Mr. Mears, counsel for the plaintiff, asked the witness, " Is not that song extremely vulgar ? " Marshall Hall was up in a moment, protesting at the epithet.

" You use epithets yourself, Mr. Marshall Hall," said the judge. " I think Mr. Mears is entitled to give it that description ? "

Mr. Marshall Hall was then understood to observe that the learned judge would naturally be a far better judge of vulgar songs than he was ; whereupon the translator of Lucan, stung to the quick, retorted, " You must remember where you are : you really must behave yourself."

But Marshall was not daunted by the judicial rebuke, and simply would not be good. The temptation to bait the already very angry judge was too strong for him. He began to argue as to the exact words used by a witness in a previous answer, and was cut short by the judge. " *I* am right, Mr. Marshall Hall," said the latter.

" Your lordship is always right," agreed Marshall sweetly.

" I think I am," replied the judge, and then, " You are almost intolerable."

Shortly afterwards, another comic song was the subject matter of one of Marshall Hall's cases. He appeared for Sam Mayo, the music hall comedian, who claimed damages from Miss Connie Crighton for breach of copyright, in singing one of his songs without his permission, and mimicking his artistry into the bargain. Each verse of the song, which was recited by the plaintiff in open court, ended with the words, " I've only come down for the day." But the case, which might have been a long one, was settled before it had gone very far, and Mr. Justice Horridge wittily observed, " he will now be able to add another verse with regard to this court—that he only came down for the day."

The last serious scene between Marshall Hall and the Bench also took place in 1916. He was appearing in a newspaper libel action, and was leading Mr. McCardie, as he then was, for the defence. The judge, Mr. Justice Bray, took a view, favourable to the plaintiff, rather early in the case, and several times interrupted Marshall's cross-examination of him. The denouncement came when Marshall Hall read to the plaintiff the whole of the article, from which the plaintiff's counsel had read the statement complained of as libellous. Marshall was instructed to do this, and maintained he was entitled to do so. The judge apparently thought this was very unfair to the plaintiff, as Marshall obviously had read the whole article in order to suggest that the plaintiff's employers, who were also attacked, were really responsible for the lawsuit being brought. At all events, he said that he would never have allowed Marshall Hall to read the whole article if he had known its contents, and that the cross-examination had been most irregular.

Marshall Hall's feelings, which had been smouldering throughout the case, thereupon flared up, and flinging down his brief on the desk, he said, " As I cannot conduct my case according to my instructions, I will retire and leave my friend Mr. McCardie to conduct it." He then strode out of court.

McCardie also refused to go on with the case. " My lord," he said stoutly, " I associate myself with every question Mr. Marshall Hall has put, and if my learned friend retires, I retire also." Thereupon, junior counsel left the court, and the case was adjourned for another judge to hear.

It was a long time since such a scene had happened. Lord Carson adopted the same procedure on a famous occasion before a committee in Ireland, but it is hard to find another instance of the kind in the English courts. As Mr. McCardie was one of the acknowledged leaders of the Junior Bar at the time, there was much discussion ; but the general opinion in the Temple was that, whether Marshall was right or wrong, McCardie had been perfectly right to support his leader. Marshall Hall felt at the moment that he could not properly present his client's case in that particular court, but probably when he reached the corridor of the Law Courts, he was already sincerely sorry for his impetuosity.

By a curious irony, McCardie, a few weeks after defying a senior judge from the back-row, himself exchanged his stuff gown for the judicial ermine. Such a change of raiment is exceptionally rare. By another chance, he happened to go on his first circuit with Mr. Justice Bray, who treated his junior " brother " with special friendliness ; and, some years later, it was Mr. Justice McCardie, summoned from the adjoining court, who, with great difficulty, persuaded Mr. Justice Bray to leave his last case unfinished, and, half-lifting him out of his chair, supported him out of court. A few hours afterwards the brave old judge died.

In 1916 Marshall Hall retired for ever from politics, leaving the House of Commons without regret, and was made Recorder of Guildford, which office he filled until his death. The judicial work at the Quarter Sessions was not heavy, and, on the first occasion, there was only one prisoner. As was to be expected, he was the most humane of judges, and his long experience as a defender caused him to study the welfare of the prisoners whom he was compelled to send to prison ; he would make enquiries and try to find work for them when they came out, and take an interest in their families in the meantime. A letter, written a few months before his death, shows how far his interest and humanity could go in this direction. His pity had been deeply aroused for the girl-wife of a man whom he had sentenced to a term of imprisonment. " DEAR MADAM," he wrote to her mother—" I am anxious, if I can, to do something for your daughter, for whom I feel very sincere sympathy in the unhappy circumstances in which she finds herself. It was my very unfortunate duty to try C. H. at Guildford, but I had no alternative but to pass sentence of imprisonment upon him in his own interests. I understand that your daughter is wishing to get back into service as housemaid, and, naturally, she would like to be somewhere in the neighbourhood so that she could see her little child. I have a small cottage at Brook, about four miles from Chiddingfold, and, although I have not mentioned the matter to my wife, I will, if you like, see if I can do anything, as, of course, it is important that, so far as possible, no mention should be made of the unfortunate circumstances under which she is obliged to go back into service. If only she could do a little cooking we could offer her a place at once."

But he could sometimes be very severe, especially in cases of cruelty. " I only wish these poor beasts could become lions and tigers and retaliate on men like you," he once said to a man brought before him for maltreatment of a dog.

He always adored dogs ; he would make friends with them in the street, or on any occasion that offered itself. He took a house in the country during the war, near Sandwich, and he there kept four dogs of different breeds, the ancestors of an amazing cosmopolitan family of charming mongrels, who afterwards inhabited the cottage at Brook, bought after his appointment as Recorder of Guildford. The letter appearing below is a specimen of a correspondence which Marshall maintained with a friend in the names of their respective dogs, and shows what a true dog-lover he was. The signatory, Bunty, was a Pekinese whom he loved dearly.

" Felder Lodge, Sandwich.

" *January 2nd,* 1917.

" GREAT CHAAKA—GREETINGS ! I am, alas, the only one of the family that can write, so I am answering your most delightful letter. I came down here with my master and mistress, but I am sorry to say that my mistress, too, has been very ill with that nasty choky thing in your throat which we dogs get some-times. They call it asthma, but it really is bronkitis (or however they spell it), but she is a little better, and master has gone to London where he has not been for a long time, and he only gave me your letter this morning as it has been waiting in London. I know you will be sorry to hear that my dear little friend Poodge, the Chinaman, has gone to his ancestors, and my master was so unhappy that he cried like a silly woman. Of course we all loved Poodge very much indeed, he was such a perfect gentleman. He never tried to take away my dinner or my bones, and always behaved so well. Williams has gone to live in Ireland at a place called Bally Hooley, and master says it used to be a famous place once for that nasty stuff called wisky, and for Mr. Robert Martin, who was a friend of master's. So there are only Judy and me left. Judy is very rheumatic and can't hold a pen to write, but she is very artful. There are some soldiers in huts quite close to us, and Judy sneaks down there at dinner time, and sits up and begs, and they all give her things, but it makes her very fat and is so bad for her figure. I would go too, but my mistress always knows if I have been down the road, as my hair is so white and shows the least little bit of mud, so I dare not go. If I did, she wouldn't let me come on her bed, and it is bad enough as it is with that nasty Persian cat and kitten that mistress has got.

" Master sends his best wishes for the New Year to your master and mistress and hopes she is better. Someday, he has said, I shall come and see you, but I know your picture well, next to mine in master's bedroom.

" Good-bye—

" BUNTY."

The death of Poodge, which is referred to in this letter, had caused his master real unhappiness, and when he died, Marshall showed his kind heart by writing the sad news to his London housekeeper, who had made much of the dead pet. " DEAR MRS. TEMPLE," he wrote,—" I know you will be dreadfully sorry to hear that poor little Poodge died yesterday morning of acute gastritis and gastric ulcer. We took him in to Dover to the vet., but nothing could be done for him, and the poor little man passed away. I cannot tell you how grieved I am, and I know how fond you were of him, so I thought I would let you know. I can hardly believe I shall never hear again his barks of joy when I come home. He was a gentleman and I loved him." These simple, artless letters about his pets show how little his long experience of life and law had affected the gentle and affectionate nature of the veteran advocate.

In 1917 Marshall Hall was knighted. His practice was at this time, in its own line, second to none, but he still hoped for judicial promotion. He had understood from the Unionist Whips that, if the party came into power, they would press the Chancellor for a judgeship for him, if his position at the Bar justified the promotion. In 1917, a Unionist, Lord Finlay, became Lord Chancellor, and Marshall hoped that his long service in the party might be given the reward which he considered was almost pledged to him. He was bitterly disappointed when his old friend Clavell Salter was given the first vacancy. " I am told that S. is to be recommended," he wrote to Lord Edmund Talbot, " Well, he is a splendid chap, and a great friend of mine of thirty years standing. I think he will tell you he owes much to me in the early days . . ." The letter is that of a bitterly disappointed man, and ends with a prophecy about his future, which came almost exactly true. " Well, I am fifty-nine ; if my health lasts, I suppose I can enjoy another ten years hard and remunerative work at the Bar." Within a few months of ten years after the date of this letter he died, almost in harness. Shortly after this disappointment he was approached as to the writing of his memoirs, and he discussed the project and even wrote a few pages. " What will you call the book ? " he was asked. " Better call it the ' Story of a Failure,' " he said sadly, and laid aside his pen.

Marshall Hall, in his sixtieth year, was still as fine looking a

man as ever. His hair was now almost completely white, but,
otherwise, he looked young for his age. His face had acquired a
greater strength, and his expression was sterner and fiercer than
in former days, although his features had not yet fined down
into the almost ascetic lines which added so much to the im-
pressiveness and grace of his appearance during his last years.
His entries into court in these days began to acquire a certain
character ; he would be preceded by a panoply of medical
apparatus. First his clerk would arrange his air-cushion ; then
there would be a row of bottles to set up on the desk containing smelling-salts and other medicines ; there would also be
some exquisite little eighteenth-century box, containing some
invaluable pill ; his noting pencils, green, red, and blue, would be
arranged in a row and, last but not least, his nose-spray would
be ready to hand, which, according to his opponents, he would be
certain to use in order to divert the attention of the jury when
the case was going against him. Finally, when all was prepared,
and the judge was waiting, the great man himself would come
in. He had become one of the great characters of the Temple.

Chapter XI

An Eventful Year

The war left other evils besides houses of remembrance and mourning throughout Britain, and a long-continuing commercial and industrial depression which has not yet passed away. Medical men say that it affected health and nerves throughout the whole population, and, while increasing the mortality, decreased the vitality of all children born during that period. At any rate it is certain that, among those who faced the frightful ordeal of modern warfare, many survived far less fortunate than those who fell. Happily, the majority of the survivors, heaving a sigh of relief, returned to their normal avocations, and tried to keep their experience out of their thoughts and conversation. But upon some the war had one of two effects— either to upset their mental balance or to produce in them an abnormal hardness and brutality of character. The strain on the nervous system from day to day, and the business of the destruction of human life, on which the combatants had been continually engaged, were certain to have their effects on some at least. It is dangerous to generalise, but it would naturally be expected that the most sensitive and excitable on the one hand, and the most naturally callous on the other, would be the most likely to be affected ; and this hypothesis perhaps accounts for many of the crimes of violence which were committed by ex-soldiers immediately after the war. " How can the men," wrote a correspondent to Marshall Hall after the Holt verdict, " who have remained at home, in quiet and safety, be competent to judge the brain-waves of a man who has seen so much death that it is almost of no importance ? . . . Why is not the jury for such cases composed of men who have been in the trenches and in Mesopotamia, and know all the horrors and how these can affect some men ? "

The case of Lieutenant Frederick Rothwell Holt, late of the Loyal North Lancashire Regiment, is an interesting one, both because his terrible crime may to some extent be attributed to mental or emotional breakdown as a result of the war, and because it raised the whole question of insanity in its relation to the

law of England. By way of [introduction it is necessary to say
a very few words. The law has always assumed all men to be
sane, but, according to English law, no man can be punished for
an act unless he performed it " with a guilty mind." If he per-
forms it in a state of unconsciousness or complete madness, he
cannot be said to have a " guilty mind." Therefore, obviously
madness can be an answer to an indictment for murder, but such
madness must be proved by the defence. Before Queen Victoria's
reign, this most difficult scientific question—the sanity or insanity of a prisoner—was left entirely to the jury as a question
of fact, and, as a rule, juries were not in advance of their times,
and only allowed insanity as an excuse in extreme cases. In
1843 a man named Daniel Macnaughton assassinated the Prime
Minister's private secretary, mistaking him for Sir Robert Peel
himself. The three judges who tried him, seeing that he was
insane, stopped the trial, and ordered him to be detained at
Bethlem. There was much public outcry at this humane decision,
and in the result the House of Lords asked for, and received,
answers from the judges, which are at present the rules laid down
to be propounded by judges to juries as to the legal responsibility
of prisoners for their actions where insanity is raised as a defence.
The judges said, in effect, that, unless a man is so mad as to be
unable to appreciate the nature and quality of his act, or, alter-
natively, unable to distinguish right from wrong, he is responsible for all breaches of the law which he may commit. The
principle was established then, as a rule of law, that an insane
man may, under certain circumstances, be criminally responsible for his actions. This is not always understood by juries
or the public, who are under the impression that the legal definition of insanity is different from the medical definition. This is
not so. It is often said that there has never been a completely
sane or a completely insane human individual, and obviously, if
there is to be criminal punishment at all, the line must be drawn
somewhere. The transition from sanity to insanity may be slow
and gradual. The principle which underlies the rules in Macnaughton's case—that insanity, being a disease of many grada-
tions, is not necessarily a defence—would be ratified as just
by most authorities ; but whether the advance in medical
research as to insanity since 1843 can legally be reflected in

LIEUTENANT HOLT

criminal practice, without a modification of the Macnaughton rules, is more open to doubt. The judges in 1843 had not at their disposal the knowledge as to insanity which is now available for every medical student. Would they, the above-mentioned principles being granted, have given the same answers as they in fact did if they had had at their disposal the results of modern medical research ? If they left something completely out of account which is to-day a commonplace, these rules may perhaps need amendment. For they have again and again been affirmed by the Court of Criminal Appeal to be the law at the present time. Undoubtedly it is undesirable that a jury should decide each case merely as a question of fact, without being given a principle of law to restrain and guide them. The rules in Macnaughton's case were a step in the right direction. But should there not perhaps be a further step in the light of modern scientific research ?

Perhaps two other rules of practice as regards our law and insanity should also be mentioned. Either the prosecution or the defence may raise the issue that the " prisoner is unfit to plead." This means that he is so insane, as he stands in the dock, that he cannot properly instruct his counsel or follow the details of the evidence. If the jury decide that he is " unfit to plead," the trial is not proceeded with, and the prisoner goes to a criminal lunatic asylum " during His Majesty's pleasure." Further, if, after sentence of death, a prisoner becomes insane, that sentence is respited, and he also is detained " during His Majesty's pleasure." For a man cannot be given a fair trial, who is unable even to instruct his own counsel, and humanity revolts from putting a madman to death, even though he was sane when he committed the crime.

Frederick Rothwell, known as " Eric," Holt was called up as a Territorial officer in August 1914. He served in the trenches, and was invalided out of the army ; he was given employment by a company in the Malay States, but he returned home to Lancashire in 1918. The outward effect which the war seems to have produced in him was a passion for gaiety and amusement ; in the prosperous middle-class circles of his native town he was a social favourite, and considered to be a pleasant, if exuberant and excitable, companion. In 1918 he met a beautiful young woman named Kitty Breaks, and a deep attachment sprang up between the two of them. She had first posed to him as a single woman, but later, in a very contrite letter, she confessed that she had been very unhappily married, and had, almost since her wedding day, lived apart from her husband. This confession did not prevent Holt from becoming her lover.

In the early morning of December 24th, 1919, Kitty Breaks was found dead, with three revolver wounds in her body, on the sandhills at St. Anne's, near Blackpool, over which there had been a wild storm of wind and rain the night before. Shortly afterwards, two gloves and a revolver, which had belonged to Holt, were found near by, and footprints were also plainly visible into which a pair of Holt's lately re-soled shoes exactly fitted. Next day Holt went to the hotel where Kitty Breaks had been staying and asked for her. There he was shortly afterwards arrested. From that moment till his death he behaved in the most curious manner.

The case, like that of Edward Lawrence, was a Christmastide tragedy; it aroused the most tremendous interest in the North of England. Marshall Hall was instructed for the defence. At the trial the Manchester Assize Court was besieged by would-be spectators, and hundreds each day were turned away from the public galleries. Sir Edward went down to St. Anne's on the Friday before the trial, and viewed the scene of the tragedy on the Sunday; and, on his return to Manchester in the evening, a long consultation was held, and it was finally decided to raise the question of " unfit to plead " as a preliminary issue. As the main defence was to be insanity in any event, a failure at the outset would certainly prejudice the prisoner's trial; after much hesitation, owing to the apparent strength of the medical evidence, Marshall Hall agreed to take this course. The case was tried by Mr. (now Lord) Justice Greer. It was the second capital case in which Marshall Hall was opposed by the Attorney-General of England. On the issue as to whether the prisoner was unfit to plead, the defence called several doctors, who were emphatic that the prisoner was insane, and it looked at one time very much as though the defence would establish this theory. The prisoner had complained that the police had sent dogs, and huge " American " flies carrying fever germs, to persecute and unnerve him as he sat in his cell.

Sir Gordon Hewart argued, for the Crown, that the prisoner had merely simulated delusional insanity, and really destroyed the case for Holt being unfit to plead by one question put to a doctor who had been sent officially to examine Holt's mental condition.

" What," asked the Attorney-General, " did the prisoner say when he was asked if he objected to a medical examination by you ? "

" He said he would like to see his solicitor first."

It is interesting that this very answer, which seemed so fatal to the plea, was set up in the appeal by another doctor as a sign of insanity, and as being consistent with Holt's " conspiracy " mania.

But the jury from this moment had obviously made up their minds that Holt was fit to plead, and, after a very short retirement, gave a verdict to that effect.

A fresh jury—the members of which, however, had been in court and heard the failure of the preceding argument—were sworn, and the trial opened. The Crown had an overwhelming case against Holt, which was built up in masterly fashion and matchless English by the Attorney-General. A double motive was put forward by the Crown ; the prisoner's desire to obtain the insurance money on Kitty Breaks's life, and to be free of an embarrassing liaison. The poor, penniless girl had recently insured her life for £5,000, and made a will leaving nearly everything to the prisoner ; he had tried in vain, earlier in the year, to insure her life for £10,000, but the company had informed him that he had, until he married her, no insurable interest in her life. Holt, like Seddon, had been an accredited insurance agent. " I will not dwell," concluded Mr. Attorney, " on the accumulated evidence. The gloves—his gloves—how did they come to be there ? The revolver—his revolver—how did that come to be there ? The footprints—his footprints—how did they come to be there ? . . . The footprints show that she walked some distance with someone. . . . I ask the jury to say that that man was the prisoner."

Holt's movements on the day of the tragedy were traced by a succession of witnesses. He and Kitty Breaks had travelled together from Bradford ; he had alighted at Ansdell station, and she had gone on alone to Blackpool, where she had changed into evening dress and dined at the hotel. She had then walked across to the Sandhills and to her death. Holt had been seen taking a tram at a place near the Sandhills between nine and ten in the evening. Marshall Hall did his best to break this damning chain of testimony, but he could do very little. He did indeed elicit from one of the witnesses that he had seen the prisoner and the dead girl fondling and making love to each other in the train journey from Bradford to Blackpool, and thus clearly presented to the jury the paradox, hard to believe, of a demonstrative lover so soon becoming the assassin of his beloved. Could this conceivably have happened ?

At all events, Holt must have been an extraordinary man ; for, after murdering this girl—with whom he had lived for two years on terms of tenderness and passion—in the most brutal manner, and leaving her half buried in the sandhills within a short distance of his home, he could still go and enjoy a few drinks, eat a good supper, and turn in unconcernedly to bed. Next morning he boarded a tram, and, passing within fifty yards of Kitty's body, he proceeded to Blackpool and bought two presents—it was Christmas Eve : one for a girl of his acquaintance at Lytham, and the other for Kitty's own sister. He was arrested that day while " waiting " for Kitty at her hotel. While in prison, he could make long statements about the police dogs and poisonous flies, but would give his advisers no statement which would assist them in his defence. Since all that he would say was " not guilty," it was quite impossible to put him in the witness box.

The prosecution closed on the Thursday with the defence in a desperate condition. Apart from the line of insanity, which was much weakened by the failure of the preliminary legal argument, the defence was an alibi. These two defences did not go well together in harness, and only the most skilful advocacy could run them both without the one destroying the other. The prisoner's attitude did not help him ; he sat throughout the trial with his arms folded, not taking the slightest interest in anything or anybody ; to all but medical men his demeanour would have suggested, not insanity, but brutal indifference. The whole of the prisoner's family was called to prove that Holt, owing to his presence at home, could not have been at the Sandhills at the time of the murder. It was most distressing to see them in the box, doing their utmost to save the life of the prisoner, and nobody in court but could feel the deepest pity for them. As to the insanity defence, it was proved that Holt's grandfather and a first cousin had been insane.

The evidence closed on Thursday night. On Friday, the fifth day of the trial, came the speech-making and the summing-up. Marshall was terribly nervous and unhappy ; never, even in the Brides in the Bath case, had he been so desperately lacking in material, and yet he was convinced in his heart that no sane man could have done the deed with which Holt was charged. As he walked down to the Salford Hundred Court with his clerk, he said, " What on earth can I say to this jury, Bowker ? They are dead against us, and I can't think how to tackle it." Afterwards, on his way from the robing-room to the court, he was jostled and pushed half way down the stairs by a mass of women, some of them fashionably dressed, whose only thought was to obtain a place in the public gallery. This disgusted him, and he went into court in a highly emotional state. It may here be observed that on the first day of the trial the judge had refused to go into court until the Bench had been cleared of privileged spectators.

Perhaps this incident gave Marshall Hall the necessary inspiration, for he made one of the most moving speeches of his life. Probably not one of his hearers on that day will ever forget his reading of the passionate love-letters written to each other by these two young people. The judge, kindest of men, and most of the jury were actually in tears. Otherwise Marshall spoke without a note, and for upwards of two hours, whenever he paused, a pin could have been heard to drop in that court, which was packed to physical discomfort. Carried away by himself almost at the outset of his speech, he glared round at the gallery and the many women spectators gathered in the court, and made a wild outburst against their presence. " It makes one's heart ache to see that gallery packed with women," he said with a gesture of unutterable disgust. " It makes me feel sick for the femininity of this country that women should come here, in their furs and their diamonds, day after day, to gloat over the

AAH

troubles of a poor demented wretch on trial for his life." The prosecution had relied on the motive of avarice, and suggested that the prisoner had killed the woman for the sake of her money. Marshall Hall said that this was incredible. " I do not suppose," he said, " that there could be a worse crime than that of a man who, under the guise of making love to a lovely woman, was really keeping her quiet until the moment came when he could murder her and put the proceeds of her insurance in his pocket. . . . I suggest to you that this theory is so improbable that it becomes impossible ; and, for the honour of our sex, thank God it *is* impossible, because we cannot conceive the Creator who created anything so vile as that man." When he had argued with all his might that the alibi was conclusive, very skilfully he passed to the other limb of the defence, and, the tears pouring down his cheeks, he told of the tragic love of Kitty Breaks and the prisoner. She had called him " Mr. Dreamer " again and again in her letters. " Eric darling . . . I want to put my arms round your neck and kiss you when you are away. I feel so lonely—you know why. You are such a dear, I love you ever so much." " Forgive me, Eric darling, you are the one person in the whole world to me, and I want to appear nice. To-day I felt hurt when you reproached me, and miserable. I know you will forgive me very soon." " Eric dear, somehow I cannot thank you nearly so much as I want for your extreme goodness to me. In my opinion, darling, you are just the biggest and whitest man I know. I want you, dearest, to try and get over as soon as you are able. No Bradford, and no friends. Just we two." " I never thought any man would make me love him as I do you." Finally, Marshall read Holt's last letter, written a few days before Kitty's death, which, he declared, was overflowing with love and tenderness. " MY DEAR, DARLING KATHLEEN,—You have no idea how lonely I feel without you, dearest. I arrived safely to-night, but I did, and do, so want you nearer me, you dear, sweet thing— you are my baby at present. You love me, I love you ; I feel I must always be near you ; you have no idea how I feel after I leave you, or you leave me, darling. I do so want you, darling. You are the one and only to me in this world, and I think the world of you, and do so want you to think the same of me. I am so sorry at what happened to us at lunch to-day, but let us both forget it, and may neither of us notice such a thing again. I know we are too fond of each other for that. I know we were at fault, because now I know you love me. . . . But you know I love you so much, darling—I do so long for you. I don't know how I shall manage without you—you are so sweet and tender. I long for Christmas and some long day ; I feel you will never leave me after Christmas. I long for some good Christmases with you in times to come, and feel that some time there will be no parting us." There is a ring of sincerity about this which is quite different in quality from Smith's abject and misspelt letters.

The prosecution had alleged avarice and a desire to be rid of a woman of whom he had grown tired as the motives of the prisoner ; Marshall Hall had another theory : if this man, in whose family there had been two undoubted cases of insanity, and whose mind had been unhinged by the war, did this deed, he did it in a fit of madness, precipitated by a frenzy of jealousy concerning the woman whom he adored. " Whatever else is unreal in this case, the one thing that is real, upon which everything hinges and turns, is his mad devotion to this woman," said Marshall Hall.

There was some evidence for such a theory ; an old and faithful lover had lately written to her begging her to marry him, and that letter was in evidence ; in the vanity-bag that was found near her body was found a letter purporting to come from Kitty, and answering this letter with a strong refusal. The letter was, however, unsigned, and was written in Holt's hand ; it had obviously been drafted for her by Holt. But she had not sent it, or any answer, to this other suitor. Might it not have been that Holt's mind, already on the brink of madness, finally gave way owing to a storm of suspicion, jealousy, and wrath ? " A man like the prisoner," urged Marshall Hall, " who has been in France, and subjected to the nerve-racking experience of the Festubert bombardment—a man who is neurasthenic, and has suffered from loss of memory and depression—is the very man who might at any moment go mad." There must be tens of thousands of men who, had they been present, would have responded in their hearts to that appeal.

Never since the trial of Marie Hermann had Marshall been moved to such a high pitch of emotion as he was then, but it was all of no avail. The Attorney-General's reply, lasting three and a half hours, was deadly and conclusive in its effect. Then followed the summing-up of Mr. Justice Greer, undoubtedly adverse to an acquittal. He allowed that Holt's letter was that of a man who seemed to prize his association with the dead woman. " Strange things," said the low, gentle voice, " happen in human life ; and it is not impossible that a man might combine with his affection for the woman feelings which might enable him, when the time was ripe, to commit a crime of this kind." This sentence might have come from Marshall Hall's own lips, but it would have been only the premises to a conclusion, not the conclusion itself. He would have added the inference that when things " so strange " and incompatible were joined in one human personality, that personality was already outside the borders of sanity and responsibility.

As regards the prisoner's alleged insanity, this, said the judge, rested on very slender evidence ; but it is of great interest that this very humane and distinguished judge " left to the jury " the question of " uncontrollable impulse," which is not covered by the Macnaughton rules. He directed the jury that if they came to the conclusion that the prisoner had done this deed while seized suddenly by some " uncontrollable impulse," they might acquit him. The Court of Criminal Appeal has since laid it down that this is not a good defence according to the law of England, and Lord Atkin's Committee on Insanity reported in 1922 that legislation would probably be necessary to make it so.

After an absence of nearly an hour, the jury returned with a verdict of " guilty." As Holt arrived in the dock to hear the verdict, he was pushing an evening paper into his pocket. He made no reply when asked by Sir Herbert Stephen, the clerk of assize, as to whether he had anything to say before sentence. He just shrugged his shoulders and looked at the clock. But there were tears in the judge's eyes and on his cheek as he pronounced sentence. When Holt was taken below, after being sentenced to death, his only remark to Major FitzClarence, the governor of the prison, was, " Well, that's over ! I hope my tea won't be late."

The appeal which followed had one unusual feature. The Court of Criminal Appeal may, in exceptional circumstances, hear additional evidence. Lord Chief Justice Reading gave

Marshall Hall leave to take this course in Holt's appeal. A Dr. Day, who had practised in the Malay Straits during Holt's sojourn there, had suddenly realised, while reading the reports of the trial, that Holt had been his patient there for syphilis. He had telegraphed to Marshall Hall on the last day of the trial too late for his evidence to be receivable at the trial, but Marshall decided that he must, if possible, be called on the appeal. It is well known that syphilis often results in general paralysis of the insane ; in the early stages of this form of insanity, caused by syphilis, the intelligence itself may work more quickly than at normal times, but the eventual degeneracy into insanity is certain. Marshall Hall gave the most impressive and dramatic reason for his application to call this evidence, which was based on the advance of medical research with regard to insanity made since the Macnaughton judgment. The Lord Chief Justice asked him to state the broad grounds of his application.

" I am going to ask your lordship," he replied, " to consider in 1920 the whole question of insanity and the subject of mental diseases. It is time the question was now settled. I am going to show that, owing to a condition of mind which was partly due to heredity and partly to syphilis, the appellant killed Mrs. Breaks as the result of uncontrollable impulse."

" What," asked the Lord Chief Justice, " is the proposition which you say is to be added to the Macnaughton case, or by which you say that case is to be modified ? "

Marshall Hall then stated very succinctly the argument of the alienists. " Will is different from reason. A man may know the difference between right and wrong and appreciate the nature and quality of his acts and the consequences thereof, and yet be deprived of that instinctive choice between right and wrong which is characteristic of a sane person. Hitherto, intellectual insanity, defective reason, has been the only insanity recognised by the law, but our contention is that a man's reason may be clear, even his judgment may be clear, yet his will-power is absent or impaired or suspended, so as to deprive the person affected of the power to control his actions or exercise his will-power."

Behind this argument lies a commonplace of modern psychology which, obvious as it is and although it is implicit in

Aristotle's ethics, was not a commonplace when Daniel Macnaughton was tried. Conduct is fundamentally dictated, not by
the intellectual or cognitive, but by the emotional faculties.
Sensation, instinct, desire, will, are the springs of conduct. The
distinction between will and intellect is clear to everybody,
although their functions overlap, and a human consciousness
cannot be regarded as a machine with separate parts. It is
possible that will may be hopelessly erratic, decayed, and
imbecile, while the intelligence still functions clearly. This is
well known to be so in the early stages of general paralysis of the
insane. If this is so, it accounts for the extraordinary combination of folly and deliberation which characterised, among
other things, Holt's revolting action. But the Macnaughton
rules only take into account intellectual perversion or decay,
and intelligence waits on will and desire. As a good servant may
serve an evil master and know it not, so a good intellect may
serve a corrupted will. Is it possible that the Macnaughton rules
ignored the main aspect of insanity ?

This, at any rate, was Marshall Hall's argument. The doctor
from Malaysia came forward to say that he had treated Holt for
syphilis, and that he had seemed at the same time to be suffering
from shell-shock. A lady who had met him in Malaysia said that
he appeared to be a typical shell-shock case. Details were given
by medical men as to the " delusions " of his two relatives.
Dr. Blair, senior medical officer of the Lancaster County Asylum,
who had given evidence at the trial, said that he had not known
at the trial of Holt's syphilis, and, in view of this fact, he now
considered that Holt had been suffering from general paralysis
of the insane at the time of the murder. Holt had, in fact, denied
that he had ever suffered from syphilis. Fresh evidence was given
of Holt's extreme excitability at trifles. All was in vain. The
Court decided that the judge had left the question of " irresistible impulse " to the jury, and that the additional evidence did
not warrant an interference with that verdict. Lord Reading
added that the rules in Macnaughton's case must be observed,
and that it was not sufficient for a medical expert to come into
court and say generally that a criminal was insane in order to
warrant a verdict of insanity.

It was easy to conclude that in the cases of Seddon and George

Joseph Smith the motive was avarice, even though in the latter
case it may have been insane avarice. But Holt's case is more
perplexing. The genuineness of his affection, which the judge
allowed ; the absurd over-insurance, which could only result in
certain detection ; the trail left by the man, which led as surely
to his arrest as if he dropped scraps of paper all the way from the
Sandhills to his home—all seemed to point to some " strange "
quality in his nature, other than a mere combination of mere
avarice, stupidity, and brutality. A legal correspondent of
The Times wrote, at the time, of the absurdity of holding as
responsible " men who see the evil to which, with a sort of
demoniac force, they are impelled ; slaves of an overmastering
idea, powerless to resist that which they know to be wrong,"
and put into the mouth of such a one the apostolic words, " O
wretched man that I am . . . what I hate, that I do . . . the
good that I would, I do not : but the evil which I would not,
that I do." May it not be that men live who, still cursed with
powers of intelligence, are, like Orestes, impelled to do some
cunning and unnatural crime by some " oracle of Loxias," some
mysterious, imperative, and fixed idea ? It is curious that just
as, after his crime, Orestes was pursued and obsessed by the
avenging Erinues, so Holt would talk of nothing but the fierce
dogs and venomous insects sent by the police to haunt him in
his cell, dreadful creatures of his imagination ; and it also
deserves mention that, in Æschylus's *Choephorœ* (ll. 273 and 301),
Orestes confesses, not only his desire for vengeance and a
barbaric superstition, but also his pecuniary need, as a reason
for the murder of his mother. If the Attorney-General of England, instead of the Furies, had prosecuted him in the trial that
followed at Athens before the divine Athena, and the goddess
had adopted as law the rules in Macnaughton's case, the jury
could hardly have acquitted him, even with Apollo as his
advocate.

Marshall Hall had not hoped that, in the present state of the
law, he could save Holt's life on the appeal ; he was deeply
unhappy about the case, and blamed himself for prejudicing the
plea of insanity by taking the preliminary point of Holt's
unfitness to plead. But, in truth, he had nothing in respect of
which to blame himself ; his efforts in both courts had been

superb. " I shall always remember," wrote Mr. Woosnam, of the firm of solicitors which instructed him, " the hours, yes, anxious hours, we spent together in doing our best—*your* very best—in a hopeless case. I don't want another quite so hopeless. I'm afraid we have shot our last bolt." A petition for a reprieve was presented ; and Marshall wrote a letter to his solicitors—to be sent, if necessary, to the authorities—which unfortunately, and contrary to his wishes and intention, found its way into the daily Press. " I feel so strongly," he wrote, " that he is now mad, and, as a man, contemplate with horror the idea of executing a madman, that I am quite willing you should, if you think fit, communicate the contents of this letter, or send the letter itself, to the Home Secretary or to the Attorney-General. As you know, I have never had any doubt in my own mind that Holt's hand fired the shot that killed Mrs. Breaks, nor have I ever had any real doubt that the deed was done under the influence of some sudden uncontrollable passion acting on a mind enfeebled by shell-shock and disease. I do not say he was mad at the time, but I do say that all the facts of the past two years point to a very strange condition of mind, and the undoubted jealousy that was existing on the 22nd and 23rd of December was, in my opinion, the actual cause of the terrible result ; but, that real madness supervened on the act, I am certain. Whether within twenty-four or forty-eight hours I cannot say, but it did supervene, and since then, and at the present time, the man is mad. I do not think the jury or the Court of Criminal Appeal could do anything. It is not a case for the lawyer, but for the medical scientist and the Home Secretary in his extra-judicial capacity. And from that point of view I do not think that sufficient weight has been given to these facts.

" 1. The doctors who examined him in February said he was suffering from delusional insanity and was mad. Subsequently, information disclosed the existence of two cases of incurable delusional insanity in his family.

" 2. The doctors at once suspected syphilis. Holt denied that he ever had it. Subsequent information disclosed that in 1917 he had suffered from generalised syphilis, which had been neglected and which had got well hold of his system.

" It is not a case of yielding to public clamour or newspaper outcry. It is a simple question. Is Holt mad now ? If he is not, then the sentence should be carried out ; but if, as I firmly believe, he is, then our Ministerial officials should be strong enough to take the line that the law of England does not execute madmen."

It only remains to say that the Home Secretary caused special medical enquiry to be made as to Holt's state of mind, and that, after their report, he was unable to advise the King to use his prerogative of mercy. Eric Holt was executed on April 13th, and was stolid and unemotional to the last. A crowd of about one thousand persons waited in the pouring rain outside Strangeways Prison, Manchester, to see the certificate of his execution posted and listen to the death-bell. " It's a great shame," said one woman in the crowd, voicing the opinion of many. But the rejoinder of another woman probably expressed the voice of the majority : " It served him right. Such a nice girl she was, too."

It might very easily be thought that Marshall Hall held extreme views with regard to the legal responsibility of insane persons : this was not so. When he was specially appointed by Lord Birkenhead to Lord Atkin's Committee on Insanity and Crime in 1922, his views were in conformity with the other members, among whom were Sir Richard Muir and Sir Archibald Bodkin. This committee heard the views of the British Medical Association and the Medico-Psychological Association. The former were in favour of retaining the existing law with a modification. The latter were advocating a far more drastic reform, behind which, according to Marshall Hall's view, loomed the extreme and erroneous principle that all criminals are mad, and which might have had the effect of emptying the prisons into the lunatic asylums. After all, murder is the rarest of all crimes, and it is better to suffer a fixed term of imprisonment for an offence than to be indefinitely detained " during His Majesty's pleasure." The committee, which was unanimous, reported according to the more conservative views of the British Medical Association, and recommended that there should be new legislation making " irresistible impulse " a defence in law. Marshall Hall was as convinced as any member of the committee that the insane impulse must not merely be victorious over a will, but be uncontrollable by it ; the will must not merely give way before an immense stimulus, but must be swept aside by an irresistible force. The recommendations of Lord Atkin's report have, however, not yet been embodied in the law of England, and the Macnaughton rules, strengthened by subsequent decisions of the Court of Criminal Appeal, remain in full Draconian force ; and insanity of the intellect is still the only form of madness of which criminal law takes official cognisance.

.   .   .   .

Sir Edward appeared, in two other murder trials, for ex-soldiers who were provoked into violence against members of their own family. One of these was infinitely sad. A young soldier had been married on Christmas Day, 1916. When he returned to his girl wife from France, he was blinded in both eyes, and could not see the baby that had been born. He was assisted by the great charity of St. Dunstan's ; but his pretty young wife lacked the character and devotion to support her great obligations. Eventually she left him in order to lead a gay life ; but he still loved her, and now and then she would visit him. Meanwhile, their little daughter, Irene, was the blind man's one joy and only companion ; somehow or other, for a time he continued to dress her, feed her, and look after her in place of her mother. " He kept her neat and tidy," said a witness ; " better than many men that can see." But eventually, in her own interests, he sent her to a home. The mother, on one of her visits, asked where the child was, and said that her proper place was with her mother. The husband went down on his knees to beg her to return to him as his wife, but she refused. Next day she called again to say that she was going abroad. He blocked the doorway to prevent her leaving him ; a struggle ensued, and the blind man seized his wife by the throat ; suddenly he felt her body relax, and heard her fall to the ground. He went in and out of the room several times before he knew she was dead. Marshall Hall, who, with Norman Birkett, lately come to his chambers, was briefed by St. Dunstan's for the prisoner, suggested graphically the ghastly picture of the blind man gradually coming to realise that his poor fickle, dearly loved wife was dead. He tried to kill himself with a razor. " Let me die," he said afterwards. " What is my life ? What have I got to live for ? " Marshall Hall was able to raise a rare defence that he had used before, in 1911. The dead woman was found to have an enlarged thymus gland in her throat. Two doctors called for the Crown stated that, in their view, the woman had died from violence, and not from *status lymphaticus*. But a doctor called by Marshall Hall said that, in his experience, a patient suffering from this complaint had died of excitement alone.

The prisoner went into the box, as pitiful a figure as Marshall had ever defended. Tears flowed from his sightless eyes as he said, " And I had done everything for her, and loved her dearly —passionately." But for his affliction, he would have been a fine young man of twenty-six ; now he stood there, before a Court he could not see, accused of murdering the wife he loved. After consulting for only ten minutes, the jury found him not guilty, both of murder and manslaughter, and gave him back life and liberty. Yet his words must have haunted his judges, when they went out into the September sunshine, as they did Marshall Hall. " What is my life ? " the blind man had said. " What have I to live for ? "

Two years later, Marshall Hall appeared at Maidstone Assizes for a young ex-officer of twenty-eight, who had served with the Buffs for two years in Mesopotamia. In the case, the defence of insanity was again raised. The mother of this man had suffered from delusions, while she was carrying him as a baby, and her sister had been a certified lunatic. After the war the man was liable to fits of temper and violence ; his wife's father helped him in every way he could, and allowed this neurasthenic and difficult man to live as a guest in his house. But his wife's nerve gave way owing to his violence ; she was afraid of him, and threatened to leave him. Shortly afterwards he took a shot-gun and shot her father in the head. A neighbour, who had seen the tragedy, said, " You villain, you have shot your best friend." The man stolidly admitted his guilt, but seemed quite unable to appreciate the gravity of what had happened. " I meant to do it," he said ; " I knew it would come to this." Like Holt, he sat in the dock and seemed to take no interest in his trial. " Do you wish to make a statement ? " asked the judge. " I don't think I could do much good," was the reply. " You have able counsel," said the judge, looking towards Marshall Hall. In this case, after

SIR EDWARD MARSHALL HALL

a deliberation of twelve minutes, the jury brought in a verdict of " guilty." He was, however, subsequently reprieved.

After the Holt trial, Marshall Hall's second capital trial in 1920 was the celebrated Green Bicycle case, in which Ronald Vivian Light was tried for murder before Mr. Justice Horridge at Leicester, on the Midland Circuit. Here again the accused was an ex-officer who had suffered badly from shell-shock, and had been through the terrible experience of the last German attack in April 1918. Happily his advocate never had to urge this ordeal as an explanation for the perpetration of an insane crime ; but he did argue that the man's shattered nerves may have accounted for the panic-stricken conduct which caused him to be apprehended and tried on a charge of murder.

Ronald Light was at the time of his arrest a mathematical master at a Cheltenham school ; he had been educated at Rugby and had qualified as a civil engineer. He was given a commission early in the war in the Royal Engineers, but later he served in the Honourable Artillery Company.

At about ten minutes to ten on Saturday, July 5th, 1919, the body of a young working girl named Bella Wright was found by the side of a country lane near Little Stretton in Leicestershire, her bicycle by her side. Although there was a pool of blood by her head, it was at first thought, by the doctor sent to attend to her, that she had died of heart failure or collapse ; but the clever village constable noticed on a gate hard by the marks of the bloody feet of a big bird. He found, in the field beyond, the dead body of a raven, which, it was thought, had died from gorging the girl's blood. This led to further investigations, and, after the blood had been washed away from her face, it was found that there was a small hole in her left cheek, and a larger one on the right side of the head. When a bullet was found half trodden into the road seventeen and a half feet away, it was thought that it had passed through her left cheek, upwards and out, leaving the larger wound on the right side of the head. It was ascertained that the girl had left her uncle's house at Gaulby, situated about two and a half miles from Little Stretton, in the company of a man riding a green bicycle and wearing a raincoat, with whom she seemed to be on friendly terms. A cycle repairer in Leicester, named Cox, gave information that he had repaired such a green

RONALD LIGHT
Rider of the Green Bicycle

bicycle and that the owner had called for it on Saturday, and had left saying " that he was going for a run in the country." Two little girls said that, at about 5.30 p.m. on July 5th, a man riding a green bicycle had tried to get into conversation with them in a road connected with the lane where the girl was found dead, and that they had been frightened by his manner.

On July 7th a police handbill was broadcast asking for information concerning a man, " age thirty-five to forty, height 5 ft. 7–9 in., dressed in light rainproof coat, said to have a squeaking voice," who had ridden, on Saturday last, " a gent's B.S.A. bicycle with a green enamel frame." But the hue and cry produced no results, and the affair was almost forgotten, except by the police, by February 1920. During that month, however, the tow-rope of a barge, passing down a canal near Leicester, raised part of the frame of a green bicycle for a minute or two. The police were told of this, and the greater part of the frame of a green bicycle was soon afterwards recovered from the canal. Though the maker's mark on the outside had been erased, there was still a secret mark which identified the machine, and it was found that Ronald Vivian Light had bought it in 1910. Light was arrested by Chief Inspector Taylor, and denied that he had ever owned a green bicycle. Afterwards he admitted that he had owned a green bicycle, but had sold it long ago. He was identified by the two little girls as the man with the green bicycle who had accosted them at 5.30 on the day of the murder, and also by the cycle repairer as the man who had taken his green bicycle away on the same day " for a run in the country." " My word," said poor Light, after he had thus been identified, " that man had me spotted." Further, a revolver holster had also been fished up from the canal, containing cartridges both live and blank ; these were of the same old-fashioned type, made for black powder and adapted for cordite, as that which had been found so near the place where the girl had fallen. The holster was almost conclusively identified as one which had belonged to Light. The meshes of a wellnigh complete net of circumstantial evidence seemed to have closed round this unfortunate man ; from this he was fondly seeking to extricate himself by denials, which could be refuted by evidence amounting to mathematical certainty.

In these circumstances Sir Edward was briefed for the defence.

This case and that of Lawrence he always regarded as his two
greatest triumphs : now he would favour the one in his recollection, now the other. The two cases have points of resemblance.
In each the defence remained a secret till after the trial had
started, and in each the prisoner was greatly prejudiced by
evidence of his own making ; in each, Marshall's great knowledge of fire-arms was the chief bulwark of the defence ; in each,
the personality of the prisoner was the determining factor. As to
the technical part of the defence in the Green Bicycle case, it is
doubtful if he took anyone, even his own junior, into his confidence before he actually rose to cross-examine the expert.
Before he went to Leicester on June 9th he visited a favourite
gunsmith's, and executed certain experiments with a revolver of
the same type as that which Light was alleged to have used, and
came to a certain and positive conclusion that Bella Wright
could not have been shot at close range either by the bullet found
in the road or by any bullet from the type of revolver which had
been traced to Light's possession within the last five years. If
this could be proved to the satisfaction of a jury, then Light
would probably be acquitted, were it not for one fact. If he persisted in denying that the bicycle was his, which the Crown
could prove to have been his on July 5th, by overwhelming
evidence ; if he still denied all knowledge of the holster and its
contents, which the police had also traced to him—the jury
might well conclude that these futile denials pointed to certain
guilt, and that, however the deed was done, however glibly his
counsel talked of the trajectories of bullets travelling at high
velocity, Light did it. Marshall Hall had not forgotten Robert
Wood's false alibi and the lying statement made by him on his
arrest, not knowing that Ruby Young had already given him
away. In the same way, Ronald Light, when he was arrested, did
not know the mass of evidence with which he was faced. Would
he, before the trial, see the futility of his denials, and confess to
ownership of the bicycle and the holster ? Both Wood and Light
were the last men to be seen with a girl found dead soon afterwards ; as Wood had gone to Ruby Young, had Light also gone
to the canal and thrown into it the evidence which would inevitably identify him with the man " on the green bicycle," after
whom there was already a hue and cry ? If only this was the

truth, and Light would admit it, Marshall Hall felt confident of an acquittal. If Light did not take this line, Marshall was a pessimist : his professional honour could not allow him to put Light into the box to repeat statements which would have, in his opinion, amounted to perjury. Meanwhile, the initiative must come from the prisoner : counsel may not suggest to a prisoner a line of defence which is in direct contradiction to the latter's instruction. Throughout the police court proceedings the prisoner made no statement, nor was any question put by the defence in cross-examination which showed any change of attitude by the prisoner ; but, during this preliminary hearing, when the Court had adjourned for lunch, Light, confined in a room in Leicester Castle with a commanding view of the surrounding country, had been observed looking out of the window towards the canal. " Damn and blast that canal," he had said hopelessly. Indeed, he had good reason to curse it.

In order to safeguard himself, Marshall Hall had no consultation, and saw Light for the first time when he came into the dock. Advocate and prisoner then conversed for a little time together.

The Crown sent down to Leicester a very strong team ; for the second time in one year Marshall Hall was opposed by the Attorney-General, who led Mr. Henry Maddocks, K.C., M.P., and Mr. Norman Birkett. Marshall's junior was Mr. A. Wightman Powers. The Crown came down with detailed and incontrovertible proof that Ronald Light was, on July 5th, 1919, the owner of the bicycle and the holster, and that he had owned at one time a revolver in which the bullet found on the road and those found in the holster could have been used. The Attorney-General's speech had that cold, reasoned, and yet dramatic quality which had characterised his conduct of the Holt case. Marshall Hall commented on its artistry to his clerk as they walked back to the hotel after the first day. The Attorney-General described the meeting of the man on the green bicycle with the girl. " Bella," he had been heard to say, " I thought you had gone the other way." He laid great stress on the word " Bella." " Their departure," said Mr. Attorney, " was at about a quarter past nine o'clock in the evening. About thirty-five minutes later Mr. Cowell found the body. Who was the man in whose company Miss Wright was last seen alive ? Who was the man with the green bicycle ? The evidence that I shall put before you will go to show that the man was Ronald Light, and his was the hand that killed the girl."

At this late stage in his speech Ronald Light's name was mentioned for the first time. The effect was most dramatic. Indeed, when he sat down, the chain of evidence seemed almost complete. Only one thing was lacking. There was no evidence of motive. But Mr. Attorney said that it was not necessary to probe into motives if the evidence otherwise was clear. Besides, the question of motive was not really a difficulty. " Suppose that the prisoner had made certain overtures to her and been rebuffed, or suppose that in anger, or, it might be, desire of concealing that which had been attempted, it is not difficult to conceive the motive."

After some preliminary evidence by the dead girl's mother and the astute village policeman, the two schoolgirls who had seen " the man with the green bicycle " were called. It was then that Marshall quietly made a dramatic announcement, which must have come as a bombshell to prosecuting counsel, spilling, as it did, gallons of midnight oil. Norman Birkett had suggested a date to one of the girls, and Marshall at once protested at his obtaining evidence from these most important witnesses by means of " leading " questions. " These young ladies," he said, " will be the only witnesses to fact as to whom there will be any cross-examination. There will be no cross-examination as to identity or ownership."

The girls' evidence was shaken without much difficulty ; it was a long time since July 1919. They had read all about the " man on the green bicycle." They had " talked the matter over and quite made up their minds that they met this man on July 5th." Moreover, one of them admitted that the police had suggested this date to them when they were first questioned. The jury were left with the opinion that, however honest, these girls might easily have been mistaken as to the date.

In spite of Marshall's announcement, there was one other important piece of cross-examination of a witness to fact. The girl's uncle said that he had heard the man say, " Bella, I thought you had gone the other way." Marshall suggested that he had not said " Bella," but " Hello." The witness would not

admit this, despite the fact that his niece had declared to him at
the time, " The man is a perfect stranger to me." This was a
point of some importance, because the murder by a man of a poor
girl whose name he does not know is, on the face of it, in the last
degree unlikely. On that word " Bella " rested the only evidence
of a possible motive.

But the important cross-examination was that of Dr. Williams
and Mr. Clarke, the gunsmith. The former produced a gruesome
" exhibit "—the actual piece of skin, preserved in formalin,
with the hole made by the bullet clearly visible. Marshall produced a slender silver pencil, and showed that this would
barely pass into the wound. The doctor's opinion was that the
bullet had been fired at a range of from five to seven feet.
Marshall put it to him that a .455 bullet, travelling at point
blank range at tremendous velocity, and starting on a flight of
1,000 yards, must make a much larger exit hole ; the woman's
head, he said, would be almost blown off. The bullet must have
been fired from a greater distance. But the doctor still maintained his opinion.

" Then how do you get out of this dilemma ? " asked Marshall.
" A bullet going in an upward direction (the wounds showed this)
at high velocity found six yards away from the body ? "

The doctor's answer was not convincing. " My theory is that
the woman was shot whilst lying on the road, and the bullet
went through her head into the ground." In his opinion the
bullet had passed through the head into the soft ground at the
side of the road, struck the hard ground underneath, and
rebounded into the road.

Then one very important admission was obtained from the
doctor. " If a bullet," asked Marshall Hall, " was fired without
any further resistance than the girl's head, it would be absurd
to suppose that it would be found only six yards away ? " The
doctor agreed.

What was begun by the cross-examination of the doctor was
completed by that of the gunsmith. Marshall asked him to look
through a microscope, and to direct his attention to a mark which
he had found upon the bullet. The witness agreed that this mark
showed the bullet to have passed through a rifled barrel, which,
whether in a rifle or a revolver, would enormously increase the

range of the weapon. Marshall, with a meaning look at the jury, asked, " This bullet could be fired from a rifle as well as a revolver ? "

" Yes," replied the gunsmith.

Though he knew his subject, and fenced very ably with Marshall Hall, he was forced to admit the bare possibility of mere accident accounting for the tragedy.

" Supposing the shot to have been fired some distance away, and that in its flight it came in contact with a fence, tree, or something else, and then struck someone on the roadway, would you expect to find that bullet within a few feet of where the person was shot ? "

" Yes," replied the gunsmith, " it is possible."

After a long technical argument of this kind, Marshall Hall suddenly rapped out a very direct and simple question.

" Have you ever seen a human being who has been shot at a distance of within five yards with a service revolver ? "—" No, sir."

" I suggest that the effect of such a bullet on the skull of a human being is almost to blow the side of the head off ? "

" It depends on the velocity, sir," replied the witness, somewhat evasively.

" Of course it does," retorted Marshall Hall.

Much had already been established, and the usual tribute, with which the reader is now familiar, must now be paid to Marshall Hall's quick eye and brain ; he had observed that mark on the bullet, and now that tell-tale bullet, found so near to the dead body, own brother to those found in the holster fished up from the canal, which had seemed to point so conclusively to Ronald Light as the murderer, was actually becoming a vital piece of evidence in his favour. The coincidences of truth are innumerable, as the Attorney-General had said, but they sometimes tell in favour of the defence. That bullet, if fired, as the prosecution would have it, so close at hand, would normally have continued its flight for a long way, even though it passed through the girl's head. Strange that it was found so near. It really began to look as if the bullet had been fired from a long way off, and, either because its normal course was nearly spent when it hit her, or else through losing direction and force by a

MARSHALL HALL'S MUSEUM OF FAMOUS REVOLVERS, KNIVES, ETC.

a. *Rex* v. *Fahmy*
b. *Rex* v. *Holt*
c. *Rex* v. *Dyer*
d. *Rex* v. *Light* (cartridges)
e. *Rex* v. *Lawrence*
f. *Day* v. *Mark Sheridan* (Mark Sheridan shot himself with this revolver)

g. *Rex* v. *Packham*
h. *Rex* v. *Kitchener*
i. *Rex* v. *Carter*
j. *Rex* v. *Doyle* (Peeping Tom case)
k. *Rex* v. *Carr*
l. *Rex* v. *Light* (holster found in canal)

ricochet, it had dropped to the ground after passing through the girl's head. Another alternative was that the bullet found on the road was not the cause of the girl's death, in which case the most vital link in the chain of evidence was broken. This was the view favoured by Marshall Hall himself.

His cross-examination had at all events opened up a wide field of conjecture. Might not the explanation of the whole affair be an accident, in view of the answers of the doctor and the gunsmith ? A girl cycling along a lane, highly flanked by a hedge ; a boy or man shooting with a rifle or revolver at a distance, either for practice or at some mark on hedge or gate ; a bullet spent on its flight from distance or ricochet—were there not here all the conditions for an accident ?

The jury were clearly puzzled by the turn which the trail had now taken, but the event was as yet far from certain. All now turned upon Light himself. If he went into the box, and repeated that he knew nothing about bicycle or holster, which appeared false to demonstration, all Marshall's brilliant questioning would have been in vain. In view of the latter's announcement at the beginning of the evidence, this course was almost ruled out. If Light remained in the dock and gave no evidence, he would be the subject of most damning comment. If he adopted the third course, and went into the box to admit the falsity of his previous statements, he would face the jury as a confessed liar. He was in a perilous predicament.

Perhaps I may here quote the instructions, in Light's own handwriting, given to Marshall Hall during the course of the trial. " Will you please ask me to tell the jury in my own words exactly why I did not come forward ? I shall say I was dreadfully worried, and for some days was quite dazed at such an unexpected blow, and could not think clearly. When I began to think, I could not make up my mind to come forward, and hesitated for days. I could not give the police any information whatever as to how the girl met her death. If the police and papers had only stated the known facts, and asked the cyclist to come forward, I shall[1] have done so, but they jumped to wrong conclusions, and I was frightened when I saw I was wanted for murder. . . . Let me do this in my own words."

[1] *Sic.*

On the afternoon of the second day, when the case for the Crown had closed, Marshall Hall said in his quietest voice :

" I desire to call the prisoner."

The prisoner, a man smartly dressed, with a clear-cut, intellectual face, then went into the witness box. All doubts as to the nature of the defence and the prisoner's capacity were soon dispelled. Hearers in court were amazed at the ease with which the bad impression created by his previous statements, far from being increased, was largely destroyed by his confession that they were all lies. He admitted so much that it was difficult to see how the prosecution could detain him very long for cross-examination. He admitted ownership of the bicycle and holster, but said that he had left the revolver itself behind in France at a casualty clearing station, when he was sent home for shell-shock. He admitted that he had met the girl at about eight o'clock on July 5th, but for the first time. She had trouble with the front wheel of her bicycle, and asked him for a spanner. They had cycled on together till they came to her uncle's house at Gaulby. She said she was only going in for ten minutes ; he took this as an invitation to wait, which he did not accept. He decided to cycle home to Leicester, but he was delayed by a puncture in his tyre. He mended it, and, as he knew he would be late for supper anyhow, he bethought him of the girl. He determined to take a short cut and see how far " that girl " had got. But he had, as it turned out, to go all the way back to Gaulby before he met her. When he arrived, she was just coming out of her uncle's house. " Hello," he had said. " You've been a long time. I thought you had gone the other way." He did not say " Bella," and, in fact, did not know her name till he read of her death in the papers. He then accompanied her till they came to a fork of the road. In a most graphic way the prisoner described their parting. " I must say good-bye to you here," the girl had said, pointing to the left. " But," said Light, pointing to the right, " that is the shortest way to Leicester." " I don't live there," replied the girl. They then parted. " I never saw her again," said Light.

The prisoner frankly admitted his fatal mistake in not telling the police ; one thing had led to another, and finally, to escape from the affair altogether and to spare the distress of his invalid mother, he had disposed of the bicycle, the holster, and the very clothes he had worn on the fatal night.

He had created an excellent impression, and the tide began to turn ; public feeling, which had begun to run very high against him, was now strongly in his favour. In spite of the high-pitched voice, by which some of the witnesses had identified him, he seemed a frank, manly fellow, and was, after all, a war veteran. On the third and last day of the trial he had to face the enquiries of the Crown. Mr. Attorney had been compelled to return to London for reasons of State, and Mr. Maddocks sat up most of the night with Norman Birkett to prepare the cross-examination of Light. But his evidence remained unshaken. The prosecution failed entirely to place him by the girl's side at the moment of her death. At the close of the cross-examination he was questioned by the judge as to the reasons of his concealment and falsehoods. " I did not make up my mind deliberately not to come forward," replied the prisoner. " I was so astounded at this unexpected thing that I kept on hesitating, and in the end I drifted into doing nothing at all. I had drifted into the policy of concealment, and I had to go on with it." The dilemma of the man who does not at first come forward, increasing as the hue and cry persists, could not have been better put.

After Mr. Maddocks's speech for the prosecution, Marshall Hall rose to address the jury. The defence was twofold : first, the impossibility, or extreme improbability, of the bullet found on the roadside being fired from near by, whether it was the cause of the girl's death or not. " First of all," said Marshall Hall, " you have got to satisfy yourselves that the girl was murdered. Even the Attorney-General has not put forward a definite theory for the crime." Secondly, there was a complete absence of motive ; the motive suggested by the Attorney-General would not bear the least critical examination. " This is absolutely and finally negatived by the evidence. There was no sign of any struggle nor of any molestation of the girl. Was it suggested that the man, having been rebuffed by word of mouth, shot her ? A man of that class would have done what he wanted first, and shot her afterwards." " I am glad," added Marshall Hall, dropping his voice low, " that there is not a tittle of evidence on this point, because the name of this poor girl remains unsullied by the evidence."

Finally, Marshall dealt with the prisoner's short association with the girl, and his fatal deceit. Why did he go back to meet her when he had once left her ? . . . Marshall then began to be carried away by the full tide of his own emotion and eloquence. He spoke of the great power of sex attraction, one of the mightiest forces in the world. To go back over a country road in the hopes of seeing an attractive girl again was but a slight instance of its power. Marshall Hall's clerk, who knew his master's temperamental nature, said to himself, " The old man's right away now," and looked forward to as fine a speech as he had made in defence of Holt.

At this moment, however, an unlooked-for interruption occurred : the judge saw a pressman about to take a photograph in court. He stopped Marshall Hall at full flood, had the culprit brought up before him, and reprimanded him severely.

But the spell had been broken, and inspiration did not return. Just as the jostling by the women at Manchester had keyed up his nerves so that he made that splendid speech, now he was quite put out of his stride by this trivial incident. Only at the very end did he seem to find himself—when he spoke of Light's anxiety to spare his mother's feelings, and his war-shattered nerves. " You must not forget that he is a man who has undergone the awful ordeal of shell-shock, an ordeal which reduces the strongest men to human wrecks, and leaves them bereft of human strength."

The judge in his summing-up warned the jury that this case deserved their special care and scrutiny, because no motive at all had been made out by the prosecution ; but one passage must have made the prisoner catch his breath. " Do you think it is credible or possible that an innocent man should have behaved in the way he did ? . . . The question you have to decide is whether that deception could have been practised by an innocent man, or whether it points the finger at the guilty man."

The jury retired at 4.35 in the afternoon, and were absent for three hours and seven minutes. The judge recalled them, and asked them if there was any prospect of their agreeing. The foreman asked for another quarter of an hour ; but in fact they returned a second time in only three minutes.

The prisoner was brought up to hear the verdict ; he had been brave throughout the trial, and afterwards confessed to having had a bet of money on the result; but for the moment he was quite unnerved; he said that the agony on this occasion was worse than anything he had undergone in France, when death had been near him for so much longer. The suspense of those three hours must have been frightful. He clung to the rail of the dock for support, and the knuckles of his clenched hands were quite white. When the foreman said, " Not guilty," he collapsed. The verdict was a popular one, and was cheered both inside the court and by the thousands gathered outside. But Light slipped out by himself, and returned home to his mother by tram alone, unrecognised by all except a friend, who lent him three-pence for his tram fare. When he reached home, he sat down at once to write the following letter to his counsel :

> " Leicester,
> " 16th *June* /20.

" DEAR SIR,—The very first letter I am writing since my release is, of course, to you.

" I cannot find words to express how deeply grateful I am to you for your great and successful efforts on my behalf. It seems rather feeble to say ' Thank you ' for saving my life, but I feel sure you will understand what I think. Your speech to the jury was simply great, and practically obliterated any previous impressions they had obtained from hearing Mr. Maddocks. . . . I shall always remember you with the deepest gratitude.

> " Yours sincerely,
> " R. LIGHT."

Marshall Hall's reply is even more interesting, and shows his character splendidly; throughout the trial he had been haunted by the thought of the prisoner's mother, an invalid old lady who had often been worried with regard to her son, and who now sat at home awaiting the result of his trial for murder. " DEAR SIR," he wrote from his cottage at Brook,—" Thank you for your letter, which I much appreciate. Quite apart from *the* matter which caused so much anxiety . . . may I in all kindness and great sincerity express the hope that you will realise that life is a serious thing, and that work and self-denial are the only means to happiness. Please convey to your mother my sympathetic regards, and you will, I am sure, forgive me if I say that you can best show your gratitude to me by making her life happier in the future than I fear it has been in the past. I am indeed glad to have been of service to you, and through you to her. Yours very faithfully, EDWARD MARSHALL HALL."

The judge sent Marshall a rare judicial compliment before he left the Judge's Lodgings at Lincoln. " Your defence of Light," he wrote, " seemed to me to be without a fault." Among the many telegrams of congratulation he received was one from his old friend, Sir Arthur Pinero : " Congratulations on the Light that did not fail." " My DEAR PIN," Marshall replied, —" I was so glad to get your telegram—for it spoke for remembrance. It was a desperate fight, and Horridge paid me a most unusual compliment, and I must say that his summing-up was most fair. . . . The coincidence of the bullet was literally astounding, as I am convinced the bullet that was found within $17\frac{1}{2}$ feet of the body never killed the girl ; but the deadly thing was that the accused man had in his possession at the time identical bullets. True, as I elicited in cross-examination, they are made in *thousands of millions*, but, for all that, it was a coincidence. Absence of motive, too, was a great asset. But, for all that, I can assure you that it wanted handling. Personally, I think it is the greatest success as an advocate I ever had. Yours, as ever, MARSHALL."

Light was acquitted, but the Green Bicycle case is unexplained. As I have said, Marshall Hall did not commit himself to any theory ; it would have been quite unnecessary for him to do so. His duty was to suggest as strongly as possible that the girl's death was susceptible of other explanations than that put forward by the prosecution. It was not for him to commit himself to murder or manslaughter, accident or design ; it was for the prosecution to prove how the girl died, and bring it home to the prisoner beyond reasonable doubt. To have put upon the defence the embarrassment of a cut-and-dried theory would have been dangerous. Several ingenious guesses have been made. Perhaps the most attractive is that of Mr. H. Trueman Humphries, who made a short story out of it for the *Strand*

Magazine. He seized upon the dead raven as the key to the story. Whoever heard of a raven dying of over-gorging or apoplexy ? It was far more likely that the bird had been shot and had bled internally. As the bird sat on the gate, he was sighted, stalked, aimed at, and shot by a reckless marksman, probably a boy, with a rook rifle ; the bullet passed through its body and through the head of a girl passing on her bicycle, and then, almost spent, dropped to the ground. The ingenious writer, from a personal visit to the place, found that from a sheep-trough, where he might have taken cover, the marksman could have seen the raven as it sat on the gate where its bloody footmarks were found ; if the marksman were lying down, so as not to alarm the bird, his bullet would be a rising one, so that it would rise in its flight so as to pass through the girl's head in its normal course. It would then drop into the road near the place where it was found ; the girl would naturally fall from her cycle into the place where Bella Wright's body was in fact found. This theory amused Marshall Hall, although he did not believe that the bullet found in the road had anything to do with the girl's death ; and, although the conclusion is sound, a great deal has to be assumed by way of premisses ; on the other hand, the Crown theory, even when a great deal had been assumed, did not warrant the conclusion sought to be drawn. At all events, the raven, whether it died of gorging human blood or revenged itself on mankind for its death by putting a human life in jeopardy, adds a sinister interest to this famous trial, and proves that life can be as strange and terrible as the most fantastic literature.

A few days before Bella Wright's violent and mysterious death, an ailing middle-aged lady, the wife of a country solicitor at Kidwelly named Harold Greenwood, had died in her bed at a quarter past three in the morning of June 16th, 1919. At half-past three in the afternoon of June 16th, 1920, Harold Greenwood, her husband, was arrested on a charge of murdering her. Local gossip had undoubtedly led to his arrest ; he had married a young and attractive woman, whom he had known for a long time, three months after his wife's death, and had also, in the interval between his first wife's death and his second marriage, proposed to another lady friend, the sister of the local doctor who had certified his first wife's death as due to heart failure.

This doctor had been sent for to attend to Mrs. Greenwood, who seemed to be suffering from a stomach upset after lunch, as a result of eating gooseberry tart. The authorities ordered the exhumation of the body, and Dr. Webster, the Home Office analyst, who had also performed the experiment for Sir William Willcox in the Seddon case, calculated by the Marsh test that there was a little more than a quarter of a grain of arsenic in the woman's body. It was known and proved that Harold Greenwood used a weed-killer, containing a strong solution of arsenic, for his garden; the police approached a girl named Hannah Williams, who had been parlourmaid to the Greenwoods at the date of the first wife's death, and obtained a statement from her that Mrs. Greenwood alone had drunk from a bottle of wine on the table at luncheon on the day of her death; that before lunch Greenwood had gone into the pantry cupboard from the garden, and that the bottle of wine which had been on the luncheon-table had disappeared by the following day. The circumstances of the death of Mrs. Greenwood were consistent with arsenical poisoning. Until the very conclusion of the trial the theory of the prosecution was that Greenwood had polluted the wine in this bottle with arsenic in order to kill his wife, and had watched her slowly die from luncheon on Sunday till **3.15** on Monday morning.

The brief for the defence was sent to Marshall Hall—his third capital case in the year 1920. Greenwood's case excited the most hostile public prejudice, and he was generally assumed to be guilty during his four months' incarceration before trial. Marshall Hall was in a favourite silversmith's shop on the day before he went down to Carmarthen Assizes. " I'm surprised at you, Sir Edward," said the silversmith, an old friend, " for defending that blackguard Greenwood. You must see he's guilty yourself. However, I suppose it's your job."

" Guilty, indeed," retorted Sir Edward. " The man's innocent, and I'll get him off—you'll see."

" Very well," said the silversmith, " whether you get him off or not, if you convince me that man's innocent, I'll make you a present of this."

As he spoke, he held out an eighteenth-century silver tankard.

Sir Edward arrived at the Ivy Bush Hotel, Carmarthen, late

ARRIVAL OF MR. HAROLD GREENWOOD AT THE COURT
to stand his trial

on a very dark night. Everybody engaged in the case was staying at the hotel, including Sir Edward Marlay Samson, leading counsel for the Crown, and Sir William Willcox. The case excited the most enormous interest in Wales, and, as Marshall drove down to see Greenwood on the following morning, the streets were lined with spectators—as they were throughout the trial—as if for a royal procession. After his interview with the prisoner, he said to his confidential clerk, Ernest Harvey, " I cannot make up my mind about calling Greenwood. I am afraid he will make a bad witness, and everything will turn on the evidence of his daughter and the cross-examination of Webster and Willcox."

A comparison of the Seddon and the Greenwood cases is unavoidable. Once again there was a duel between Willcox and Marshall Hall as to arsenical poisoning ; once more Marsh's test was to be examined and criticised for hours ; once more the methods of the police in obtaining evidence were to be attacked. In the course of the trial, Marshall Hall again created an amazing transformation of feeling ; at the beginning, as Greenwood was driven to the assize courts, his carriage was given special police protection, and he was the subject of angry demonstrations. Towards the end, the police witnesses almost needed protection themselves.

It is difficult to select from this really historic trial the essential and vital episodes. There were so many exciting and dramatic moments which contributed materially to the result. Sir Edward himself was a very sick man throughout the trial ; he could neither stand up nor sit down without acute physical discomfort, and, for this reason, his conduct of the defence was not only masterly but heroic. But the physical strain told terribly on his nerves, and resulted in frequent outbursts on his part against the witnesses, and even in vehement protests at the periodical interventions from the Bench. It was only when his old friends, the experts, were in the box that he exercised the admirable restraint which had characterised the whole of his conduct of the Seddon case.

On the mere facts of the case there were two important witnesses whose evidence it was essential to challenge ; the doctor who had certified death, and the parlourmaid. The latter was a pretty, rather complacent young lady ; Marshall Hall sought to show that her whole evidence was coloured by questions put by the burly policeman who had approached her months after her late mistress's death. She altered the details of her story again and again, and finally said that the bottle of wine from which Mrs. Greenwood had helped herself at lunch was labelled " Port Wine." " Whoever heard of such a thing? " commented Marshall. " A little touch of the domestic servant." She also said that she had never known Mr. Greenwood to wash his hands in the pantry cupboard before that morning, but she was quite certain he had done so that Sunday on one—or was it two occasions ? Miss Irene Greenwood never drank wine, on this occasion or at any time ; nevertheless, she had put out two pink glasses, one for Miss Irene and one for her mother. " Poor little girl ! Poor little frightened thing ! " Marshall observed in his final speech, and that was undoubtedly the impression created by her on the minds of the jury. She had been led to make statements about details which she could not be expected to remember after the lapse of months, and had tried in vain to adhere to them. But if she was frightened by the big, burly policeman, she was still more frightened by the big, burly counsel for the defence. She seemed to consider herself on her defence for having drunk the remainder of the wine herself. In answer to the question, " Are you a teetotaller ? " she said, " Yes, I am. I am having a name for having drunk it, but I am not drunk to-day."

Marshall Hall was defending a man's life, and he pressed the girl still further, for her defensive attitude was extremely helpful and interesting to him. She was clearly thinking, not of the prisoner, but of her own position. Finally the judge intervened. " You were shouting at the witness," he said. " I have to see that witnesses are not addressed in a vehement way."

" Why," retorted Sir Edward, " it is my duty to be vehement."

If this girl's evidence had remained unshaken, it might have gone hardly with the prisoner ; but there was another witness for the prosecution whom Marshall Hall was to put upon the defensive—the local doctor who had given the certificate of death. The doctor had prescribed a mixture of bismuth, and also, according to his evidence at the police court, two morphia pills, which had been administered by the trained nurse to the patient at 1 p.m., after which she was violently sick, and fell into a state of coma, from which she never recovered. It was suggested to the doctor at the police court that these pills might have been the cause of death. Now, a morphia pill contains half a grain of morphia, and a grain of morphia would be a dangerous dose to a woman who, like Mrs. Greenwood, suffered from a weak heart. Marshall Hall, when he read this in the depositions, realised that here lay a strong line of defence. If Mrs. Greenwood took, under doctor's orders, a drug in a dangerous quantity, and soon afterwards sank into a state of coma—the natural result of such a dose of morphia—from which she never recovered, it would be difficult to attribute her death to her husband, whether arsenic was found in her body months after her death or not. Naturally, Marshall Hall had prepared a heavy cross-examination on this point for the doctor. But an unpleasant surprise was in store for him ; things were not to be so easy as that. When the doctor went into the box, he explained that when he had said morphia pills at the police court he had meant opium pills. Now, an opium pill only contains one-fortieth of a grain of morphia, and it would be absurd to suggest that these two pills could have caused death even to a woman with a weak heart.

Marshall Hall was on his legs in a moment, protesting at this apparent change of front, and demanded that his cross-examination should be deferred till the morrow. He did, however, ask the doctor one interesting question that afternoon.

" If you had given her two half-grains of morphia, you would not be surprised that she died at four o'clock ? "—" Yes, I would."

Now, this answer was a surprising one, and provided Marshall with all the ammunition which he needed, in view of the doctor's explanation of his previous statement. On the next day the battle was resumed, and the doctor said that opium pills were often called morphia pills, because they contain morphia.

" Now, doctor," said Marshall, " there is an enormous difference between opium and morphia."—" I know that."

" You said that, in your opinion, there would have been no danger in giving this woman two half-grains of morphia ? "— " I meant two half-grains of pure opium."

" I asked you the question last night purposely before the Court rose. I asked you if it would have been safe to give this woman two half-grains of morphia, and you said it was perfectly safe. Did you think I meant opium then ? "—" Yes."

Then Marshall spoke slowly and deliberately. " I give every allowance to every witness who says what I don't expect him to say. Have you the smallest doubt whatever that if you, as a medical man, were accurate when you said you gave her two half-grains of morphia after ten o'clock that she would have been dead before four o'clock ? —" If I had given her morphia she would, but I did not give her morphia."

Later Marshall Hall asked the doctor for the prescription of the tonic given by him to Mrs. Greenwood. He could only produce a piece of paper which he had copied from his prescription book. He undertook to produce the book itself on the next day. When the time came, he had to admit that the prescription book had been destroyed. It must have been destroyed, he said, when he retired from practice at the end of 1919. But Marshall was able to show from the doctor's own statement that the latter had copied the prescription from the book in June 1920.

" Why was it destroyed ? " asked Marshall.

" I don't remember," said the doctor.

At one point the Court was thrown almost into a frenzy of excitement. The police had taken down a statement from Greenwood in a notebook, and he had signed it. When the statement was read out in court, he said that it differed from the signed one in several particulars. The differences really came to very little, but a most unusual scene took place. Marshall saw a little piece of paper sticking up from the binding of the book, which indicated that some pages might have been torn out. He flourished his magnifying-glass. The inspector in the box took exception to the suggestion, and was very positive that the book had been in good order before it passed to Sir Edward, and added that he had seen Sir Edward handling it roughly. Marshall Hall flew into a temper, and demanded to be put into the witness box. The judge calmed him down ; but he again became excited when the clerk of assize went into the witness box to count the pages of another police notebook, and found ten more pages in it than in the Greenwood book. However, the incident was only a passing storm, and nothing hinged upon it.

On the fourth and fifth days of the trial Marshall Hall cross-examined the Crown experts. Dr. Webster produced a series of glass tubes, or " mirrors," which proved the arsenic present in Mrs. Greenwood's body on exhumation. The amount found was much less than that found in Miss Barrow's body, and the cross-examination was so much the easier. Marshall again argued that a very slight mistake in observation or calculation in performing the Marsh experiment would make the most vital difference, and embarked on a long mathematical discussion with Dr. Webster, during which the judge made some observations to him.

" I may not know much about the law, but I know something about decimals," he said, and went on with his calculations.

The duel with Sir William Willcox was again a triumph of patience and skill. Marshall hardly received a contradiction from either of these two witnesses ; his questions were so cunningly framed that it was hard to disagree with them. When he was putting forward the wildest improbability, he would ask whether such a thing were barely possible, and the doctor would have to agree. An admirer of Marshall Hall's said that his propositions sounded hardly less innocent and unimpeachable than such a question as, " Do you agree with me, doctor, in believing that arrowroot is better for infants than arsenic ? " This constant assent by the Treasury experts gave the jury the impression that Marshall was winning them over to his views.

After quietly asking Sir William Willcox if he had ever given evidence for the defence, and referring to the Seddon case, Marshall Hall asked :

" You gave evidence before the magistrates in this case, and expressed the opinion that the cause of death was arsenical poisoning ? "—" Yes."

" Is that the opinion you expressed some months ago ? "—" Yes."

" Has the evidence you heard in this case weakened or strengthened your opinion ? "

Sir William, who always uses a slow, rather deliberate manner, paused very noticeably before replying, " I am *still* of the opinion that death was caused by arsenical poisoning."

This hesitation of the chief witness for the Crown was one of the strong points of Marshall Hall's opening speech for the defence.

Even more important was another question and answer: " The utmost deduction that you can draw against the accused here is that something on the border-line of the possible fatal dose had been administered ? "—" Approximately the minimum fatal dose had been administered."

And yet again :

" When Dr. Griffiths says that morphia pills are often called opium pills, is that news to you ? "—" Yes."

Marshall Hall very skilfully used the suggestion that the arsenic from the weed-killer might conceivably have got on to the skins of the gooseberries which Mrs. Greenwood had eaten for lunch ; that the arsenic might even have been blown up from the grass by the wind, and that Mrs. Greenwood might have inhaled it ; he also put to the witness a number of mysterious and curious instances of arsenical poisoning.

The most dramatic moment, however, of the cross-examination was the result of Marshall's own enterprise. He remembered, as he lay awake in some pain on the night after the local doctor had given his evidence, that the latter had said that he kept both bismuth and Fowler's solution of arsenic in his dispensing-room, and had prescribed bismuth for Mrs. Greenwood on the day of her death. An idea occurred to him. " I wonder if that is a possible theory ? " he thought. " They look exactly the same." The next morning at nine o'clock he was down at the chemist's, and bought two little bottles, one containing bismuth, the other Fowler's solution of arsenic. They were almost indistinguishable in appearance. While Willcox was in the box, Marshall innocently asked him what Fowler's solution of arsenic looked like. " Oh," said the doctor, " it is a reddish liquid."

" Rather like this ? " said Marshall, producing his little bottle of bismuth before anyone could stop him. " Yes," said Sir William.

Marshall then showed his other little bottle to the witness and the jury, and suggested that a mistake was quite possible in regard to them. It was in vain for the prosecution to protest that these little bottles were not official exhibits of the court. They had had their effect, and Sir William had been cross-examined as to them.

" If, by some unfortunate mistake, he, in the anxiety and hurry, gave her four teaspoonfuls of Fowler's solution, you would have got all the arsenic you found, or more than you found ? "—" Yes."

" And there would be practically no distinction in colour in the mixture, whether the mixture were of bismuth or a solution of arsenic ? "—" No ; they resemble each other."

He persisted in this suggestion till the trial ended, not in any way as a charge against the ministrations of the local doctor, but as an alternative hypothesis (which he was under no obligation to prove) to account for the presence of the arsenic in the body. It was in the last degree unlikely that the doctor had in fact made such a mistake ; but was it not still more unlikely that a respectable solicitor should murder his wife in this brutal manner ? Each hypothesis was improbable ; the true explanation in all probability was still unguessed; for arsenic can get into the human body in a number of extraordinary ways. But, when one hypothesis postulates murder, it is the duty of the defence to call attention to all the possibilities on the face of the case. It was a brilliant " red herring " dragged across the case for the prosecution, and very typical of Marshall Hall's quick and original mind.

It is interesting to go behind the scenes and discover that this long duel between the Crown expert and the defending advocate was only made physically possible by the skill and kindness of the former. Sir William had been giving medical treatment and assistance at the Ivy Bush Hotel throughout the trial to Marshall Hall, and, if it had not been for this, the latter would never have fought his way through this strenuous case as he did.

Marshall Hall began his opening speech for the defence with an allusion to the fact that local gossip had been the first origin of this case. Adapting the lines from *Othello*, he said :

> " Trifles light as air
> Are, to the jealous, confirmation strong
> As proofs of Holy Writ."

He said that he would call two doctors for the defence—Dr. Toogood and Dr. Griffiths of Swansea—the prisoner, and his

CCH

daughter, Irene Greenwood. These two distinguished physicians both said that in their opinion Mrs. Greenwood had died of a dose of morphia. Greenwood himself went into the box on the sixth and seventh days. Marshall Hall examined him in a most unexpected and dramatic way, only asking him a few direct questions, of which the last were these :

" Had you anything to do with your wife's death ? "— " Nothing whatever."

" After your wife's death, what happened to her private means ? "—" They went to her children."

" You have been in prison for four and a half months, and are you now ready to answer any questions my friend may ask relative to his case ? "—" Yes."

Greenwood spoke very low, and his evidence added no new aspect to the case. But he survived his long ordeal of cross-examination without breaking down in any important particular. Yet, on trial for his life as he was, the most important witness for the defence was to come after him.

When the case for the prosecution had closed, Marshall Hall had held a long and earnest consultation with the prisoner's daughter, Miss Irene Greenwood, a slim girl twenty-two years old, after which he told his clerk that everything depended upon her evidence ; with this dreadful responsibility on her shoulders she went into the witness box. Her great nervousness showed that she was fully aware of this responsibility ; she made a most moving and convincing witness, constantly referring to the prisoner as " my daddy." The great importance of her testimony was that she said that she also had drunk from the bottle of wine from which, as the prosecution alleged, her mother had been poisoned by her father. She gave her evidence with great certainty as to detail. When asked how her memory was so good, she replied that she remembered everything so well because her mother died that day. Marshall Hall afterwards said that she had saved her father's life. As the judge said in his summing-up, " If she also drank from the bottle, there is an end of the case."

Marshall Hall's final speech lasted over three hours. It had been very doubtful the night before whether he would be able to make it, but " as the prisoner was a member of his own profession " he made a supreme effort. He contended that the case for the prosecution had been utterly exploded, begun by local gossip, depending for its circumstantial details on the prompted and uncertain memory of a servant girl, and for its scientific justification on the finding in the body of the bare minimum quantity of arsenic necessary for a fatal dose by means of an elaborate and fallible experiment. Once again he performed " Hall's Scales of Justice Act " ; once again he had his opportunity to refer to the vital spark of human life. " Your verdict is final. Science can do a great deal. These men, with their mirrors, multipliers, and milligrams, can tell you, to the thousandth or the millionth part of a grain, the constituents of the human body. But science cannot do one thing—that is, to find the final spark which converts insensate clay into a human being."

And then the advocate dropped his voice to a whisper, and closed his masterly defence, as he had opened it, with a quotation from *Othello*—the words of the Moor when he stole into Desdemona's chamber :

> " Put out the light, and then put out the light.
> If I quench thee, thou flaming minister,
> I can again thy former light restore,
> Should I repent me ; but once put out thy light,
> Thou cunning'st pattern of excelling nature,
> I know not where is that Promethean heat
> That can thy light relume."

" Are you going, by your verdict, to put out that light ? " he said, still speaking low. Then he stood erect, and his words rang out loud and clear : " Gentlemen of the jury, I demand at your hands the life and liberty of Harold Greenwood."

After his speech, Marshall Hall was compelled by sheer physical pain to leave the court. Greenwood was furious, perhaps thinking that his life and mental anguish were more important than any physical pain of his advocate.

The concluding speech for the Crown lasted three hours, and Marlay Samson attempted to broaden the case for the Crown. He pointed out that the dead woman, besides drinking wine at lunch, had taken tea and brandy, and the poison might equally well have been poured by the prisoner into these beverages. This change of position did not strengthen the case for the prosecution. The motive suggested throughout the trial was Greenwood's physical passion for his second wife ; and during the course of his speech this experienced advocate made a bad slip in referring to the fact that the lady had not been called to give evidence--a comment which is prohibited under the Criminal Evidence Act.

Immediately after Mr. Justice Shearman's summing-up on the following day, Marshall Hall left, again for reasons of health, in a special car, to catch the London train at Cardiff ; and, as he was walking with his clerk on the platform, anxiously speculating on the result of the verdict, a porter came up and spoke to him.

" I see you got him off, Sir Edward," he said.

The jury, whose foreman, by a fortunate chance, was a manufacturing chemist—Mr. E. Willis Jones—had acquitted the prisoner after a deliberation of over an hour.

The verdict was an exceedingly popular one ; but, although Sir Edward probably received more congratulatory letters and telegrams on this case than any other, none came from the prisoner himself—the only one of all his prisoners who never thanked him by word or letter. Perhaps his counsel's absences were still rankling in Mr. Greenwood's mind. It is certainly a fact that he refused to pay him his fee, or " refresher," for the last day of the trial. As Marshall Hall was there for such a short time, he was perhaps within his strict legal rights.

Soon after Marshall Hall returned home, he received a parcel from his friend the silversmith containing a tankard, which was inscribed, " I dared you to do it, and you did it." By an amazing and romantic coincidence, this piece had been the property of Sir Edward's own grandfather, and bore his name.

The Greenwood case was only one of many cases, in these latter years, when Marshall Hall was prepared to go through the ordeal of great physical pain, and tax his endurance to the utmost, for the sake of his client. A letter to A. M. Bremner reveals his wonderful pluck in this respect. " I am hoping to get back to some sort of work next week as they are letting me get up to-morrow, but I have practically had four weeks of it. I was a fool to get up, as I did, and go to Bury St. Edmunds Assizes to do that case there, but my clients were in such a state of anxiety, and it meant so much to them to lose it, that I made a desperate effort and went. Bailhache let me sit down all the time, and I

THE FIELD AND GRAY CASE 421

had my leg on a rest, but it was most unpleasant. It took two
long days—10-7 on the second day—but I won it, and got
£750 for my poor lady, so that was some consolation, and, as it
was all surgical and medical work, it would have been a difficult
brief to hand over. But I had to go straight back to bed, where I
still am."

The Greenwood trial was over on November 10th, and a
month later Marshall Hall was well enough to conduct another
capital defence—this time on his own circuit, at the old assize
town of Lewes, where he had first made his name. The leading
counsel for the Crown was Sir Charles Gill, who had returned to
the Bar after a retirement, and this assize must indeed have
seemed like old times to Marshall Hall. The two veterans dined
together in mess one night at the White Hart, Marshall, as the
senior King's counsel, presiding. Many memories, personal and
professional, must have come to their minds as they sat over
their wine together.

Gill conducted his case with his old extraordinary thorough-
ness, but with advancing years he had become exceedingly
nervous ; he did practically the whole of the prosecution himself,
and only allowed to his juniors, Mr. Henry Curtis Bennett and
Mr. Cecil Whiteley, the mere formalities of the case.

The case of Field and Gray is a story of callousness and
brutality. If Holt may be taken as an instance of nature softened
and unstrung into abnormality by the horrors of war, Gray's
mind may have been hardened into brutality by the same
experience. Field was a mere lad of nineteen, and probably under
Gray's influence ; but both were ex-service men. They had settled
down at Eastbourne after the war, and become regular boon
companions.

A pretty typist, only seventeen years old, went down to
Eastbourne for a holiday in August 1920. She was seen on several
occasions with two young men dressed in grey—for the last time
on the afternoon of August 19th, as she was walking gaily with
them across the lonely region known as the Crumbles, towards
Pevensey. The three young people were talking and laughing
together as they went along. Next day a little boy was playing
on the Crumbles, and stumbled over a human foot. The body of
Irene Munroe was discovered buried in the shingle, her head and

face horribly wounded and mutilated. According to a statement made by Gray's wife after the trial, she had come home late that afternoon and found Field and Gray unconcernedly playing a game of cards. Afterwards they certainly went for entertainment to the Eastbourne Hippodrome. In the course of time Field and Gray were both arrested, but were released afterwards—after they had made their statement. They had tried to induce another young girl, whose acquaintance they made, to say that they had been with her at Pevensey on the afternoon of August 19th. She, however, told them that she was shortly going to leave Eastbourne, as she " was afraid of being murdered herself." Strong evidence of the identification of Field and Gray with the two young men last seen with Irene Munroe had now been collected, and they were again arrested.

The case for the prisoners would not have been so hopeless had it not been for Gray's second attempt to create an alibi. While he was in Maidstone Gaol he got into communication with a fellow-prisoner named Dallington, and asked him to give him an alibi for August 19th. According to another prisoner, named Smith, Gray made an even more unwise statement. " I was with the girl almost till the hour it happened," he said, " but that does not mean to say I done it." Smith afterwards asked him how the murder was done, and Gray said, " By dropping a stone on her head." Smith then asked, " How do you know that ? " and Gray replied, " I have seen the stone." In fact, a great brick was found near where the girl's body was lain, upon which Dr. Cadman had actually sat while he examined the body of the poor girl on August 20th.

Marshall Hall defended Gray, and Mr. J. D. Cassels held a separate brief to defend the younger man. There was abundant evidence of identification, and there was only one real doubt to be resolved from the start. Were both these young men murderers, or was one of them a murderer and the other an accessory. Would each of them seek to blame the other ?

In the trial before Mr. Justice Avory the two prisoners instructed their counsel to defend them on lines which were not inimical to each other. They had been in each other's company at Pevensey on the afternoon of August 19th. They had not been to the Crumbles at all, and they had not been in the company of any girl. Field went into the witness box to tell his story, but Gray remained in the dock.

It was an almost hopeless case to defend, but Marshall Hall made one very good point. Dr. Cadman had examined the body at eleven o'clock on the night of the 20th. At the inquest he gave as his opinion that, from the state of the girl's body and the blood upon it, she had died at eleven o'clock on the night of the 19th at the earliest. If this opinion were correct, she could not have died during the afternoon, shortly after she was seen with Field and Gray. The doctor very candidly adhered to his previous opinion at the trial, and this was a really good point for the defence. Marshall Hall made the most of this medical "opinion." in his speech, and reinforced it by a vivid argument.

" How was it possible," he urged, " for Irene Munroe to have been struck in the face, or suddenly smashed with that brick, without giving an awful scream of terror or apprehension. . . . Would not the scream and the shifting of the shingle have been heard ? Was it credible that two men would commit a murder of that kind in the broad glare of the sun in the middle of the afternoon ? Is it not a right inference that this is not a day crime? It is a night crime, committed under cover of darkness and, if it is a crime committed at night, you have absolute corroboration of Dr. Cadman's evidence."

But this argument, cogent as it was, did not prevail. In the face of the rest of the evidence the Sussex jury concluded that the doctor must have made a mistake. Their verdict was, however, a remarkable one. They found both prisoners—who heard the verdict with absolute composure—guilty, but recommended them to mercy because, in their opinion, " the crime was not premeditated." Yet it is difficult to imagine a more cold-blooded crime. Although he fought the case with all his usual force and energy, Marshall Hall confided to a friend afterwards that he hoped the two men would swing ; and this was a rare thing for Marshall Hall to have said. Nevertheless, the jury meant that the two young roughs had not intended, when they set out that afternoon, to kill poor Irene Munroe, but had had a different purpose. Yet if they killed her simply because she would not yield to them, or were afraid that she might complain and get them into trouble, their lack of premeditation does not excuse their crime from being almost the most brutal and callous murder on record.

The real interest of this trial lies in the fact that in the Court of Criminal Appeal the whole case was virtually retried on an entirely different basis from the lines of defence at the assizes. When Field and Gray went back to prison under sentence of death, and began to realise that their " recommendation to mercy " was not likely to have effect, they began to remember things ; and in the Court of Criminal Appeal they were each allowed to go into the witness box and to accuse the other of sole responsibility for the murder. Field, the younger man, admitted that he had walked with Irene across the Crumbles, but said that she was far more interested in Gray than in himself, and that he had walked on alone to Pevensey, leaving Gray alone with the girl. On his return, Gray had virtually confessed to murdering and burying her, and he had agreed to protect Gray right through the trial. Gray, on the other hand, adhered to his original alibi, and said that Field had left him after the performance at the Hippodrome, and had afterwards confessed to killing a girl later that evening as a result of a quarrel. Throughout the appeal the two men were separated by two warders, and the spectators in the Lord Chief Justice's Court saw two men, under sentence of death, go into the witness box in turn and denounce one another in the hope of saving his own neck. Both appeals were dismissed.

So ended the year 1920—a most memorable year in the career of Edward Marshall Hall. Rarely has a counsel been engaged in four capital cases in one year which aroused, for different reasons, such widespread public interest, and, by his wonderful conduct of these cases, he had now achieved that extraordinary prestige which surrounded his name till the day of his death. For the future he was to be counted among the Olympians.

Chapter XII

In Harness

BEFORE turning to Marshall Hall's latest triumphs, one more disappointment must be mentioned. When his old chief, Sir Forrest Fulton, decided to retire from the Recordership of London in 1922, he informed Marshall Hall before anybody, " so that he might make his arrangements." Nearly twenty years before this, it will be remembered, a young junior, Mr. F. E. Smith, had asked for Marshall Hall's assistance on his application for a North-Country recordership ; now their rôles were reversed and Marshall Hall, a petitioner in his turn, went down to ask Lord Chancellor Birkenhead for his help in obtaining the Recordership of London. But the gift of the Recordership lies with the aldermen of the City of London, and Marshall notified them that he desired to stand for election. " It has always been the ambition of my career," he wrote to each alderman, " to be Recorder of London, and I hope you will help me to attain to it." But he was afterwards informed that a very old friend, Sir Henry Dickens, the Common Serjeant, wished to stand, and that there was a strong wish on the part of the electors that he should be Recorder. Marshall was informed that his own candidature would embarrass that of the Common Serjeant ; he therefore wrote to the Lord Mayor withdrawing his name. " He (Sir Henry Dickens) is an old and valued friend of mine," he wrote, " and I know, who have practised before him, how admirably he has discharged his judicial duties. If, therefore, my candidature is in any way likely to prejudice his chance of appointment, so far as he is concerned, I would wish to withdraw. I am sure that his appointment to this great office would give great pleasure to the Bar, as it would to me personally." Although Sir Ernest Wild was actually elected to the Recordership, Marshall's withdrawal, so as not to handicap his old friend's chances, deserves to be noticed here as not the least unselfish action of his life. Two of his old chiefs, Sir Charles Hall and Sir Forrest Fulton, had both held the position, and Marshall Hall dearly wished to follow them. As far back as 1915, he was writing that this was the post which he really coveted ; and it must have been a wrench to deny himself for ever the chance to realise this long cherished ambition. He longed for the quiet and ease of the bench, and he would have discharged the duties of the Recorder of London with distinction. Such preferment might, indeed, have lengthened his days, but, perhaps, after all, his wonderful career as a lifelong advocate is more notable, as it was, than if his last years had been spent as a judge. It may have been a consolation to him to know that there were some among those who had gained the preferment denied to him, who admired and envied him. " The position of a great advocate," wrote Lord Sankey to him in 1920, " is splendid, but it must take it out of one. My job was usually to try and convince a few old gentlemen that an Act of Parliament didn't mean what it said. Yours I envy and admire." Marshall Hall was a man of moods, and might talk of himself as a failure, but he knew, very well, that this was not so. At about this time he received a bitter letter from an old acquaintance, Mr. Sholto Douglas, whom Marshall had, as the reader will remember, both examined and cross-examined.

" My failure," Marshall Hall proudly replied, " as you call it, is to me more of a success than any of the careers which, in your view, might have been open to me—I am more than content."

If in Marshall Hall's opinion the Green Bicycle and the Lawrence cases were his greatest triumphs in the Criminal Courts, the jury's verdict in the Russell divorce suit in 1923 was regarded by him as his greatest victory in a civil case. The Hon. Mrs. John Russell had married Lord Ampthill's heir ; a child was born, whose paternity the latter denied ; the husband brought a suit for divorce, and, in the first trial, he engaged the services both of Sir John Simon and Sir Douglas Hogg. Several co-respondents were cited but, despite all the advocacy of the two greatest leaders at the Bar, the jury disagreed, and all the co-respondents were dismissed from the suit. Mr. John Russell was, however, determined to persist with a new co-respondent, and his wife was equally determined to defend the suit. When the date for the second trial approached, Mr. Russell was in an unfortunate position. Sir Douglas Hogg had become Attorney-General and could no longer take a private brief, and Sir John Simon was unable, for other reasons, to appear for the petitioner. His advisers came round, almost in despair, to see Sir Douglas, and to ask his advice with regard to the counsel to be employed. " Well," he said, " John Simon and I both failed where several co-respondents were cited. Now there's only one. There's only one man at the Bar who might pull it off for you. He might win you a brilliant victory, or he might make a terrible mess of it. But I really believe he's the only man who can do it—Marshall Hall."

Marshall was approached, and he was, at first, very unwilling to take the brief. " I do not like," he said, "to take a brief which has been hawked all round the Temple." Finally, Lady Ampthill herself came to see him in Temple Gardens : she was very distressed, and Marshall Hall was on the point of refusing, when he saw in Lady Ampthill a resemblance to his own mother. His emotional nature was touched, and he made up his mind to do the case.

On January 2nd, 1923, he writes to Pinero, " I am at my cottage at Brook, working hard at the Russell case, which comes on next term, and I am going to do Simon's brief. I don't like doing cases after they have been tried once."

His cross-examination of Mrs. Russell was a wonderful performance. A clever, brilliant woman, she was no " butterfly on the wheel." Marshall Hall's instructions were, that the child could not have been her husband's ; she swore to the contrary, and, for four hours, stood up to Marshall Hall's ruthless cross-examination as to the intimate details of her life and character and demeanour in the witness-box. Marshall, at one point, cross-examined her as to tears which had been in her eyes on one occasion when she had parted from her husband.

" Did they come genuinely to your eyes ? "

" I do not know any other way of bringing tears to your eyes, except by smelling onions."

" Do you think that our great actresses smell onions on the stage to produce tears ? " asked Marshall Hall.

" I am not an actress," parried Mrs. Russell.

" Are you not ? " retorted Marshall Hall, " I suggest you are, Mrs. Russell, and were throughout the whole of your married life."

Later on, Mrs. Russell began to mimic the tone and manner of her interrogator.

" You are not acting, are you now ? " he asked.

" No," she replied, " I was only imitating *you*."

Again, Mrs. Russell began to talk with great emotion of her child. "Affection grows, and one would do anything for the child, and *die* for it if necessary."

Marshall Hall took advantage. "Would you *lie* for the child?" he asked.

"It is not necessary," boldly answered Mrs. Russell.

"I see. You would die for it, but would not lie for it?" persisted the advocate.

"Exactly."

After four hours, Marshall Hall sank back among his papers, and the slender young woman, whose nerve never gave way and must be like steel, left the witness-box, and, perhaps, the most remarkable court duel of Marshall's whole life was concluded.

After a long hearing, in which the child itself was produced as evidence to show its likeness to the petitioner, and many doctors and domestic servants were called, Marshall Hall passionately addressed the jury for the husband. "I ask you," he concluded, "to find a verdict in favour of John Russell, and free him from the tie which he once hoped would be a tie of love, but which is now a rusty chain that burns into his soul."

After an absence of four hours, the jury dismissed the co-respondent from the suit, but found that Mrs. Russell had committed adultery with a man unknown. In itself, a very extraordinary verdict, this was the more surprising in face of the great public prejudice which had been excited in favour of the "mother fighting for her child," and to which the jury, as ordinary members of the public, must have been susceptible. Marshall Hall had achieved something which the combination of Simon and Hogg had failed to do, with much more material at their disposal.

But a victory of this kind may be bought too dearly; the verdict of the jury depended on the evidence of the husband himself, that, although he had lived in the same house with his wife at the relevant period, the child could not be his. An appeal followed, in which the point was taken that, under the Common Law, neither party to a marriage has the right to give such negative evidence as to their life together as man and wife in order to obtain a divorce, but that the law presumes the ordinary results of marriage, when the parties live together in the same house as man and wife. The Court of Appeal dismissed the appeal, which was argued by Marshall Hall, and the case went further, to the supreme legal tribunal, the House of Lords : Marshall Hall was in a panic, since he had never yet argued a case in the House of Lords. The point was essentially one of law, and Marshall Hall felt no confidence in himself. Sir Douglas Hogg was now again in private practice, owing to the defeat of the Government in the 1923 election, and he, as an ex-law officer, at Marshall's earnest request, led him for the petitioner. Marshall Hall " followed " Sir Douglas Hogg, with a short argument of no great profundity ; but he had, at last, almost at the end of his career, addressed " their Lordships' House." The argument, however, in which he took part, was one of the most memorable ever heard in the House of Lords. This *cause célèbre* had changed from the most sensational suit of the year, brimful of the pitiful interest and paradox evoked by the mutability of fleeting human affections and the circumstances of this amazing modern marriage, into a dry, legal argument in which learned lawyers were citing at each other eighteenth-century cases. But, behind the arid atmosphere of the law, the drama was nevertheless present. Behind it all, the lawyers and the public knew that here, on one side, was a great English family fighting to the last for the honour of its name, and, on the other, a woman doing battle for her own honour and that of the little child whose mysterious birth had given rise to all this fierce and protracted litigation, and that on the decision of a dry, legal point, rested this desperately fought and very human issue. Lord Birkenhead has said that the argument between Mr. Stuart Bevan and Sir Douglas Hogg was the finest legal argument ever heard by him, and as the last named sat down, Lord Birkenhead whispered to Lord Dunedin, " How can that possibly be wrong ? " Nevertheless, after the judgments were reserved, Lord Birkenhead was among the majority which allowed the appeal, on the ground that Mr. Russell's evidence was inadmissible, and the verdict of the jury was annulled. A new trial was ordered, but the family at last bowed to the inevitable.

Marshall Hall had now achieved his ambition as an advocate ; quite apart from his criminal practice, he was one of the foremost advocates of the day in the civil courts. He could now write to Pinero, " I am now declining all sensational criminal cases, and hope to confine myself in future to the High Court, except on circuit." He could, indeed, well afford to adopt this course, but, as the reader will see, he was never allowed to avoid, nor, indeed, could he resist, the less lucrative but more sensational call of the Old Bailey. In his Christmas letter to Pinero at the end of the year, he wrote, " I know you have always taken such an interest in my career, that it may please you to know that this year has been my record professional year in every way, and sixty-six has sounded never to sound again."

It was about this time that I began to know Marshall Hall, and he would always wave me enthusiastic greeting whenever I met that vigorous and impressive figure hurrying down Middle Temple Lane, and dominating that narrow thoroughfare with his exuberant personality.

" Hullo, Edward," he would exclaim, " How's work ? " little knowing he was saluting his biographer ; and my fellow fledglings of the profession would smile a little scornfully at my apparent intimacy with the great man, but, nevertheless, be a trifle impressed. He vigorously tried to secure me junior briefs to him in Treasury prosecutions from that incorruptible man, Sir Douglas Hogg, when he was Attorney-General. Marshall thought that the State could easily afford to give an extra brief to an inexperienced youth, who was at once a kinsman of Mr. Attorney and a friend of his own. But here I am afraid that even Marshall Hall's power of advocacy was unsuccessful.

On one occasion, however, he actually did lead me in a civil case, on Armistice Day, 1924. Lady Terrington had been elected as Liberal Member for Maidenhead at the last General Election. During her campaign, the *Daily Express* had starred her as the " Best Dressed Woman M.P.," and published an interview, in which Lady Terrington was reported to have said that she intended to brighten the atmosphere of Westminster. To the report of this interview her feminine susceptibilities took exception, and she sued for libel. I was given a third brief to Mr. J. B. Melville and Sir Douglas Hogg. But the sands of the Labour Government were running out, and it was merely a question of time before Sir Douglas became Attorney-General once more. If the case came on before his appointment, he could have fought it through and presented me with " a red bag " in the last case of his private practice. We held a consultation in New Court.

" What do you think about the case, Sir Douglas? " asked the solicitor.

" I think it is a borderline case—I think it is a case which might be lost."

" Do you think we had better settle then, Sir Douglas ? Lord Beaverbrook doesn't want to lose this action."

" Settle ? " replied Sir Douglas, with a smile, " No, I didn't say that. I said it was a case which might be lost. We will have to go very warily. I'm told she's a very charming lady. But now, I think, Mr. Marjoribanks had better go over and watch Lord Darling's court."

The previous case lasted out the Labour Government, and Douglas Hogg returned the brief : it was delivered to Marshall Hall overnight. Very different was the last-minute consultation held in the little consulting room, opposite Court 4, with Marshall as the presiding genius, from the wary atmosphere of New Court. The solicitor was entirely unable to restrain him. " We'll win this case—not a doubt of it. She won't stand up to cross-examination. She's *sure* to break down, she won't get a farthing." The solicitor begged him to be cautious—Lord Beaverbrook really did not wish to lose the action—but he might as well have wasted his breath on the desert air.

In the cross-examination that followed, Marshall Hall was at his very worst. He succeeded in making the plaintiff burst into tears, but that made the case for the defendants no better. But Marshall Hall unconcernedly sailed on from indiscretion to indiscretion, doing the case almost as badly as it could be done, apparently with blissful ignorance of the mistakes he was making—and turning round now and then for our approval of his sallies. One very pathetic answer, in view of later events, he did, however, wring from her. " My husband," she said, " works for every penny he earns."

" He's only inflaming the damages," said a journalist, sitting behind me. The day ended not very hopefully. The morrow was Armistice Day, and it so happened that the two minutes' silence at 11 o'clock found Marshall Hall on his feet in the most vital part of his address to the jury, speaking with a voice raised high in argument. He stopped dead in the middle of a sentence. Everybody rose and stood. Sir Edward's expression, as he stood facing the jury was transfigured ; from an eager, argumentative advocate, he became like a statue of mourning, the tall figure erect, the great head bowed, and on his fine ascetic face an expression unutterably sad. The jury and most of us in court looked only at him. After the two minutes had elapsed, Marshall was still silent; then he began to speak in a low voice, making no attempt to round off the interrupted argument.

"Members of the jury," he said, "we have just been celebrating the anniversary of the greatest national sacrifice which the world has ever seen. We have all suffered loss in the war ; you have suffered, I have suffered, we have all suffered, and every year comes this two minutes' silence for remembrance's sake. . . . And now, turning from this great national ceremony, we find ourselves in this court, and have to address ourselves to the trifling grievances of this lady, who, by an unfortunate chance on this very day. . . . "

Sir Ellis Hume-Williams for the plaintiff was at once on his feet protesting, but Marshall Hall waved him aside. From that moment, his unconventional eloquence rose to its highest pitch, and he poured out, in a torrent of words, the full force of his rhetoric and irony. The poor lady's grievances had been set against the most momentous happening in history, and they could not stand the test. Marshall Hall had been right after all. There was a verdict for the defendants, and Lady Terrington did not get a farthing.

But Marshall Hall did not like the rôle of inquisitor to charming ladies, nor did he always succeed as well as he did in the Russell case. Mrs. Russell was a match for any man ; the jury saw this, and did not resent Marshall Hall's hard hitting. However, when he embarked on an attack on Mrs. Dennistoun, the " little brown mouse " of the celebrated society suit in 1926, the effect was very different. The jury, perhaps, did not know that Marshall Hall was in desperately bad health, and would never have appeared in the case at all if his client had not been a lifelong friend, to whom his appearance in the case seemed to be of vital importance. So much has been whispered in the Temple to the contrary, that this much, at least, can be said :

MARSHALL HALL AT 68

it was to Sir Edward's deep regret that the case came before the courts at all. Nothing destroys the nerve and balance of an advocate so completely as the knowledge that on his advocacy depends the near interests of an intimate friend ; it destroys his objective position on which so much of his power depends, and leads him into indiscretion. When this was accompanied by ailing health, and even great physical suffering, it is perhaps not hard to understand why Marshall Hall, always a mass of nerves, made mistake after mistake, and no doubt seemed to the jury a very different person from the *preux chevalier* who had pleaded for the life of Madame Fahmy. Sometimes courage and friendship try to achieve the impossible, and this was the case with Marshall Hall in the Dennistoun suit. So much has been said in criticism of him, for the manner in which he conducted this case, that something deserves to be said about the courage and self-sacrifice which brought him into court at all, and the conditions under which he did his best.

But if Marshall was at his worst in the Dennistoun case, as the inquisitor of a beautiful woman, he had been at his very best when he appeared as the defender of another at the Old Bailey three years before. Of all Marshall Hall's great cases, this was perhaps the most dramatic. Even nature seemed in conspiracy to set for the tragedy a scene of gloom and splendour worthy of any play of Æschylus or Shakespeare.

On July 10th, 1923, readers of the morning newspapers saw that London was visited at midnight by a violent thunderstorm —the most severe that had occurred for many years. " The outbreak appeared to travel from the direction of Kingston and Richmond. Soon afterwards the storm reached London itself, and broke with all its fury at a time when, luckily, most of the theatre-goers had been able to reach their homes in safety. The lightning was vivid to a degree. For over two hours the sky was illuminated by brilliant, continuous flashes, that gave the buildings an eerie appearance, and at least once what seemed to be a gigantic fireball broke into a million fragments of dazzling fiery sparks. Equally dramatic were the heavy crashes of thunder which grew in a mighty *crescendo*, intense and majestic, and then into a *diminuendo* as the storm swept irresistibly over the city. The storm followed a day of almost tropical heat."[1] It was, as

[1] *Daily Telegraph*, July 10th, 1923.

DDH

Sir Edward said later at the Old Bailey, a weird and awful night.

A remarkable trio had been staying for a few days at the Savoy Hotel, London : an Egyptian, " Prince " Fahmy Bey, his Parisian wife, and his faithful secretary and companion, Said Enani. The prince was the son of a great Egyptian engineer, a young man of twenty-two, and had inherited his father's colossal fortune. He had purchased his title by the most lavish generosity to charity. While attached to the Egyptian Legation in Paris, he had met a fascinating and ultra-Parisian lady named Madame Marguerite Laurent, whose maiden name had been Alibert. She had gone out to Egypt at his invitation, and married him in December 1922. This woman, essentially a citizeness of the most cultured city of the Western world, went out, as she wrote to an English friend, to enjoy *une vie de rêve* with this charming man, who was so very kind and considerate in all ways, and loved her so dearly. Many months of unhappiness lay behind her, when she sat at luncheon with her husband and his secretary in the restaurant of the great London hotel. Ignorant of this, and wishing to do honour to the prince and his wife, the leader of the orchestra went up to her, as she sat at luncheon on July 9th, and asked her if she would like anything to be played. " Thank you very much," was her strange reply. " My husband is going to kill me in twenty-four hours, and I am not very anxious for music."

The polite musician had heard many strange things, and bowed gravely. " I hope you will still be here to-morrow, madame," he said.

After two o'clock next morning, when the storm was at its height, a porter wheeling luggage along one of the corridors of the Savoy Hotel heard above the thunder three pistol shots fired in quick succession ; he found Prince Fahmy lying dressed in his pyjamas on the ground, with blood trickling out of his mouth. His wife had thrown down a Browning automatic pistol, and three empty cartridges lay at her feet. The night manager was summoned, and she cried out to him in French, " What have I done ? What will they do to me ? Oh, sir, I have been married six months, and I have suffered terribly." According to Dr. Gordon, who was immediately called in, she said, also in French, " I have pulled the trigger three times." It was known that she kept a pistol constantly by her to protect her jewels.

Mr. Freke Palmer, one of Marshall Hall's oldest clients, was instructed to defend Madame Fahmy, and he retained Marshall Hall. In the face of the three pistol shots and the lady's statements after her husband's death, apart from the pitiful situation of the beautiful foreign woman charged with the murder of her husband, there seemed at first sight very little to say in answer to the capital charge. The woman must no doubt have been very unhappy to have done such a thing. " The lady forgot she was not in Paris," many people said. " There, no doubt, she would have been acquitted—*crime passionnel*, you know—but one cannot behave like that in London." But the farther Marshall Hall, with his colleagues Sir Henry Curtis-Bennett and Mr. Roland Oliver, enquired into the whole story of this marriage, the more it became obvious to them that the circumstances of the case not merely provided evidence of great provocation, but of a complete answer to the apparently overwhelming case for the prosecution. Madame Fahmy was alone in London and without money, but she had devoted friends, and a romantic story could be told as to the help which was forthcoming to her in her hour of peril. Enquiries of the most expensive kind were made in Paris and elsewhere as to the manner of life of the late prince, and the results of these appeared to corroborate in every way the dreadful and almost incredible story of the poor woman herself. Two youths who had been associated with him were actually brought over, to be present in court in case there should be any doubt as to the " prince's " true character. " Take any opinion from anyone you like," said Marshall, " this lady's life is in peril. Three shots were fired—three shots, remember that. We are entitled to procure *any* evidence to get at the truth and save her life."

Marshall Hall had in this case 652 guineas marked on his brief, and, as usual, he left nothing undone which could help the defence. He went down to Whistler's, in the Strand, and borrowed an automatic Browning pistol such as had been in Madame Fahmy's possession, and with Mr. Stopp, the manager, an old friend of fifty years' standing, he minutely examined and manipulated the weapon. He remembered that Lawrence's life had been saved many years before by a revolver demonstration. This case was a very delicate one to handle, and, as usual, he changed his mind again and again as to the tactics to be employed. For instance, in Madame Fahmy's civil marriage contract the clause which entitled her to divorce Fahmy had been struck out at his instance, whereas Fahmy could at his will divorce her, in the brusque Oriental manner, simply by " repudiating " her. Would this circumstance help her or not ? Would it not be said that this clause, cruel as it was, added tremendous weight to her motive for killing him ? After all, as long as Fahmy wanted her with him, there was no escape for her but through his death. On the other hand, this fact showed clearly the dreadful life-trap in which this Western woman had been entangled, and it was certain to excite the deepest pity and sympathy for her. Marshall at one time was positive that reticence on this point was right ; then he swung round completely in the opposite direction. As usual, it was a bewildering experience to hold a junior brief to this strange, mercurial genius of an advocate.

The case began on September 10th, 1923, before Mr. Justice Rigby Swift, who had often sat behind Marshall Hall as a junior. Mr. Percival Clarke and Mr. Eustace Fulton appeared for the prosecution, and it was considered that they had a strong case. The pith of the case for the prosecution was admirably put by Mr. Percival Clarke at the end of his opening speech. " Coming to this country, persons are bound by the laws which prevail here. Every homicide is presumed to be murder until the contrary is shown. From her own lips it is known that she it was who caused the death of her husband. And, in the absence of any circumstances to make it some other offence, you must find her guilty of murder."

Swarthy Egyptian lawyers sat in court cheek by jowl with members of the English Bar. The dead man's family was represented by highly distinguished advocates ; perhaps they considered that their kinsman's memory could be protected in this way ; but in England no official intervention is allowed to the holder of a " watching brief " during the course of a trial. Something can occasionally be done by tactful suggestion, or as a favour from one brother advocate to another, but in this case Marshall Hall was not amenable to tact or requests of any kind directed to the object of sparing the memory of the dead man.

LIGHT AND ITS SHADOW

On the first day, Said Enani, the secretary, was called. In a Cairo newspaper there had been a caricature depicting three profiles, one against the other. It was entitled, " The Light, the Shadow of the Light, and the Shadow of the Shadow of the Light." They represented Fahmy, his secretary Said Enani, and Said Enani's secretary. Marshall Hall pressed the " Shadow of the Light," the dead man's devoted secretary, for four hours for the true story of his master's life with the accused woman.

" You told Inspector Crosse that you tried to dissuade the prince from marrying her ? "—" Yes."

" Did you say he was an Oriental, and passionate ? "—" Yes."

" You were very much attached to Fahmy ? "—" Yes."

" Was he infatuated with her at that time ? "—" Yes, very much in love with her."

Then Marshall read out a letter from Fahmy written in abject and sickening terms of flattery, begging her to come out to Egypt. " Your presence everywhere pursues me incessantly. . . . Torch of my life, you appear to me surrounded by a halo. I see your head encircled by a crown, which I reserve for you here. It is a crown I have reserved for you on your arrival in this beautiful country of my ancestors."

Then he passed to the treatment of the French woman after marriage ; he quoted from a letter which Fahmy wrote to his wife's sister : " Just now I am engaged in training her. Yesterday, to begin, I did not come in to lunch or dinner, and I also left her at the theatre. This will teach her, I hope, to respect my wishes. With women one must act with energy, and be severe." This millionaire made his wife ride in a public tram. Marshall Hall now passed from the moral to the physical persecution that followed.

" On February 21st was there a very serious scene ? Do you know that he swore on the Koran that he would kill her? "—" No."

" Do you know that she was in fear of her life ? "—" I never knew."

" On the 23rd, did Fahmy take her on his yacht at Luxor, ten days' journey from Cairo ? "—" Yes."

" Were there six black servants on board ? "—" Yes."

" I suggest that from that moment Fahmy began to treat her with persistent cruelty ? "—" I cannot say cruelty ; he was a bit unkind."

" Was not the Madame Fahmy of 1923 totally different from the Madame Laurent of 1922 ? "—" Perhaps."

" From being a gay, cheerful, entertaining, and fascinating woman, was she not sad and broken, miserable and wretched ? "—" They were always quarrelling."

" Did she say you and Fahmy were always against her, and it was a case of two to one ? "—" Yes."

Marshall Hall also put to the witness that Fahmy was a man of vicious and eccentric sexual appetite, but this the secretary loyally denied.

The cross-examination of the secretary had been a very delicate matter ; if Marshall, always excitable and indiscreet, had in any way attacked the man's character, this would have entitled the prosecution to attack that of Madame Fahmy, and it was of vital importance that she should not be distressed by the introduction of other matters. She needed all her strength and balance to answer questions as to this one grievous matter. Whereas it was essential to attack the character of Fahmy, it would have been a fatal mistake to attack that of his secretary. After all, the man was only his hired " shadow." Mr. Roland Oliver had sat like a watch-dog by him to restrain his leader, and in the end Marshall Hall obtained all that was necessary from Said Enani without once attacking the witness himself. The secretary did not admit a great deal ; it was, after all, natural that a paid servant should be loyal to the memory of his friend and patron ; but he had admitted enough to create an atmosphere of intense sympathy for the prisoner, this fragile creature who had been in the power of this decadent Oriental millionaire. But still it only appeared as if she had been driven by extreme provocation into taking her husband's life. This might reduce the verdict to one of " manslaughter," but nothing had as yet been established which would justify a clean acquittal.

On the next day the main line of defence was foreshadowed in the cross-examination of the gunsmiths. In this case the weapon used was an automatic magazine pistol, and not a revolver, as in the Lawrence and Jeannie Baxter cases. The way in which these weapons operate is as follows. When the magazine is loaded with cartridges it is necessary, in order to bring the first cartridge into firing position in the breach, to pull back the

breach cover by hand and release it. A pull of the trigger will then
fire the first shot ; thereafter the force of the explosion of each
successive shot fired will operate to eject the empty cartridge-
case and to bring the next cartridge automatically into firing
position. It will thus be seen that whereas for the first shot it is
necessary to pull back the breach cover, after one shot has been
fired this function is performed automatically. If, however, the
breach cover is only partially pulled back, exposing the ejecting
slot at the side, it is just possible to shake out or extract by hand
the cartridge in the breach, and it will be necessary to pull back
the breach cover once more to the full extent to get the next
cartridge into firing position.

Marshall Hall cross-examined the gunsmith, Mr. Robert
Churchill, at length with regard to the mechanism of this weapon,
and suggested to him that, when the pistol was tightly gripped,
a very small pressure on the trigger would discharge each shot,
and also that an ignorant person might easily reload the weapon
by firing a shot, thinking that in fact he might be emptying it.

Dr. Gordon, who had been summoned to the scene of the
tragedy, then gave evidence, which was very material to the
defence. Madame Fahmy, on the day after her husband's death,
had told him the cause of their quarrel. It was necessary that
Madame should undergo a most painful operation ; she wished
to have it performed in Paris. She had no money, and her
husband refused to let her go there. Worse than this, he had
brutally handled and pestered her; in great pain already, she was
panic-stricken, loathing and dreading what she knew he meant
to do. Mortally afraid of her cruel and abnormal husband, she
had picked up a pistol, fired one shot out of the window to empty
it, and, as her husband was advancing on her, she threatened
him with the pistol, meaning only to hold him away. But somehow it had gone off. " The accused's condition," said the doctor,
" was consistent with the conduct on the part of her husband
which she alleged."

" Oh, sir," the lady had said, " I have been married six months
and I have suffered terribly." The jury were beginning to understand some measure of the suffering she had endured. There
were three women in the jury box.

On the third day Marshall Hall opened the case for the

defence. He talked of the extraordinary pride which an Eastern man took in the possession of a Western woman. He spoke of the meanness and cruelty of this Oriental, who demanded a slave-like obedience from his wife, who treated her with such continual and systematic brutality that she had become a nervous wreck. While staying at the Savoy Hotel, she had received an anonymous letter, which said, " Do not agree to return to Egypt. A journey means a possible accident, poison in a flower, a subtle weapon which is neither seen nor heard. Remain in Paris with those who love you, and will protect you." This husband found it amusing to fire a pistol over her head in order to terrify her, and kept a guard of black men to watch over her. There was a great Hercules of a negro, named Costa, whose life Fahmy had saved, of whom she was especially afraid. On the night of his death, Fahmy had held money before her eyes which would take her to Paris and pay for her operation, but he had refused to give it to her unless she submitted herself to his unnatural will. On that same night he had threatened to kill her, and had seized her by the throat. " I submit," Marshall Hall concluded, " that this poor wretch of a woman, suffering the tortures of the damned, driven to desperation by the brutality and beastliness of this man, whose will she had dared to oppose, thought that he was carrying out the threat he had always made, and that when he seized her by the neck he was about to kill her."

Madame Fahmy was then called in her own defence. She was a small and dark woman, and her appearance had great distinction, even beauty, though she was not " pretty " in an English sense. Through the medium of an interpreter, Marshall Hall took her through the tragedy of her life with Fahmy until the three fatal shots were fired. Even before she had married him, she had wished to return to France. " I began to understand," she said significantly. " He was not very sincere." In January, Fahmy, now her husband, had taken in his hand the Koran. " I swear on the Koran that I will kill you, and that you shall die by my hand." he had said. Later she wrote to her lawyer in France saying that she bore on her arms " the marks of her husband's gentleness." During the course of her evidence Marshall after all decided to bring out the fact that the clause for divorce had been deleted from the civil contract.

MADAME FAHMY

Then came the pistol demonstration ; she had, she said, never fired a pistol till the night of her husband's death. Her husband had given it to her, loaded, saying, " It is all ready to fire." She had often seen her husband unload his own pistol by opening the breach and taking a cartridge out ; on that dreadful night, when he had tried to strangle her, and she had been in an agony of fear, she had tried to do the same thing. But her hands had not been strong enough to pull back the breach cover fully, and she had struggled to extract the bullet by shaking the weapon in front of the window. While she was thus engaged, somehow the first cartridge went off and spent itself harmlessly out of the window. She thought that this would have the same effect as if she had taken the bullet out by hand, as she had intended to do, but, unknown to her, the second cartridge had automatically come up into position. " I know nothing about automatic pistols," she said. Marshall Hall handed up the pistol to her ; she shrank back from it at first, but finally she took it in her hands, and seemed to be quite unable to pull back the breach cover.

She sobbed pitifully as she related her terrible life with her husband, culminating in his last attempted assault. She had become terrified of him. Very skilfully Marshall Hall appealed to the chivalry of a British jury.

" Why," he asked, " did you assent to come to London, when you were so frightened ? "—" I had to come to London for family reasons. I had always hoped he would change. Every time I threatened to leave him, he cried, and promised to alter. I also wished to see my daughter, who was at school near London."

" Did you think you would be *safe* in London ? " asked Marshall Hall, turning to the jury.

" I passed from despair to hope, and from hope to despair," answered Madame Fahmy naïvely, missing the point of the leading question, which, however, the jury had clearly understood.

With a sob punctuating every phrase, she told the story of the final scene. " He crouched to spring on me, and said, ' I will kill you.' . . . I now lifted my arm in front of me, and, without looking, pulled the trigger. The next moment I saw him on the ground without realising what had happened. . . . I do not know how many times the pistol went off. I did not know what had happened, and I asked the people what was all the trouble. I saw

Fahmy on the floor, and I fell on my knees alongside of him. When I saw him lying on the floor, I caught hold of his hand, and said to him, ' Sweetheart, it is nothing. Speak, oh, please speak to me.' While I was on my knees the porter came up, but I was so touched that I understood nothing."

Then came the last two questions in her examination.

" When the pistol went off, killing your husband, had you any idea that it was in a condition to be fired? " asked Marshall Hall.

" None," she replied. " I thought there was no cartridge when you had pulled the barrel, and that it could not be used."

" When you threw your arm out, as the pistol was fired, what were you afraid of ? "—" That he was going to jump on me. It was terrible. I had escaped once. He said, ' I will kill you, I will kill you ! ' It was so terrible."

Mr. Percival Clarke then rose to cross-examine ; when he asked her, " Madame, were you not very ambitious to become his wife ? " she replied, " Ambitious ? No. I loved him so very much, and wished to be with him."

Marshall, himself a very fluent French speaker, thought that the interpreter was not able to convey the exact meaning of Madame Fahmy's words. He had won the Hermann case on his interpretation of the words, " Speak, speak, speak," and Madame Fahmy had used almost the same words to her husband when he lay dead at her feet. He had received on the previous day a very remarkable offer of help through the letter of Helena Normanton, a lady barrister. A young lady member of the French Bar, Mlle. Odette Simon, who was by chance in England, had been sitting in court during the trial. " Mlle. Simon," wrote Helena Norman-ton, " says she too much reveres your great position at the English Bar to proffer you any advice, but she has just author-ised me to offer you her aid as witness or otherwise, if you care to avail yourself of it. . . . I hope you don't think it any pre-sumption on my part to send this note ; it is only intended in a spirit of humility and helpfulness."

Marshall at once saw the immense advantage it would be to the prisoner to have a fellow-countrywoman, and trained French lawyer at that, by her side to interpret her testimony, who would pass on to the jury not only her words, but every *nuance* of meaning and every inflection of her tone. The romantic situation, too, of one gifted young Frenchwoman helping another in her hour of extreme peril in a strange country, made an irresistible appeal to him. Next day he made an application that Mlle. Simon should act as interpreter. The judge granted the application. " I cannot allow an accused person to think there is anything unfair during the trial." Mlle. Simon was thereupon sworn as interpreter, and acted as such for the remainder of Madame Fahmy's evidence.

Mr. Clarke also questioned the prisoner as to her knowledge of firearms ; his suggestion was that she had fired the first shot out of the window to see if the weapon was in working order. " I never intended," she said, " to shoot it out of the window. I just wanted to get the ball out, and I tried to pull the thing back, but I had not the strength to do it. As I was shaking it, it went off, and I felt perfectly safe."

Marshall Hall had reserved for her re-examination two most important documents. The first was a telegram sent at 9 p.m. on July 9th by the prisoner to Paris, saying that she was returning to Paris the next day ; then he read out a " secret " document which his client had written in Egypt on January 22nd, and which she had then left with her Egyptian lawyer, only to be opened in the event of her death :

> " I, Marie Marguerite Alibert, of sound mind and body, formally accuse, in the case of my death by violence or otherwise, Ali Bey of having contributed to my disappearance. Yesterday, January 21st, 1923, at three o'clock in the afternoon, he took his Bible or Koran—I do not know how it is called—kissed it, put his hand on it, and swore to avenge himself upon me to-morrow, in eight days, a month, or three months ; but I must disappear by his hand. This oath was taken without any reason—neither jealousy, nor bad conduct, nor a scene on my part. I desire and demand justice for my daughter and my family."

When she had sworn to the truth of this document, the prisoner left the box after an ordeal of nearly seven hours.

After the prisoner's sister and her chauffeur had been called to prove the prince's violence to his wife, Marshall Hall began his final speech on the afternoon of the fourth day. " This woman," he said, " made one great mistake—she married an Oriental. I dare say the Egyptian civilisation is, and may be, one of the oldest and most wonderful civilisations in the world. But if you strip off the external civilisation of the Oriental you get the real Oriental underneath." He made his hearers' flesh creep by describing how Fahmy had enticed the Western woman into his " Oriental Garden." Somehow the word " garden " sounded terrible after the evidence which had been heard. " Do not forget," he said, " that great black Hercules who came day after day for orders—who owed his life to Fahmy. . . . Why was this woman afraid ? The curse of this case is the atmosphere which we cannot understand—the Eastern feeling of possession of the woman, the Turk in his harem . . . that is something almost unintelligible, something we cannot deal with. . . . "

Next day he resumed his speech. " One almost smiled," he said, " when my friend asked yesterday, ' Why did you not get Said Enani to protect you ? ' You have seen him, and you have heard something about him." Then, in dramatic accents, he referred to " The Light, the Shadow of the Light, and the Shadow of the Shadow of the Light."

He dealt with the storm. " Imagine," he said, " its effect on a woman of nervous temperament who had been living such a life as she had lived for the past six months—outraged, abused, beaten, degraded."

When he came to the actual shooting, he performed the most wonderful physical demonstration of his forensic career ; he imitated the crouch of the stealthily advancing Oriental. " In sheer desperation—as he crouched for the last time, crouched like an animal, like an Oriental, retired for the last time to get a bound forward—she turned the pistol and put it to his face, and to her horror the thing went off." As he spoke the last words he held the pistol up and pointed it towards the jury ; and, when he described how the man fell, he paused and dropped the heavy weapon so that it clattered to the floor of the Old Bailey, just as it must have clattered on to the floor of the corridor in the Savoy Hotel. No words can describe the effect of this daring demonstration. But Marshall Hall always said afterwards that the actual dropping of the pistol was an accident.

Then came the peroration, and the literary allusion—not this time from *Othello*, though this would not have been inappropriate, but from a modern best-seller. Yet there was no bathos whatever in the reference. " You will remember, all of you, that wonderful work of fiction written by Robert Hichens, *Bella Donna*. . . . You will remember the final scene, where this woman goes out of the gates of the garden into the dark night of the desert. Members of the jury, I want you to open the gates where this Western woman can go out, not into the dark night of the desert, but back to her friends, who love her in spite of her weaknesses ; back to her friends, who will be glad to receive her ; back to her child, who will be waiting for her with open arms. You will open the gate, and let this woman go back into the light of God's great Western sun."

Marshall looked up and pointed at the skylight, where the bright English September sun was streaming in, and diffusing the packed court with its warmth and brightness. Quite unconsciously, in throwing down the revolver and in pointing to the sunlight, Marshall had reproduced in one speech the historic gestures of two great House of Commons orators, Burke and Pitt. Probably, if any other living advocate had done either of these things, he would have made himself ridiculous ; but with Marshall it was sublime.

Finally, turning towards Mr. Percival Clarke, he said, " To use the words of my learned friend's great father, in a case in which I heard him many years ago at the Old Bailey, ' I don't ask you for a verdict : I demand it at your hands.' "

After the final speech for the prosecution, and the summing-up by the judge, who pointed out that there were three verdicts which could be found, " murder," " manslaughter," and " not guilty," the jury were out for a little over an hour. Marshall Hall talked anxiously with Percival Clarke during this time, playing as he did so with Madame Fahmy's pistol. When the jury came back, and the foreman announced that the prisoner was not guilty of murder, there was such a storm of cheering that the court was cleared by order of the judge. There was therefore a delay of some minutes before the clerk could ask if the jury found her guilty of manslaughter. Of this offence, too, the jury found the prisoner not guilty, and she was discharged. She was quite overcome by emotion, and covered her face in her hands, and Marshall Hall, understanding completely, quietly slipped out of court without speaking to her. He, too, was utterly exhausted by his effort ; after his speech he was sweating all over his body to such an extent that before he left the Old Bailey he had made a complete change of clothing.

On this occasion his client was all gratitude. Marshall Hall went down that afternoon to his cottage at Brook to rest, and received a telegram from her the same evening : " De tout mon cœur je vous suis profondément reconnaissante.—MARGUERITE ALIBERT." As soon as she reached Prince's Hotel that evening she wrote him a letter :

" *Septembre* 15*me*, 1923.

" CHER MAÎTRE,—J'arrive, et dans cette ambiance de bonheur un regret m'attriste, celui de n'avoir pu vous prendre la main et de vous dire merci. Mon émotion était si grande que vous me pardonnerez d'avoir fermé les yeux et de m'être laisser emmener.

" Votre profondément reconnaissante,

" M. FAHMY."

A few days afterward she saw Marshall Hall and thanked him personally, and before leaving England she wrote to him again :

" CHER MAÎTRE,—Je ne veux pas quitter Londres, sans vous dire combien j'ai été ravie de vous voir, et je vous prie de me croire toujours

" Votre très reconnaissante,

" M. FAHMY.

" P.S.—Les journaux d'hier sont meilleurs, pour moi la vérité va se connaître enfin ! ! "

The day after the trial was a Sunday, September 16th, and Marshall celebrated his sixty-sixth birthday with the knowledge that he had added one more great victory to his wonderful record. He replied to Madame Fahmy's letter and telegram in his best French :

" CHÈRE MADAME,—Je vous remercie beaucoup pour votre depêche, et votre lettre si bien reconnaissante. Quant à moi, je n'ai fait rien au dessus de mon devoir, et c'était à vous, et le témoignage que vous avez si bravement donnée au cour que le résultat si heureux était en effet dû. Je regrette aussi que je ne pouvais pas vous féliciter personellement après le ' verdict,' mais j'ai bien compris que vous étiez enfin à peu près épuisée par les évènements des six derniers jours. J'espère que l'avenir vous donnera beaucoup de moments heureux pour remplacer les misères passées. C'est encore une fois que ' la vérité c'est triomphante.' Agréez, madame, mes sentiments bien empressés à vous.

"EDWARD MARSHALL HALL."

Madame Fahmy came to see Marshall Hall on several other occasions when she came to London, once having tea at Temple Gardens, and she continued to correspond with him. At the time of the Vacquier trial she wrote to him from Karlsbad : " J'ai suivi avec émotion le procès Vacquier. Je savais par les journaux que vous étiez contre l'accusé, et de ce fait je me plaignais—mais oui ! ! ! Mais il ne semble pas un personnage bien intéressant, et ses moyens de défense sont faibles. Une fois de plus, j'ai compris, devant ce jugement, combien vous aviez fait d'effort pour ma défense et les mots me manquent pour vous exprimer ma reconnaissance."

Immediately after the Fahmy trial Marshall Hall also wrote a letter to M. le Bâtonnier de l'Ordre des Avocats du Barreau de Paris, thanking the French Bar for Mlle. Odette Simon's invaluable services to him during the trial. " Les nuances," he wrote, " d'expression d'une femme française, déjà difficiles à rendre pour une autre française, sont, à mon avis, tout à fait impossibles pour un homme qui de plus n'est pas français. . . . Je salue le Barreau français au nom du Barreau anglais."

Congratulations poured in from old friends and from strangers all over the world. One of these was addressed to " Marshall Hall, the Greatest Lawyer on Earth," and the Post Office was equal to the occasion. Everywhere the public had been profoundly moved by the trial of this Parisian woman ; she indeed was a butterfly on the wheel, a butterfly who had been made to suffer for one terrible year to the utmost limit of human endurance. During the course of the trial she received innumerable messages of sympathy and " God-speed " from Englishwomen. From the moment that she married her Eastern lover, until she stepped from the dock at the Old Bailey, her life had been one long torture. When the case was all over, it was, no doubt, considered by many that Marshall Hall had had an easy task to perform, but this was far from true. As an English friend of the accused wrote to Marshall Hall, " We knew her story was true, but you had to make the judge and jury understand." Provocation, self-defence, and accident are very different matters; they do not go well together in harness, and only the last two can secure an acquittal. Madame Fahmy had, on the face of it, killed with a lethal weapon an unarmed and defenceless man. Long provocation such as she had endured may come dangerously near to proving, not self-defence, but motive, not accident, but revenge. The manner in which Marshall Hall, by exposing the long story of her frightful provocation, showed why she had come to seize the pistol in self-defence, and how, owing at once to her ignorance of mechanism and her mortal terror at the moment, the pistol, which she thought harmless, was fired by accident, is beyond all praise. The three lines of defence, inconsistent as they seemed at first, could only stand with each other, and together they had the unmistakable ring of truth.

The story was no afterthought, no advocate's reconstruction long after the event. The prisoner had told, in effect, the same story immediately after her arrest. In pathetic sentences, which I have translated into very literal English, she wrote at the first opportunity her pitiful story, speaking of herself in the third person. Like many people in great trouble, she seemed to see herself from outside, as another person, perhaps as a figure in one of the great operas, most of which she could sing by heart. Who, in deep personal misfortune, is not familiar with that strange, haunting feeling, " Could this really have happened to me ? "

" In London in July," she wrote, " we are in the presence of a woman who has suffered mentally for six months, she is weak and nervous ; she sees dying, day by day, the hope she had conceived of reforming her husband. She realises that all is useless. She explains to them—to Aly and Said—her contempt, and wishes to go away, feeling herself no longer mistress of her nerves ; sickness and sufferings have got the better of her courage. She has no longer the strength to struggle. She has now only one desire—to escape. She loves her child. She has friends. She is young and can make her life again. If she remains with Aly Fahmy, it means either brutal death or slow agony which will lead her fatally and speedily to suicide. She realises all this, and uses her last energy in arranging her departure. . . . This woman cannot speak English, she has no friends in London ; it is therefore natural that she should wish to return home, to her family and to her friends. Aly feels, this time, that the comedy is finished, that she is going to escape him, that he will not find her again. He becomes fierce. . . ." " I had seen my husband load and unload his revolver several times ; either the bullet rose or it came out at the side. . . . I wish to make the bullet come out at the side, to unload it. Unfortunately I could not succeed, for lack of strength. I try two or three times—impossible —the shot goes off. It was the first shot that ever has gone off in my hands in my life. . . . I believe the weapon, therefore, harmless since the bullet has gone out."

Marshall's dramatic statements concerning the marriage of a Western woman to an Eastern man, and his description of Fahmy as " crouching for his final spring—like a beast—like an Oriental," had imperial repercussions. The Bâtonnier of the Egyptian Bar immediately sent a long cable, which reached the Attorney-General of England, complaining of Marshall Hall's license " in allowing himself to generalise, and to ' lash ' all Egypt and, indeed, the whole East. . . . A great advocate like Hall is not ignorant that it is unjust and disloyal to judge a whole nation by the conduct of a single individual. The Egyptian Bar protests with all its force against the principle followed by Sir Marshall Hall, in his defence, as unjust and deplorable." Sir Douglas Hogg replied, " I am quite confident that Sir Edward Marshall Hall would not willingly hurt the feelings of any foreign people, and he is far too distinguished and experienced an advocate to transgress the limits properly restraining the conduct of his client's case. I hope, therefore, that you may have been misled by a newspaper summary."

Marshall Hall replied :

" MY DEAR ATTORNEY-GENERAL,—I am afraid the Press must have published reports which I have not seen, and which

are not accurate. Any attack I made was, on express instructions received through Egyptian sources, on the man Ali
Fahmy, and not on the Egyptians as a nation. If my instructions were, as I believe them to be, accurate, anything I said
about that person was more than justified. The only thing that
I remember saying that might be misunderstood was that it
was a mistake for the Western woman to marry this Eastern
man, and his idea of his rights towards a wife were those of
possession instead of mutual alliance. . . . If, by any chance,
in the heat of advocacy I was betrayed into saying anything
that can be construed as an attack on the Egyptians as a
nation, I shall be the first to disclaim any such intention, and
express regret if I was so represented.

" I am, my dear Attorney-General, yours very sincerely,

" EDWARD MARSHALL HALL."

In fact, as the reports show, Marshall had expressly limited
his attack to the prisoner's husband, though, in fact, he was so
completely carried away by his own eloquence in this case that
he might have said anything. He told me afterwards that a
strange idea came into his head as he was demonstrating with the
pistol : he was conscious that he was pointing it at the judge.
" Suppose, I thought, a cartridge were still left in the magazine,
and I were to pull the trigger and it were to kill the judge !
What a scene ! " he said. " I would indeed have ended my career
at the Bar in a blaze of glory. But," he added with a mischievous smile, " I should have had a perfectly good defence. I
would have said the same thing had happened to me as happened to Madame Fahmy, and we would both have got off." I
wondered afterwards whether this idea, flashing for an instant
through his brain, was the real reason why he dropped the pistol.

.   .   .   .

In July 1924, Marshall Hall appeared in a most unusual rôle
before Mr. Justice Avory at the Guildford Assizes. As Madame
Fahmy had read with surprise at Karlsbad, he was briefed as
second string for the prosecution of another French subject,
Jean Pierre Vacquier. Vacquier was an inventor, and had met
Mrs. Jones, the wife of an English publican, in the South of
France. Unable to speak each other's language, they had made

love with the aid of a French-English dictionary. He came over to
England, and stayed with the lady and her husband at their
hotel at Byfleet ; during the visit the husband died an agonising
death from a dose of strychnine, which he took in place of his
medicine. The lady, or the money Vacquier thought that he
would gain with her, were the motives suggested for this crime,
and he was convicted, still protesting his innocence. " I can only
say that I am innocent," he said. " I swear on my mother's and
father's graves that I am innocent of the crime with which I am
charged."

It is not necessary to deal with this case at length in a life of
Marshall Hall ; he played a very subsidiary part in the proceed-
ings, all the heavy work of the prosecution being done by the
Attorney-General, Sir Patrick Hastings, who was called to the
Bar nearly twenty years later than his distinguished junior.
Marshall Hall, however, was repelled in the same way by the
dark-bearded Frenchman as he had been by Smith. Vacquier had,
like the English Bluebeard, uncanny and magnetic eyes, and
Marshall felt convinced that this murder was by no means the
first crime which he had committed.

In November 1924, Sir Edward secured another victory in a
capital case at the Old Bailey. He defended a man named
Alfred Solomon, who had killed a boxer named " Barney Blitz "
in a scuffle at the Eden Social Club, Eden Street. All the parti-
cipants in the affray were members of the racing fraternity, and
Blitz had attacked a friend of the prisoner's named Emmanuel
with a drinking glass ; Blitz considered that Emmanuel was
responsible for a prosecution which had been brought against
him in respect of his activities on the Turf, and wanted his
revenge. A scuffle ensued in which the prisoner drew a knife,
" ran amok," and killed the boxer. Alfred Solomon's friends, with
the loyalty of their race, raised a subscription for his defence,
and actually came down to Sir Edward's flat in Welbeck Street,
with the notes in their hands, in order to persuade the great
advocate to appear for the prisoner. Did they think that he
would be more amenable to reason if they approached him direct,
instead of through the medium of his lynx-eyed and vigilant
clerk ? At any rate, Marshall appeared for Solomon, and pleaded
self-defence. The feature of the defence was again the vivid

re-creation by Marshall Hall of the atmosphere in which the crime was committed. A drinking glass (with which the dead man had begun the affray) does not seem, on the face of it, a very dangerous or lethal weapon, but when Marshall took one up, from which he had been drinking for refreshment, and crashed it down on the desk before him, the jury began to revise their opinion. Glass, after all, was capable of inflicting the most dreadful injuries, was almost the most dangerous artificial substance in daily use. It could mutilate the face beyond recognition, and sever the vital arteries. In the end the prisoner was convicted of manslaughter only, and sentenced to three years' penal servitude.

In the " Peeping Tom " case the prisoner, a young miner and ex-service man, was supported in his defence by the voluntary contributions of his fellow workers, and Marshall Hall was instructed for the defence. The case came on before Mr. Justice Branson in March 1925, at Leeds Assizes. The circumstances of this case were most extraordinary. " Peeping Toms " may deserve an ignominious punishment, but hardly death. It appeared that two young Doncaster men named Needham and Throstle found it an excellent evening's amusement to hide behind a wall skirting the Doncaster cricket-ground, and watch the mutual endearments of courting couples who came up to the ground in order to make love to each other. They provided themselves with limelight in the form of a flash-lamp, and one of them had tied round his leg a rubber knee-cap to make his stealthy approach comfortable and noiseless. When, about 10.30 on a December night, James Doyle walked up to the cricket-ground with his fiancée, the lovers were interrupted in some way by the two " Peeping Toms." Doyle, who was carrying a knife, killed one of them. The question for the jury was, How did this terrible result occur? Allowing for all the outraged anger of a lover pestered by such vile people, the mere curiosity and laughter of " Peeping Toms " armed with a flash-lamp does not justify murder. The main evidence for the defence consisted in muddy footmarks which were found after the affray on Doyle's waistcoat.

" Do you really tell the jury," asked Marshall Hall of the surviving " Peeping Tom," who was the chief witness for the

Crown, " you were sufficiently expert a kicker to kick this man so high, when he was standing up ? "

In his evidence in chief this youth had said, with unashamed frankness, " The latter part of the evening we generally spent in the cricket-field, spying on couples."

" Why did you do that ? "—" For amusement—hobby."

The two watchers were each of them bigger than Doyle himself, and Marshall Hall urged the jury to decide that Doyle, finding himself one against two, and admittedly very angry, thought it necessary to draw a knife in self-defence against these contemptible roughs. The auburn-haired sweetheart came forward to give evidence for her lover, as did his father. " A father could not have a better lad," he said. Sir Herbert Nield, however, for the Crown, persisted in the murder charge, but after a retirement of an hour and a half the jury decided in favour of a clean acquittal. It is remarkable that in neither of these two cases, in each of which the prisoner undoubtedly killed a man with a dangerous weapon, was the accused called to give evidence on his own behalf.

In Marshall Hall's last year at the Bar he appeared for the defence in three capital cases. Since the case of Eric Holt, he had not been so deeply troubled as he was concerning the first of these.

In the early hours of December 2nd, 1925, a call came through to the Birkenhead telephone exchange, and a confused, foreign voice was heard to say, " I have shot my wife and child." The speaker was immediately put on to " Police," and P.C. Drysdale heard the same voice say, " Tam—shot—kill wife and child."

" Who is that speaking ? "

" Lock Ah Tam," was the answer. " Send your folks, please. I have killed my wife and child. My house is 122 Price Street."

The police knew the house and its master well, but the news to them was incredible. Police officers at once went round, through the empty shop, to the luxurious rooms behind, where their friend Lock Ah Tam, one of the most respected and influential of all the Chinese community in England, lived. The door into the shop was always open, so that he was at all times accessible to his countrymen of any sort and condition ; but, since his visitors were sometimes very peculiar people, he always kept a loaded automatic and revolver close at hand. When the police arrived they were confronted by a ghastly scene. Tam's wife, a Welshwoman whose maiden name had been Catherine Morgan, and his youngest child, Cecilia, aged eighteen, lay dead, both killed by gunshots ; and his daughter Doris, aged twenty, lay mortally wounded. Tam seemed quite calm, and smoked a cigarette and said, " Shot my wife." To Kwok Tsan Chin, a Chinese friend and neighbour who had come in, he said quite calmly, " I am in trouble. You will look after the business ; do your best. If I am hung, get my body out, and bury me by my wife and daughter." Up to this moment the man had seemed calm and collected ; but, when he was brought to the police station, he was so wild and excited, and his eyes stared and protruded so curiously, that the superintendent refused to charge him. When he was finally charged and asked if he had anything to say, he said, " Nothing at present, nothing at present, nothing at the present time."

The police were distressed and amazed. Born in 1872 in Canton, Tam came to England as a young ship's-steward in 1895 ; in thirty years he had risen to a great position among his fellow countrymen, had amassed at one time considerable wealth, and was respected wherever he went in the country of his adoption. With his Welsh wife, his son, and his daughters he was ideally happy. He was the European representative of the Jack Ah Tia, an organisation of Chinese stevedores with headquarters in Hong-Kong, and was, besides, appointed superintendent of Chinese sailors for three British steamship lines. Owing to the influence which his position gave him over innumerable Chinese seamen, he was of great assistance to the police ; he would see that undesirable Chinamen left the country, or returned to their ships, without any expense to the British taxpayer. It was understood that he was president of the Kock Man Tong, a world-wide Chinese Republican organisation, and that he had served the great Sun Yat Sen himself as a secret service agent in England. His word had great prestige with Chinese sailors far and wide, and he even dispensed justice on behalf of the Kock Man Tong to his fellow countrymen. He had recently presided over a secret court to punish a Chinaman for beating his English wife. But he was not the sinister " King of Chinatown " of detective romance ; a kindly, gentle person, he distributed much in charity and hospitality, giving Christmas treats to the poor children of Birkenhead and Liverpool, and renting a shoot where he entertained his English friends.

He had founded the Chinese Progress Club in Liverpool; in 1918 he had been stunned and rendered unconscious on the premises of the club owing to a blow on the head from a drunken Russian sailor. In 1924 he launched out on a large commercial undertaking, lost many thousands of pounds, and filed his own petition in bankruptcy. This disaster broke his heart, and, though he still lived in an extravagant way, all was not well with the man: he would suddenly fly into uncontrollable tempers; he would jump up and break crockery. On these occasions, saliva would flow from his lips, and his eyes would bulge from their sockets; soon afterwards he would be weeping at the sight of poor children with bare feet, and pressing largesse upon them; he also began to drink heavily. In October 1925, Catherine Tam wrote to a friend that he was pining away and that she sometimes thought he was going mad. He often frightened her; but she worshipped her Eastern husband, and she preferred to remain at his side.

On December 1st, however, Lock Ah Tam's cares sat lightly on him. His son Lock Ling Tam was lately home from his nine years' course of education in the East, and his father gave a dinner-party to celebrate his coming of age. There had really been quarrels between father and son, but on this night of nights all was forgotten. Speeches were made in the son's honour by his father and mother, and all seemed festive and happy. Perhaps the host had drunk a little more than was good for him, but to the last of his guests leaving after midnight he had said, "Ring me up to-morrow morning, and let me know how your daughter is."

When all the guests were gone, Lock Ling Tam heard his father's voice angrily addressing his mother; he was stamping his feet and gesticulating wildly: Ling went down and told his father to leave her alone. Ah Tam withdrew, but later he called for the maid, Margaret Sing, to bring him his boots: as she crept downstairs she saw the reflection of her master in the mirror; he was loading a revolver. Soon afterwards dreadful things began to happen. In a short space of time, Ah Tam got out his sporting-gun, shot his wife, and his youngest daughter. He then took his revolver, walked round the room, and saw his other daughter cowering with the maid behind the door. " Isn't it awful," poor Doris cried. " Do save me." Pulling the door back, he shot her twice. The son, quite terrified by his father's wild demeanour, had run for help to the neighbours ; the one futile act which he did to prevent the tragedy was to hurl a kettle through the window at his father, missing his mark.

As in the cases of Solomon and Doyle, a defence fund was raised. When it was known that Lock Ah Tam, the good, the strong, the generous, was to be tried for murder, and that all his money was gone, the word went round, and subscriptions flowed in from the Chinese community from all over England and beyond. Over a thousand pounds was raised, and Marshall Hall, whose attack on the Eastern character had been such a feature of the Fahmy defence, was instructed to defend the life of this Oriental. He, too, had married a European wife, and the marriage had ended in a catastrophe, though so different, even more tragic and pathetic than the scene in the Savoy Hotel. In this case, for over twenty years the affectionate Chinese husband had lived happily with his British wife ; then something had happened to end it all. The figure of Medea, standing over her dead children, could not have been more tragic than Lock Ah Tam as he sat in that silent house on that dreadful morning, his life in ruins, after so much prosperity.

As it was incontrovertible that Lock Ah Tam had killed these three poor women, there was only one defence to put forward, that of irresponsibility. The contention of the defence was that the prisoner had done those acts while in a state of " unconscious automatism " brought on by an epileptic fit. It was suggested that the blow to his head in the Liverpool club in 1918 had affected his brain, and made him subject to epilepsy. Epilepsy frequently induces a desire for alcohol, and alcohol in turn precipitates and aggravates the fits. His bankruptcy had caused him great un-happiness, and worry would further disturb his mental balance. At any rate, from 1918 onwards there was a certain amount of evidence of moodiness and sudden violence ; and certainly the man had behaved in a peculiar way since he had been confined to prison. On one occasion he had flung his clothes on the fire and said, " Me want new clothes," and then fallen into a deep sleep.

It was a superhuman task to save the Chinaman under the

present English law of insanity. For he had immediately rung up the police and reported what he had done, showing clearly that he both remembered his deed and knew that it was wrong. The main refrain of Marshall Hall's defence was that no sane man, absolutely without motive and immediately after a happy family celebration, could have perpetrated this awful crime ; least of all could this man have done so whose normal character was generous and kindly in the extreme, and whose love for his wife and family was so notorious. The man had asked to be buried by the side of his wife and daughter, " if he should be hung." Marshall at once saw the importance of this strange and pathetic request ; and, deeply interested as he was in the survival of the personality after death, he pursued the matter at some length with one of the Chinese witnesses.

" In China," he asked, " a man and his wife are buried side by side ? "—" Yes."

" With regard to the belief in the after-life, does the question where you are buried make any difference to you ? If a man and his wife are buried together, does it make any difference, in your religious beliefs, as to the chance of their meeting in the after-life ? "—" Some of us say so."

One of the guests of the birthday party was called by the prosecution.

" Was he," asked Sir Edward, " a man who was very popular amongst all his friends in the neighbourhood ? "—" Yes."

" May I put it higher than that ? He was loved by everyone that knew him ? "—" That is correct, sir."

" Have you any doubt that Mrs. Tam was very fond of her husband ? "—" I think they were both fond of each other. The girls were very fond of him also, and kissed him every night before going to bed."

The wretched Lock Ling Tam, who had run away "to get help" at the time of the tragedy, was strongly pressed by Marshall Hall as to his father's terrifying condition and appearance.

" Have you ever seen a man in the East ' running amok ' ? " he asked. " Did you ever see your father look like he looked that night ? "—" No."

" Didn't the sight of your father, and what you saw, absolutely terrify you ? "--" Well, it did, sir."

Then there was a pause.

" He has been a very good father to you, and your mother has been a good mother to you ? "—" Yes, sir."

Marshall thus obtained from the man's son the almost irreconcilable contrast between the prisoner's usual affectionate nature and his terrible demeanour on that one night. " I do not suppose," said Marshall Hall, in opening the case, "if you were to search the tragedies of the Greek poets, you would find anything more poignant than this tragedy. It is admitted here that he was loved by everyone, a peaceable, quiet citizen, devoted to his wife and children, and a man who earned the respect of everyone who came into contact with him. . . . Some minute happening in his brain caused a change for which none of us can account. It turned a man—a mild, lovable, and peaceable man—into a raving madman, and under the influence of this he did an act, which was the last act in the world which he would have done. Absolutely and entirely motiveless, he killed those whom he loved best. . . . Yes, there is no doubt he did it, but at the time he did it he was insane."

Evidence was called for the defence that the Tam family was one of the happiest in Birkenhead, but this had already been proved beyond doubt. The main evidence for the defence was that of Dr. Ernest Reeve, an expert on mental diseases, whose opinion it was that the prisoner had been in a state of " unconscious automatism " as a result of epilepsy, caused by a blow on the head, and induced by alcohol. An epileptic fit and epileptic automatism are quite different things, said the doctor ; often the latter state is preceded by a fit, but epileptic automatism can supervene without a fit at all. It was not difficult for a lawyer to riddle this hypothesis by a series of common-sense questions. How could the man be unconscious when he had telephoned for the police and said, " I have shot my wife and child ? "

" Yes," replied the doctor, " he said that in a condition of automatism. He would know everything. A patient in that condition is like a sleep-walker. A sleep-walker may walk on the parapet of a roof and may do all sorts of things apparently with conscious knowledge. But afterwards he has no recollection of what he was doing." The doctor gave remarkable instances of epileptic automatism where the subject behaved in a perfectly rational way during the attack, and remembered nothing about the matter afterwards ; to the lay minds of the jury, unused to the infinitely various phenomena of the abnormal mind, these instances may have sounded more like fairy-tales than medical evidence. The diagnosis of insanity, especially of this rare kind, must largely be arrived at only by the study of the subject's outward behaviour ; the mysterious reaction of the physical on the mental which produces insanity is not a matter of exact science, and it was impossible for any doctor to put forward a cut-and-dried theory of insanity, to account for Lock Ah Tam's abnormal behaviour, which was not open to attack from every quarter. "The Devil himself knoweth not the thought even of a normal man," as a judge said many centuries ago. How, then, could a doctor do anything but speculate as to what went on in the mind of Lock Ah Tam, from the night of the murder till he was brought to sit in the dock ?

Rebutting evidence was called for the Crown, and Dr. Watson, senior medical officer at Brixton, said he could hardly imagine how Dr. Reeve, or anybody else, could form the theory of an epileptic seizure.

Any hope which the prisoner's friends now had depended on Marshall's speech. The prisoner himself, who had sat like a statue throughout the trial, could not be called. Marshall again addressed himself to the crime itself. " Let us put doctors and everything else on one side for a moment," he said. " Is not the real difficulty you have to face, this ?—How can any man who is a sane man believe that a sane man could do this thing. . . . ? " Marshall Hall, who had been allowed to sit down while he cross-examined the witnesses, was now standing erect, and speaking with immense earnestness and energy. He believed passionately in his case. " *Could* any sane man have done it ? *Would* any sane man have done it ? Are you not constrained to look for some explanation which is negative of sanity ? You are ! " he shouted. " You must be ! You can't believe that this sudden revolution in a man's mind, which converted him from a loving father into a murderer, was not the result of his reason being dethroned." During his peroration he turned and pointed to the impassive figure in the dock, and caught sight of some of Lock Ah Tam's friends, weeping, and apparently praying in some fashion, near the dock. He made a strange appeal, not for the man himself, but for his friends. " I am struggling almost for a matter of sentiment," he said. " I do not think we can get into the mind of an Oriental. I do not suppose, if we got into his mind, that which happens now really matters to him one iota. He is here, and knows that whatever the verdict is his days of liberty are at an end. Fatalists as all Orientals are, he must know that he must walk from this place to some place of detention in some circumstances or other, but the nature of that place is of some moment to those who know him and were fond of him. . . . To those who have rallied round him at the last, to try and provide him with such humble efforts as we can make on his behalf, it will be some consolation to feel that the man who was their friend, the man whom they loved, was safe. They would gladly welcome the verdict ; they would join in grateful thanks if you could say . . . that, though he was guilty of the act, he was insane at the time he did it."

Marshall had used every inflection of his voice, every gesture of hand and arm and body to drive home this passionate appeal. In great contrast came the grave reply of the Crown. " The upraised hand and the uplifted voice is not for the prosecution," said Sir Ellis Griffiths. " The defence to this crime is the crime itself . . . never was there such a paradox as this."

The jury were only out for twelve minutes before they returned a verdict of " guilty," the shortest consideration which a jury ever gave to a plea by Marshall on the capital charge. The judge, Mr. Justice Mackinnon, lately appointed to the Bench, and very little used to criminal business, was deeply affected as he pronounced sentence.

" You have been convicted by your adopted countrymen of this crime," he said. " I can only ask you to use the time that remains for you, so that, when that time comes, you will meet it with the bravery that a man should show."

The exhortation was unnecessary, and even inappropriate. Without a sign of emotion on his mask-like face, the prisoner was taken below. The appeal that followed was futile, as was the agitation for a reprieve, in which Marshall Hall joined wholeheartedly. He recalled the case of Henry Patrick, who had murdered his sweetheart for no apparent motive, in whose case

LOCK AH TAM

the defence of an epileptic seizure had been raised unsuccessfully by Marshall and Fulton at the trial, and whose sentence had been respited owing to subsequent epileptic seizures in prison. But no such deliverance came to poor Lock Ah Tam, who soon followed his beloved wife and daughters to the grave, doubtless with stoical indifference.

How deeply Marshall Hall felt about this case appears from letters written at the time. " I came back from Chester on Saturday night, dead beat and very disappointed at the verdict : it was a wrong verdict. The scene in court was extraordinary— most dramatic, and, amidst the sobbing of the women and the tear-broken voice of the judge, that inscrutable Chinaman stood, still steady and apparently unconcerned, with a face like a mask, and a mysterious smile hovering round his lips. Mr. Wu over again. . . . " " It looks like a mystery which will never be solved in all its details. Poor Mr. Wu ! I'm afraid he will fail in his appeal, not that he minds. When asked if he wished to come to London, to hear the appeal as he is entitled to, he merely shook his head as he had done when the clerk of assize, after verdict, had asked him if he had anything to say why he should not be sentenced to death—merely moved his head slowly from one side to the other. Life cannot be such an important thing if all the millions and millions of Easterns treat it with such unconcern."

In June 1926, Marshall Hall appeared, at the Worcester Assizes, for another man who suddenly and for no apparent reason killed a member of his family. Edward Flavell's mother had married again. He was a young man who had never shown any promise, and was employed as a crane-driver. His half-brother, aged fourteen, was an intelligent and clever boy, and was being sent to an art school. This may have caused some jealousy in Flavell's mind, and he took a chopper and brutally killed his brother while he slept. He afterwards said, " He never had any pain. I did it while he was asleep. I did it after it got light this morning." Evidence was called which showed there had been instances of insanity in his family, and that he had been abnormally cruel, even as a child : he had once imprisoned a cat in an oven. He was very slow and stupid.

Marshall Hall in this case became irritated with one of the

medical men, who was very positive as to the sanity of the prisoner.

" Are you one of the class who believes that no one is mad ? " —" No."

Here Mr. Justice Avory interposed : " I hope you are not one of the class, doctor, who believes that everybody is mad ? "

Flavell was sentenced to death ; but Marshall Hall made a passionate appeal to the Court of Criminal Appeal on his behalf, begging the judges once again to give a wider interpretation to the Macnaughton rules, and even saying that he would apply to the Attorney-General for a fiat to take the case to the House of Lords. But the Court of Criminal Appeal was obdurate, and ruled that no extension of the Macnaughton rules could be made under the present law. An agitation for a reprieve followed, and in this case the Home Secretary decided to advise His Majesty to exercise his prerogative of mercy, but it is significant that the sentence was commuted to penal servitude for life, and he was not sent to a criminal lunatic asylum. His insanity, therefore, was not the ground of his reprieve.

It was not inappropriate that Marshall's last capital case of all also should be before Mr. Justice Avory, whose work at the Criminal Bar, like that of the defender himself, dated back over forty years, they had met so often that each must have been familiar with every professional characteristic which the other possessed. This appearance was for the defence of Alfonso Austin Smith, who was charged with the murder of John Derham. Both the dead man and the prisoner had been at Eton and Cambridge. The prisoner was the grandson of a Canadian millionaire, had been an officer in the Dragoon Guards, and had at one time been master of a very large fortune. He had served bravely throughout the war, and had married after it a very attractive lady, who had borne him three children. He was devoted to his family. About six months before the tragedy, he met Derham, a married man, and the two men quickly became great friends. His new friend fell in love with his young wife, and this deeply distressed Smith. Man and wife had not definitely decided to separate on August 12th, 1926, and Smith was, in fact, staying with his wife at a villa named " Stella Maris " at Whitstable. But their matrimonial future was still very uncertain ; and, on

the 12th, Smith sent, in his wife's name, an " urgent " telegram
to Derham, asking him to come down to " Stella Maris." These
three unhappy people dined together at an hotel. They then
returned home, and at 11 p.m. a shot was heard. Mrs. Smith's
young sister went down to the drawing-room and saw Derham
holding Smith down on the floor, and hitting him wildly with a
revolver. Mrs. Smith was trying to pull Derham away, and
eventually he desisted, staggered out of the house, and collapsed
in the street. He was mortally wounded, a bullet having entered
his left side, and came to rest in the right side of his stomach.
Two bottles of beer were on the table, and playing-cards were
scattered all over the room ; altogether the disordered scene was
worthy of the pencil of a modern Hogarth. Mr. Roland Oliver
was briefed by the Crown, and Marshall Hall, with 350 guineas
on his brief, motored down one very foggy November morning to
conduct his last capital defence. The fog made him late, and he
arrived just as the Court was sitting. Mr. Roland Oliver's opening
showed that the prisoner had written menacing letters to the
new friend, who, in his opinion, was robbing him of his beloved
wife ; counsel quoted a letter written that summer to his wife :
" MY DEAR, DEAR GIRL,—This problem can only be solved in
one way, the removal of your lover Derham or myself. . . . May
God forgive me for what I am about to do, and may he forgive
you. . . . I have no more to say. My heart is broken and there is
nothing in life for me. If you hold anything sacred, in this world or
the next, look after the children." To the dead man he had written
in July : " You damned swine, I only wish you had the courage
to meet me. . . . You must realise that you have ruined, not
only a very sweet girl, but the woman I, and not you, love."

All this, however sad and moving to any hearer or any reader,
seemed to be little legal assistance to Smith. His defence was
shortly expressed in his own words soon after the shooting. " I
intended to shoot myself, but in the struggle for the revolver
it went off and shot Derham."

If this could be established, the prisoner was guilty neither of
murder nor manslaughter. The chief evidence against the
prisoner's account of the matter was that of a passer-by, who
said that he heard a shot, and *afterwards* saw Derham and the
woman rushing at Smith. But Marshall suggested to him that

his mind had subconsciously inverted the sequence of events, there being, at most, only a fraction of a second between the two happenings. The doctor admitted that it was possible for the wound to have been caused while Derham was struggling to seize the revolver, by its barrel, out of the other man's hand, when the latter was in the act of withdrawing it from his hip pocket. The curious place of the wound on the left side might be explained by the twisting of his body in the struggle.

Marshall Hall was very much in his element in this case : he took the big Webley revolver in his hands, and several times he left counsel's benches and went into the well of the court to demonstrate with his old friend Robert Churchill (the gunsmith), the doctor, and even with Mr. Roland Oliver himself, in order to show that the wound might easily have been inflicted by an accidental explosion of the revolver as Derham leapt forward to prevent Smith from killing himself. Indeed, Marshall gripped Churchill's wrist with such force that the latter begged him to let go. A discussion took place at some length with Mr. Churchill as to the holes which had been made by the bullet in the dead man's clothes. It was sought to fix the range at which the shot had been fired by the nature of the injury to the material. During this discussion Marshall stood with a jeweller's lens in his eye, examining minutely the dead man's clothing which he held in his hands, and testing the gunsmith's evidence with all manner of technical questions.

On the second day the prisoner went into the box : Marshall had handed him the usual alternative form—" I wish to give evidence. I do not wish to give evidence "—but the prisoner wrote back saying that he preferred to put himself unreservedly in the hands of his counsel. Marshall was furious, and explained to Smith that the responsibility was entirely the prisoner's and not counsel's in this matter, and sent the prisoner a second form. The prisoner struck out the latter part of the alternative, and decided to give evidence. Marshall Hall went over to Smith and said to him, " I feel bound to tell you that I defended a man named Seddon who would have been acquitted, but for his own evidence. He insisted on doing it." But Austin Smith had made up his mind : he was confident that no jury could convict him of murder. If sympathy had been with the prisoner before, it was far more so after his evidence. He said he had procured the revolver in order to kill himself. The really wonderful letters which he had written to his wife were read to him. " MY OWN ADORABLE LITTLE WIFE,—You have made me happier than I ever hope to be. I have been mad lately and in hell. You asked me to forgive you last night, and I could only say, ' I love you,' and that covered everything. I feel like a man who has been in a terrible fever, delirious and wandering, and am just waking from a deep, refreshing, and life-giving sleep. Do not throw a life-belt to me and then draw it away at my last gasp. You have a great heart and courageous. I need it always and I want it."

" That," asked Sir Edward, " was an honest expression of your feelings to your wife on Wednesday, August 11th, 1926 ? "

The prisoner replied, " It is."

Then a most dramatic thing happened : one of the two women on the jury screamed and collapsed, and other women in court began to sob. The woman juror went out and returned in about five minutes, during which time the trial stood adjourned and the prisoner sat waiting in his chair in the witness box.

Sir Edward then dealt with the agony in the prisoner's mind when he saw that the reconciliation with his wife was not permanent. He went and possessed himself of his revolver.

" What was your state of mind ? " asked Sir Edward.— " Impossible to describe."

" The life-belt had been withdrawn ? "—" Yes."

He described how he had sent for Derham so that the three of them could talk the matter over. It was apparently suggested by the other two that Smith should go away.

" Where were you to stay ? " asked Sir Edward. " Oh, it didn't matter where I went," replied the prisoner.

He said the tragedy had occurred in a flash, when Derham and his wife were sorting the cards for a game. He told them he was going to shoot himself. " It did not appear to distress them. They did not believe it."

The prisoner then told and demonstrated how he had felt for the revolver in his hip pocket. " The next thing that happened— all I know is—there was a terrific struggle. I was struck on the head, the revolver went off, and the next thing I was absolutely conscious of was speaking to Inspector Rivers."

His last answer in examination in chief was, " I swear I never touched the trigger."

Mr. Oliver's first question was a most dramatic one :

" Do you think a man who behaved as Derham behaved deserves to be killed ? "

The accused replied, " I do not think any man deserves to be killed." This was the key-note of Mr. Oliver's very fair cross-examination, and he put to the prisoner other letters written to his wife. " I cannot live without you, nor do I intend to. . . . For the children's sake send him away. Chappie won't want to have fingers pointed at him as the son of the murderer of an unfaithful wife and her lover, and a suicide. Come back to me, my girl, my little white heather." The prisoner during the trial had worn a little sprig of white heather in his button-hole. In another letter he wrote of his children, " If only you knew how I long to see you and them. Is it fair that they should have no daddy ? "

When the judge questioned him about the possibility of a reconciliation, the prisoner said earnestly, " She had become reconciled the day before. . . . I thought I could even persuade Derham to see the folly of it. . . . Derham was a gentleman. I might have appealed to his better nature."

The prisoner had made a most convincing and moving witness, and, by the time he had left the box, Marshall Hall felt sure that the jury had believed his account of what had happened, and would acquit him on his own evidence. But there was still the speech to be made, and, since he had only called the prisoner, Marshall Hall had the last word.

It was a fine speech, a worthy coping stone to his great career, but it is exceedingly scantily reported. " Is it conceivable," he said, " that a man who was going to murder another would manufacture evidence against himself by sending a telegram, drafted in his own handwriting, under his wife's name, and that he would show the reply to the telegram to his wife ? Had Smith had any intentions of murdering Derham, he could have done so while walking home from the Marine Hotel. . . . Smith found himself with the only things in the world which he loved and adored, his wife and children, being taken away from him, and he had come to a stage when it seemed wellnigh hopeless to go on under existing conditions. The only solution which appeared

to him was to take his own life, but even up to the last he was
hoping—desperately, perhaps—for a reconciliation, and deferred
the moment till the time when hope was no longer a possibility."
Sir Edward concluded with a passionate appeal to set free a man
who had been so cruelly buffeted by fate. " He begged his wife
not to withdraw the life-belt, which she had thrown him as he
was struggling in the water. That life-belt has been withdrawn
once. Members of the jury, it is now for you to say whether you
will throw him that life-belt once more, give him the chance of
grasping it and being pulled ashore to resume his old happy life
with the woman he loves, which has been so long denied to him."

Curiously enough, Smith had almost been drowned in the
river at Thames Ditton after long and fruitless efforts to rescue a
friend, and had only just been " pulled ashore " in time for his
life to be saved.

In his summing-up, the judge observed, " The law you have to
administer in this case is the law of this country and not of any
other, and, above all, not that which is erroneously called the
" unwritten law." That is merely a name for no law at all. It is
the name given to the proposition that every man and woman is
a law unto himself or herself, and that reverts us to a state of
barbarism. I have told you the law of this country, as it must be
applied. If you apply any other law or notions of your own you
are violating the oaths you have taken."

The jury were out of court for two hours and eleven minutes
before they came to their decision. They declared the prisoner
not guilty, both of murder and manslaughter. The judge entered
the two verdicts ; everybody in court thought that he was about
to discharge the prisoner ; but it was not so.

" There is another charge on the calendar against the
prisoner," he said.

It appeared that the prisoner was also charged, under a
statute, with " possessing fire-arms and ammunition with intent
to endanger life." On his own evidence he had intended to take
his own life, and the judge held that the statute applied. The
prisoner pleaded " guilty " to this charge, and he was sentenced
to twelve months' imprisonment with hard labour. In this
rather unexpected way ended the " Stella Maris " trial. Once
again Marshall Hall had run, in dangerous combination,

provocation and accident ; once more he brought them into harmony, and so his last victory was won. He had fought the case with all his usual vigour and vitality. In no single particular did his powers seem to be failing. It was as if he were still in the prime of life.

During his stay at Maidstone, Marshall Hall went over part of Maidstone Gaol, and, while he was passing through one of the workrooms, he suddenly caught sight of a familiar figure, an old client on whose behalf he had appeared for over twenty years. This man had been a member of Parliament and in his way a great national figure. The two men's eyes met for an instant : it would have been unlawful for Marshall Hall to have spoken to a prisoner, but it would also have been impossible for a man of his generous nature not to make some gesture of recognition ; he raised his hand to his mouth, blew his old client a kiss, and passed on.

A few days after the " Stella Maris " trial, Marshall came to lunch with me at a famous London hotel. He could talk of nothing but this case, and we were only too anxious to hear him. It was not very long before he was repeating to us the peroration of his final speech ; and when he reached the ' life-belt ' passage, Mr. J. C. Squire, who was sitting opposite to him, said, quite carried away, " My God, Marshall, that's poetry," while a musical comedy star of twenty-five summers, who was sitting next to him, whispered to me, " Take this man away—he's breaking my heart." Meanwhile, the waiters had gathered round, and were scandalously neglecting their obligations to other patrons. Of course, June's heart was not broken ; that was her way of saying, " This is a wonderful man." And, of course, Marshall's rhetoric was not poetry ; but for a moment it seemed to be so to one who is both a poet and a critic of poetry.

In December 1926, Sir Edward had been extremely busy, and he had a cold which he could not shake off ; nevertheless, he did not allow this to interfere with his work. The last occasion on which I saw him was at the end of December, when we went together to a first night. Out of one of the pockets of a capacious fur coat, he produced an eighteenth-century tortoiseshell snuff-box. " I couldn't get you that Treasury brief," he said, " so I thought I'd give you this." For it gave him real pleasure to bestow presents, especially at Christmas time ; and there were few of his friends who had not in their possession some token of his generosity and exquisite taste.

It was his last Christmas ; in the preceding year he had lost a great and lifelong friend, Sir Squire Bancroft, and had felt his loss keenly. He wrote to Sir Arthur Pinero, on Christmas Eve, 1926 :

" MY DEAR OLD FRIEND,—Somehow it has happened that always at this time of year there have been two letters which I always write, and this year there is only one. None the less, though you and I will both miss our old friend very much, there remains very keen and vivid the happiness of friendship and remembrance for us. It is more than forty years, my dear Pin, since I saw those shaggy eyebrows, and well remember the many kindnesses that I received at your hands ; for, though I am years and years older than you, you were *you* then, and I was literally unknown. Well, we have had many years of friendship, and I hope we shall have many more—but I never shall forget that evening when, after the early days of the famous *Second*, I came to supper at your house, and, being given a certain charming lady to take in to the festive spread, I addressed her as Mrs. Tanqueray ! Was ever compliment so gauche and so sincere ' My love to you and good health and happiness.

" Yours as always,

" MARSHALL."

Perhaps another Christmas letter may be quoted, written to Marshall on Christmas Eve by a solicitor and lifelong friend. " You and another friend have made Christmas Eve what it is to me—an afternoon stolen from the current rough and tumble and given to thoughts of old days and things that last and are worth having. How other things do slip away, and what a rotten world this would be but for what you call the things you cannot buy, the things one thinks of on Christmas Eve. I saw the *Strand* last night, the picture of you at twenty, the Good Fairy had done her work all right and life was before you. You've grasped some of the things that aren't worth having, and missed others ; but, of the things you can't buy, you've got your full share." These two letters show what genius for friendship the man possessed.

He had only a short Christmas holiday : on January 10th he was down in Wales at Bridgend police court to defend, for a fee of 500 guineas, the officials of Messrs. Cory Brothers, who were charged, under a new statute, with " setting a man-trap calculated to destroy human life upon the trespasser or other person coming into contact with it." The company had protected their property by " live " electric wires, and the public were warned by conspicuous notices not to approach them. A young collier went ratting with some friends ; and, although their dogs passed unscathed through the " live " wires, when the boy came against it he was electrocuted. A prosecution for manslaughter was launched against the officials by the relatives of the dead boy ; and the object of the defence was, if possible, to dispose of the charge of manslaughter at the police court. This was an impossible task under the circumstances, but Marshall Hall's cross-examination laid the foundations for the afterwards successful defence which was conducted by Mr. Norman Birkett at the next Cardiff Assizes.

For the last time, he cross-examined Sir William Willcox, who admitted that, if death was caused by the electric current of so low a voltage as was used here, it was a very exceptional and unfortunate occurrence.

One observation made in this case by Marshall Hall was remarkable in view of the sequel. Sir William said that unexpectedness in an electric shock was a very important factor.

Sir Edward then said, " It is like funk in a case of an influenza epidemic : that probably kills more people than the influenza itself."

He was not at all well during this case, and he returned to London on the eleventh. While he was in London he seemed to have a premonition that he would not live long. "Somehow I feel," he said to a dear friend, " that I shall not live much longer. Do not grieve for me too much. I am very, very, tired." But next morning, resuming the rush of his busy life, he took the early morning train to Derby, and enjoyed on it " the best breakfast he ever had in his life." He was briefed to defend, at the police court, a man on a charge of false pretences. After this was over he held a consultation with his clients in a heavy " receiving " case which began on Thursday before the recorder at Quarter Sessions. This case, his last appearance in court, caused great interest in Derby, the defendants all being well-known men. A considerable number of motor-cars had been stolen, and the defendants were charged with receiving them, " well knowing them to have been stolen." It will be remembered that the very first occasion on which Marshall ever addressed a jury was in the defence of two tradesmen for " receiving " at Lewes Quarter Sessions. Speaking of that occasion, he had said, " I did not know whether I was standing on my head or my heels," and his fee had been four guineas. Now, forty-three years afterwards to the very day, he was defending another tradesman for "receiving," this time as the most experienced jury advocate of his time, with two hundred and fifty guineas marked on his brief. It is interesting, too, that the venue of his last case was Derbyshire, in which his family had been settled for many generations. The case was tried in the spacious council chamber, and big crowds gathered round the town hall every day and admired the celebrated defending advocate as he went in and out. The recorder sat very late, as it was a long and difficult case. Marshall dined in the Bar mess one night, where he was full of high spirits and anecdotes, but otherwise he spent his time quietly, as he needed all his strength for the case. His last letter to his daughter was written from Derby. " As far as I can see at present, it will be late on Saturday night at the earliest before we shall get away, if then. There are over a hundred witnesses in this case, and six defendants and ten counsel, so goodness only knows when we shall get through. It is stuffed full of perspiring and deep-breathing humanity, and the result is most unpleasant : we are sitting each day from ten till six, and we are jolly tired. . . . This case is about Morris-Cowley cars. The man Lewis, who has bolted and is not here to stand his trial, made a habit of watching these cars just after they had been bought, stole them, altered their numbers, forged their books of reference, and sold them to dealers who resold them. Now they are all charged with receiving stolen cars. There are no less than thirty-six of them outside the town hall here, all parked up in charge of the police. . . . I hope you are all right. Everyone in Derby has got the flu. . . . Well, love to all the dogs."

The case was still part heard on Saturday : at 4 p.m.,

Marshall Hall returned to London without taking his luggage, expecting to be back again on Monday. But he never put on wig or gown again. His last illness had struck him down during the progress of a case ; he was in harness to the very end. This was as he would have wished.

.   .   .   .

Many years before, in the later 'eighties, a young barrister named Moresby was sitting in the Bar room of the "White Hart" at Lewes during the Assizes. A very handsome young colleague, brimful of vitality, rushed into the room in a state of high excitement. It was young Marshall Hall. " I've got a fifty-guinea brief for murder," he said.

" I wouldn't do it for a hundred," said Moresby.

" Wouldn't you just," replied Marshall Hall scornfully.

" No," persisted Moresby, " I hate crime, and wouldn't take the responsibility."

" I mean to specialise in the two biggest gambles there are," said Marshall, with great earnestness : " life and death—freedom and imprisonment. Facts, not principles, for me. I don't know much law, but I can learn what there is to be known about men and women."

The words of his friend were so striking and vivid that Moresby took them down at the time and wrote them in his diary. Indeed, the conversation inaugurated a long friendship between the two men, who, widely different in their fields of advocacy, yet had one taste in common. Both were enthusiastic connoisseurs and collectors of precious stones. Occasionally, too, their profession brought them together. Forty years after their meeting in the " White Hart," Marshall and Moresby, both grey in the service of the law, sat together in a final consultation before a civil trial. The client was an excitable foreign doctor, whose whole professional future, together with a large sum of money, depended on the result of the case. Owing to Marshall Hall's illness, the consultation took place in his flat, and, although the case was to be called on within the hour, the great man was still in his dressing gown. The consultation was difficult, and there was much discussion. Suddenly Marshall made up his mind in the middle of a sentence. He broke off suddenly, and produced an immense blue stone from one of his pockets.

" By the way, Moresby," he said, " what do you think of this sapphire ? "

The bewildered little foreigner was aghast at his leading counsel's apparent callousness to his vital interests. How could he know that Marshall had made up his mind and that there was no more to be said ? When Moresby took the stone and examined it eagerly, his composure broke down completely. " Sapphires ! " he almost screamed, dancing up and down the room. " What has my case to do with sapphires ! " His impatience was excusable, and yet the result of the action which he had confided to these two legal jewellers was far from unfavourable to him.

During the forty years which had elapsed between these two episodes, it can truly be said that Marshall Hall had achieved what he had set out to do. In his simple direct way he knew most things about men and women, and this knowledge had worked wonders for those whom he was called upon to serve. His vivid advocacy, informed by his great experience, had on innumerable occasions saved fortune, regained freedom, vindicated honour, and, as the reader must now appreciate, often preserved life itself. If it were possible to assemble all those who owed one of these precious things to Marshall Hall there would indeed be gathered together a large and varied company of human beings. I have endeavoured to let the man speak for himself, and reveal himself and his art to the reader by his own words and actions ; but it will surely have been appreciated that Marshall Hall's advocacy was no ordinary thing. Never content, like most advocates, merely to work on his " instructions," when once he was briefed on behalf of a client, so passionately did he enter into his duty that he became, not merely counsel, but also detective, showman, rhapsodist, actor, friend, and even father confessor.

Nor did he reserve his gifts of sympathy and understanding of the human heart to mere professional engagements. As the writer knows full well, he was always ready to give counsel and consolation to those in trouble. " The great big man," wrote Spiro Mavrojani to me, " could be as tender as a woman to anyone who needed sympathy and help." His papers are full of evidence of his munificence and generosity to those who came to him for other assistance than comfort and advice. This book has to a great extent, of necessity, been a legal biography ; but the writer has tried to place before the public the man himself. He was a much admired and a much envied figure. The public took him at his face value, and probably did not credit him with a care in the world. The great splendid figure had seemed to stride so triumphantly through life, dying, as " Cheiro " had prophesied, at a ripe age, but at the zenith of his powers and reputation. Few knew or remembered the difficulties which had faced him in his long career, or how near failure had come ; only his intimate friends knew how sensitive he was ; hardly a soul guessed at the secret battle which the man had fought in order to put so bold a face before the world. Although this book has chiefly been the story of his cases, a man's soul is expressed more in his work than in any other activity, and the measure of my success will be whether or no I have been able to present in these pages an adequate portrait of the man himself.

On Sunday, January 16th, he went to bed, and never got up again. On Monday he sent for Archibald Bowker, and told him that he would not be able to go back to Derby. His two faithful clerks visited him frequently that week, and it was obvious to them that he was terribly ill. In spite of his brave rallies, to those who knew him best, and saw the change in him, the end appeared inevitable. For although his stormy and strenuous life had tired him out, he was too brave a warrior to give in, even to death, without a mighty struggle. Bronchitis and pneumonia followed on influenza, which the doctors said he had had on him for weeks. But still he held out for over a month. With his incurable optimism he said to his clerk at the end of January, " I should think I should be able to see somebody next week. Life is wretched, but mending I think. . . . " But next week came, and he dictated, for a letter to Ernest Harvey : " Judges and doctors and big swells at the Bar and the Bench and all manner of men, including ' Pin,' are calling and leaving a message, ' Say your time, Marshall, and I will come.' The answer is, ' All time forbidden.' "

There were numberless enquiries as to his condition, from the King of England himself, who had lately listened enthralled to Marshall's stories at a shooting-party at Lord Burnham's, to the humblest of men and women whom he had served in one way or another. At the Garrick Club, which had been almost a home to him for forty years, the question, " How is Marshall ? " was being asked from morning till night. But never again would he, with the premature optimism that his cronies knew so well, fling down his cards on the table and say, " The rest are mine."

His wife and daughter were by his side, and he sent for his favourite dog, a tiny Pekinese mongrel, Lulu, of great vivacity and charm. He had loved dogs all his life, and he would have one with him at the last. His memory wandered over his long and successful legal career ; yet the case to which he would always return in his talk was not a triumph, but a failure, the case of Lock Ah Tam. He confidently looked forward to doing the Welsh Colliery case at the next Cardiff Assizes. On February 1st he looked up and said to his wife, " This was poor Ethel's birthday," and his mind was, perhaps, recalling the raptures and agonies of forty years ago. There was no bitterness in his voice ; it was February 1st ; this had been her birthday, and she had died thirty-seven years ago ; now he was dying, and his gentle sentence showed that he remembered. During these last days, when he was conscious, his strong belief in a future life must have been a great strength to him. " How utterly incomplete," he had recently written in a letter, " would the best things in this life be, if the grave were to be the end of all these things ! I do believe that our souls are immortal." His very concrete mind, puzzled and bewildered by the injustice and incompleteness of human life, impressed by its wonders and not able to believe in their total extinction for the individual by death, had undoubtedly found consolation in the rather material evidences of a future life alleged by the Spiritualists. This search for concrete evidence of the greatest hope which humanity cherishes was the outcome of his optimistic and still youthful spirit, and of the ardent earnestness which had marked his every activity. " To sum it up in a few words," he had himself written, " my knowledge is *nil*, my belief strong, my hope infinite." We may be sure that this hope was with him to the last. About midnight on February 23rd the long battle was over, and the brave and gentle heart stopped beating.

On the day after his death the flag over the Inner Temple flew at half-mast, and the Bench and Bar of England gathered in the Lord Chief Justice's court to do honour to his memory. Mr.

Justice Avory, who presided, speaking with great emotion, said, " I am constrained to make reference to the great loss which the public and the profession of the law have sustained by the death of Sir Edward Marshall Hall. Of the gallant fights which he made as an advocate at the Bar, none has been more gallant than the fight which he has made against the malady which recently overtook him, and which, unfortunately, has ended fatally. No one who has known him as a personal friend, as an opponent at the Bar, as an advocate practising before one, as I have, can have failed to recognise his many sterling qualities, his striking individuality, and, above all, his great qualities as an advocate." It was a long time since Horace Avory had won that " iniquitous " verdict from Marshall Hall in the county court; but, perhaps, it and many other incidents were recalled by the learned judge as he spoke.

Sir Douglas Hogg, the Attorney-General, an advocate of so different a type and a generation apart from Marshall Hall, spoke on behalf of the Bar. " We at the Bar," he said, " regarded Sir Edward Marshall Hall, with pride, as a fearless advocate ; and we who knew him loved him as a great-hearted gentleman. By his loss the profession is robbed of a brilliant personality, and its members lose and mourn a very loyal friend."

A great crowd, composed of all manner of men and women, collected to see the coffin of the great defender carried in and out of St. Marylebone Church, and his brother lawyers did him honour by a special memorial service in the Temple Church. His ashes were laid, like those of an antique hero, by the side of his mother and father at Frant. Indeed, there was something heroic about him. He was the last of his kind ; his mantle has fallen on no successor. Through understanding of life, and the unfailing courage with which he used his commanding personality and great natural talents in his calling, he fought his way to a leading position among his fellow countrymen. In all reverence, having regard to his long career of service to others, this book may not inappropriately close with the words of the Master to the faithful servant, both for the sake of his fine achievement and of the great hope which he cherished : " Well done, thou good and faithful servant : enter thou into the joy of thy Lord."

INDEX

PORTWAY & NEW PORTWAY

NON-FICTION

Anderson, Verily	Beware of children
Anderson, Verily	Daughters of divinity
Armstrong, Martin	Lady Hester Stanhope
Arnothy, Christine	It's not so easy to live
Asquith, Margot	The autobiography of Margot Asquith
Barke, James	The green hills far away
Bentley, Phyllis	The Pennine weaver
Bishop, W.A.	Winged warfare
Blain, William	Home is the sailor
Brittain, Vera	Testament of experience
Brittain, Vera	Testament of friendship
Brittain, Vera	Testament of youth
Buchan, John	The clearing house
Cobbett, William	Cottage economy
Crozier, F.P.	Ireland for ever
Day, J. Wentworth	Ghosts and witches
Dunnett, Alastair M.	It's too late in the year
Edmonds, Charles	A subaltern's war
Evans, A.J.	The escaping club
Falk, Bernard	Old Q's daughter
Fields, Gracie	Sing as we go
Firbank, Thomas	A country of memorable honour
Gandy, Ida	A Wiltshire childhood
Gary, Romain	Promise at dawn
Gibbons, Floyd	Red knight of Germany
Gibbs, Philip	Realities of war
Gough, General Sir Hubert	The fifth army
Grant, I.F.	Economic history of Scotland
Hart, B.H. Liddell	Great captains unveiled
Hart, B.H. Liddell	A history of the world war 1914—18
Hart, B.H. Liddell	The letters of private Wheeler
Hart, B.H. Liddell	The other side of the hill
Hecht, Hans	Robert Burns: the man and his work
Holtby, Winifred	Letters to a friend
Huggett, Renee & Berry, Paul	Daughters of Cain
Jones, Ira	King of air fighters
Jones, Jack	Give me back my heart
Jones, Jack	Me and mine

Jones, Jack	Unfinished journey
Kennedy, John F.	Why England slept
Kennedy Shaw, W.B.	Long range desert group
Keyes, Frances Parkinson	St. Teresa of Lisieux
Keyhoe, Donald	The flying saucers are real
Lawrence, W.J.	No. 5 bomber group
Lethbridge, Mabel	Against the tide
Lethbridge, Mabel	Fortune grass
Masefield, John	The battle of the Somme
Neumann, Major Georg Paul	The German air-force in the great war
O'Mara, P.	The autobiography of a Liverpool Irish slummy
Pound, Reginald	Arnold Bennett
Price, Harry	The end of Borley rectory
Price, Harry	The most haunted house in England
Raymond, Ernest	In the steps of the Brontës
Raymond, Ernest	In the steps of St. Francis
Stoker, Bram	Famous imposters
Tangye, Derek	Time was mine
Tanner, J.R.	Tudor consitutional documents (1485—1603)
Vigilant	Richthofen — red knight of the air
Von Richthofen	The red air fighter
Whipple, Dorothy	The other day

PORTWAY & NEW PORTWAY

FICTION

Albert, Edward	Herrin' Jennie
Aldington, Richard	All men are enemies
Aldington, Richard	Death of a hero
Anand, Mulk Raj	Seven summers
Andersch, Alfred	Flight to afar
Anderson, Verily	Our square
Anderson, Verily	Spam tomorrow
Anthony, Evelyn	Imperial highness
Anthony, Evelyn	Victoria
Arlen, Michael	Men dislike women
Arnim, Elizabeth von	Elizabeth and her German garden
Arnim, Elizabeth von	Mr. Skeffington
Ashton, Helen	Doctor Serocold
Ashton, Helen	Family cruise
Ashton, Helen	Footman in powder
Ashton, Helen	The half-crown house
Ashton, Helen	Letty Landon
Ashton, Helen	Swan of Usk
Barke, James	Bonnie Jean
Barke, James	The land of the leal
Barke, James	Major operation
Barke, James	The song of the green thorn tree
Barke, James	The well of the silent harp
Basso, Hamilton	Pompey's head
Bates, H.E.	The purple plain
Baum, Vicki	Berlin hotel
Benson, R.H.	Come rack come rope
Benson, R.H.	Lord of the world
Bentley, Phyllis	Love and money
Bentley, Phyllis	A modern tragedy
Bentley, Phyllis	The partnership
Bentley, Phyllis	Sleep in peace
Bentley, Phyllis	Take courage
Bentley, Phyllis	Trio
Birmingham, George A.	General John Regan
Birmingham, George A.	The inviolable sanctuary
Blackmore, R.D.	Mary Anerley
Blain, William	Witch's blood

Blaker, Richard	The needle watcher
Bottome, Phyllis	Murder in the bud
Bromfield, Louis	Early autumn
Bromfield, Louis	A good woman
Bromfield, Louis	The green bay tree
Bromfield, Louis	The rains came
Bromfield, Louis	Wild is the river
Brophy, John	Gentleman of Stratford
Brophy, John	Rocky road
Brophy, John	Waterfront
Broster, D.K.	Child royal
Broster, D.K.	A fire of driftwood
Broster, D.K.	Sea without a haven
Broster, D.K.	Ships in the bay
Broster, D.K. & Taylor, G.W.	Chantemerle
Broster, D.K. & Forester, G.	World under snow
Buchan, John	Grey weather
Buchan, John	The Runagates club
Buck, Pearl S. *(Trans.)*	All men are brothers (2 vols.)
Buck, Pearl S.	Fighting angel
Buck, Pearl S.	The hidden flower
Buck, Pearl S.	A house divided
Buck, Pearl S.	Imperial woman
Caldwell, Erskine	Place called Estherville
Caldwell, Taylor	The arm and the darkness
Caldwell, Taylor	The beautiful is vanished
Caldwell, Taylor	The final hour
Caldwell, Taylor	Let love come last
Caldwell, Taylor	Melissa
Caldwell, Taylor	Tender victory
Callow, Philip	Common people
Chandos, Dane	Abbie
Chapman, Hester W.	To be a king
Church, Richard	The dangerous years
Collins, Wilkie	Armadale
Collins, Wilkie	The dead secret
Collins, Wilkie	The haunted hotel
Collins, Wilkie	Poor miss Finch
Common, Jack	Kiddar's luck
Comyns, Barbara	Our spoons came from Woolworths
Cookson, Catherine	Maggie Rowan
Cookson, Catherine	Mary Ann's angels

Cookson, Catherine	Rooney
Cookson, Catherine	Slinky Jane
Cooper, Lettice	Black Bethlehem
Cooper, Lettice	The new house
Cooper, Lettice	Private enterprise
Cooper, Lettice	We have come to a country
Cordell, Alexander	Race of the tiger
Cost, March	The dark star
Cost, March	The year of the yield
Costain, Thomas B.	The tontine
Crockett, S.R.	The black Douglas
Crockett, S.R.	The raiders
Croker, B.M.	The youngest miss Mowbray
Cusack, Dymphna & James, F.	Come in spinner
Dane, Clemence	The arrogant history of white Ben
Dane, Clemence	The Babyons
Dane, Clemence	The moon is feminine
Davenport, Marcia	East side, west side
Davies, Rhys	The black Venus
Davies, Rhys	Honey and bread
Davies, Rhys	Jubilee blues
Davies, Rhys	The red hills
Davies, Rhys	Rings on her fingers
Davies, Rhys	The trip to London
Deeping, Warwick	Apples of gold
Deeping, Warwick	Doomsday
Deeping, Warwick	Lantern lane
Deeping, Warwick	Martin Valliant
Deeping, Warwick	Old Pybus
Deeping, Warwick	Orchards
Deeping, Warwick	Suvla John
Dehan, Richard	The dop doctor
Dehan, Richard	The man of iron
Dehan, Richard	That which hath wings
Douglas, George	The house with the green shutters
D'Oyley, Elizabeth	Play me fair
Dumas, Alexandre	The Corsican brothers
Fanu, Sheridan Le	In a glass darkly
Feuchtwanger, Lion	The day will come
Feuchtwanger, Lion	The Jew of Rome
Feuchtwanger, Lion	Jew Süss
Feuchtwanger, Lion	Josephus

O'Brien, Kate	The flower of May
O'Brien, Kate	The land of spices
O'Brien, Kate	Mary Lavelle
O'Brien, Kate	Pray for the wanderer
O'Brien, Kate	Without my cloak
O'Flaherty, Liam	The assassin
Oliver, Jane	Crown for a prisoner
Oliver, Jane	Isle of glory
Oliver, Jane	The lion and the rose
Oliver, Jane	Queen of tears
Oliver, Jane	Sing morning star
Oliver, Jane	Sunset at noon
Onstott, Kyle	Drum
Onstott, Kyle	Mandingo
Ouida	Moths
Page, Gertrude	Paddy-the-next-best-thing
Pain, Barry	The exiles of Faloo
Pargeter, Edith	The assize of the dying
Pargeter, Edith	The city lies four-square
Pargeter, Edith	The eighth champion of Christendom
Pargeter, Edith	Holiday with violence
Pargeter, Edith	A means of grace
Pargeter, Edith	Most loving mere folly
Pargeter, Edith	Ordinary people
Pargeter, Edith	Reluctant odyssey
Pargeter, Edith	The scarlet seed
Pargeter, Edith	The soldier at the door
Park, Ruth	The harp in the south
Prior, James	Forest folk
Porter, Jeanette Stratton	Freckles comes home
Proctor, Maurice	No proud chivalry
Prouty, Olive Higgins	Now voyager
Pym, Barbara	Jane and Prudence
Pym, Barbara	Less than angels
Raymond, Ernest	Child of Norman's End
Raymond, Ernest	Daphne Bruno
Raymond, Ernest	The five sons of le Faber
Raymond, Ernest	The fulfilment of Daphne Bruno
Raymond, Ernest	For them that trespass
Raymond, Ernest	A song of the tide
Renault, Mary	The friendly young ladies
Riley, William	Jerry and Ben

Riley, William	Laycock of Lonedale
Roberts, Kenneth	Arundel
Roberts, Kenneth	Oliver Wiswell
Roche, Mazo de la	Delight
Roche, Mazo de la	Growth of a man
Roche, Mazo de la	The two saplings
Sandstrom, Flora	The midwife of Pont Clery
Sandstrom, Flora	The virtuous women of Pont Clery
Seton, Anya	The mistletoe and sword
Seymour, Beatrice K.	Maids and mistresses
Shellabarger, Samuel	Captain from Castile
Sherriff, R.C.	The Hopkins manuscript
Shiel, M.P.	Prince Zaleski
Sienkiewicz, Henryk	The deluge (2 vols.)
Sienkiewicz, Henryk	With fire and sword
Sinclair, Upton	Boston
Sinclair, Upton	The flivver king
Sinclair, Upton	The jungle
Sinclair, Upton	Oil!
Sinclair, Upton	They call me carpenter

WORLD'S END SERIES

Sinclair, Upton	World's end
Sinclair, Upton	Between two worlds
Sinclair, Upton	Dragon's teeth
Sinclair, Upton	Wide is the gate
Sinclair, Upton	Presidential agent
Sinclair, Upton	Dragon harvest
Sinclair, Upton	A world to win
Sinclair, Upton	Presidential mission
Sinclair, Upton	One clear call
Sinclair, Upton	O shepherds speak
Sinclair, Upton	The return of Lanny Budd
Smith, Betty	A tree grows in Brooklyn
Smith, Eleanor	Caravan
Smith, Sheila Kaye-	The children's summer
Stone, Irving	Love is eternal
Stone, Irving	Lust for life
Sue, Eugene	The wandering Jew (2 vols.)

PORTWAY JUNIOR

Armstrong, Martin	Said the cat to the dog
Armstrong, Martin	Said the dog to the cat
Atkinson, M.E.	August adventure
Atkinson, M.E.	Going gangster
Atkinson, M.E.	The compass points north
Aymé, Marcel	The wonderful farm
Bacon, Peggy	The good American witch
Baker, Margaret J.	A castle and sixpence
Blackwood, Algernon	Dudley and Gilderoy
Coatsworth, Elizabeth	Cricket and the emperor's son
Edwards, Monica	Killer dog
Edwards, Monica	Operation seabird
Fenner, Phyllis R.	Fun, fun, fun
Haldane, J.B.S.	My friend mr. Leakey
Hill, Lorna	A dream of Sadler's Wells
Hoke, Helen	Jokes, jokes, jokes
Hoke, Helen	Love, love, love
Hoke, Helen	More jokes, jokes, jokes
Hoke, Helen & Randolph, Boris	Puns, puns, puns
Hourihane, Ursula	Christina and the apple woman
Lemming, Joseph	Riddles, riddles, riddles
Lyon, Elinor	Run away home
Parker, Richard	The sword of Ganelon
Pudney, John	Friday adventure
Pullein-Thompson, Christine	Ride by night
Pullein-Thompson, Diana	The secret dog
Pullein-Thompson, Josephine	Janet must ride
Pullein-Thompson, Josephine	One day event
Pullein-Thompson, Josephine	Show jumping secret
Manning-Sanders, Ruth	Children by the sea
Manning-Sanders, Ruth	Elephant
Saville, Malcolm	All summer through
Saville, Malcolm	Christmas at Nettleford
Severn, David	Burglars and bandicoots
Severn, David	Dream gold
Severn, David	The future took us
Sperry, Armstrong	Frozen fire
Sperry, Armstrong	Hull-down for action
Sperry, Armstrong	Thunder country
Stucley, Elizabeth	Springfield home

PORTWAY EDUCATIONAL & ACADEMIC

Abbott, W.C.	Colonel Thomas Blood
Abrams, Mark	The condition of the British people 1911—45
Adams, Francis	History of the elementary school contest in England
Andrews, Kevin	The flight of Ikaros
Balzac, Honoré de	The curé de Tours
Bazeley, E.T.	Homer Lane and the little commonwealth
Bowen, H.C.	Froebel and education by self-activity
Braithwaite, William J.	Lloyd George's ambulance wagon
Brittain, Vera & Taylor, G. Handley	Selected letters of Winifred Holtby and Vera Brittain
Cameron, A.	Chemistry in relation to fire risk and extinction
Clarke, Fred	Education and the social change
Clarke, Fred	Freedom in the educative society
Caldwell-Cook, H.	Play way (1 map, 14 illustrations)
Crozier, F.P.	A brass hat in no man's land
Crozier, F.P.	Angels on horseback
Crozier, F.P.	The men I killed
Dewey, John	Educational essays
Dewey, John	Interest and effort in education
Duncan, John	The education of the ordinary child
Fearnsides, W.G. & Bulman, O.M.B.	Geology in the service of man
Ferrier, Susan	Destiny (2 vols.)
Galt, John	The provost
Gates, H.L.	The auction of souls
Gilbert, Edmund W.	Brighton old ocean's bauble
Glass, David V.	The town — and a changing civilization
Gronlund, Norman E.	Sociometry in the classroom
Geological survey	The geology of Manchester and the south-east Lancashire coalfield (H.M.S.O.)
Hadow report 1933	Report of the consultative committee on infant and nursery schools (H.M.S.O.)
Harrison, G.B.	The life & death of Robert Devereux Earl of Essex

Smith, Norman Kemp	A commentary to Kant's "critique of pure reason"
Smith, P.W., L. Broke	The history of early British military aeronautics
Smollett, Tobias	The adventures of Sir Launcelot Greaves
Stocks, Mary	The workers' educational association—the first fifty years
Strutt, Joseph	Sports and pastimes of the people of England
University of London Institute of Educ.	The bearing of recent advances in psychology on educational problems
Wall, W.D.	Child of our times
Watson, Francis	The life and times of Catherine de Medici
Watson, Francis	Wallenstein — soldier under Saturn
Wells, H.G.	Crux ansata
Yoxall, Ailsa	A history of the teaching of domestic economy